LEGAL ENGLISH
An Introduction to the Legal Language and Culture of the United States

Teresa Kissane Brostoff
Ann Sinsheimer

Oceana Publications, Inc.
Dobbs Ferry, New York

Information contained in this work has been obtained by Oceana Publications from sources believed to be reliable. However, neither the Publisher nor its authors guarantee the accuracy or completeness of any information published herein, and neither Oceana nor its authors shall be responsible for any errors, omissions or damages arising from the use of this information. This work is published with the understanding that Oceana and its authors are supplying information, but are not attempting to render legal or other professional services. If such services are required, the assistance of an appropriate professional should be sought.

You may order this or any other Oceana publications by visiting Oceana's website at http://www.oceanalaw.com

Library of Congress Cataloging-in-Publication Data

Brostoff, Teresa Kissane
    Legal English : an introduction to the legal language
and culture of the United States / by Teresa Kissane Brostoff, Ann Sinsheimer.
        p. cm.
    Includes bibliographical references.
    ISBN 0-379-21424-5 (alk. paper)
    1. Law—Study and teaching—United States. 2. Law—United States—
Language. 3. Culture and law. 4. English language. I. Sinsheimer, Ann.
II. Title.

KF272.B76 2000
349.73—dc21

                                        00-32643

TABLE OF CONTENTS

Acknowledgments

We would like to thank a few people for their assistance in preparing this book. We would first like to thank Dean David Herring for his support of our research on this project. We also offer our thanks to Professor Ronald Brand for giving us the opportunity to teach the English for Lawyers course, which inspired this text. We would also like to thank Professor Vivian Curran and Ms. Bessy Lochbaum for their assistance with the English for Lawyers course and for their encouragement. Professor Harry Flechtner generously gave us permission to use his Contracts examination as an example and we thank him. Thank you as well to Susan Reinhart for reviewing early drafts of this text. Our research assistants have given us invaluable help. They are: Meghan Ford; Arthur Sandel; Kathleen Matthews, Gerry Shoemaker, and Rebecca Titus. LuAnn Driscoll and Barbara Salopek, Darleen Mocello, Karen Knochel and Valerie Pompe at the Document Technology Center at the University of Pittsburgh School of Law made the final work on this manuscript a pleasure. Thank you also to John Kissane for his expert legal advice. And finally we would like to thank our families and friends for their love and support during this endeavor.

INTRODUCTION

This text is written for an LL.M. preparatory course that we teach at the University of Pittsburgh School of Law. It can be used as the blueprint for an Introduction to Law and Law School course for LL.M. students, law students or other students of legal studies at the graduate or undergraduate level. This text takes the student into the new world of the study of law by carefully guiding the student through the use of English in legal settings. This text was designed with non-native English speakers in mind, and thus it carefully discusses the vocabulary necessary to understand each new concept or case.

After completing this text, the student should feel comfortable reading and understanding case law and statutes. The students will also be exposed to techniques for predicting an answer to a legal problem and persuading an audience of a particular legal perspective. Each new problem presented in the text will also expose the students to a different subject area in the law. While this exposure is necessarily brief, due to the introductory nature of this type of course, students should find the broad array of legal topics interesting and intriguing, finding themselves well-prepared to take on LL.M. or first year law school classes.

This text comes to the student after testing and use by LL.M. students preparing to enter their course of study. These students report an increased comfort level in reading and understanding their law school assignments. They are also better able to communicate their ideas and analyses about the law both verbally and in writing. Students using this text will gain mastery of both English grammar and usage and the use of legal terms, concepts and ideas. With this mastery will necessarily come the beginnings of understanding about American culture and life as it is reflected in the law. In a shrinking world marketplace, it is an advantage for non-American attorneys to understand the language and culture of American law. This text will help these students to begin to understand American law and the American law school classroom.

SECTION I:
The Law School Classroom

CHAPTER 1—SKILLS

Conversation Skills

In American law schools, the students get to know each other very well. In their first year, students are grouped together to take all classes. While law school may be stressful at times, the students provide friendship and support for each other. In this exercise, you will begin to get to know the other students in your class while practicing your conversational English as well as public speaking skills.

✓ Assignment

Interview another person in your class asking some of the following questions and some of your own questions. In America, it is polite to offer some details about your life when inquiring into the life or profession of another. Try to ask open-ended questions to keep the conversation flowing and to gather as much information as possible. Also try to volunteer information about yourself. Typically, we ask about work, school, interests or hobbies, the weather, weekend activities or general questions about family. It is considered impolite to inquire as to a person's marital status, salary, age, weight, religion, or politics. After your interview is complete, introduce that person to the class.

I. Sample questions and conversations:

1. Hi, my name is _____. What is your name?

2. What country do you come from? I come from _____.

3. What is your area of legal practice or expertise? My field of law is _____. (Add any details that you would like to include about your legal practice.)

4. Are you in the United States to complete an LL.M. program? Which law school will you attend? Why are you seeking an LL.M.? I will be attending _____. I would like to receive an LL.M. because _____.

5. Are you in the United States alone or are you with your family? (Then give details about your family life to encourage the other student to discuss his or her family.)

6. What kinds of things do you like to do in your spare time? I _____ _____. Suggestions: Do you like American food? Will you be

traveling while in the United States? Do you have hobbies that you will continue while studying in the United States? What type of sports do you enjoy?

II. Introducing your partner

After completing your interview, you will introduce your partner to the class. Make sure you understand all of the information you have gathered in your interview. Ask further questions if you are unsure of an answer to a particular question.

Example of the start to an introduction

Hello, my name is Alejandro Ruiz, I would like you to meet Claudia Perez. Claudia will be an LL.M. student at the University of Pittsburgh School of Law. She is from _____ .

Then, continue to give an orderly presentation of the details you have collected in your interview of your fellow student.

III. Using these skills

While you may not regularly be conducting formal interviews of your fellow students, you will have to meet many new people. Using the questions you have practiced in class will make the meeting process easier. When you engage in "small talk" or casual conversation with your fellow students, remember the conversation will flow or move back and forth better if you ask open-ended questions rather than questions that require a yes or no answer.

Examples of open-ended vs. yes-no questions

Yes-No	**Open-ended**
Do you like sports?	What sports do you like?
Do you enjoy your job?	How is your job going?
Did you like that class?	What did you think of your class?
Have you been in the U.S. a long time?	How long have you been in the U.S.?
Do you like American food?	What kind of food do you like?

Also keep in mind that you can encourage conversation by using verbal cues or prompts that tell your conversation partners that you are interested in them.

Examples

How about you?
What about you?
What do you think about _____ ?
I love pizza, hot dogs and hamburgers. What about you?
I thought the reading last night was very difficult. What did you think of it?

Finally to keep conversations moving, give full answers to the questions you are asked. Avoid giving only one-word answers as this may discourage your conversation partner from asking further questions.

Your Role in the Law School Classroom

You will be expected to be an active participant in class. This means that you will need to pay careful attention to what the professor says and you must be sure to follow the comments and questions from your classmates. You will be expected to participate in the classroom discussions and will often need to take detailed notes. You will be expected to finish assignments prior to class and to review notes from the previous class so that you are prepared for the upcoming class. You will also need to tell your professors if you are confused about a particular point or did not hear something. Similarly, you should indicate that you understand and are following a lecture. Usually, this is done through body language such as maintaining eye contact with the speaker or nodding your head slightly from time to time during the lecture.

American students have been encouraged throughout their education to ask questions and actively participate in classroom discussions. They are usually comfortable with this interactive style and comfortable acknowledging confusion and asking questions even in large lecture classes. International students, particularly those who are nonnative speakers of English, may not be so comfortable with this style and often have a difficult time knowing when and how to break the lecture. They may also feel self-conscious about their language ability and feel reluctant to "slow the class down" by asking questions. Nevertheless, professors in the U.S. will expect the students to ask questions and not just passively write down information. For the most part, professors will welcome questions and comments from the class. Professors often view questions and comments positively, as a sign that the students are involved in the class and engaged in the learning process.

The following pages explain techniques for participating in a classroom discussion and for listening to a lecture. Please study this information and be prepared to practice these techniques throughout this course and in your law school classes.

Listening to a Lecture

1. Try to familiarize yourself with the topic before you listen to the lecture.
Do the assigned reading before class and look up unfamiliar terms. Think about
what the professor wants you to get out of the assignment.

2. Take notes even if you are taping the lecture.

3. Try to understand the main idea. Don't worry if you don't hear every word
clearly or don't understand the meaning of every word. Try to paraphrase ideas
and look up unfamiliar words after class. You don't need to write down
everything.

4. Pay attention to the way the speaker presents the information. Your law
professor will typically use the "First tell them what you're going to tell them,
then tell them, and then tell them what you have said" method to present
information.

The main idea will usually be stated at the beginning and followed by the details.
The details may be organized in a variety of styles. Try to identify the style your
professor uses since the style will give you clues to what he or she thinks is important. Identifying the style will also help you follow the lecture since you may
be able to predict what type of information the professor will present.

A speaker may use one or a combination of several of these styles to organize
information:

   a) Analytical—large subjects are broken into small parts, and the nature of the
   parts or the relationship of the part are identified.

   b) Chronological or sequential—information is ordered into the events or
   steps in which they occur in time.

   c) Problem/Solution—a problem is presented and the solution is explained or
   potential solutions are evaluated.

   d) Compare and Contrast—the similarities and differences between two similar concepts are presented or the advantages and disadvantages of two concepts are discussed.

   e) Cause and Effect—the various causes which lead up to a particular effect
   are examined or the various effects of a particular cause or effect are
   examined.

   f) Hypothesis and Support—an assertion/claim is made and justified by
   bringing in evidence, supporting arguments, and refuting counter-arguments.

   g) Case Study—a particular example or hypothetical situation (a "hypo") is
   used to help establish, prove, or disprove a generalization.

5. Organize your notes while you are taking notes in class by trying to categorize information and then after class reorganize your notes. As you take notes, try

to fit your notes into an outline format. A sample outline of a class lecture may look something like this:

Sample Outline of a Class Lecture

I. Opening of Class

A. Greeting and getting everyone's attention

B. Announcements

C. Review of previous class

(*language cues*: "In our last class . . .", "If you recall . . .")

II. Body of the Lecture

A. Introduction of topic for this lecture

(*language cues*: "Ok. I'd like to move on to . . .", "Let's move on to today's topic . . .," "Today, I will discuss . . .", "In the next several classes, we will be covering . . .")

B. Background information relevant to topic

    1. Give important contextual information

    2. Define important terms

    (*language cues*: "Before I start, I'd like to mention . . .", "Keep in mind . . .", "How many of you are familiar with . . .?", "First of all . . .")

C. Presentation of main ideas which make up the topic

    1. Main ideas may be

        a) explicitly stated (i.e., a roadmap or statement of principles)

        b) indirectly presented through questioning of students (ie, the Socratic method.)

        (*language cues*: "Now, let's take a look at . . .", "The key point is . . ." "First, Second, . . . Third, . . .", "What was the holding in . . . ?", "Tell me about . . .")

    2. Main ideas are illustrated with supporting details by

        a) examples

        b) presenting hypothetical problems.

        (*language cues*: "For example . . .", "For instance . . .", "What were the facts in . . .", "Suppose . . .", " What if . . .", "Consider . . .")

D. Summary of important points

(*language cues*: "To summarize . . .", "In conclusion . . .", "Let me just end by saying . . .", "So, to recap . . .", "Today we looked at . . .")

III. End of Class

A. Question period

    1. Feedback to students

    2. Get feedback from students

    (*language cues*: "Any questions . . .?", "Is that clear?", "OK?")

B. Closing

    1. Preview of upcoming class

    2. Homework assigned

    3. Signal end of class

    (*language cues*: "The next class will focus on . . .", "For the next class, please read . . .", "Thank you.", "See you . . .", "We've run out of time . . .")

---

6. Understand the details.

a) in class: listen for the examples; pay attention to the questions the professor asks and the answers students give.

In law school, professors often use the Socratic method in which the details are raised through a series of questions and answers. Like Socrates, the professor raises ideas indirectly by asking more questions than either the professor or student can answer. The professor's questions will indicate what information is important. The questions will also help you to decide what information to investigate further and study more carefully.

b) after class: look up unfamiliar words after class; compare notes with classmates; reread portions of the previous assignment; do additional reading if necessary, and talk to the professor if you are still confused.

7. Fit your notes into a larger context. Consider how this lecture fits with previous lectures and future lectures.

✓ Exercise

You will now listen to a lecture on the U.S. legal system. Take careful notes, and ask your instructor if there is any vocabulary you do not understand. Following the lecture, you should compare notes with a classmate, and try to organize your information into an outline form. This style of note taking is sometimes referred to as making a "reverse outline" because you are trying to reconstruct the outline that the professor used. You can finish working on your outline at home. Look up anything you do not understand and review the concepts presented. Hand in this outline in tomorrow's class.

✓ Matching Exercise

Please match the terms on the left with the definitions on the right. Write the term number in the blank.

Terms:
1. Matter of law
2. Appellate cases
3. Appeal
4. Treatises
5. Pass
6. Prima facie case
7. Monetary damages
8. Plaintiff (¶)
9. Defendant (∆)
10. Interrogatories
11. Genuine issue
12. Statute
13. Material fact
14. Cite
15. Intermediate courts
16. Assigned seats
17. Decedent
18. U.S. Supreme Court
19. Multiple-choice question
20. Seating chart
21. Trial courts

Definitions:

A. ___ Reference to legal authorities.

B. ___ Person who brings the lawsuit.

C. ___ Seeking compensation in the form of money.

D. ___ The court of original jurisdiction where all evidence is first received and considered.

E. ___ A test question that forces a student to select the best of several answers.

F. ___ Issues which can be sustained by substantial evidence and creates the slightest doubts as to the facts.

G. ___ Lawsuits that have been appealed.

H. ___ Resort to a superior court to review the decision of an inferior court or administrative agency.

I. ___ Instructing the professor that you do not wish to speak in class.

J. ___ Whatever is to be ascertained or decided by the application of statutory rules or the principles and determinations of the law.

K. ___ Facts which constitute a legal defense or affect the result of the action.

L. ___ A methodical explanation of law.

M. ___ Person against whom a lawsuit is brought.

N. ___ A formal written enactment of a legislative body.

O. ___ The deceased.

P. ___ Written questions used during discovery.

Q. ___ A case that has sufficient evidence so that the case can go to the jury.

R. ___ Appellate courts; courts of appeal.

S. ___ Court of last resorts.

T. ___ Listing of where people sit usually in alphabetical order.

U. ___ Seat the registrar selects for each individual student.

Active Listening

In law school classrooms, professors expect students to be active listeners. Even in very large classes, professors expect students to not only attend class but come prepared and to show they are alert. Active listening takes a lot of effort, particularly for nonnative speakers of English. Listeners have little control of the situation. The pace, content, and word choice are determined by the speaker. Depending on the size of the class or temperament of the speaker, listeners will have limited or no opportunity to stop the speaker and ask for clarification. Listeners can easily get distracted and confused.

Here are some things you can do to develop your active listening skills and hopefully minimize your confusion:

1. Prepare for the lecture. Do the reading so you'll be familiar with the topic and the vocabulary.

2. Act like an active listener. Sit toward the front of the class. Sit straight. Turn toward the speaker. Remain relatively still and quiet. Look at the speaker. Make eye contact if you can. Show signs that you understand by nodding yes or no. Professors will often pay attention to student's body language to see if the class understands the material.

3. Pay attention to the speaker's verbal and nonverbal behavior. Listen for the words which are stressed. Listen for language that signals a transition or indicates the organization of the lecture. Watch how the speaker uses body language or gestures to emphasize a point or to indicate a shift in the topic.

4. Take notes. Listen for the main ideas and try to find the examples the speaker uses to illustrate those main ideas. Note any key terms.

5. Try to connect the specifics to the speaker's general theme. Try to get beyond the isolated facts and figures. Try to relate the information to what you already know.

6. Make a note of what you don't understand or where you get lost. Write this down in the margin of your notes or make some mark to indicate that there is a gap in your understanding of the lecture. Then, force yourself to move on with the speaker. (You may want to ask a classmate or the speaker for clarification after the lecture.)

7. Avoid getting distracted. Pay attention to the speaker not the environment in the classroom.

8. Think critically. Try to distinguish any biases on your part or on the part of the speaker. Think about what the speaker is telling you. What more information would you like? Are there other ways to view the situation?

9. Generate questions. Think of questions you'd like to ask the speaker. If you have the opportunity, ask those questions.

10. Practice whenever you can! Apply these same skills while you watch or listen to the news.

11. Remember this will be hard work and demands lots of energy but you will improve with practice and time. Allow yourself that time. You may find you have days when you can't understand anything, days when your brain just won't function in English. Take a short break if you need to but then get back to practicing. Language learning is a process but not always a linear one.

Participating in Classroom Discussions

1. First, get the professor's attention:

   eye contact
   gestures (nodding, raising hand)
   posture (lean forward)

2. Next, politely interrupt:

   Pardon me . . . .
   Excuse me . . . .
   Excuse me for interrupting . . . .
   Professor?
   I'm sorry, I didn't catch what you just said.
   I have a question.
   Could I ask a question?
   I'm sorry, I didn't understand/ hear that.

3. Then, ask for clarification or more information by restating or rephrasing:

   You were saying . . . .   Could you give an example of . . . ?
   You said that . . . .   Could you say that again slowly?
   If I understand you correctly . . . .   Do you mean that . . . ?
   As I understand it . . . .   Does that mean . . . ?
   So what you're saying is that . . . .   Did you mean . . . ?
   Could you please repeat that?
   Could you please rephrase that?
   I'd like to know . . . .
   Could you explain more about . . . ?

4. You may be able to communicate your understanding or add to the discussion:

   Another example might be . . . .
   I think that makes sense because . . . .
   I can agree that . . ., but what about . . . ?
   But what about . . . ?
   Well, it seems to me that . . . .
   But I think . . . .

5. Be prepared to restate your question or comment by self paraphrasing:

I mean . . . .   What I mean is . . . .
To put it another way . . . .   What I mean to say is . . . .
What I'm saying is . . . .   What I meant to say was . . . .
Let me rephrase what I just said . . . .
So, in other words . . . .

6. Add examples if necessary:

For example . . . .
The reason I say that is because . . . .
I think that this may be true because . . . .

Defining/Explaining a Term or Concept

We will be discussing two interrelated skills: defining and rephrasing. You will need to identify these defining and rephrasing skills as you listen to lectures so you can follow the lecture. You will also want to incorporate these skills into your own speech so that you can be more easily understood.

When you listen to a lecture, you'll probably find that much of the lecture is about explaining a concept or theory. To explain a concept or theory, we typically use a definition. First we use a formal definition and then an extended definition depending on how complex a term is. This process tends to be very redundant. Native speakers, are as a whole, more redundant than nonnative speakers. This lack of redundancy or repetition, often causes problems in communication for nonnative speakers.

Think about how you act in your native language, and pay attention to how often native speakers define and rephrase. Native speakers will negotiate meaning. We may, for example, give a definition, see that the listener is confused, and then we might immediately rephrase or add an example. In an effort to communicate and express an idea, we may compare and contrast, make generalizations, repeat ourselves, or use synonyms.

When you are listening to a lecture, remember that a certain proportion of what you hear will be repetitious. A speaker may, for example, introduce a concept, define it with a formal dictionary definition, then a speaker may add an example or discuss a case which illustrates the meaning of the concept. Many of the law lectures you will hear will involve some form of defining and explaining. Professors' lectures will often involve defining and explaining terms or concepts. In the class, you may be called on to define a term or concept using a short or extended definition. You might be asked to compare and contrast the definitions of two terms or several cases or concepts. You may be asked to very broadly define a term or concept or to state a more narrow definition. Speakers will often define or rephrase a term or concept to make sure they are being clear. Redundancy helps people to understand each other. As you listen to a lecture, you should try to listen for what is the definition and what it the expansion or rephrasing of that definition. Listen also for the ways in which the professor defines and rephrases.

Building redundancy into your own speech will also allow you to be better understood. If you can rephrase your ideas, you have a better chance of being understood accurately. If someone is not understanding you, you will need to get your message across another way. Listeners rarely understand every word a speaker says. Rather, they fill in a great deal based on prior conversations or a general understanding of the language. They also will ask a speaker to clarify and rephrase so that they can understand the exact meaning. Repetition can also be a strategy to compensate for any pronunciation problems you might have.

The following materials will help you to practice this idea of formal definitions and expanded definitions.

Techniques for Defining/Explaining a Term or Concept[1]

I. Use a formal or dictionary definition—explain a term by referring to the general category or class of the term followed by a relative clause to add more specific detail about the term.

Example: A *(term)* is (a) *(class)* which/that *(specific detail)* .

"A will is an instrument by which a person can dispose of property after death."

II. You may need to go beyond the formal definition to clarify your meaning or because your pronunciation is not clear. In these situations, you may want to try extending the definition. Begin with the formal definition, and then give more specific details using one of the following methods.

1. Give more specific example of a general term.

"For example, in a will, a person can direct money to a particular friend or relative or even an animal."

Describe a hypothetical or give the facts from a case you have read which deals with wills: "You know, like that person in . . . (name of a case.)"

2. Add more information about the term—look at meaning of term from a different perspective.

"Wills allow people to decide where property will go as opposed to the state directing the property distribution."

---

1   Based on information in JAN SMITH ET AL., COMMUNICATE: STRATEGIES FOR INTERNA-TIONAL TEACHING ASSISTANTS 44 (1992).

3. Add redundancy—rephrase or repeat information you have already given.

"a will . . . an inheritance device . . . and inheritance instrument . . . ."

4. State the context in which the term is used.

"You know, it is used when someone with lots of money dies."

5. Give words which are commonly associated with the term.

"a last will and testament"

6. Use synonyms.

"an inheritance device"

7. Use an antonym—contrast with an opposite term.

"A person might have a will or they might die intestate."

8. Demonstrate the term. Show somebody a copy of a will.

9. Write it or spell it.

"W-I-L-L"

The following phrases may be helpful as you listen to lectures and as you practice these defining and rephrasing techniques.

Language which indicates an example:

for example	specifically
for instance	that is/that means
in particular	to illustrate this concept

Language which indicates additional information:

additional	furthermore
also/too	in addition
and	moreover

Language which indicates rephrasing:

in other words	to state this another way
more simply	what I mean by that is
that is	

Language which indicates comparison:

also	in the same way/manner
as we saw/as in	similarly

Language which shows contrast:

alternatively	on the other hand
but	rather
conversely	unlike
however	yet
on the contrary	

Language which indicates emphasis:

certainly	in fact
clearly	more importantly

Language which indicates uncertainty or hedging:

allegedly	questionably
arguably	

Language that indicates sequence or cause and effect:

as a result	recently
because	since
consequently	so
finally	subsequently
first, second, third	then
hence	thereafter
later	therefore
meanwhile	thus
next	

Language which indicates conclusion:

finally	to conclude
in conclusion	to recap
in short	to sum up

English Stress Patterns

Stress within words and phrases—part 1:[2]

Studying English stress and intonation patterns will help you master English pronunciation and will increase your ability to communicate. Understanding the way native speakers use stress and intonation will also help you to follow lectures and conversations since stress and intonation are used to convey meaning in English.[3]

In English, stress can be on a syllable or a word. It is irregular, and is produced by volume and timing. For example, a speaker may stress a word or syllable by using the following stress elements:[4]

1. LOUDER (more air)

2. L-O-N-G-E-R (take more time)

3. Pause (there is a pause before or after the stressed element to make it stand out from the non-stressed parts).

✓ Exercise

Single Words

With the help of your professor, practice putting stress on the correct syllable. Remember to make the stressed element longer, louder and then add a pause. Stress the portion of word in boldface.

plaintiff	con**vic**tion	juris**pru**dence
de**fen**dant	sus**tain**	ac**com**plice
appeal/appellate	in**tent/inten**tional	ju**dic**iary/**judic**ial
negligence	ad**min**istrative	**pro**ximate
verdict	**prec**edent	legislation
cul**pabil**ity	li**abil**ity	com**plaint**
executory	juris**dic**tion	**hy**po/hypo**thet**ical
EU	**EPA**	**NLRB**
UCC	**DOE**	**ABA**

---

2   Based on information by Peggy Heidish, The Intercultural Communication Center, Carnegie Mellon University, Pittsburgh, Pa.

3   Information on stress is based on the work by Gary Esarey. *See generally* GARY R. ESAREY, PRONUNCIATION EXERCISES FOR ADVANCED LEARNERS OF ENGLISH AS A SECOND LANGUAGE (1977).

4   For more detailed information on English Stress patterns, see JAN SMITH ET AL., COMMUNICATE: STRATEGIES FOR INTERNATIONAL TEACHING ASSISTANTS (1992).

Two Word Expressions

Try the following two word nouns. Remember to give slightly more stress to the first word and to pause between words.

*Example: Criminal //case (to get the stress, answer the question, What kind of case? A **criminal** case.)*

jury instruction	discretionary appeal	federal statute
gross negligence	causal connection	expert testimony
common law	legal system	directed verdict
good faith	wrongful death	exclusionary rule
trial court	superseding cause	legislative intent
en banc	civil law	involuntary manslaughter

Stress in longer titles

In titles, all of the terms are important, so all need to be stressed:

Court of Common Pleas
Pennsylvania Superior Court
Pennsylvania Supreme Court
Federal District Court
United States Circuit Court of Appeals
United States Supreme Court
Rules of Civil Procedure
Restatement (Second) of Torts
Brown v. Board of Education
Pennsylvania Bar Association
Harvard Law Review

Stress within English Sentences—part 2:

As you saw in exercise 1, English stress within a word in isolation will vary. The stress falls irregularly on the word or syllables within the word. Additionally, when words appear within sentences, some words receive more stress than others. This is because in English, stress is linked to meaning, and so a speaker needs to stress the words which carry the most meaning or importance.

Basic Emphasis Rule for English Stress Patterns:

1. Stress content and not function words

2. The most important word has the most stress

3. When a conversation begins, main focus word is the final content word

4. New information usually gets the main stress

What are these content and function words?

Content (meaning) words are stressed

1. nouns

2. verbs (but not helping or auxiliary verbs): will, can, have

3. adverbs and adjectives

4. questions words: who, what, why

5. demonstratives: this, that, these

6. negatives: no, not, don't, can't, impossible

Function words are not stressed

1. prepositions: of, in, at

2. pronouns: I, you, his, my who

3. articles: a, the

4. some verbs: to be

5. conjunctions: and, but

6. auxiliaries: do, can, will, have

✓ Exercise

The following drills are based on the work of Carolyn Graham.[5] These drills were designed to help nonnative speakers learn to lengthen the stressed elements, pause and to minimize pronunciation of the non-stressed elements. Each sentence should be read in the same amount of time. Although there are more words, native speakers can stress the same three content words in the same time by de-emphasizing the function words. To a listener, the function words may get lost or swallowed. To practice these sentences, you may want to tap three steady beats for each sentence.

1.   a. Dogs eat bones.
   b. The dogs eat bones.
   c. The dogs will eat bones.
   d. The dogs will eat the bones.
   e. The dogs will have eaten the bones.
2.   a. Boys need money.
   b. The boys need money.
   c. The boys will need some money.
   d. The boys will be needing some of their money.

Now practice using stress to emphasize the content words in the dialogues below. The following exercises are based on exercises from *Clear Speech*.[6]

1. X: I lost my BOOK.
   Y: What KIND of book? (Book is now an old idea. Kind is the new focus)
   X: It was a TEXT book.
   Y: What COURSE was it for?
   X: It was for CONTRACTS.
   Y: There was a contracts book in the CAR.
   X: WHICH car?
   Y: The one I SOLD.

(Note that the question intonation is carried by the stressed words in questions.)

2. X: I want some FOOD.
   Y: What KIND of food?
   X: Fast food.

---

5   *See* CAROLYN GRAHAM, SINGING, CHANTING, TELLING TALES: ARTS IN THE LANGUAGE CLASSROOM (1992).

6   *See* J. GILBERT, CLEAR SPEECH (1984).

Y: BAGELS or PIZZA?

X: Neither. I'm TIRED of bagels and pizza. I want a HOAGIE.

You decide where to stress:

3. X: Where are you going?

   Y: California.

   X: Where in California? To the north or to the south?

   Y: Neither. I've already been north and south. I'm going to central California.

4. X: What've you been doing?

   Y: I've been studying.

   X: Studying what? Torts or Contracts?

   Y: Neither. I'm sick of Torts and Contracts. I'm studying Property.

Using Stress for Special Purposes—part 3:

After you have mastered the rules for the normal use of stress in English, you can learn to use stress for special emphasis. In English, stress is an important part of the meaning; as the stress changes, so can the meaning of the sentence.

There are three basic uses for special stress:

1. Emphatic stress (to show that something is of special importance)

2. Contrastive stress

3. Corrective stress

✓ Exercise

The following exercises examine each type of stress.

1. Emphatic Stress:

Stress can change the focus (and meaning) of a sentence. For example, the sentence below can take on several different meanings depending on what word receives the stress.

Example: Did John take International Law last semester? (normal stress)

1. Did John take International Law LAST semester? (no, this semester)

2. Did John take INTERNATIONAL LAW last semester? (no, Contracts)

3. Did John TAKE International Law last semester? (no, he taught)

4. Did JOHN take International Law last semester? (no, Bob did)

Change the stress in the following questions. Ask as many logical questions as you can:

1. Did you go to the movies in Squirrel Hill last weekend?

2. Can Bob come to our house for dinner next week?

3. Will you have a presentation at the end of your seminar?

4. Did Alice buy a new color TV for her apartment?

2. Contrastive Stress

Stress can be used to indicate information which is in contrast or conflict. By stressing certain words in English, a speaker can draw attention to ambiguities or points which require clarification or elaboration.

1. Did you research STATE or FEDERAL law? FEDERAL law

2. Did you say WITH or withOUT consent? WithOUT consent

3. Is that INductive or DEductive reasoning? DEDUCTIVE

4. Is the exam OPEN or CLOSED-book? OPEN-book

5. Did you like or dislike your class?

6. Was the result favorable or unfavorable?

7. Is England a common or civil law country?

8. Was it a criminal or civil action?

9. Was she guilty or not guilty?

10. Was the law constitutional or unconstitutional?

3. Corrective Stress

When you are correcting mistakes, you must use stress to highlight the correction.

Try the following:

1. Pittsburgh is a state.   No, it's a CITY.

2. Tokyo is in Korea.   No, it's in Japan.

3. Ellen can speak French fluently.   No, she speaks German fluently.

4. The book is on the desk.   No, it's in the desk.

5. You can buy books in the library.   No, you buy them in a bookstore.

6. The garage is behind the building.   No, it's beside the building.

7. Tom can play the piano quite well.   He can, but he doesn't. He lost interest in music.

8. The exam will be on the 15th of April.   Actually, it's on the 16th.

9. Let's invite Mike; he loves Italian food.   He told me he hates it.

10. Rush hour is usually over by 4:00.   Actually, it starts at 4:00.

Correct the following (each sentence contains at least one mistake):

1. George Washington is the President of the U.S.

2. Pittsburgh is the capital of Pennsylvania.

3. The court of common pleas is the highest court in Pennsylvania.

4. Our legal system is based on an unwritten constitution.

5. The LL.M program is five years long.

6. Common law uses only statutory law.

7. Everybody has the right to appeal to the U.S. Supreme Court.

8. The Law School has no library.

9. Pittsburgh is always sunny.

10. In the U.S., all judges are elected officials.

Articles

Articles in English signal definiteness (the) or indefiniteness (a, an) in certain nouns. Articles help us to identify what information has already been given to listeners or readers and what is new information. Given information is usually definite; new information is typically indefinite. To determine what is given versus new information, we need to look at the context in which a noun occurs.

Is it a proper noun?

Besides context, we also need to consider whether a noun is a common or proper noun. In their singular form, proper nouns generally do not take articles because proper nouns are by their very nature definite (i.e., John Brown, Canada). In their plural form, proper nouns use "the" (i.e., the Browns).

Is it a countable noun?

Common nouns generally do require articles, but to determine what article, we need to decide if the noun is countable (i.e., book) or uncountable (i.e., information). Countable nouns have singular and plural forms. Uncountable nouns are not distinguishable as singular or plural. To indicate definiteness with an uncountable noun, we use "the" (i.e., the information). To indicate indefiniteness, we use no article or a determiner such as "some" (i.e., some information).

Is it singular or plural?

Countable nouns, in their plural form, act like uncountable nouns. To indicate definiteness, we use "the" (i.e., the books). To indicate indefiniteness, we use no article or a determiner (i.e., books, some books). When countable nouns occur in singular form, definiteness is indicated with "the" (i.e., the book). Indefiniteness is indicated with "a" or "an" (i.e., a book, an apple).

Does it have a unique referent?

As mentioned above, to decide whether a noun is definite or indefinite, we need to consider the context in which the noun occurs and examine whether the noun refers to given or new information. Specifically, we need to consider if we are talking about a noun that is familiar to both the speaker/writer and the listener/reader. A noun might be familiar because:

- everybody knows about it (i.e., the sun, the moon);
- it is unique by nature or by our description of it (i.e., the crash, the dog with no teeth, the book in the car I sold);
- it occurs in a given or shared setting (i.e., the blackboard);
- we point to it or mentioned it previously.

To decide if the noun refers to given information, ask if the noun has a specific referent: Is it a particular noun? If the answer is "yes," use the definitive article "the" to indicate this. If the answer is "no," the noun does not have a specific referent to either or both the speaker or the listener. Use the indefinitive article "a" or "an" to indicate this.

✓ Article Exercise

Please fill-in the blank with the appropriate article ("a," "an," or "the") or leave it blank to indicate that no article is necessary.

"George Pavlicic is not asking for _____ damages because of _____ broken heart or _____ mortified spirit. He is asking for _____ return of _____ things which he bestowed with _____ attached condition precedent, _____ condition which was never met. In demanding _____ return of his gifts, George cannot be charged with _____ Indian giving. Although he has reached _____ Indian summer of his life and now at _____ 80 years of age might, in _____ usual course of human affairs, be regarded as beyond _____ marrying age, everyone has _____ inalienable right under his own constitution as well as that of _____ United States to marry when he pleases, if and when he finds _____ woman who will marry him. George Pavlicic believed that he had found that woman in Sara Jane. He testified that he asked her at least 30 times if she would marry him and on each occasion she answered in _____ affirmative. There is nothing in _____ law which required him to ask _____ 31 times. But even so, he probably would have continued asking her had she not taken his last $5,000 and decamped to another city. Moreover he had to accept _____ 30 offers of marriage as _____ limit since she now had married someone else. Of course, mere multiplicity of _____ proposals does not make for _____ certainty of acceptance. _____ testimony, however, is to _____ effect that on _____ occasion of each proposal by George, Sara Jane accepted—accepted not only _____ proposal but _____ gift which invariably accompanied it.

_____ Act of 1935 in no way alters or modifies _____ law on _____ ante-nuptial conditional gifts as expounded in _____ 28 C.J. 651, and quoted by us with approval in _____ case of *Stanger v. Epler*, 382 Pa. 411, 415, 115 A.2d 197, 199, namely:

'_____ gift to _____ person to whom _____ donor is engaged to be married, made in _____ contemplation of _____ marriage, although absolute in _____ form, is conditional; and upon breach of _____ marriage engagement by _____ donee _____ property may be recovered by _____ donor.' "

Excerpt from Pavlicic v. Vogtsberger, 136 A.2d 127, 131 (Pa. 1957).

For more information on articles, see Marianne Celce-Murcia & Diane Larsen-Freeman, The Grammar Book: An ESL/EFL Teacher's Course (1983). *See also* Thomas N. Huckin & Leslie A. Olsen, Technical Writing and Professional Communication for Nonnative Speakers of English (2d ed. 1991).

✓ Preparing Presentations

Prepare a presentation about the legal system in your country. In preparing your presentation, consider the following points. In evaluating your classmates' presentations, consider how effectively they have addressed these points.

1. Consider your audience and your purpose in planning your presentation. Ask yourself who your audience will be and what they need or want to know.

> What background knowledge does your audience have?
> How much detail will they want?
> What type of information will they find interesting?
> How can information be presented to them in an interesting way?
> How can information be put into context or related to their experience?

2. Consider your purpose in planning your presentation. Ask yourself why you are making this presentation and what information you want to convey.

> What are your goals?
> What do you want your audience to learn?
> How can you accomplish your goals?

3. Consider your audience when making your presentation.

> Maintain eye contact. Look at your audience to see if they are understanding you. Ask questions if you sense they are having trouble following you. Ask your audience occasionally if you are speaking slowly enough or if they are following you.

> At the beginning of your presentation, make sure your audience has the appropriate background knowledge. During the presentation, be sure to define unfamiliar terms for your audience.

> Slow down or try to rephrase a point you think is causing confusion. Be prepared to rephrase complicated ideas.

> Leave time for questions. Ask the audience questions to make sure they have understood your main points.

4. State your purpose when making your presentation. Begin by telling your audience what you will be covering.

> Use transitional phrases to make the purpose of the information clear and to guide your audience through the presentation: "Today I would like to talk about . . .", "First . . .", "For example, . . .", "The next thing I'd like to mention is . . .", "Compare this to . . .", "To sum up, ..."

> End your presentation by highlighting the major points again.

> Pace yourself. Be sure you have time to cover your main points and accomplish your goals.

5. Make your presentation clear.

Prepare a detailed outline. Make sure your information is presented in a logical, orderly manner. Make this organization obvious to your audience. Try to organize information into 3-4 large categories. Present these categories as the key points you'd like to cover.

Focus your presentation. Consider what specific facts you want to present and include only information that is relevant to the topic.

Be concise. Eliminate information that does not support your main points.

Be thorough. Try to include the most important information on the topic. However, remember that your audience cannot learn everything you know in just one brief presentation. Don't try to cover too much.

Give examples and details to support your key points. Consider how to make these examples interesting to your audience: Can you use visuals? Can you draw on the audience's experience?

6. Practice your presentation.

Practice your presentation in front of a mirror. Practice with a friend. Practice with the teaching assistants.

Do not try to read or memorize your presentation. Strive for a conversational style. Prepare notes in a way that will be easy for you to find your place if the audience asks you questions.

Monitor your grammar. Tape record a few minutes of your presentation and listen carefully for grammatical errors or ask the teaching assistant or native speaker to listen carefully for errors.

Pay attention to your verbal and nonverbal language. Use stress to emphasize key points. Use your body language to emphasize key points. Try to sound enthusiastic. Speak loudly enough (but not so loudly that you sound hostile or unapproachable).

Watch your pronunciation. Write key terms on the blackboard so that you are sure the audience understands you. If there are words you know you have trouble pronouncing, be prepared to use another word to clarify or give an example.

7. Prepare for questions. Consider what questions your audience might ask you. Think about how you might answer potential questions.

Presentation—Peer Review

Use the following form to evaluate your classmates' presentation.

I. Audience
   1. Did the speaker select appropriate information for the audience?

   2. Did the speaker give sufficient background information?

   3. How did speaker make the presentation interesting to the audience?

II. Purpose
   1. Did the speaker tell you the purpose of the talk?

   2. What was the purpose? (Try to write a one sentence summary of the purpose.)

III. Style
   1. Did the speaker present the information in an original form?

   2. Is the information clearly presented?
      A. Organization: what organizational pattern(s) did the speaker use?

      B. Transitions: what transitions did the speaker use to connect main ideas?

      C. Examples: what examples/details did the speaker use to illustrate the main ideas?

      D. Grammar: what, if any, grammatical problems did you detect?
      (word form, plurals, articles, tense, subject-verb agreement, vocabulary use)

      E. Pronunciation: was the speaker's stress and intonation varied? Did the speaker use stress for emphasis?

   4. Delivery: was the delivery effective?
   (eye contact, gestures/body language, volume, enthusiasm)

IV. What did you like about the presentation?

V. How could speaker improve the presentation?

VI. Questions for the speaker:

Exam Taking[7]

Throughout this course, we use the law to predict and persuade. In your law school classes, your professors will be asking you to practice these same skills. At the end of the term, you will probably have to take exams which will test your ability to predict and persuade by asking you to apply the law to a new set of facts. These facts are often referred to as a fact pattern.

Most courses in law school have only one examination at the end of the semester. The exam may be closed book, which means you cannot take any materials into the exam, or it could be open book, which means you will be allowed to bring into the exam notes, course materials, or whatever materials the professor allows. Some professors will ask you to write a take-home exam, which means that you will have a defined period of time, typically between 12 and 72 hours, to answer and return the exam to the professor, but you are free to work on the exam at home or the library as specified by the professor.

Examinations are stressful for almost all law students, but it might help you to consider the following as you prepare for your exams. Remember first of all that law deals with conflict, disputes, and ambiguities so you can be sure that your professor will be testing you on these ambiguities in some manner. In other words, in answering your exam questions, you will have to predict how the law will apply, and you will have to persuade your reader that your analysis is sound. To do this effectively, you must consider all plausible interpretations of the law regarding the fact pattern.

There could be disputes or ambiguity in the law and in the facts. When considering where the disputes arise in the law, you should consider rules and counter-rules or exceptions, traditional and modern law, and different views of the same rules. When considering factual disputes, you will need to look carefully at the fact pattern in the exam and consider how the facts can be used to support or defeat a given argument. To do this, you will need to consider what facts were relevant in the cases you studied in your course. Compare the facts in your exam to those facts in the cases you've studied. Are the facts similar or different? How might these similarities or differences influence a court trying to resolve a dispute?

To practice identifying these conflicts, you should look at prior examinations by your professor. Many law school libraries will keep prior examinations or you may want to ask your professor for a copy of his or her old examination. Use these old exams to simulate exam conditions and to practice writing an exam. The old exams may help you to understand important issues covered in the

---

7   For additional information on law school exams, see RICHARD MICHAEL FISHER, JEREMY R. PAUL, GETTING TO MAYBE: HOW TO EXCEL ON LAW SCHOOL EXAMS (1999).

course but remember that professors will often emphasize different information from year to year.

The tips which follow are based on the advice of several past and present law students.

Before the exam:

- write your *own* outlines[8]
- find ways to make material easily accessible during the exam (for open book exams)
- find arguments for both sides of an issue (studying with a group is good for this)
- attend review sessions
- take practice exams (most professors will allow you to review old exams)
- study hard
- get at least 6-7 hours of sleep
- eat something before the exam

Bring to the exam:

- a watch (but not one that beeps)
- sweater or sweatshirt
- more than one pen
- outline and textbook if allowed
- tissues, gum, water, or whatever you think you might need (so you don't have to leave the room and waste valuable time)

Taking the exam:

- relax
- give yourself time limits for each question, and don't go over the limit
- sit at least every other seat
- read the question thoroughly

After the exam:

- don't talk about the exam
- don't second guess yourself
- don't let the past exam interfere with studying for the next exam

---

8   An outline is an integrated summary of all the material covered in a course.

The following is a sample examination from a contacts course taught by Professor Flechtner at the University of Pittsburgh School of Law.

CONTRACTS
Section C

Final Examination   3 Hours
December 18, 1997   9:00-12:00

Instructions

Directions: This examination is three hours in duration. It consists of three questions, each of which must be answered and each of which is weighted equally for grading purposes. This is an open book exam.

If you believe you have discovered a mistake in the question, simply indicate your discovery and resolve the mistake in a reasonable manner. The questions do not necessarily contain all pertinent information. If you need further information to answer a question, indicate what is needed and how it would be relevant to your analysis. Assume that the jurisdiction whose law governs the transactions described in this exam applies generally accepted principles of the common law of contracts, and has adopted the Uniform Commercial Code ("U.C.C.") as well as a general statute of frauds similar to that found in most U.S. jurisdictions.

Support all your answers with legal analysis of the facts. The grade for this examination will constitute one hundred percent (100%) of your final grade in this course.

QUESTION I
(One Hour)

Anna Bell and Bill Bell, brother and sister, were each 50% co-owners of a combination bookstore and candle store called the Bell Book and Candle Shop. Anna had primary responsibility for bookstore operations and Bill took the lead in the candle part of the business. The shop had been in business a little over 10 years when Anna and Bill began to disagree over the future direction of the business. Tensions built until, one day, Bill stormed into Anna's office and announced that he wanted out of their partnership so he could open his own candle store. Anna, also quite angry, said that she too wanted to end their joint venture so she could launch her own book store. Anna suggested that the two of them sit down on the spot to determine how the assets of their current business should be divided between them. Bill noted that each of them had used his or her own money (not the business's) to purchase the furnishing's in their respective offices, so that each was entitled to keep those items; but he pointed to an expensive leather chair in the comer of Anna's office and said: "When I gave you that chair on the tenth anniversary of the store, I never dreamed that you would turn out to be so short-sighted and pig-headed about expanding our candle department. I want it back" Anna replied: "Fine with me."

The two then began to go over the property owned by the business and decide who would get what. As the discussion proceeded, Bill began to write down which of the siblings was to get the various items. Anna received the store's stock of books and Bill got the inventory of candles. Cash and accounts were divided equally. Because the stock of books was considerably more valuable than the candles in inventory, Anna agreed that Bill could have the store's fixtures (display racks, a cash register, etc. . . .) as well as the lease on the premises where the store was located. (Anna planned to open her bookstore at a different location.) When they were done, Bill told Anna to review the list he had made to make sure it was accurate. The list did not mention office furniture. Anna read over the list, then each signed it. After making a copy of the signed list and giving it to Anna, Bill stomped out of her office.

Anna did not come to the Bell Book and Candle store for the next several days because she was busy making arrangements for opening her new bookstore. When those arrangements were complete she returned to the old store with the movers she had hired to haul the book inventory and her office furniture to her new location. Bill, however, refused to allow them to take the books, saying he had changed his mind about splitting up the business. He did permit Anna to take her office furniture, but he had moved the leather chair to his own office where Anna could not get it. Anna has filed suit to recover the books and the leather chair. Please answer both of the following questions: (a) Is there consideration or any other validation device (and if so, what is it) for Bill's agreement to give Anna the book inventory and half the cash and accounts of Bell Book and Candle? (b) Assuming there is an enforceable contract between Bill and Anna to divide up the assets of Bell Book and Candle, will the parol evidence rule prevent Bill from proving that Anna agreed to give him the leather chair from her office?

QUESTION II
(One Hour)

On July 15, X Landscaping Inc. agreed to landscape the grounds of the suburban headquarters of Y Telecommunications Corp. in exchange for $40,000. X's duties included devising a landscape plan, using a bulldozer to recontour the land and create a small pond, planting trees and shrubs (the plantings were purchased separately by Y Corp.), and laying down sod for grassy areas. The written contract signed by both parties required all work to be completed by November 15, after which date the weather would likely be too cold to permit the landscaping to be completed until the following spring. Y paid X $10,000 when the contract was signed, and the balance was due within 10 days after the work was completed.

X completed the landscape plan on schedule by the end of August. A remarkable span of rainy weather throughout September, however, slowed the progress of the actual landscaping work. At the very end of September a fire in X's main storage garage heavily damaged much of its equipment. Although its losses were covered by insurance, it took some time for X to deal with the calamity and replace the damaged equipment. It was the middle of October before X was ready to go back to work on the Y headquarters project. At that point an unprecedented cold snap combined with a freak snowfall delayed resumption of the project until after the beginning of November. X then made an all-out attempt to complete the project: It required its employees to work overtime, it rented extra equipment, and it even brought in portable lighting so the work could proceed at night. While it managed to finish the recontouring, dig the pond and install several trees, it fell well short of completing the project before winter weather set in on November 20 and stopped all progress until spring. At that point X had spent $25,000 on the project, including about $5,000 in "extra" costs caused by its crash attempt to complete the work. The work that X had completed would survive the winter in its unfinished state, and the project could be completed in the spring, but in the meantime Y's grounds were an unsightly mess. It would cost Y $20,000 to hire someone else to complete the project in the spring.

Answer all of the following questions: (a) Can X successfully invoke an excuse doctrine or doctrines (and if so, which one(s)) to escape liability for damages for its failure to complete the project by the November 15 deadline? (b) Assuming X could successfully claim an excuse, is X entitled to further compensation for the work it did (and if so, how much)? (c) Assuming X could not successfully claim excuse for failing to finish the project on time, would Y have the right to cancel the contract and hire a new landscaper to complete the project in the spring?

QUESTION III
(One Hour)

On June 1, Buyer Corp. faxed to Seller Inc. a purchase order for 500 compressors. Buyer and Seller are located in the same city. Buyer's purchase order specified a price of $100 per compressor ($50,000 total), called for a delivery date of June 20, and required payment for the compressors to be made within 10 business days of delivery. The purchase order also stated that Seller had to respond to it by June 10. It said nothing about methods or procedures for handling disputes. On June 8, Seller mailed to Buyer an acknowledgment form covering Buyer's order for 500 compressors at a price of $100 per compressor ($50,000 total) for delivery by June 20, with payment due within 10 business days after delivery. The acknowledgment form contained a preprinted clause requiring any dispute concerning the transaction to be submitted to arbitration. The following language also appeared on the form: "We hereby accept your order on the terms and conditions stated herein." The acknowledgment form reached Buyer on June 12. On June 15, Buyer faxed to Seller a message objection to the arbitration clause in Seller's acknowledgment form. The message said that Buyer was withdrawing its purchase order and would refuse to accept delivery of any of the 500 compressors. Seller inquired again on June 20 whether Buyer would take delivery of the 500 compressors, but Buyer again refused.

Answer both of the following questions: (a) Was a contract for the sale of 500 compressors formed between Buyer and Seller? (b) Could Buyer argue successfully that any contract for compressors was unenforceable because it was not evidenced by a sufficient writing?

Professor Flechtner

Culture Shock

Culture shock refers to the anxiety a person feels when he or she moves to a completely new environment.[9] This term expresses the confused feelings of not knowing what to do or how to do things, and not knowing what is appropriate or inappropriate in a new culture. Culture shock for most foreign students begins within the first few weeks of arriving in a new country.

We can describe culture shock as the physical and emotional discomfort one suffers when coming to live in another country. Sometimes, aspects of the lifestyle you enjoyed in your home country are not accepted or not present in your host country. More often, there are little differences and idiosyncracies in your host culture that you have difficulty reconciling. At first, these small details do not bother you, but trouble you more over time. Some examples of difficulties, large and small, are not speaking the language, not knowing how to use banking machines, and not knowing how to use the telephone.

Culture shock affects different students in different ways. Some of you may feel severe anxiety, especially if you have never been outside your home country. However, if you have traveled abroad before, especially to the United States, you might only be mildly affected, and may not even notice any symptoms. While culture shock can be the cause of some emotional and psychological pain, it is also an opportunity to redefine your life objectives. It is a great chance to learn and acquire new perspectives. Culture shock can help you develop a better understanding of yourself and stimulate your legal learning.

Symptoms
- Sadness or loneliness
- Changes in temperament, depression, feeling vulnerable, feeling powerless
- Lack of confidence
- Loss of identity
- Feelings of inadequacy or insecurity
- Developing stereotypes about the host culture
- Trying too hard to absorb everything in the host culture or country
- Longing for family
- Idealizing one's home country
- Feelings of being lost, overlooked, exploited or abused
- Preoccupation with health

---

9   *See* Association for International Practical Training, *Conquering Culture Shock in the U.S.* (Apr. 13, 2000) <http://www.aipt.org/news03.html>; *Culture Shock* (Apr. 12, 2000) <http://www.atsadc.org/nafsa/shock.html>.

- Developing obsessions such as over-cleanliness
- Aches, pains, and allergies
- Sleeping disorders
- Anger, irritability, resentment, unwillingness to interact with others
- Unable to solve simple problems

Stages of Culture Shock[10]

A student that comes into a new cultural environment (such as the United States, or more specifically, an American law school) will typically show signs of the following stages of culture shock. The intensity and duration of each stage vary significantly from student to student.

Honeymoon Stage

The student may feel euphoric and be excited by all of the new things found in the host country and culture.

Disintegration Stage

The student may begin to experience some crises in daily life. For example, a student may discover some communication difficulties, such as not being understood. In this stage, there may be feelings of anger, sadness, impatience, or incompetence. This occurs when the student is trying to adapt to the host culture, which might be very different from the culture of origin. Transition between these cultures is a difficult process and can take a long time to complete. During the transition, there can be strong feelings of frustration and dissatisfaction.

Reintegration Stage

The student may now gain some understanding of the new culture. The student may sense a new feeling of pleasure or excitement. He or she may no longer feel quite as lost, and may begin to feel balanced and focused. The student is more familiar with his or her host environment and wants to belong.

Autonomy Stage

The student begins to establish an objective and impartial view of his or her situation and experiences, leading to more advanced reintegration. The student may develop a new sensitivity to the host culture and greater self-awareness in relation to others. The student is less dependent on others for things such as communication. The student is much more relaxed, and even comfortable, in the host environment.

---

10   *See* University of South Florida, *International Student & Scholar Services Culture Shock Material* (Apr. 12, 2000) <http://ctr.usf.edu/isss/shock.htm>.

Home (Interdependence) Stage

This is where a foreign student feels at home in the new environment. This stage represents the culmination of the multicultural goal of study-abroad programs. It is characterized by a sense of belonging, trust, and sensitivity to the host culture. The student feels integrated in the culture and travels through it with an air of confidence. The student may now even identify himself or herself more with the host culture than with the culture of origin.

Re-Entry Stage

The student may experience "re-entry shock" when he or she returns to his or her home country. One may find that things are no longer the same in the country of origin. Things that were once familiar become strange. The student may experience the same symptoms and stages as when he or she arrived in the host country.

Culture Shock and Law School

The effects of culture shock can be compounded by the anxiety of law school. Law school in the United States has traditionally been very stressful. Law school can be very competitive. Some of the more "cutthroat" law schools in the U.S. see students trying to do whatever they can to succeed, even if that means sabotaging or destroying another student's work. Fortunately, most law schools today are much more relaxed. There are a few students who are extremely competitive and "cutthroat," but you will find that most students help each other. They will study together, make outlines together, and celebrate together at the end of the semester. You will also find that most American law students are willing to help international students adapt to American culture, as well as to law school.

Remember that while you may be experiencing anxiety from culture shock, the American students are experiencing it too, in a way. Law school is a different culture for many American students. Several often unfamiliar factors found in law school contribute to law school anxiety:

- being called on randomly in class (Socratic Method)
- not knowing how you are doing because of lack of performance feedback (the final exam is usually 100% of your grade)
- imagined competition (belief that you are the only one who does not understand a concept; belief that everyone is smarter than you; etc.)
- fear of not doing well
- studying
- waiting for grades
- looking for a job
- school-related financial stress (tuition, debt, financial aid)

Even American law students show some of the familiar symptoms of culture shock—depression, low self-esteem, lack of confidence, insecurity, sleeplessness, regret, anger, and resentment, for example. The feelings which law students, American and international alike, experience are normal. Of course, this does not make dealing with these emotions any easier. What can make coping with culture shock and law school easier is to realize that you are not alone. All law students feel stress and anxiety in law school. It helps to remember the old American axiom, "misery loves company." Talk to your law school friends, both American and international, about what you are feeling. You might find that they feel the same way.

Understanding Your Needs and Motives[11]

Before confronting culture shock and law school anxiety, it is useful to understand your personal "hierarchy of needs." The modern concept of a hierarchy of needs was first developed by the psychologist Abraham Maslow a few decades ago. Maslow described five levels of human need. A person must satisfy the first level of need before worrying about the second level; a person must satisfy the second level of need before worrying about the third; and so on. For example, if you are hungry, you should worry about eating before you worry about studying for an exam.

Maslow's Hierarchy of Needs[12]

Level 1: Physiological Needs
Food, water, air

Level 2: Safety Needs
Security, stability, protection, freedom from fear, freedom from anxiety, freedom from chaos, structure, order, law

Level 3: Belonging and Love Needs
Friendship, affectional relationships, social and interpersonal acceptance

Level 4: Self-Esteem Needs
High self-evaluation, self-respect, self-esteem, esteem of others, strength, achievement, competency, reputation, prestige, status, fame, glory

Level 5: Self-Actualization Needs
Doing what one is fitted for doing, self-fulfillment, realizing one's potential

Understanding your own needs can help you organize your time and priorities. Having a sense of how these needs relate to one another can help you overcome the difficulties of culture shock and law school anxiety. Remember, it is important to understand yourself, and not lose sight of who you are in the coping process.

---

11   *See* JOSEPH A. DEVITO, THE ELEMENTS OF PUBLIC SPEAKING 378 (6th ed. 1997).

12   *See* MASLOW, MOTIVATION AND PERSONALITY (1970).

How to Fight Culture Shock

Most students can successfully confront the obstacles of a new environment. Here are some ways to help combat culture shock and law school anxiety:

- Be patient. Studying abroad, especially in an American law school, means constantly adapting to new situations. It is going to take time, but you will get through.

- Learn from negative social experiences. If you encounter a negative environment, try not to put yourself in that specific situation again.

- Don't try too hard to beat culture shock. Overcoming culture shock means taking the path of least resistance.

- Learn to include some physical activity in your daily routine. This will help combat the sadness and loneliness in a constructive manner. Join, or start, an intramural soccer team at your university; go to the gym; run or jog.

- Find a hobby.

- Relaxation and meditation are proven to be very helpful for people who are passing through periods of stress.

- Maintain some contact with your ethnic group, especially if some members have already acclimated to the new environment. This will give you a feeling of belonging, reduce your feelings of loneliness and alienation, and assist you with your own integration process.

- Maintain contact with the new culture. Practice your language skills. Volunteer in community activities that allow you to practice English. This will help you feel less stressed about language, and useful at the same time. Many students have also participated in language exchanges, where you can help an American learn your language while practicing English with that American.

- Do not keep your feelings bottled up inside. Allow yourself to feel sad about the things that you have left behind, like your family and friends. Allow yourself to feel anxiety about American culture and law school.

- Maintain close contact with your family and friends at home. They will serve as support for you in difficult times.

- Establish simple goals and evaluate your progress. Take it a day at a time.

- Organize your time. You need time to study, relax, eat, exercise, and enjoy your hobbies. Studying should not dominate your life. Take time out for yourself.

- Prioritize. First do what is most important for that day or week. Then concentrate on things that are less important.

- Take steps toward becoming a successful law student: Go to class, take notes, study, make semester outlines, and never be afraid to ask questions.

- Find ways to live with the things that do not satisfy you completely.

- Maintain confidence in yourself. After all, you have made it this far. Follow your ambitions and continue your plans for the future.

- If you feel confused or stressed, ask for help. There is always someone available to help you. Do not hesitate to talk to your professors or teaching assistants.

Law School Slang Vocabulary

Instructions: To better understand this material, be sure you know the definitions of the following terms. Be prepared to define these terms for your classmates, using the techniques described in "Defining/Explaining a Term or Concept." (pg. 14)

1. Cutthroats
2. Slack off/Slacker
3. Burn out
4. Cram
5. Snob
6. Make a fool of myself
7. All-nighter
8. Clueless
9. Lame
10. Stress out
11. Bonding
12. Ace
13. What's up?
14. Hang out
15. Nerd
16. Cool
17. Cheesy

✓ Law School Vocabulary Exercise

Terms:
1. Lawyer/attorney
2. Concurring opinion
3. Socratic method
4. One (1) Ls
5. Two (2) Ls
6. Three (3) Ls
7. Brief a case (briefing)
8. Case report (opinion)
9. Substantive history (the facts)
10. Procedural posture
11. Issue
12. Holding
13. Reasoning/Rationale
14. Rule of law
15. Dicta (dictum)
16. Dissenting opinion
17. Assumpsit
18. Precedent (stare decisis)
19. Common law
20. Administrative law
21. Statutory law

Definitions:

A. ___ A promise or engagement by which one person assumes or undertakes to do some act or pay something to another.

B. ___ A systematic method of questioning of another to reveal his hidden ignorance or to elicit a clear expression of a truth supposed to be known by all rational beings.

C. ___ Outlining a case into parts such as Facts, Procedure, Issues, Holding, Rule, and Reasoning.

D. ___ First year of law school.

E. ___ Law constructed by the judicial branch; case law.

F. ___ The procedural history of the case; the tracking of the case through the court system.

G. ___ The question(s) asked of the court.

H. ___ One whose profession is to conduct lawsuits for clients or to advise as to legal rights and obligations in other matters.

I. ___ Second year of law school.

J. ___ Law constructed by the legislative branch.

K. ___ The court's decision for that particular case.

L. ___ Third year of law school.

M. ___ Judicial written decision of a case.

N. ___ Judicial commentaries in the written opinion; not law.

O. ___ The relevant facts of the case (the human story).

P. ___ Policy of courts to stand by settled decisions.

Q. ___ The courts analysis of why the case was decided the way it was.

R. ___ The general law that came out of the case; binding law.

S. ___ Opinion that agrees with the majority decision but is written separately and is not regarded as binding law.

T. ___ Law made by the executive branch.

U. ___ Written opinion disagreeing with majority.

CHAPTER 2—THE LEGAL SYSTEM

The U.S. Legal System

In order to understand the materials you will be reading in this text and in your law school or practice experience, you should first understand the basic structure of the American system of government. You must be able to identify the sources from which the law emanates and feel comfortable addressing case law, statutes and regulations. In order for you to practice your listening skills, your instructor may present this information in a lecture format.

American Legal System

Since the United States is a federalist system, it has a central or federal government structure and each state within the union also has corresponding government structures. The federal government and state governments share powers and functions within their government institutions.[1] The federal government has powers specifically enumerated in the United States Constitution.[2] The states have all other government powers and functions not specifically reserved for the federal system.

The Constitution

The United States and each individual state have a constitution.[3] A Constitution is a document drafted at or near the formation of each unit, whether state or United States.[4] A constitution specifically defines, empowers, and imposes limits on each part of the governmental structure. Constitutions also impart substantive and procedural rights to the citizens within its jurisdiction.[5]

---

1   For example, both the federal government and state governments have Departments of Education. The federal government can allocate funds for states to use in education programs and can provide guidelines for the use of the funds. The state government Department of Education will be more intimately involved with the workings of the educational system in that particular state. It may provide licensing boards to credential schools and teachers, pass on the curricula from various school districts and it will oversee the spending of federal funds.

2   *See* Appendix B.

3   *See* Appendix B.

4   The constitutions of the United States and each individual state are formal written documents ratified and endorsed by the citizens of each jurisdiction through their representatives.

5   *See* U.S. CONST. amend. I-X, commonly called the "Bill of Rights."

Governmental Structure

In both state and the federal governments, the power within the government is divided into three separate sections. Each section functions both independently of and interdependently with the other two sections. Each branch of government interacts with the other two branches to gives the government structural and functional balance. The three branches of government are the judicial, executive, and legislative branches. (See Diagram 1.) Each branch of government is a source of a different type of law.

The Judicial Branch of Government

The judicial branch of government is the court system.[6] The courts decide cases presented to them by private citizens or the government. The courts can create legal doctrines through the cases. This is called common law. The courts can also decide controversies based on statutes by interpreting and deciding the meaning of statutes in various factual situations. This is called case law.

The judicial branch interacts with the other branches of government in several ways. Only the courts can decide whether a statute is constitutional. The courts are also accorded great deference in deciding the meaning of statutory language. Courts also interpret the language of regulations and assign them meaning in particular factual contexts. In the rarest of instances, the chief justice will preside over an impeachment trial of the chief executive in the Senate.

Structure of United States Court System

There are two coexisting court systems, the federal courts and the state courts. Each court system has its own areas of jurisdiction. The federal system is limited in its subject matter jurisdiction, while the state courts have broad subject matter jurisdiction. All court systems have a hierarchy or tiered system of courts within them. Usually, the systems have three levels of courts: the trial court, usually divided by geographic areas, the intermediate appellate court, and the highest court. (See Diagram 2.) The federal court system is further divided into eleven numbered geographic circuits plus the DC circuit and the Federal Circuit. Each circuit has trial courts assigned by geographic districts and an intermediate level of appellate court. The United States Supreme Court is the highest court for the entire federal court system. (See Diagram 3.)

The trial court is where the parties present their case to a court for an initial disposition. The trial court can dispose of the case after a trial or pursuant to pre-trial motions. In the trial court, juries sometimes decide the fate of the parties. A jury is usually a 12-person body comprised of the geographic peers of the parties in a civil case or the defendant in a criminal case. A jury is sometimes

---

6   *See* U.S. CONST. art. III, § 1.

called "the fact-finder." Juries are empowered to listen to evidence[7] presented at trial and decide what are the true facts of the case. They then apply the law to those facts. The law is always defined for the jury by the judge. Judges always make any decisions on questions about the law. Judges can also sit as fact-finders and can hear a case without a jury.[8]

If a party or a criminal defendant is unsatisfied with the legal decision in the trial court, he or she may appeal. In an appeal, a party takes a contested legal question to a higher court for a decision. Appellate courts will only decide questions of law and will defer to the trial court on questions of fact. There is no new trial and the parties present no new evidence on appeal. Rather, the parties present an alleged error[9] in the trial court's legal decision-making for the appellate court to review. Most jurisdictions have an intermediate appellate court to which all parties have the right to appeal and a highest court which will only grant discretionary appeals. If a party has an automatic right to an appeal, it is called an appeal as of right. In a discretionary appeal, a party must petition the court and explain why the court should hear the case. Then, the court will decide if it will hear the case. Each jurisdiction has a specific name for this petition to the highest court. In the United States Supreme Court, it is a writ of certiorari. In Pennsylvania, for example, the petition is a petition for allocatur. Highest courts receive many more petitions for appeal than they accept. The highest court in a jurisdiction is usually the court of last resort, and the last chance for a party to appeal. However, in some instances where the legal issue involves the United States Constitution or a federal statute, the United States Supreme Court can hear an appeal from a state's highest court.

Once the highest court decides the case, the law and the controversy are considered settled and the decision becomes binding precedent for all lower courts. When courts defer to the rulings of the highest court or prior courts, they are following the doctrine of stare decisis. Stare decisis provides consistency and some predictability throughout the common law. However, the highest court of a jurisdiction can choose to change settled principles of common law, if justice, or changing societal needs require it.

While this is but a general guide to the hierarchy of the state and federal court systems, it will help you to begin to understand the case law that you will be reading in law school.

---

7   Evidence is any information that is introduced during a trial. Evidence can take the form of witness testimony, scientific data, visual information such as pictures, graphs or videos and tangible objects such as a gun.

8   When a judge sits as the finder of fact without a jury, the trial is called a bench trial.

9   When parties allege an error of law, they claim this as a legal truth. In an appeal, the appellate court will decide whether the legal question or claim of error has merit.

The Executive Branch of Government

The main function of the executive branch is to enforce the law. The chief executive holds ultimate executive power and makes policy and law enforcement decisions.[10] The president, as chief executive of the federal government is also Commander-in-Chief of the armed forces and is empowered to enter into treaties with other nations. The chief executive also has the power to appoint the cabinet and heads of administrative agencies. The administrative agencies are part of the executive branch of government and are the source of administrative law in the form of regulations. Regulations are the rules and guidelines that implement the words of a statute. Generally the statute itself would authorize an agency to make these regulations. One would typically say that an agency promulgates regulations. Some examples of executive agencies are the Department of the Treasury and the Environmental Protection Agency.

The executive branch of government interacts with the other branches of government in several ways. The president or governor, as chief executive, can introduce legislative proposals and can veto legislation passed by the legislative branch. The vice-president sits as President of the Senate and has the power to cast a tie-breaking vote there. The chief executive can also influence judicial decision-making in the courts through the power to appoint federal judges, United States Attorneys, and Federal Public Defenders.

The Legislative Branch of Government

The legislative branch of government[11] enacts statutes as a source of law. The federal and state systems of government have bicameral legislatures.[12] The number of members of the House of Representatives or the lower house of the state legislature are elected based on population within each jurisdiction. The Senate, in the federal system, has two members from each state. The United States Constitution defines the subject matter on which the legislature can enact statutes.

The legislative branch also interacts with the other branches of government. The Senate must approve the chief executive's appointments of the judiciary, agency heads, and other important government officials. The legislature can also override a veto with a two-thirds majority vote, and it can refuse to act on the chief executive's policy or legislative initiatives. In the rarest of situations, the legislature can act to impeach, convict, and remove a chief executive from office. Further, the legislature can enact statutes that will override decisions of even the highest courts. If constitutionally sound, these statutes will always prevail as binding authority over inconsistent judicial opinions on any subject.

---

10   *See* U.S. CONST. art II, § 1.

11   The entire federal legislature is called the Congress.

12   U.S. CONST. art. I, § 8 empowers the federal legislature.

Diagram 1
FEDERAL SYSTEM OF GOVERNMENT

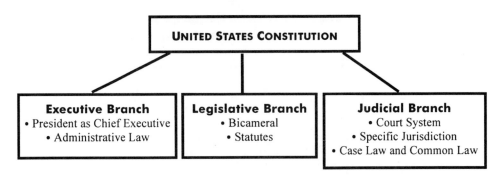

STATE SYSTEM OF GOVERNMENT

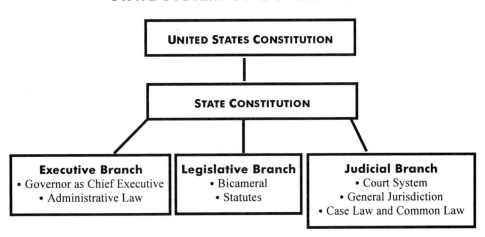

Diagram 2
FEDERAL COURT SYSTEM (simplified)

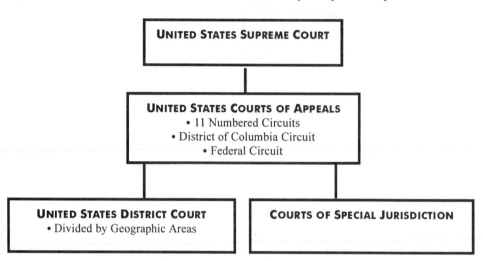

UNITED STATES SUPREME COURT

UNITED STATES COURTS OF APPEALS
- 11 Numbered Circuits
- District of Columbia Circuit
- Federal Circuit

UNITED STATES DISTRICT COURT
- Divided by Geographic Areas

COURTS OF SPECIAL JURISDICTION

Diagram 3
STATE COURT SYSTEM
(using Pennsylvania Court System as an example)

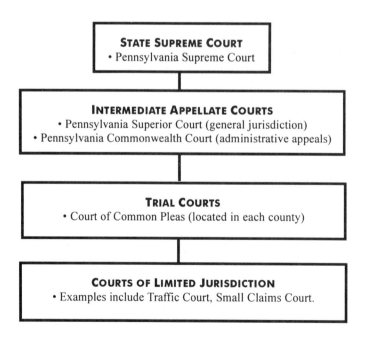

STATE SUPREME COURT
- Pennsylvania Supreme Court

INTERMEDIATE APPELLATE COURTS
- Pennsylvania Superior Court (general jurisdiction)
- Pennsylvania Commonwealth Court (administrative appeals)

TRIAL COURTS
- Court of Common Pleas (located in each county)

COURTS OF LIMITED JURISDICTION
- Examples include Traffic Court, Small Claims Court.

✓ The Corpus Juris Game

Americans love quizzes and games. Now is your chance to see why. The Corpus Juris Game will test your knowledge of the United States legal system. Work in small groups and use your notes from your reading and class discussion to formulate a grammatical question for which the description in the quiz is the answer.

The Corpus Juris Game

	Executive Branch	Judicial Branch	Legislative Branch	Court System I	Court System II	Verbs
100 points	The chief law officer and representative in legal matters of a national or state government, and the legal advisor or the executive	Defines the power of courts to inquire into facts, apply the law, make decisions, and declare a judgment	The legislature of the U.S. consisting of the House and the Senate	The process by which a higher court examines a lower court proceeding to ensure that no prejudicial mistakes were made	An adjudged case or decision of a court, considered as furnishing an example or authority for an identical or similar case afterwards arising or a case with a similar question of law	To affect one in a constraining or compulsory manner
200 points	To put into execution; to cause to take effect; to compel obedience to	The aggregate of reported cases as forming a body of jurisprudence, or the law of a particular subject as evidenced or formed by the adjudged cases	The lower chamber of the U.S. legislature comprised of 435 members	The court of original jurisdiction where all evidence is first received and considered; the first court to consider litigation	Sources of law which must be taken into account by a judge in deciding a case; also known as precedent	To appoint, designate, name, or propose a candidate for office
300 points	A department, division, or administration within the federal government	The set up of the U.S. court system that gives both federal and state courts their own jurisdiction	A formal written enactment of a legislative body, whether federal, state, city, or county; an act of the legislature declaring, commanding, or prohibiting something	An issue which arises where evidence is undisputed and only one conclusion can be drawn	An innocent verdict; a release, absolution, or discharge from an obligation, liability or engagement	To refuse to sign into law a bill that has been passed by a legislature
400 points	The power to select or designate a person, to fill an office or public function	A certain number of men and women selected according to law, and sworn to inquire of certain matters of fact, and declare the truth upon evidence to be laid before them	The name of the upper chamber, or less numerous branch of the Congress of the U.S.; comprised of 100 members—two from each state	The policy of courts to stand by precedent and not to disturb a settled point	Authorities that are explanation or commentary on primary sources of law	To improve; to change or modify for the better by removing defects or faults
500 points	The approval sought by the president when choosing appointments to various federal positions	To conquer; defeat; ruin; what the judiciary may do to regulations made by agencies if found to be unconstitutional	To surpass or prevail over; to disregard, overrule or nullify; Congress may do this to a presidential veto	A formal written application to the U.S. Supreme Court asking for review of a lower court decision; analogous to a discretionary appeal	An error of the court in applying the law to the case on trial. These are the only issues that can be argued on appeal	To do something opposite in nature, order, or direction; when judges behave in opposition to the President who appointed them

✓ Matching Exercise

Please match the terms on the left with the definitions on the right. Write the term number in the blank.

Terms:

1. Closed memo
2. Open memo
3. Demurrer
4. Bargain
5. Judgment
6. Estoppel
7. Replevin
8. Summary judgment
9. Directed verdict
10. Depositions
11. Discovery
12. Legal doctrine
13. Legal theory
14. Torts
15. Podium/Lectern
16. Consideration

Definitions:

A. ___ Final and determinative utterance by a court on a lawsuit.

B. ___ Party with the burden of proof has failed to present a prima facie case for jury consideration so the trial judge orders an entry of a verdict without allowing the jury to consider it, because, as a matter of law, there can be only one such verdict.

C. ___ Structure of the rules.

D. ___ An action seeking the return of goods rather than monetary damages.

E. ___ Writing a memo in which all of the cases are provided.

F. ___ Small stand in the front of the class from which the professor lectures.

G. ___ Writing a memo in which none of the research has yet been done.

H. ___ A mutual undertaking, contract, or agreement.

I. ___ The cause, motive, price, or impelling influence which induces a contracting party to enter into a contract.

J. ___ Allegation that the evidence against the defendant is insufficient in point of law (whether true or not) to make out his case or sustain the issue.

K. ___ A principle that provides that an individual is barred from denying or alleging a certain fact or state facts because of that individual's previous conduct, allegation, or denial.

M. ___ Broad conceptions of purpose underlying an area of law.

N. ___ Case is decided during pretrial by the judge because there is no dispute as to either material fact or inferences to be drawn from undisputed facts, or if only a question of law is involved.

O. ___ The disclosure of coming to light of what was previously hidden.

P. ___ A legal wrong.

CHAPTER 3—READING AND BRIEFING CASES

Reading Cases[1]

Learning to read and understand cases is a fundamental task that you must master as you begin law school. While you have been reading for most of your life, reading cases will be a different experience from the kind of reading you do everyday. When you read a case, you must pay attention to all of the details of the case including its social context and background. You must also be aware of the reasoning or principles that result from the court's decision, even if those principles are not fully articulated in the text of the opinion. Remember that the court communicates its decision on the case to the parties in the form of an order, a short document communicating the precise procedural disposition of the case. The case opinions that you will be reading are pieces of advocacy in which the courts explain their rulings. The court wants the reader to accept the ruling as the inevitable outcome to that legal dispute. However, your job, as law student and lawyer, is to read critically and try to understand how the case follows and departs from existing law in the jurisdiction. Now it is time to start to develop your skill in reading cases.

Before you begin to analyze the case, read it once. Define for yourself any words that are unfamiliar to you. Use an American English dictionary and a law dictionary. Examine the introductory material in the case before reading any of the substance of the case. You must understand the case in its historical context and its context within the court system. Once you have read the case for a general understanding of its content, reread it using the following steps.

1. Read the case name: What kind of controversy is before the court; is it a criminal or civil case? Who are the parties? What are the designations of the parties? Parties in the trial court are the plaintiff and defendant. Parties in an intermediate appellate court are the appellant and appellee, and those in the highest court are the petitioner and respondent. Where might you find this case in the library? What is the case citation?

---

1   For more information on reading and understanding cases, see Mary A. Lundberg, *Metacognitive Aspects of Reading Comprehension: Studying Understanding in Legal Case Analysis*, READING RESEARCH QUARTERLY 407 (1987); Laurel Currie Oates, *Beating the Odds: Reading Strategies of Law Students Admitted through Alternative Admissions Programs*, 83 IOWA L. REV. 139 (1997).

2. Which court decided the case? Is this a mandatory or persuasive authority? Who was the authoring judge or justice?

3. When did the court decide this case? What was the historical setting of the case? What was the social and political setting of the case?

4. Remember to read the case critically and with a particular focus. Try to read the case with a particular purpose, even if the purpose is "what will my professor ask me about this case in class tomorrow?" Imagine how a reviewing court might read the opinion. Imagine how counsel for each party might read the case.

5. Begin to understand the usual structure of court opinions, although sometimes these sections will appear in a different order.

　　a. Discussion of the procedural posture of the case.

　　b. Summary of the facts

　　c. Legal issue before the court, sometimes followed by the legal theories of each party

　　d. Court's decision or the holding in the case

　　e. Court's reasoning

　　f. Rule emerging from this decision

　　g. Procedural order

6. Try to fully understand the procedural posture of the case. This is the history of this case through the legal system. The procedural posture will, in part, determine the standard of review the court will apply in making its decision. It is usually written in the past tense. Even if you are tempted, do not skip the court's discussion of procedure to jump to the substantive material in the case.

7. What are the substantive facts of the case? These facts tell the human story of the parties. They recount the controversy that brought these parties into the court system. You must determine which substantive facts are determinative to the legal dispute. To do this, you must understand which facts are critical to the court's decision. You must distinguish the determinative facts from those that merely add details about the parties' story. The substantive facts are often written in the past tense.

8. What legal issue is before the court? Think of this as the narrow, factually specific question that the litigants are asking the court to decide. Do not extrapolate a broad legal question as the issue in the case. Remember the court's decision will be guided by the facts of this case. The court may phrase the legal issue as a direct or an indirect question. For example: Is Sleepy a dangerous dog? The question is whether Sleepy is a dangerous dog.

9. What is the court's decision? This is called the holding in the case. Think of the holding as the narrow, factually specific answer the court gives to the

question that these litigants have put before it. When trying to discern the holding in a case, be alert to language such as: "We decide . . . .," "We hold . . . .," "We are constrained to follow . . . .," "We adopt . . . .," "We agree . . . .," "We reject . . . ." The holding is usually written in the present tense.

The court may also refer to itself as "this court."

You can distinguish the legal decision from the factual findings through the use of the verb "find." A court will "find" facts.

10. Determine what rule or legal principle the court applies when making its decision. Is the rule drawn from common law or statute? On what authority does the court rely? Be aware of language that signals when the court relies on a rule. Examples of this language are: "The rule is well established . . . .", "The law in this area is settled . . . .", "The rule is undisputed . . . ."

11. If the court is examining a legal issue for the first time, the case will be "one of first impression." The court may look to other jurisdictions to formulate its rule. Look for language such as: "We have reviewed . . . and we adopt the rule in . . . ." "We reject the rules adopted in . . . ."

12. What was the court's reasoning? Why did the court apply the rule as it did? If the court could have chosen a different rule or interpreted the statute differently, why did it decide as it did? What reasons does the court give to explain its decision.

13. What is the rule that emerges in this case? The rule is usually stated as an abstract legal principle that is not factually specific. Is the rule from the case different from the rule that the court examined in making its decision? Has the court modified the existing law in this jurisdiction or made new law?

14. What is the court's procedural decision? What is the order emerging from this case? The order usually appears at the end of the case and contains language such as: "affirmed," "denied," "reversed," "quashed," "vacated" and "remanded."

15. Read any concurring or dissenting opinions carefully. What reasoning does the concurring or dissenting author put forth? Assess the merit of the majority and dissenting reasoning. Which is more persuasive to you? Why?

After completing the steps above, review your understanding of the case. Could you explain the facts, holding, and reasoning of this case to someone else? Could you briefly articulate the legal principle for which the case stands? If not, read the case again and repeat the steps above. When you first begin to read cases, you may have to read them several times in order to fully understand them. The more cases you read, the more familiar you will become with their language and structure.

Some law students find study groups helpful. A study group can be two or more students from the same class or classes who choose to work together to prepare for class and for exams. Reading cases and discussing them in a study group can help you to better understand various viewpoints on the law articulated in the cases. Studying together with others can also help you anticipate questions and concerns that your professor may raise in class.

Briefing Cases

Case briefs are useful tools for law students. A brief is an organized way to express the material contained in any case. Case briefs are individual tools that students use to better understand and remember any case for class participation and exam preparation. While you will develop your own style of case briefing over time, begin with this format.

1. Introductory Materials—case name, citation, court, authoring judge or justice.

2. Facts:

    a. Procedural Posture—This is the history of the case through the legal system. Include everything that has happened in the courts.

    b. Substantive Facts—This is the human story or dispute that brings the parties before the court. What is the personal, business or other problem that made the parties seek legal intervention.

3. Issue—What is the question that the parties bring before the court? Make this a narrow, factually specific legal question.

4. Holding—What is the narrow, factually specific legal answer that the court gives to the question that the parties ask? How did the court decide this particular controversy?

5. Rule—What is the broad legal principle for which this case stands? Did the court articulate a new legal principle or build upon existing legal principles? How did this case add to the body of existing law in the jurisdiction?

6. Rationale—What was the court's reasoning? How did it explain its decision? The court may use several lines of reasoning. If so, you should explain each one thoroughly.

7. Dissenting Opinions—discuss alternate reasoning on this issue by other members of the court.

8. Evaluation—This section should contain your thoughts, ideas and questions about the case.

✓ Exercise

Read and brief the *Groner* case using the briefing format described above. Look up definitions of any unfamiliar words contained in the case. Then, compare your brief to the sample contained in Appendix C.

Groner v. Hedrick[2]

Regional Reporter
169 Atlantic Reporter, 2d series 302

Official Reporter Cite

403 Pa. 148

Bertha GRONER, Appellant,
v.
Frank W. HEDRICK and Dorothy Ann Hedrick.

Caption of the case

Supreme Court of Pennsylvania

Court deciding the case

March 28, 1961

Rehearing Denied April 20, 1961.

Action by housekeeper for injuries received when knocked down by the defendants' Great Dane which had jumped on her. The Court of Common Pleas of Chester County at No. 60, April Term, 1959, Samuel Lichtenfeld, J., entered a judgment for the defendants notwithstanding the verdict, and the housekeeper appealed. The Supreme Court, No. 91, January Term, 1961, Bok, J., held that the evidence presented a jury question as to whether housekeeper had assumed risk of being jumped upon by dog.

Summary of the case

Reversed and remanded with directions to dispose of motion for new trial.

Bell and Cohen, JJ., dissented.

1. Animals ⚖ 74(5)

Evidence showed that the owners of Great Dane had knowledge that he might jump up on people.

2. Animals ⚖ 74(8)

Headnotes

Evidence presented a jury question as to whether housekeeper, knocked down when employers' Great Dane had jumped on her, had assumed risk of being jumped upon by the dog.

Reilly & Fogwell, G. Clinton Fogwell, Jr., West Chester, Jacques H. Fox, Johnson, Fox, McGoldrick & Prescott, Upper Darby, for appellant.

MacElree, Platt & Marrone, Richard Reifsnyder, West Chester, MacElree, West Chester, of counsel, for appellees.

Before CHARLES ALVIN JONES, C.J., and BELL, MUSMANNO, BENJAMIN R. JONES, COHEN, BOK and EAGEN, JJ.

Judges on the court

BOK, Justice.

Authoring Justice

First Friend, as Kipling called Wild Dog, was in this case a large Great Dane named "Sleepy". It jumped upon the plaintiff, who was seventy-four years old, five feet two in height, and 105 pounds in weight, and knocked her down so that she broke her arm and leg.

Introductory Facts

The jury gave her $17,000 but the court below entered judgment for defendants n.o.v., on the theory that plaintiff had assumed the risk of Sleepy's temperament. A motion for a new trial was also filed but not disposed of.

Procedural Posture

What happened was that defendants hired plaintiff to come and be housekeeper and companion for Mrs. Stanley, Mrs. Hedrick's mother, while Mrs. Hedrick went to Europe. Mr. Hedrick stayed behind. The term of employment was five weeks at $100 or $125, and the accident happened after she had been on the job four weeks. She carried a little whip "because he acted as if he was inclined to jump. I was afraid he would jump and knock me over." She also took hold of things when the dog was near, to steady herself, and once, when she told Mr. Hedrick that she was afraid Sleepy would jump on her, he replied: "Be careful; he might." He jumped or brushed against her on several occasions. She said: "I

Detailed Facts of the case

---

2   *Atlantic Reporter*, West Group. Reprinted with permission.

don't think he was vicious, "I'm not sure", and that nothing but his jumping indicated that he was trying to hurt her. He did not growl. Another witness, who said that the dog had jumped on her twice, called him "friendly".

Facts of the case

On the day of the accident, plaintiff and her patient were preparing to sit down to lunch when Mrs. Stanley asked to let Sleepy in, in order to keep him off the highway. She called him from the porch, and "when he got beside me I started to go inside the house with him, through the living room door, and that is when he just turned suddenly and just jumped on me * * * he just went past me, then he suddenly turned and jumped." By jumping she meant that the dog "raised up with his front paws against here * * * left shoulder, left chest." He often put his paws up when plaintiff sat on the sofa, and she kept a rolled magazine to keep him away.

Court's Legal Analysis Rule

[1] We have no doubt that enough appears to establish defendant's negligence, and indeed this point has not been argued. A large, strong, and over-friendly dog may be as dangerous as a vicious one, and our recital of the dog's behavior at home is enough to bring knowledge to his owners, when considered together with its size and their apparent knowledge that it might jump up on people. Andrews v. Smith, 1936, 324 Pa. 455, 188 A. 146. In Fink v. Miller, 1938, 330 Pa. 193, 198 A. 666, the opinion refers to the dog's viciousness or playfulness as undisclosed by the evidence. We can find no Pennsylvania case of harm by *mansuetae natura*, or tame and domesticated animals, resulting from their excessive affection. Since intention forms no part of an animal's assault and battery, the mood in which it inflicts harm is immaterial, so far as the owner's duty goes. An Alabama case argues

what seems to us the correct rule. Owen v. Hampson, 1952, 258 Ala. 228, 62 So.2d 245, 248, in which the Court said:

Court relies on case law from other jurisdictions

"Based on a review of our cases, as well as those from other jurisdictions, it is our opinion that the law makes no distinction between an animal dangerous from viciousness and one merely mischievous or dangerous from playfulness, but puts on the owner of both the duty of restraint when he knows of the animal's propensities. Crowley v. Groonell, 73 Vt. 45, 50 A. 546, 55 L.R.A. 876; State v. McDermott, 49 N.J.L. 163, 6 A. 653; Knowles v. Mulder, 74 Mich. 202, 41 N.W. 896; Hicks v. Sullivan, 122 Cal.App. 635, 10 P.2d 516; Mercer v. Marston, 3 La.App. 97; Hartman v. Aschoffenburg, La.App., 12 So.2d 282.

"In 3 C.J.S. § 148 c, p. 1250, under the title Animals the rule is stated thus:

Court relies on legal encyclopedia definitions and the Restatement of Torts

"'A vicious propensity is a propensity or tendency of an animal to do any act that might endanger the safety of the persons and property of others in a given situation. Although an animal is actuated solely by mischievousness or playfulness, rather than maliciousness or ferociousness, yet, if it has a tendency to do a dangerous or harmful act, it has a vicious propensity within the meaning of the rule holding the owner or keeper liable for injuries resulting from vicious propensities of which he has knowledge.'"

See Restatement, Torts, § 518(1), and Stevenson v. United States Express Co., 1908, 221 Pa. 59, 70 A. 275, where the temperament of a horse was held to be a matter for the jury.

We regard the rule as different so far as the victim's reaction to the animal is concerned. People trust a dog sooner than a tiger, and they would trust a friendly dog before a vicious one. In life the firmest friend, Byron said of

Analysis of the facts

the dog: the first to welcome, foremost to defend. It is likely that plaintiff would have acted very differently if Sleepy had been a growler and a biter. A bite is a bite, but a dog's display of affection may be greater or less. And plaintiff had successfully evaded the animal's amiable lunges for four weeks.

Reference to the standard of review

Hence, when we give her the benefit of all favourable facts and inferences, as we are told to do while considering judgment n.o.v. by such cases as Rutovitsky v. Magliocco, 1959, 394 Pa. 387, 147 A.2d 153, we think that the entry of summary judgment was error. In Esher v. Mineral R.R. & Mining Co. (No. 1), 1905, 28 Pa. Super. 387, the Court said:

> "Where the facts are disputed, where there is any reasonable doubt as to the inference to be drawn from them, or when the measure of duty is ordinary and reasonable care and the degree varies according to the circumstances, the question cannot in the nature of the case be considered by the court; it must be submitted to the jury."

The Superior Court then added:

> "It cannot be successfully contended that the risk of injury from the vicious mule was so obvious that Esher ought not to have continued in the service of the company in the tunnel where the mule was used or that if he did so he assumed the risk of injury. If he knew the vicious disposition of the mule, it was still the province of the jury to determine whether from the character of his duties he assumed the risk of injury from this source."

The court below quotes Section 521 of the Restatement of Agency 2nd:

> "In the absence if a statute or an agreement to the contrary, a master is not liable to a servant for harm caused by the unsafe state of the premises or other conditions of the employment, if the servant, with knowledge of the facts and understanding of the risks, voluntarily enters or continues in the employment."

Court's legal decision on the facts of this case

[2] We think that it was for the jury to say whether plaintiff, under the economic pressure of the job, had knowledge of the facts and understanding of the risks, when the facts and the risks were dependent upon Sleepy's mood, and hence whether she can be held to have assumed them, There are too many variable factors in the dog and in the person and in the enclosing circumstances. Even this court has taken an advanced position of trust about dogs, when we said, in Andrews v. Smith, supra (324 Pa. 455, 188 A. 146, 148):

> "Of all animals, dogs have probably been the longest domesticated and the vast majority of them can be allowed their freedom without imperilling the public safety."

Order of the court

The judgment is reversed and the record is remanded with directions to dispose of the motion for a new trial.

BELL, Justice (dissenting)

Dissenting Opinion

The majority and I agree that a dog is man's best friend; after that we part. It is likely that dogs were originally tamed and used for protection, later for the chase, then for "beasts of burden", and now principally for companionship and affection. A dog exhibits obedience but not affection by lying in the corner. Those who understand or love dogs know that very often they show their affection by putting their paws on or licking or playfully jumping onto persons they like or love. I cannot understand how a Court can equate a dog's act of affection with viciousness. It will come as a bitter blow to all dog lovers, and their numbers are legion, to learn that man's best friend is malum in se and that the only dog they can safely keep, even in their own home, is a sleeping dog or a dead dog.

Assuming, arguendo, that this dog's affectionate actions amounted to legal misconduct, plaintiff admittedly knew well the dog's dangerous propensities and clearly and certainly assumed the risk.

COHEN, Justice (dissenting).

I fail to seek the relevancy of debating whether the injury was caused by Sleepy's affectionate or vicious action. I also fail to see how the majority can imply that "the economic pressure of the job" negated the plaintiff's "knowledge of the facts and understanding of the risks" incident to her employment. This case falls within the clear and precise language of Section 521 of the Restatement, Agency (2d ed. 1958). See also Jerdon v. Sirulnik, 1960, 400 Pa. 423, 162 A.2d 202. Since the defendants have violated no duty that they owed to the plaintiff I would affirm the judgment of the court below.

Groner Vocabulary

Instructions: To better understand this material, be sure you know the definitions of the following terms. Be prepared to define these terms for your classmates, using the techniques described in "Defining/Explaining a Term or Concept" (pg. 14).

> 1. Assumption of the risk
>
> 2. Disposition
>
> 3. Immaterial
>
> 4. Inference
>
> 5. Intention
>
> 6. Judgement n.o.v.

✓ The *Groner* Quiz

	Procedural Terms	Substantive Terms	Parts in a Case
100 points	The party in a case against whom an appeal is taken; that is, the party who has an interest adverse to setting aside or reversing the judgment.	Not material, essential, or necessary; not important or pertinent; of no substantial consequence; of no material significance.	It is immaterial whether an animal is vicious or overly friendly. Only the animal's ability to cause injury to persons or property is important.
200 points	Abbreviation for the Latin phrase non obstante veredicto, meaning judgment notwithstanding the verdict. It is a judgment entered for the plaintiff or defendant after the jury has entered a verdict for the other party. It is now called a directed verdict.	The doctrine means legally that a plaintiff may not recover for an injury to which he assents, because he or she is said to have voluntarily exposed himself or herself to the risk.	"It jumped upon the plaintiff, who was a seventy-four year old, five two in height, and 105 pounds in weight, and knocked her down so that she broke her arm and leg."
300 points	An indication that a decision of one court has been vacated by a higher court in the same jurisdiction.	In the law of evidence, a truth or proposition drawn from another which is supposed or admitted as true.	The court must draw all conclusions in favor of Ms. Groner, the appellant, when reviewing a judgment n.o.v.

Verb Vocabulary

Instructions: To better understand this material, be sure you know the definitions of the following terms. Be prepared to define these terms for your classmates, using the techniques described in "Defining/Explaining a Term or Concept" (pg. 14).

1. To affirm
2. To argue
3. To arrest
4. To bind
5. To consider
6. To contend
7. To decide
8. To deny
9. To determine
10. To dispute
11. To distinguish
12. To find
13. To follow
14. To grant
15. To hold
16. To implicate
17. To overrule
18. To present
19. To rely
20. To reverse
21. To review
22. To vacate

✓ Exercise

Read and brief this case.

George J. PAVLICIC

v.

**Sara Jane VOGTSBERGER, a/k/a Sara Jane
Slesinski, a/k/a Sara Jane Mills, Appellant.**
Supreme Court of Pennsylvania.
136 A.2d 127 (Pa. 1957)

[Some footnotes may have been omitted.]

MUSMANNO, Justice.

George J. Pavlicic has sued Sara Jane Mills[1] for the recovery of gifts which he presented to her in anticipation of a marriage which never saw the bridal veil. At the time of the engagement George Pavlicic was thrice the age of Sara Jane. In the controversy which has followed, Pavlicic says that it was Sara Jane who asked him for his hand, whereas Sara Jane maintains that Pavlicic, following immemorial custom, offered marriage to her. We are satisfied from a study of the record that it was Sara Jane who took the initiative in proposing matrimony—and, as it will develop, the proposal was more consonant with an approach to the bargaining counter than to the wedding altar.

George Pavlicic testified that when Sara Jane broached the subject of holy wedlock, he demurred on the ground that he was too old for her. She replied that the difference in their ages was inconsequential so long as he was "good to her." Furthermore, she said that she no longer was interested in "young fellows"—she had already been married to a young man and their matrimonial bark had split on the rocks of divorce. Hence, she preferred an older man. George qualified. He was 75. Sara Jane was 26.

The May-December romance began on a very practical footing in April, 1949, when Sara Jane borrowed from George the sum of $5,000 with which to buy a house, giving him a mortgage on the premises. In three and one-half years she had paid back only $449 on the mortgage. On the night of November 21, 1952, she visited George at his home and advanced the not illogical proposition that since they were to be married, there was no point in their having debts one against the other and that, therefore, he should wipe out the mortgage he held on her home. George said to her: "If you

---

[1] The defendant was married twice and her name appears in various spellings in the record. For convenience in this discussion, she will be referred to as Sara Jane. For similar convenience the plaintiff George J. Pavlicic will be referred to as George.

marry me, I will take the mortgage off." She said: "Yes," and so he promised to satisfy the mortgage the next day. To make certain that there would be no slip between the promise and the deed, Sara Jane remained at George's home that night; and on the following morning drove him in her automobile to the office of the attorney who was to make, and did make, arrangements for the satisfaction of the mortgage.

Being enriched to the extent of $4,551 by this transaction, Sara Jane expatiated on another rational thesis, namely, that since they were going to be married and would be riding around together she should have a better car than the dilapidated Kaiser she was driving. She struck home with her argument by pointing out that in a new car he would not fall out, for it appears this was an actual possibility when he rode in her worn-out Kaiser. Thus, without any tarrying, she drove George from the Recorder of Deed's Office, where she and the mortgage had been satisfied, to several automobile marts and finally wound up at a Ford agency. Here she selected a 1953 Ford which she said would meet her needs and keep him inside the car. George made a down payment of $70 and on the following day he gave her $800 more, the latter taken from his safety deposit box. Still later he handed her a check for $1,350, obtained from a building and loan association—and Sara Jane had her new car.

Less than a year later, Sara Jane complained that her feet got wet in the Ford and she proposed the purchase of an Oldsmobile. She explained that by trading in the Ford, which she characterized as a "lemon," she would need only $1,700 to acquire the Oldsmobile. George was not averse to transportation which would keep his future wife's feet dry, but he said that since they were to be man and wife, and he apparently was paying for all the bills, it might be more businesslike if title to the car were placed in his name. This suggestion, according to George's testimony at the trial, made Sara Jane "mad" and he practically apologized for being so bold and inconsiderate as to ask title to an automobile which he was buying with his own money. Accordingly he withdrew his suggestion, said: "Al right," and made out a check in Sara Jane's name for $1,700. And thus Sara Jane got her new Oldsmobile.

In January, 1953, in the enthusiastic spirit of an anxious swain, George presented Sara Jane with a $140 wrist watch. Sara Jane selected the watch.

In February, 1953, Sara Jane represented to George that they would both make a better appearance if she had an engagement and wedding ring. George took her to a jewelry store and she made a selection consistent with discretion. George paid $800.

Sara Jane then asked George to take care of the repairing of a ring she had received from her mother. It was a mere matter of adding a diamond. George paid the bill.

Even before George's bank book became Sara Jane's favorite literature she had prevailed upon him to advance substantial sums to her. In June, 1952, she told George she needed $800 to cover her house with insulbrick. George gave her $800 to cover her house with insulbrick.

It is not to be said, however, that Sara Jane was completely lacking in affectionate ante-nuptial reciprocity. In June, 1953, she bought George a wedding ring for him to wear. She conferred upon him at the same time a couple of woolen shirts. There is no way of learning how much the ring and shirts cost because she did not take George into her confidence or into the store where she purchased the items.

George testified that when he wore the wedding ring people laughed and asked him when he was to be married. He replied: 'Pretty soon.' He tried to live up to the prediction and asked Sara Jane for the wedding date. She said she could not name the month. In view of what was to develop, she could have added with truth that she could not name the year either.

In October, 1953, Sara Jane expounded to George the economic wisdom of purchasing a business which would earn for them a livelihood in his old and her young age. She suggested the saloon business. George agreed it was a good idea. She contacted a saloon-selling agent and George accompanied her to various saloons which the agent wished to sell. George was impressed with one saloon called the "Melody Bar," but the price was above him. Sara Jane then said that if he would give her $5,000 she would buy a cheap saloon outside of Pittsburgh. George gave her $5,000. And Sara Jane disappeared—with the $5,000.

The next time she was heard from, she was in Greensburg operating Ruby's Bar—with George's $5,000. From Ruby's Bar she proceeded to the nuptial bower where she married Edward Dale Mills. Although she had many times assured George she would marry him because she liked the idea of an old man, the man she then actually married was scarcely a contender for Methuselah's record. He was only 26—two years younger than Sara Jane.

When George emerged from the mists and fogs of his disappointment and disillusionment he brought an action in equity praying that the satisfaction of the mortgage on Sara Jane's property be stricken from the record, that she be ordered to return the gifts which had not been consumed, and pay back the moneys which she had gotten from him under a false promise to marry. Sara Jane filed an Answer and the case came on for trial before Judge Marshall of the Allegheny County Court of Common Pleas. Judge Marshall granted all the plaintiff's prayers and entered a decree from which the defendant has appealed to this Court.

The defendant urges upon us the proposition that the Act of June 22, 1935, P.L. 450, 48 P.S. § 171, popularly known as the "Heart Balm Act," outlaws the plaintiff's action. This is the first time that the Act of 1935 has come before this Court for interpretation and ruling. Although the Act contains several sections, the heart of it lies in the first sentence, namely, "All causes of action for breach of contract to marry are hereby abolished."

There is nothing in that statement or in any of the provisions of the Act which touches contracts subsidiary to the actual marriage compact. The Act in no way discharges obligations based upon a fulfillment of the marriage contract. It in no way alters the law of conditional gifts. A gift given by a man to a woman on condition that she embark on the sea of matrimony with him is no different from a gift based on the condition that the donee sail on any other sea. If, after receiving the provisional gift, the donee refuses to leave the harbor,—if the anchor of contractual performance sticks in the sands of irresolution and procrastination—the gift must be restored to the donor. *A fortiori* would this be true when the donee not only refuses to sail with the donor, but, on the contrary, walks up the gangplank of another ship arm in arm with the donor's rival.

The title to the gifts which Sara Jane received, predicated on the assurance of marriage with George, never left George and could not leave him until the marital knot was tied. It would appear from all the evidence that the knot was fully formed and loosely awaiting the ultimate pull which would take title in the gifts from George to Sara Jane, but the final tug never occurred and the knot fell apart, with the gifts legally falling back into the domain of the brideless George.

The appellant in her argument before this Court would want to make of the Act of June 22, 1935, a device to perpetuate one of the very vices the Act was designed to prevent. The Act was passed to avert the perpetration of fraud by adventurers and adventuresses in the realm of heartland. To allow Sara Jane to retain the money and property which she got from George by dangling before him the grapes of matrimony which she never intended to let him pluck would be to place a premium on trickery, cunning, and duplicitous dealing. It would be to make a mockery of the law enacted by the Legislature in that very field of happy and unhappy hunting.

The Act of 1935 aimed at exaggerated and fictional claims of mortification and anguish purportedly attendant upon a breach of promise to marry. The legislation was made necessary because of the widespread abuse of the vehicle of a breach of promise suit to compel overly-apprehensive and naive defendants into making settlements in order to avoid the embarrassing and lurid notoriety which accompanied litigation of that character. The legislation was intended to ward off injustices and incongruities which often occurred when, by the mere filing of breach of promise suits innocent defendants became unregenerate scoundrels and tarnished plaintiffs became paragons of lofty sensibility and moral impeccability. It was not unusual in threatened breach of promise suits that the defendant preferred to buy his peace through a monetary settlement rather than be vindicated by a trial which might leave his good name in shreds.

There is no doubt that in the history of romance a nation could be populated with the lovers and sweethearts (young and old) who have experienced genuine pain and agony because of the defection of their opposites who promised marriage and then absconded. Perhaps there should be a way to compensate these disillusioned souls, but it had been demonstrated that the action of breach of promise had been so misemployed, had given rise to such monumental deceptions, and had encouraged blackmail on such a scale, that the Legislature of Pennsylvania, acting in behalf of all the people, concluded that the evil of abuse exceeded to such an extent the occasional legitimate benefit conferred by a breach of promise suit that good government dictated its abolition.

Thus the law of 1935 prohibited, but prohibited only the suing for damages based on contused feelings, sentimental bruises, wounded pride, untoward embarrassment, social humiliation, and all types of mental and emotional suffering presumably arising from a broken marital promise. The Act did not in any way ban actions resulting from a tangible loss due to the breach of a legal contract. It could never be supposed that the Act of 1935 intended to throw a cloak of immunity over a 26-year old woman who lays a snare for a 75-year old man and continues to bait him for four or five years so that she can obtain valuable gifts and money from him under a false promise of marriage.

George Pavlicic is not asking for damages because of a broken heart or a mortified spirit. He is asking for the return of things which he bestowed with an attached condition precedent, a condition which was never met. In demanding the return of his gifts, George cannot be charged with Indian giving. Although he has reached the Indian summer of his life and now at 80 years of age might, in the usual course of human affairs, be regarded as beyond the marrying age, everyone has the inalienable right under his own constitution as well as that of the United States to marry when he pleases, if and when he finds the woman who will marry him. George Pavlicic believed that he had found that woman in Sara Jane. He testified that he asked her at least 30 times if she would marry him and on each occasion she answered in the affirmative. There is nothing in the law which required him to ask 31 times. But even so, he probably would have continued asking her had she not taken his last $5,000 and decamped to another city. Moreover he had to accept 30 offers of marriage as the limit since she now had married someone else. Of course, mere multiplicity of proposals does not make for certainty of acceptance. The testimony, however, is to the effect that on the occasion of each proposal by George, Sara Jane accepted—accepted not only the proposal but the gift which invariably accompanied it.

The Act of 1935 in no way alters or modifies the law on ante-nuptial conditional gifts as expounded in 28 C.J. 651, and quoted by us with approval in the case of *Stanger v. Epler*, 382 Pa. 411, 415, 115 A.2d 197, 199, namely:

> "A gift to a person to whom the donor is engaged to be married, made in contemplation of marriage, although absolute in form, is conditional; and upon breach of the marriage engagement by the donee the property may be recovered by the donor." *See also* 38 C.J.S. Gifts § 61.

In the case of *Ruehling v. Hornung*, 98 Pa. Super. 535, 538, the Superior Court quoted with approval from Thornton on Gifts and Advancements as follows:

> "If the intended husband makes a present after the treaty of marriage has been negotiated, to his intended wife, and the inducement for the gift is the act of her promise to marry him, if she break off the engagement he may recover from her the value of such present."

As already stated, the Act of 1935 provides that "All causes of action for breach of contract to marry are hereby abolished." This language is as clear as the noonday sun. The appellant would darken it with the eclipse of artificial reasoning. The appellant would want us to read into the statute the provision that "All causes of action *for the recovery of property* based on breach of contract to marry are abolished." The appellant would want the statute to be read: "All actions *resulting from* a breach of contract are abolished." But we cannot so read or so interpret the statute. The abolition is confined to actions *for* breach of contract to marry, that is, the actual fracture of the wedding contract.

It thus follows that a breach of any contract which is not the actual contract for marriage itself, no matter how closely associated with the proposed marriage, is actionable.

After a thorough review of the pleadings, the notes of testimony, the briefs and the lower Court's Opinion, we come to the conclusion that the final decree entered by Judge Marshall is eminently just and in accordance with established principles of law and equity. It is accordingly

Decree affirmed at appellant's costs.

Pavlicic Vocabulary

Instructions: To better understand this material, be sure you know the definitions of the following terms. Be prepared to define these terms for your classmates, using the techniques described in "Defining/Explaining a Term or Concept" (pg. 14).

1. Action in equity
2. Mortgage
3. Record
4. Matrimony
5. Subsidiary
6. Condition Precedent
7. A fortiori
8. Fraud
9. Legislature
10. Offer
11. Acceptance
12. Donor
13. Donee
14. Unjust enrichment
15. Answer
16. Heart Balm Act
17. Decree
18. Promise
19. Breach
20. Cause of action
21. To pray (for relief)
22. To grant
23. To compensate

SECTION II:
Using the Law to Predict and Persuade

CHAPTER 4—USING CASES

> ✓ **Exercise: The *Niederman v. Brodsky* Case**

To practice the art of reading and briefing cases, carefully read the *Neiderman v. Brodsky* case. Then carefully re-read and brief the case. Be prepared to discuss the case in class. Turn in your completed brief to your professor.

Henry NIEDERMAN, Appellant,
v.
Gerald BRODSKY
Supreme Court of Pennsylvania
261 A.2d 84 (Pa. 1970)

[Some footnotes may have been omitted.]

ROBERTS, Justice.

Appellant, Harry Niederman, alleges that on November 4, 1962 he was walking with his son at the corner of 15th and Market Streets in Philadelphia. At that time appellant's complaint asserts, appellee was driving a motor vehicle in a reckless and negligent manner as a result of which the automobile skidded onto the sidewalk and destroyed or struck down a fire hydrant, a litter pole and basket, a newsstand and appellant's son, who at that time was standing next to appellant. Almost immediately after this destructive path was cut by appellee's car, appellant claims that he suffered severe chest pain and that upon examination in the hospital, where he was confined for five weeks, appellant was diagnosed to have sustained acute coronary insufficiency, coronary failure, angina pectoris, and possible myocardial infarction. Consequently, appellant sought recovery from appellee for both these severe disabilities and the accompanying shock and mental pain.

Appellant's complaint was reluctantly dismissed on preliminary objections for failing to state a cause of action under the "impact rule" which provides that there can be no recovery for the consequences of fright and shock negligently inflicted in the absence of contemporaneous impact. Appellant admitted that the careening automobile had never struck his person. The judge noted "The impact rule will, no doubt, eventually be rejected as was the formerly well-entrenched rule of charitable immunities. It is regrettable that Harry Niederman, the plaintiff in this action, may not be afforded the opportunity to prove that his injuries are just as real, just as painful, just as disabling as if he had been struck physically by defendant's motor vehicle. However, we are bound by the law as set forth by the Supreme Court."

Today we decide that on the record before us, appellant may go to trial and if he proves his allegations, recovery may be had from a negligent defendant, despite the fact that appellant's injuries arose in the absence of actual impact. "It is fundamental to our common law system that one may seek redress for every substantial wrong. 'The best statement of the rule is that a wrong-doer is responsible for the natural and proximate consequences of his misconduct * * *'." *Battalla v. State*, 10 N.Y.2d 237, 240, 219 N.Y.S.2d 34, 36, 176 N.E.2d 729, 730 (1961). By our holding today Pennsylvania proceeds along the path recently followed by our neighboring jurisdictions, see *Falzone v. Busch*, 45 N.J. 559, 214 A.2d 12 (1965); *Robb v. Pennsylvania Railroad Company*, 210 A.2d 709 (Del. 1965); *Battalla v. State, supra*, and removes this ancient roadblock to appellant's recovery.

Were we to do otherwise, appellant and those who are severely injured in a like manner would be barred from recovery in our courts. But the gravity of appellant's injury and the inherent humanitarianism of our judicial process and its responsiveness to the current needs of justice dictate that appellant be afforded a *chance* to present his case to a jury and perhaps be compensated for the injury he has incurred. The Restatement has adopted a view in harmony with this approach: "§ 436 * * * (2) If the actor's conduct is negligent as creating an unreasonable risk of causing bodily harm to another otherwise than by subjecting him to fright, shock, or other similar and immediately emotional disturbance, the fact that such harm results solely from the internal operation of fright or other emotional disturbance does not protect the actor from liability." Restatement (Second), Torts § 436(2).

We believe that it is not sufficient to perpetuate the old impact rule simply in the name of precedent. Each and every objection raised in the past which would preclude appellant in this case from going to trial can now be answered effectively and persuasively.

An analysis of the prior case law indicates that there have been three basic arguments which in the past would have defeated appellant. The first deals with medical science's difficulty in proving causation between the claimed damages and the alleged fright. The second involves the fear of fraudulent or exaggerated claims. Finally, there is the concern that such a rule will precipitate a veritable flood of litigation. *See, e.g., Knaub v. Gotwalt*, 422 Pa. 267, 220 A.2d 646 (1966) (not the view of a majority of the court); *Bosley v. Andrews*, 393 Pa. 161, 142 A.2d 263 (1958); *Huston v. Freemansburg Borough*, 212 Pa. 548, 61 A. 1022, 3 L.R.A., N.S., 49 (1905);

Ewing v. Pittsburgh C. & St. L. Railway Co., 147 Pa. 40, 23 A. 340, 14 L.R.A. 666 (1892).

The first objection has been variously stated but the quotation set out below is representative of some earlier judicial sentiments. "In most cases, it would be impossible for medical science to prove that these subjective symptoms could not possibly have resulted from or been aggravated or precipitated by fright or nervous shock or nervous tension or emotional disturbance or distress * * *. Medical science, we repeat, *could not prove* that these could not have been caused or precipitated or aggravated by defendant's alleged negligent act." *Bosley v. Andrews*, 393 Pa. at 168-169, 142 A.2d at 267. (Emphasis supplied.) While we agree that this might have been an appropriate conclusion because of the lack of sophistication in the medical field when the impact doctrine was first announced in 1888, it would presently be inappropriate for us to ignore all of the phenomenal advances medical science has achieved in the last eighty years. Today diseases of the heart, for example, are comprehended much more fully (to the extent that open heart surgery is almost an everyday occurrence), and the effects of hyperemotional states of the human body no longer are shrouded in mystery or myth.

New equipment and research, improved education and diagnostic techniques, and an increased professional understanding of disease in general require us now to give greater credit to medical evidence. Other jurisdictions have also recognized that this advancement in the medical arts should and could be legitimately reflected in changes in the legal field. *See, e.g., Battalla v. State*, 10 N.Y.2d 237, 219 N.Y.S. 34, 176 N.E.2d 729 (1961) ("we must * * * rely to an extent on the contemporary sophistication of the medical profession"); *Robb v. Pennsylvania Railroad Company*, 210 A.2d 709, 712 (Del. 1965) ("the early difficulty in tracing a resulting injury back through fright or nervous shock has been minimized by the advance of science"). Finally, The American Law Institute through a deletion of a caveat from one of its comments, has expressed a similar view.

The logical invalidity of this objection to medical proof can be demonstrated further by noting that the rule has *only* been applied where there is absolutely no impact whatsoever. Once there is even the slightest impact, it has been held that the plaintiff can recover for any damages which resulted from the accompanying fright, even though the impact *had no causal connection* with the fright-induced injuries. The rule has been stated: "However, where, as here, a plaintiff sustains bodily injuries, *even though trivial* or minor in character, which are accompanied by fright or mental suffering directly traceable to the peril in which the defendant's negligence placed the plaintiff, then mental suffering is a legitimate element of damages." *Potere v. City of Philadel-phia*, 380 Pa. 581, 589, 112 A.2d 100, 104 (1955).

It appears completely inconsistent to argue that the medical profession is absolutely unable to establish a causal connection in the case where there is no impact at all, but that the slightest impact (e.g., a bruised elbow and sprained ankle in *Potere*) suddenly bestows upon our medical colleagues the knowledge and facility to diagnose the causal connection between emotional states and physical injuries. It can easily be urged that recent advances in medical science have bestowed this ability upon physicians; but it is illogical to argue that the presence of some slight injury has accomplished the same effect! As the Supreme Court of our neighboring state of Delaware recently said: "* * * the line of cases permitting recovery for serious injuries resulting from fright, where there has been but a trivial impact in itself causing little or no injury, demonstrate that there is no insuperable difficulty in tracing causal connection between the wrongdoing and the injury via the fright." *Robb v. Pennsylvania Railroad Company*, 210 A.2d at 712.

Finally, even if we assume *arguendo* that a great deal of difficulty still remains in establishing the causal connection, this still does not represent sufficient reason to deny appellant an *opportunity* to prove his case to a jury. There is no reason to believe that the causal connection involved here is any more difficult for lawyers to prove or for judges and jurors to comprehend than many others which occur elsewhere in the law. "We realize that there may be difficulties in determining the existence of a causal connection between fright and subsequent physical injury and in measuring the extent of such injury. However, the problem of tracing a causal connection from negligence to injury is not peculiar to cases without impact and occurs in all types of personal injury litigation. * * * in any event, difficulty of proof should not bar the plaintiff from the opportunity of attempting to convince the trier of fact of the truth of her claim." *Falzone v. Busch*, 45 N.J. 559, 561, 214 A.2d 12, 15-16 (1965). We recognize the recent view of the New Jersey Supreme Court as representative of current jurisprudence.

The second major objection includes the fear of fictitious injuries and fraudulent claims. It has been expressed with varying degrees of politeness: first, in *Huston v. Freemansburg Borough*, 212 Pa. 548, 550-551, 61 A. 1022, 1023 (1905), the Court indicated its lack of respect for claims like this by observing: "In the last half century the ingenuity of counsel, stimulated by the cupidity of clients and encouraged by the prejudices of juries, has expanded the action for negligence * * *. It requires but a brief judicial experience to be convinced of the large proportion of exaggeration, and even of actual fraud, in the ordinary action for physical injuries from negligence; and if we opened the door to this new invention the result would be great danger, if not disaster, to the cause of practical justice." In recent cases, that concern has been expressed in a more charitable manner but the *same* denial of recovery for severe injuries has been the result. "For every wholly genuine and deserving claim, there would likely be a tremendous number of illusory or imaginative or 'faked' ones." *Bosley v. Andrews*, 393 Pa. at 169, 142 A.2d at 267.

The charge that fraudulent claims will arise is not unique to this Commonwealth. Every court that has been confronted with a challenge to its impact rule has been threatened with the ominous spectre that an avalanche of unwarranted, trumped-up, false and otherwise unmeritorious claims would suddenly cascade upon the courts of the jurisdiction. The virtually unanimous response has been that (1) the danger of illusory claims in this area is no greater than in cases where impact occurs and that (2) our courts have proven that any protection against such fraudulent claims is contained within the system itself—in the integrity of our judicial process, the knowledge of expert witnesses, the concern of juries and the safeguards of our evidentiary standards.

For the first proposition, the New Hampshire Supreme Court provides us with significant support. "From the viewpoint of analogy, allowance for mental pain, and for injury to mind and nerve as well as body, is given as items of damage in all cases of liability for personal injury where there is impact. It would seem practically as easy to pretend them and as difficult to disprove them in such cases as in cases where there is no impact and fright is the intervening agency of transmittal." *Chiuchiolo v. New England Wholesale Tailors*, 84 N.H. 329, 150 A. 540, 543 (1930). See *Savard v. Cody Chevrolet, Inc.*, 126 Vt. 405, 234 A.2d 656, 659 (1967) (quoting *Chiuchiolo*). In addition, it is abundantly clear that in the *Potere* case, *supra*, where the injury was slight and unrelated, the opportunity for fraud was just as great; yet in that situation recovery was allowed. See *Battalla v. State*, 10 N.Y.2d 237, 240, 219 N.Y.S.2d 34, 36, 176 N.E.2d 729, 730 (1961) ("fraudulent accidents and injuries are just as easily feigned in the slight-impact cases").

Furthermore, we are unable to accept the proposition that our courts and the judicial system in general cannot deal with fraudulent claims when they arise. Factual, legal, and medical charlatans are unlikely to emerge from a trial unmasked. This same thought has been given compelling exposition in recent opinions by the highest courts of our neighboring states, Delaware, New Jersey, and New York. We, of course, join these and other authorities in rejecting as patently fallacious the argument that would bar actions such as appellant's because some other litigants might present false or feigned claims. "Public policy requires the courts, with the aid of the legal and medical professions, to find ways and means to solve satisfactorily the problems thus presented—not expedient ways to avoid them." *Robb v. Pennsylvania Railroad Company*, Del., 210 A.2d at 714.

The last argument urged by the proponents of the impact rule is that: "If we permitted recovery in a case such as this, our Courts would be swamped by a virtual avalanche of cases for damages for many situations and cases hitherto unrecoverable in Pennsylvania." *Knaub v. Gotwalt*, 422 Pa. at 271, 220 A.2d at 647. However, it is our view that this argument is currently refuted on two grounds. First, it is not at all clear that the flood of litigation has occurred in states without the impact rule. "The truth of the matter is that the feared flood tide of litigation has simply not appeared in states following the majority rule allowing recovery of psychic injuries without impact. The volume of litigation has been heaviest in states following the *Mitchell* doctrine and its impact rule. See McNiece, *Psychic Injury and Tort Liability in New York*, 24 St. John's L. Rev. 132 (1949) * * *." Lambert, *Tort Liability for Psychic Injuries*, 41 Boston U.L. Rev. at 592. Even those who do not believe that the amount of litigation is *greater* in jurisdictions with the impact rule, maintain that there has been *no increase* in those states which have abandoned this doctrine. *Okrina v. Midwestern Corp.*, 165 N.W.2d 259, 263 (Minn. 1969) ("there is no indication it [the abandonment of the impact rule] has either spawned a flood of litigation or bred a rash of fraudulent claims since its adoption in 1892"); see Smith, *Relation of Emotions to Injury and Disease*, 30 Va. L. Rev. 193 (1944); Comment, *Injuries From Fright Without Contact*, 15 Cleve.-Mar. L. Rev. at 336 (1966).

Secondly, and more compelling than an academic debate over the apparent or real increases in the amount of litigation, is the fundamental concept of our judicial system that any such increase should not be determinative or relevant to the availability of a judicial forum for the adjudication of impartial individual rights. "It is the business of the law to remedy wrongs that deserve it, even at the expense of a 'flood of litigation'; and it is a pitiful confession of incompetence on the part of any court of justice to deny relief upon the ground that it will give the courts too much work to do." Porsser, *Intentional Infliction of Mental Suffering: A New Tort*, 37 Mich. L. Rev. 874 (1939). We obviously do not accept the "too much work to do" rationale. We place the responsibility exactly where it should be: not in denying relief to those who have been injured, *but* on the judicial machinery of the Commonwealth to fulfill its obligation to make itself available to litigants. Who is to say which class of aggrieved plaintiffs should be denied access to our courts because of speculation that the workload will be a burden? Certainly this Court is unwilling to allow such considerations to influence a determination whether a class of litigants will be denied or permitted to seek adjudication of its claims. See *Robb v. Pennsylvania Railroad Company*, 210 A.2d at 714 (Del. 1965) ("if there be increased litigation the courts must willingly cope with the task"); *Falzone v. Busch*, 45 N.J. 559, 214 A.2d at 16 (1965) ("the proper remedy is an expansion of the judicial machinery, not a decrease in the availability of justice"); *Battalla v. State*, 10 N.Y.2d 237, 242, 219 N.Y.S.2d at 36, 176 N.E.2d at 731 (1961) ("it is the duty of the courts to willingly accept the opportunity to settle these disputes").

* * *

We have carefully examined the arguments in support of the old impact rule. It seems clear to us that even if these rationales may have had validity in earlier years, in 1969 continued adherence to the rule makes little sense. We believe that our analysis of the underpinnings of the impact doctrine proves that they are now so weak and that the arguments opposing the doctrine are so strong that an overruling of earlier cases is compelled.

We today choose to abandon the requirement of a physical impact as a precondition to recovery for damages proximately caused by the tort in only those cases like the one before us where the plaintiff was in personal danger of physical impact because of the direction of a negligent force against him and where plaintiff actually did fear the physical impact. Since appellant's complaint alleges facts which if proven will establish that the negligent force was aimed at him and put him in personal danger of physical impact, and that he actually did fear the force, this case must proceed to trial.

The order of the Court of Common Pleas of Philadelphia County is reversed and appellee's preliminary objections are dismissed.

BELL, Chief Justice (dissenting).

The Majority too often forget that an emotionally-appealing or heart-rending claim often produces bad law and sets a dangerous precedent.

Pandora's Box

The majority Opinion commits three tremendous and grievous errors in overruling Pennsylvania's "impact rule." The first regrettable and disastrous error is that they open Pandora's famous Box, out of which will flow a multiplicity of trespass suits for personal injuries and/or diseases. These will include the most fictitious or false or exaggerated claims that the imagination can conceive—based upon (as the Majority assert) the *direction* of a negligent force so near a plaintiff that he feared a dangerous physical impact.

A Guessing Game

The second major error of the Majority is that they not only substitute a "medical guessing game" for Pennsylvania's clear and definite and well-established "impact rule," but add a "Judicial guessing game." Few writers and few States can agree on a clear and definite formula for recovery, and the Majority itself cannot formulate a clear, specific, definite and boundarized rule or standards for recovery in this so-called "impact" field, which the Majority now abolish. It is difficult to imagine stronger reasons for not abandoning Pennsylvania's clear and well-established impact rule than the jumble of diverse, indefinite and farfetched views set forth in the majority Opinion.

Stare Decisis

The third major error of the Majority is that they deal another fatal or nearfatal blow to stare decisis. Once again a majority of the present Supreme Court has cavalierly buried or ignored the basic principle and the fundamental precept upon which the House of Law was built and maintained. Upon this Rock of Gibraltar, all Judges and all public officials, as well as all the people of Pennsylvania, can see and know and rely on their respective rights, their powers, their duties, their obligations and limitations. It is regrettable to be compelled to say that a decision of the present Court of Pennsylvania is good "for this day and this train only." What a catastrophe, and what a mockery of Law and of Justice!

What this Court said was well-established and sound law as recently as 1966 has today been rendered by the Majority obsolete and worthless by "all of the phenomenal advances medical science has achieved in the last 80 years." Can anything be more ridiculous than the argument that because of the phenomenal advances of medical science in the last 80 years something has miraculously come to light in this particular medical field in the last three years?

In *Knaub v. Gotwalt*, 422 Pa. 267, page 270, 220 A.2d 646, page 647 (1966), we said: "The rule is long and well established in Pennsylvania that there can be no recovery of damages for injuries resulting from fright or nervous shock or mental or emotional disturbances or distress, unless they are accompanied by physical injury or physical impact: *Koplin v. Louis K. Liggett Co.*, 322 Pa. 333, 185 A. 744; *Ewing v. Pittsburgh C. & St. L. Ry. Co.*, 147 Pa. 40, 23 A. 340, 14 L.R.A. 666; *Fox v. Borkey*, 126 Pa. 164, 17 A. 604; *Huston v. Freemansburg Borough*, 212 Pa. 548, 61 A. 1022, 3 L.R.A., N.S., 49; *Morris v. Lackawanna and Wyoming Valley Railroad Co.*, 228 Pa. 198, 77 A. 445; *Howarth v. Adams Express Company*, 269 Pa. 280, 112 A.2d 536; *Hess v. Philadelphia Transportation Co.*, 358 Pa. 144, 56 A.2d 89; *Potere v. Philadelphia*, 380 Pa. 581, 112 A.2d 100; *Gefter v. Rosenthal*,

384 Pa. 123, 119 A.2d 250; *Bosley v. Andrews*, 393 Pa. 161, 164, 142 A.2d 263. This rule was reaffirmed as recently as *Cucinotti v. Ortmann*, 399 Pa. 26, 159 A.2d 216 (1960)."

In *Cucinotti v. Ortmann*, 399 Pa. 159 A.2d 216, *supra*, Justice COHEN, speaking for all the members of this Court except Justice MUSMANNO, said (page 29, 159 A.2d at 218): "It is the well-settled rule in Pennsylvania that there can be no recovery of damages for unintentional injuries resulting from fright or nervous shock or mental or emotional disturbances or distress, unless they are accompanied by physical injury or physical impact. *Bosley v. Andrews*, 1958, 393 Pa. 161, 142 A.2d 263 (1958); *Koplin v. Louis K. Liggett Co.*, 1936, 322 Pa. 333, 185 A. 744 (1936); *Ewing v. Pittsburgh C. & St. L. Ry. Co.*, 1892, 147 Pa. 40, 23 A. 340, 14 L.R.A. 666 (1892)."

Mr. Justice Oliver Wendell HOLMES repeatedly and eloquently emphasized that "the life of the law has not been logic; it has been [human] experience." Holmes, *The Common Law. In Homans v. Boston El. Ry. Co.*, 180 Mass. 456, 62 N.E. 737, 57 L.R.A. 291, that Court, speaking through Justice HOLMES, reaffirmed the so-called "impact rule," and aptly said "that [it] prevents a recovery for visible illness resulting from nervous shock alone."

In *Huston v. Freemansburg Borough*, 212 Pa. 548, 61 A. 1022, 3 L.R.A., N.S., 49, Chief Justice MITCHELL, speaking for a unanimous Court, stated there can be no recovery of damages for fright or other mental suffering unconnected with physical injury, and said: "*It requires but a brief judicial experience to be convinced of the large proportion of exaggeration, and even of actual fraud, in the ordinary action for physical injuries from negligence; and if we opened the door to this new invention the result would be great danger, if not disaster, to the cause of practical justice. Spade v. Lynn & Boston R.R. Co.*, 168 Mass. 285, 47 N.E. 88, 38 L.R.A. 512, 60 Am. St. Rep. 393; *Mitchell v. Rochester Ry. Co.*, 151 N.Y. 107, 45 N.E. 354, 34 L.R.A. 781, 56 Am. St. Rep. 604. If, therefore, the question were new, we should see no reason to reach a different conclusion. But it is settled for this state, and is no longer open to discussion. * * *"

This Court has iterated and reiterated this well-established rule or principle of Stare Decisis based on Judicial experience numerous times before and since *Huston*, 212 Pa. 548, 61 A. 1022, 3 L.R.A., N.S., 49 (1905), *supra*.

In *Burtt Will*, 353 Pa. 217, pages 231, 232, 44 A.2d 670, page 677, 162 A.L.R. 1053, the Court said: "The doctrine of *stare decisis* still prevails in Pennsylvania. * * * This Court has always rigidly adhered to the rule of *stare decisis*. * * * All of the cases reciting our policy to adhere strictly to the rule of *stare decisis* need not be collected and reviewed. What was said by us in a few of the latest cases will suffice: Mr. Chief Justice Maxey said in *Monongahela St. Ry. Co. v. Philadelphia Co. et al.*, 350 Pa. 603, 616, 39 A.2d 909, 915, 'The doctrine of stare decisis is recognized and applied by the courts of this Commonwealth. * * *'; and in *Davis v. Pennsylvania Co.*, etc., 337 Pa. 456, at page 464, 12 A.2d 66, at page 70: 'An interpretation of law consistently followed by an appellate court over so long a period that it has become fundamentally imbedded in the common law of the Commonwealth should not be changed except through legislative enactment, which is a remedy always available and the proper one under our scheme of government. Otherwise the law would become the mere football of the successively changing personnel of the court, and "the knowne certaintie of the law," which Lord Coke so wisely said "is the safetie of all," would be utterly destroyed.' "

In *Bosley v. Andrews*, 393 Pa. 161, pages 168-169, 142 A.2d 263, page 266, this Court (in a decision with only two dissents) said: "To allow recovery for fright, fear, nervous shock, humiliation, mental or emotional distress—with all the disturbances and illnesses which accompany or result therefrom—where there has been no physical injury or impact, would open a Pandora's box. * * * For every wholly genuine and deserving claim, there would likely be a tremendous number of illusory or imaginative or 'faked' ones."

By permitting recovery in cases such as this—for alleged mental, emotional, psychic or physical injuries, without physical impact, the Majority will, we repeat, open wide the doors to an avalanche of fraudulent or emotional or imaginary illness claims which will unfairly delay thousands of meritorious claims, and will swamp our already tremendously overburdened Courts and make a joke out of Justice.

One enormously important problem which the Majority blithely ignore is that while medical science has made tremendous progress in this century, it has not yet reached a stage of knowledge where it can prove with any certainty—or without a tremendous diversity of sincere opinion which would therefore amount to nothing but a guess—both medical and legal causation, especially in the emotional disturbance and heart disease fields.

I will give a few of the very many examples that will occur to everyone: A plaintiff might be driving her car alertly or with her mind preoccupied, when a sudden or unexpected or exceptionally loud noise of an automobile horn behind or parallel with her car, or a nearby sudden loud and unexpected fire engine bell or siren, or a nearby sudden unexpected frightening buzz-saw noise, or a nearby unexpected explosion from blasting or dynamiting, or a nearby unexpected nerve-wracking noise produced by riveting on a street, or the shrill and unexpected blast of a train at a spot at a nearby crossing, or the witnessing of a nearby horrifying accident, or the approach of a car near or over the middle line, even though it is driven to its own side in ample time to avoid an accident, or any one of a dozen other everyday nearby events—each of these can cause or aggravate fright or nervous shock or emotional distress or nervous tension or mental disturbance and physical ills. If any one of these and other events are compensable, without physical impact, it may cause normal people, as well as nervous persons and persons who are mentally disturbed or mentally ill, to honestly believe that the sudden and unexpected event nearby and believed by them to be threatening, caused them fright or nervous shock or nervous tension with subsequent emotional distress or suffering or pain or heart attack or miscarriage, or some kind of disease or physical injury. In most cases, it would be impossible for medical science to prove that these subjective symptoms could or could not possibly have resulted from or been aggravated or precipitated by fright or nervous shock or nervous tension or emotional disturbance or distress, each of which can in turn produce an ulcer or headaches or fainting spells or, under some circumstances, a heart attack, or a serious disease or other injurious results. Medical science, I repeat, could not prove but *could only guess* whether these could or could not have been caused or precipitated or aggravated by defendant's alleged negligent act.

Here the plaintiff alleges that he suffered a variety of heart attacks immediately after defendant's car *skidded* onto the sidewalk and struck down a fire hydrant, a litter pole and basket, a newsstand, and injured plaintiff's son who was standing next to the plaintiff when the accident occurred. While the chain of events may have contributed to or caused Mr. Niederman's heart attacks, there are innumerable other possible situations which could have contributed to plaintiff's alleged heart attacks but in which no legal causation could be established. Equally important, it is a matter of universal medical knowledge that numerous people walk the streets and countrysides engaged in their normal daily pursuits who have had heart disease for months or for several years without its having manifested itself.

Should we say to Stare Decisis, Quo Vadis? Or is Stare Decisis like Antaeus, who was lifted from but returned to the earth, or like Mohammed's coffin, which is suspended between Heaven and earth, with no one knowing when or which way it will fall? Or is it like Nineveh and Tyre, which were destroyed, but every now and then are restored to temporary glory? Today, no one knows from week to week or from Court session to Court session what the law is today or yesterday (retroactive decisions) or what it will be tomorrow. How can anyone know today what the law will be tomorrow, or what anyone's rights, privileges, powers, duties, responsibilities, limitations and liabilities are, or will be?

The basic principle of Stare Decisis which is the bedrock for all our Law is not as immutable as the law of the Medes and the Persians. It may be changed by the Legislature and, under some circumstances, it may be changed by the Courts. I would hold that the principle of Stare Decisis should always be applied, *irrespective of the changing personnel of this (or any Supreme) Court,* except (1) where the Supreme Court of Pennsylvania is convinced that prior decisions of the Court are irreconcilable; or (2) the application of a rule or principle has *undoubtedly* created great confusion; or (3) a rule of law has been only fluctuatingly applied; or (4) to correct a misconception in an occasional decision; or (5) in those rare cases where the Supreme Court is *convinced that the reason for the law undoubtedly no longer exists, and modern circumstances and Justice combine to require or justify a change, and no one's present personal rights or vested property interests will be injured by the change.* Change of circumstances or modern circumstances does not mean, nor has it ever heretofore been considered as the equivalent of change of personnel in the Court, or the substitution of the social or political philosophy of a Judge for the language of the Constitution or of a written instrument, or for well-settled principles of law.

Mr. Justice OWEN J. ROBERTS, Pennsylvania's most illustrious member of the Supreme Court of the United States, in a dissenting Opinion in *Smith v. Allwright,* 321 U.S. 649, 669, 64 S. Ct. 757, 768, 88 L. Ed. 987, thus aptly and strikingly expressed his views concerning the erosion or abolition of the principle of Stare Decisis: "The reason for my concern is that the instant decision, overruling that announced *about nine years ago,* tends to bring adjudications of this tribunal into the same class as a *restricted railroad ticket, good for this day and train only.* I have no assurance, in view of current decisions, that the opinion announced today may not shortly be repudiated and overruled by justices who deem they have new light on the subject."

Mr. Justice FRANKFURTER, in his concurring Opinion in *Green v. United States,* 356 U.S. 165, 192, 78 S. Ct. 632, 648, 2 L. Ed. 2d 672, said: "To say that everybody on the Court has been wrong for 150 years and that that which has been deemed part of the bone and sinew of the law should now be extirpated is quite another thing. * * * The admonition of Mr. Justice Brandeis that we are not a third branch of the Legislature should never be disregarded."

Mr. Justice DOUGLAS, who is generally regarded as the leading opponent of Stare Decisis, in an article written for the Columbia Law Review of June 1949, Vol. 49, p. 735, said: "Uniformity and continuity in law are necessary to many activities. If they are not present, the integrity of contracts, wills, conveyances and securities is impaired. And there will be no equal justice under law if a negligence rule is applied in the morning but not in the afternoon. Stare Decisis provides some moorings so that men may trade and arrange their affairs with confidence. Stare Decisis serves to take the capricious element out of law and to give stability to a society. It is a strong tie which the future has to the past."

Mr. Justice EAGEN well expressed the same concern for Stare Decisis in the recent case of *Commonwealth v. Woodhouse*, 401 Pa. 242, 253, 164 A.2d 98, 104 (1960): "Unquestionably, in a republican form of government as we are privileged to enjoy, order, certainty and stability in the law are essential for the safety and protection of all. Stare Decisis should not be trifled with. *If the law knows no fixed principles, chaos and confusion will certainly follow.* * * * If it is clear that the reason for a law no longer exists and modern circumstances and justice require a change, and no vested rights will be violated, a change should be made."

What Chief Justice BLACK said for this Court in *McDowell v. Oyer*, 21 Pa. 417, 423 (1853), concerning Stare Decisis, is presently most apposite, viz., "It is sometimes said that this adherence to precedent is slavish; that it fetters the mind of the judge, and compels him to decide without reference to principle. But let it be remembered that *stare decisis* is itself a principle of great magnitude and importance. *It is absolutely necessary to the formation and permanence of any system of jurisprudence.* Without it we may fairly be said to have no law; for law is a fixed and *established rule*, not depending in the slightest degree on the caprice of those who may happen to administer it."

Moreover, I may add that which is often forgotten by the Majority—it is one of the most important duties of an appellate Court to erect legal signposts with language inscribed thereon so clearly, definitely, wisely and well that they who read may easily understand. This the Majority have likewise failed to do, in this case.

For the above reasons, I very strongly dissent.

––––––––––––––––

Niederman Vocabulary

Instructions: To better understand this material, be sure you know the definitions of the following terms. Be prepared to define these terms for your classmates, using the techniques described in "Defining/Explaining a Term or Concept" (pg. 14).

1. Allege
2. Complaint
3. Appellant
4. Appellee
5. Recovery
6. Reckless
7. Negligent
8. To dismiss
9. Cause of action
10. To bind
11. Common law system
12. Wrong
13. Wrong-doer
14. Responsible
15. Natural and proximate consequences
16. To bar (from recovery)
17. Precedent
18. Causation
19. Fraudulent claims
20. Damages
21. Mental suffering
22. Arguendo
23. Trier of fact
24. Claim
25. Fictitious injuries
26. Unmeritorious claims
27. Safeguard
28. Charlatan
29. To refute
30. To abandon
31. To remedy
32. Aggrieved plaintiff
33. Adjudication
34. To overrule
35. Stare decisis

Drafting the Legal Memorandum

A legal memorandum is a document that communicates information and analysis on a specific legal problem. An attorney or a law student will usually write a memorandum for another attorney's use. The memorandum will predict a court's answer to a particular legal question. A well-written memo will give a fair and objective appraisal of the law and will fully consider and discuss both sides of the legal issue.

Purpose of the Legal Memorandum

Lawyers use legal memoranda for a variety of purposes. They may want to clarify issues before drafting contracts or while planning a litigation strategy. Some attorneys also use memoranda to inform clients about the status of a legal problem or question. Sometimes, a legal memorandum will be used and shared by several law firm members who are working on different aspects of the same case or a memorandum may be used as a basis of knowledge if a similar legal issue arises at a later date. In short, legal memoranda are important documents that you will draft frequently as a practicing attorney.

Your Audience

Since you will usually not be drafting a memorandum for your own personal use, you must keep your reader in mind when you are writing. You will usually be writing for another attorney. So, you can safely assume that your reader is an intelligent, legally-trained individual. Do not assume that your reader is familiar with the law you will be discussing or with the specific facts of your controversy. You should fully describe the facts and law related to your controversy or case with particularity and clarity.

Your reader probably will not ask you to write a legal memorandum merely for his or her own edification. Your reader will be a busy person who needs to make a decision. You must be firm and definitive about the predictions you make in your memo. Do not equivocate. Your reader also needs to know the dangers of following a particular legal course. Your memorandum must fully discuss any arguments that oppose your reasoning and outcome and should evaluate the strength of those arguments. Your memorandum will make your reader's job easier, if you clearly communicate your ideas in your writing.

Parts of a Legal Memorandum

Heading

To: The immediately intended reader
From: You, the author
Date: Of completion
Re: Concisely identify the subject matter of the memorandum or give case name

Question Presented

The question presented is usually a single clearly-written sentence. It should not include the legal conclusions that you reach in your memorandum. Rather, it should define the precise legal question you answer in the memorandum. Make the question narrow and factually specific.

Remember each question before a court is framed by the facts of the controversy. Facts make a difference in the court's legal decision-making. Do not extrapolate a broader legal issue, as the court will not decide your case in the abstract. If you have more than one question, number them to make it easier for the reader to use your memorandum as a tool.

Brief Answer

The brief answer will give your prediction. You should try to predict as clearly as the law allows, remembering that you cannot guarantee a particular outcome in the courts. Try to answer the question with a yes or no. Then, explain your answer in several clear, concise sentences. The reader should have some understanding of the legal principle and how it will apply to your case. Give a separate answer for each question you ask. Number them in a way that corresponds to the questions.

Fact Section

State the facts as a clear, chronological narrative. Include all facts that are relevant to the resolution of the legal questions that you are addressing. Try not to dwell on insignificant facts, unless they give needed context to your narrative. Never analyze or characterize the facts. Do not omit facts negative to your controversy. If facts essential to the controversy are unknown, you must indicate this in your fact section. The facts should be written objectively rather than in the light most beneficial to your client. Include no legal conclusions in the statement of the facts. The fact section can be one or two pages long and should include properly-formatted paragraphs comprised of clearly-written sentences.

Discussion/Analysis Section

In the discussion/analysis section of the memorandum, you will fully explain and analyze your predictions. Make the discussion section easy to read. Use subheadings, if appropriate and number each argument in a way that corresponds to your questions and brief answers. When setting forth your analysis, many legal writers use the following format.[1]

> 1. Prediction—In a sentence, state your conclusion or prediction for the question or the subpart of the question.

> 2. Legal Principle—State the rule of law and cite to the authority from which you draw the legal principle. You may draw the legal principle from one controlling authority or from several authorities. You should fully define the applicable legal principle for the reader. Properly cite to all authority.

---

[1]   This format generally follows that explained in RICHARD K. NEUMANN, LEGAL REASONING AND LEGAL WRITING: STRUCTURE, STRATEGY AND STYLE (3d ed. 1998), a text we recommend for its clear explanation of legal analysis and writing.

---

3. Examples of the legal principle in prior case law—In this part of your analysis, you should show the reader examples from the important case law that apply the legal doctrine or statutory language. Explain the cases completely giving the reader a good understanding of the facts, holding and reasoning of each case. Use two to three sentences to explain each case. Do not discuss how the precedent influences your case until the reader fully understands how the courts have applied the legal principle in prior cases. Of course, you will cite to all authority that you explain.

4. Analysis—In this section of the discussion, you will demonstrate how the law will apply to the facts of your case. Show your reader how the precedent cases will influence the court's reasoning in your case. Discuss whether the facts of your case are similar or dissimilar to those in the precedent cases. Would the court be bound by the prior case decisions or are there enough factual differences between your case and the precedent cases to allow the court to apply the rule of law differently?

5. Counter-analysis—For each legal issue you address, you should present the arguments against the legal position that you have predicted will prevail. If your prediction benefits your client (always desirable), present the arguments against your legal position. If your prediction does not benefit your client, present the best legal analysis that you can that will benefit the client. With rare exceptions, every argument will have a corresponding counter-analysis. However, if your question only has one clearly defined, irrefutable answer, do not make up a counter-analysis.

6. Conclusion—for each legal issue or subpart of a legal issue, tie your analysis together in one sentence that reminds your reader of what you predict as the court's answer to the legal question.

Use this writing format for each issue and sub-issue you address.

Conclusion Section

In this section of the legal memorandum, you will restate your predictions briefly but with a bit more detail that you place in the brief answer. If you have reservations about your predictions, state them here. If the case law suggests a certain strategy for presenting the case, you may suggest it here.

Editing

The last step in drafting a legal memorandum is editing. Re-read your work many times, checking for grammatical and typographical errors. Edit your sentences to make them clear and concise. Make sure your paragraphs are focused and not overly long. The memorandum should be easy to read and the reader should understand it completely after reading through it once. After editing your work, let someone else read and edit it as well. As with other new tasks that you learn in law school, writing a legal memo is difficult at first, but will become easier with practice.

Using Predictive Language

When you are drafting a legal memorandum, you will usually predict how a court will rule on a particular legal question under particular factual circumstances. You should always be as definitive as you can be when you give your answer to the reader. Sometimes, the answer to the legal question will be clear, and you can answer with great certainty; however, at other times, you may not be able to give the reader an unqualified answer to the legal question. The following chart will help you to become familiar with the use of verbs, adverbs and adjectives that indicate your certainty about the answer you give to a legal question. All of the examples in the chart come from the *Niederman* case. Use this chart when you draft your memorandum addressing Mrs. Hope's legal problem and keep as a reference for use in future memoranda.

Language of Prediction

(Examples from *Niederman*)

Positive Prediction Language

Degree of Authority and Conviction	Verbs	Adverbs, Adjectives	Examples from *Niederman*
50%	Could (be) Might (be)	Possibly Potentially Plausible Conceivable	"Other jurisdictions have also recognized that this advancement in the medical arts . . . could be legitimately reflected in changes in the legal field."
	May (be)	Perhaps Quite possibly Colorable	"As to the possibility of actions based on fictitious injuries, a court should not deny recovery for a type of wrong which **may** result in serious harm because some people **may** institute fraudulent actions."
			"But the gravity of appellant's injury and the inherent humanitarianism of our judicial process and its responsiveness to the current needs of justice dictate that appellant be afforded a chance to present his case to a jury and **perhaps be** compensated for the injury he has incurred."
	Should (be)	Likely Seemingly	"Other jurisdictions have also recognized that this advancement in the medical arts **should . . . be** legitimately reflected in changes in the legal field."
	Must (be)	Necessarily Inevitably	"Since appellant's complaint alleges facts which if proven will establish that the negligent force was aimed at him and put him in personal danger of physical impact, and that he actually did fear the force, this **must** case proceed to trial."
100%	Will (be)	Certainly Doubtlessly Undoubtedly No doubt Unquestionably Clearly Surely Definitely	"The impact rule **will, no doubt,** eventually **be** rejected as was the formerly well-entrenched rule of charitable immunities."

Negative Prediction Language

Degree of Authority and Conviction	Verbs	Adverbs, Adjectives	Examples from Niederman
50% 100%	Might not (be) May not (be)	Questionable Debatable	"the plaintiff in this action, **may not be** afforded the opportunity to prove that his injuries are just as real, just as painful, just as disabling as if he had been struck physically by defendant's motor vehicle."
	Should not (be)	Unlikely Doubtfully Improbably	"in any event, difficulty of proof **should not** bar the plaintiff from the opportunity of attempting to convince the trier of fact of the truth of her claim."
			"As to the possibility of actions based on fictitious injuries, a court **should not** deny recovery for a type of wrong which may result in serious harm because some people may institute fraudulent actions."
			"Factual, legal, and medical charlatans are **unlikely** to emerge from a trial unmasked."
	Must not (be) Can not (be) Could not (be) Will not (be)	Impossibly Futile Hopeless	"there **can be no** recovery for the consequences of fright and shock negligently inflicted in the absence of contemporaneous impact."
			"In most cases, it would be **impossible** for medical science to prove that these subjective symptoms **could not possibly** have resulted from or been aggravated or precipitated by fright or nervous shock or nervous tension . . ."

✓ Exercise: Using a Case as Precedent

Use the *Niederman v. Brodsky* case as precedential authority. Draft a memorandum predicting how a court will rule on the Mrs. Hope problem. Turn in your memorandum to your professor.

Case Analysis: Applying the Rule to the Facts

Our client, Mrs. Hope, seeks the advice of our firm. Hope wishes to bring suit against an allegedly negligent driver for injuries that she and her son have suffered.

> On the afternoon of June 13, Mrs. Hope was outside her suburban Pittsburgh home watching her ten year old son, Robert, riding his bicycle up and down their street. At approximately 3:00 p.m., Hope walked over to her front porch to make a phone call on her cordless phone. While she was talking on the phone and looking at the ground, she heard the screeching of brakes and a crash. Immediately after hearing these noises, Hope looked up and ran to see her son lying on the ground in front of a stopped automobile. The bicycle was crushed beneath the wheels of the auto. There were skid marks from the car's tires on the street.

> Fearing the worst, Hope fainted from the shock of seeing her son lying on the street. Hope fell to the ground and struck her head on the concrete sidewalk. She suffered a severe concussion and head trauma that required treatment in the hospital for one week. Hope claims that she now suffers from painful recurrent headaches that began after her head injury.

> Robert managed to jump away from his bike just before the car hit it. He suffered cuts and abrasions but was otherwise physically unharmed by the incident. However, since the incident, Robert has had nightmares and remains fearful of riding a bicycle.

Evaluate Robert's cause of action and his chances for recovery against the driver of the automobile. You should also determine whether Mrs. Hope can bring a negligence action to recover damages from the driver of the automobile for her injuries.

Assume that the *Niederman v. Brodsky* case is binding precedent in your jurisdiction. Extract the legal rule from *Niederman*. Analogize or distinguish the facts of this case from those of *Niederman*. Predict whether the Hopes can sustain causes of action against the driver of the offending automobile. You may assume that the car in this situation constituted a "negligent force." Where applicable, make your best argument for extending the law as the attorney in *Niederman* did.

Chapter 5—Using Statutes

Reading Statutes

American law develops through judge-made case law and legislatively-enacted statutes. If a statute exists addressing an area of law, it will be considered the ultimate primary mandatory authority.[1] A court applying a statute is not free to change the provisions contained in it. A court is limited to interpreting the statute in light of the facts of the case before it or trying to understand what the legislature intended the words of the statute to mean. The court must consider every word in the statute to be important and may not ignore any statutory language. Moreover, the court cannot disregard or otherwise change the meaning of statutory language, even if the statute changes decades of well-established common law.[2]

However, the courts will usually not look to the words of the statute alone to determine how to apply it in a particular controversy.[3] The court must consider the prior court decisions interpreting that statute. If the highest court has interpreted the language of the statute under similar circumstances, lower courts will consider that interpretation to define the meaning of the statute's language.[4] In the absence of a decision of the highest court, the courts may consider any interpretation by a court of that jurisdiction when making its decision.

When interpreting statutes in the absence of prior case law, courts will usually look first to words of the statute and try to give the words their plain, everyday

---

[1]   Primary authority is the law of a certain jurisdiction. Primary authority can be constitutions, statutes, regulations, and case law. Mandatory authority is primary authority that binds a court to follow the legal rules that the authority articulates. For example, a decision of the highest court in a jurisdiction will bind all other lower courts to follow the law as articulated by the highest court.

[2]   See Lawrence C. Marshall, *The Canons of Statutory Construction and Judicial Constraints: A Response to Macey and Miller*, 45 VAND. L. REV. 673, 674-5 (1992) for an interesting view of the role of the court in interpreting statutes.

[3]   See Cass R. Sunstein, *Formalism and Statutory Interpretation*, 66 U. CHI. L. REV. 636 (1999) for an interesting discussion of formalist and nonformalist ways to interpret statutes. Courts and individual judges differ in how much material outside the text of the statute should affect the interpretation of the statute.

[4]   This means that a lower court will accept the highest court's interpretation of the statute, even if it disagrees with it. This is part of the precedential system of authority that the courts follow or stare decisis.

---

meaning.[5] If the language of the statute is clear, the court may look no further and will then apply the words of the statute to the facts at hand.[6] Sometimes, however, the language of a statute is less than clear when applied to certain factual situations. Under those circumstances, the court uses well-accepted techniques for interpreting ambiguous statutory language.[7]

The courts will look to the entire statute and the statutory compilation. The statute itself may contain a definition section to help the court find meaning in the language of the statute. Words in statutes may take on meanings different from those used in non-legal speech. The compilation of statutes may also have a general statutory construction act which give rules the courts should use in construing the meaning in the language of statutes in that jurisdiction.[8]

Courts will also consider the words of the legislature at the time it enacted the statute. This is called the legislative history of the statute. Courts may consider the remarks of the committee that worked on drafting the language of the statute or any comments of record from any of the legislators at the time of the statute's passage. In considering the remarks of legislators, a court will also have to be mindful of the time in history and during which the legislature enacted the statute and the societal problems that the statute was meant to address.

Finally, the courts may look to other jurisdictions with similar statutes that have interpretive case law. While a court in one jurisdiction will never be bound to follow a court decision in another jurisdiction, it may be persuaded by the reasoning of a court addressing similar factual circumstances and a similarly-worded statute.

The courts use these and other tools to intertwine statutes and case law to arrive at what they hope will be a clear and definitive decisions to the cases before them. The following exercise will expose you to a statute with its interpretive case law. Consider the first hypothetical situation below. Apply the plain language of the statute without consulting the interpretive case law to arrive at your

---

5   See William N. Eskridge, Jr., *The New Textualism*, 37 UCLA L. REV. 621 (1990) for further discussion of the plain meaning test.

6   See Frederick Schauer, *The Practice and Problems of Plain Meaning: A Response to Aleinikoff and Shaw*, 45 VAND. L. REV. 715 (1992) for an interesting discussion about the role of the plain meaning of the statute in courts' statutory interpretation.

7   The maxims called the *Canons of Statutory Construction* that many judges use to construe statutes are controversial. See Karl N. Llewellyn, *Remarks on the Theory of Appellate Decision and the Rules or Canons About How Statutes Are To Be Construed*, 3 VAND. L. REV. 395 (1950) for perhaps the most famous critique on the canons that advocates a practical reason approach to appellate decision-making. See also Edward L. Rubin, *Modern Statutes, Loose Canons, and the Limits of Practical Reason: A Response to Farber and Ross*, 45 VAND. L. REV. 579 (1992) for a continuing discussion of the issues that Llewelyn raises.

8   See WILLIAM N. ESKRIDGE, JR., PHILIP P. FRICKEY ET AL., LEGISLATION AND STATUTORY INTERPRETATION 211-284 (2000) for a thought-provoking discussion of various theories of statutory interpretation.

---

legal decision. Then, read the cases. Does your interpretation and application of the statute change? Consider the second hypothetical problem in light of the statute and the cases. How would you decide the case?

✓ Exercise: Aggravated Assault Hypothetical

Sally Robbins is a tenth grade student at Penguin Valley High School. She has a small build and is five feet, two inches tall. On May 3, while Sally was standing in the lunch line in the school cafeteria, Bob Morrison approached her and began to tease her. Bob, also a tenth grade student, is a six-foot tall football player with a large athletic build. Bob proceeded to loudly tease Sally for her failure to make the cheerleading squad in front of everyone in the cafeteria. Sally attempted to ignore Bob, but his taunting only grew worse when he began poking her with his hand and laughing at her. Humiliated and intimidated by the size of Bob, Sally put down her tray and began to walk toward the cafeteria door. Bob caught up with Sally before she could leave the cafeteria and grabbed her arm. He was teasing her and holding her arms roughly to keep her from leaving when she lost her balance and fell hard onto the floor. Sally was taken to Greater Igloo Hospital where doctors examined her and found that her right shoulder had been dislocated and her right arm had been broken. To recover, Sally had to wear a cast and a splint on her right arm for two months.

1. Look at 18 Pa. Cons. Stat. Ann. § 2702(a)(5) and divide the subsection into its elements. Determine whether Bob can be convicted of aggravated assault.

2. Now add your review of *Commonwealth v. Scott* and *In the Interest of D.S.* to your understanding of the statute. How does this change your analysis?

3. Now assume that both Sally and Bob were in line at a local fast food establishment when the incident occurred. How would this change the analysis? Also consider 18 Pa. Cons. Stat. Ann. § 2702 and *Commonwealth v. Bryant* while formulating your response.

Pennsylvania Statutes (Selected)

18 Pa. Cons. Stat. Ann. § 2702 (West 1983 & Supp. 1998). Aggravated assault

(a) **Offense defined**. A person is guilty of aggravated assault if he:

(1) attempts to cause serious bodily injury to another, or causes such injury intentionally, knowingly or recklessly under circumstances manifesting extreme indifference to the value of human life;

*   *   *

(5) attempts to cause or intentionally or knowingly causes bodily injury to a teaching staff member, school board member, other employee or student of any elementary or secondary publicly-funded educational institution, any elementary or secondary private school licensed by the Department of Education or any elementary or secondary parochial school while acting in the scope of his or her employment or because of his or her employment relationship to the school; or

*   *   *

18 Pa. Cons. Stat. Ann. § 2301 (West 1983). Definitions

"**Bodily injury**." Impairment of physical condition or substantial pain.

"**Deadly weapon**." Any firearm, whether loaded or unloaded, or any device designed as a weapon and capable of producing death or serious bodily injury, or any other device or instrumentality which, in the manner in which it is used or intended, to be used, is calculated or likely to produce death or serious bodily injury.

"**Serious bodily injury**." Bodily injury which creates a substantial risk of death or which causes serious, permanent disfigurement, or protracted loss or impairment of the function of any bodily member or organ.

"**Serious provocation**." Conduct sufficient to excite an intense passion in a reasonable person.

§ 104. Purposes

The general purposes of this title are:

(1) To forbid and prevent conduct that unjustifiably inflicts or threatens substantial harm to individual or public interest.

(2) To safeguard conduct that is without fault from condemnation as criminal.

(3) To safeguard offenders against excessive, disproportionate or arbitrary punishment.

(4) To give fair warning of the nature of the conduct declared to constitute an offense, and of the sentences that may be imposed on conviction of an offense.

(5) To differentiate on reasonable grounds between serious and minor offenses, and to differentiate among offenders with a view to a just individualization in their treatment.

1972, Dec. 6, P.L. 1482, No. 334, § 1, effective June 6, 1973.

§ 105. Principles of construction

The provisions of this title shall be construed according to the fair import of their terms but when the language is susceptible of differing constructions it shall be interpreted to further the general purposes stated in this title and the special purposes of the particular provision involved. The discretionary powers conferred by this title and, in so far as such criteria are not decisive, to further the general purposes stated in this title.

Legislative History of 18 Pa. Cons. Stat. Ann. § 2702

Mr. RICHARDSON offered the following amendments:

Amend Sec. 1 (Sec. 2702), page 2, line 9, by striking out "~~or~~"

Amend Sec. 1 (Sec. 2702), page 2, line 9, by inserting after "~~directors~~" or student

On the question,

Will the House agree to the amendments?

The SPEAKER. The Chair recognizes the gentleman from Philadelphia, Mr. Richardson.

Mr. RICHARDSON. Mr. Speaker, this is a very simple amendment. What it does is it adds the word "student." In the school district of Philadelphia in the sixth district where I live and where my legislative district encompasses, we have a serious problem concerning the fact that a number of people who come from outside the school into the school may not only inflict harm upon any school board employee or a teacher or someone who works for the board would also inflict that same harm upon a student who enters inside the building who is a student of the school. We feel there needs to be some protection to protect the student inside the classroom who attends that school so that he is protected from being beaten up also inside the school, and I, therefore, Mr. Speaker, ask for an affirmative vote on this amendment.

The SPEAKER. The Chair recognizes the gentleman from Philadelphia, Mr. Salvatore.

Mr. SALVATORE. Mr. Speaker, I rise in support of this amendment.

On the question recurring,

Will the House agree to the amendments?

The question was determined in the affirmative, and the amendments were agreed to.

In the Interest of D.S.
Appeal of D.S., Appellant
Superior Court of Pennsylvania
622 A.2d 954 (Pa. Super. Ct. 1993)

[Some footnotes may have been omitted.]

KELLY, Judge:

In this appeal, we are called upon to determine whether a juvenile resident of "Cumberland House" was properly adjudicated guilty of aggravated assault under 18 Pa. C.S.A. § 2702(a)(5)[1] for punching a roommate once in the jaw. We hold that there was insufficient evidence to sustain appellant's conviction of aggravated assault under 18 Pa. C.S.A. § 2702(a)(5). Accordingly, we vacate the adjudication of delinquency based upon aggravated assault.

FACTS AND PROCEDURAL HISTORY

The facts and procedural history of this case may be summarized as follows. Appellant and T.T. both lived at "Cumberland House." At approximately 7:30 p.m., appellant walked downstairs to the living room, approached T.T., who was watching television, and punched T.T. once in the jaw, knocking him to the ground. T.T. was taken to a medical center the following day, and his jaw was wired shut for the next four weeks.

Appellant was charged with simple assault, aggravated assault, and recklessly endangering another person. At the bench trial, after the parties stipulated to the aforementioned facts, appellant demurred to the charges of aggravated assault and recklessly endangering another person.

Before ruling on appellant's demurrer, the court asked if Cumberland House was a school for the purpose of satisfying 18 Pa. C.S.A. § 2702(a)(5). Defense counsel stated that, to the best of her knowledge, Cumberland House was not a school and did not fall within the purview of the statute. The Commonwealth requested that the court take judicial notice that Cumberland House was a school. However, unsatisfied that it was a school, the court called a recess to allow the attorneys for both sides to ascertain Cumberland House's status. The court noted that if appellant could be convicted

---

[1] **§ 2702 Aggravated Assault**

(a) offense defined.—A person is guilty of aggravated assault if he:

(5) attempts to cause or intentionally or knowingly causes bodily injury to a teaching staff member, school board member, other employee or student of any elementary or secondary publicly-funded educational institution, any elementary or secondary private school licensed by the Department of Education or any elementary or secondary parochial school while acting in the scope of his or her employment or because of his or her employment relationship to the school.

under 18 Pa. C.S.A. § 2702(a)(5), the parties would not have to argue, nor the court decide, whether appellant's one punch to the victim's jaw was an aggravated assault pursuant to 18 Pa. C.S.A. § 2702(a)(1).

After trial reconvened, the Commonwealth requested the court to take judicial notice that Cumberland House was a school, because it was accredited. The court took judicial notice that it was a school, denied appellant's demurrer to aggravated assault,[2] adjudicated appellant guilty under 18 Pa. C.S.A. § 2702(a)(5) and committed him to the Department of Public Welfare for placement. After appellant timely appealed, the trial court, in its opinion, requested that we remand for a hearing to determine whether Cumberland House is an accredited school.

On appeal, appellant presents the following two issues for our consideration:

> 1. MUST NOT THE JUVENILE APPELLANT'S AGGRAVATED ASSAULT ADJUDICATION BE REVERSED WHERE AN ELEMENT OF THE OFFENSE WAS NEVER ESTABLISHED; WHERE THE ADJUDICATING COURT TOOK "JUDICIAL NOTICE" OF A DISPUTED FACT OF WHICH ALL PARTIES ACKNOWLEDGED PERSONAL IGNORANCE, AND WHERE THERE IS NO STATEMENT ON THE RECORD BY THE PROSECUTOR OF HOW, WHERE, WHEN, FROM WHOM, OR EVEN WHETHER SHE HAD "ASCERTAINED" THE FACT IN ISSUE DURING A BRIEF RECESS?

> 2. DID NOT THE EVIDENCE ESTABLISH THAT JUVENILE APPELLANT HAD COMMITTED NO MORE THAN A SIMPLE ASSAULT WHERE AT 7:30 P.M. HE PUNCHED ANOTHER YOUNG MAN ONE TIME IN THE JAW IN THE LIVING ROOM OF CUMBERLAND HOUSE, WHERE THE TWO RESIDED?

Appellant's Brief at 2.[3]

FACTUAL FINDING OF CUMBERLAND HOUSE AS A SCHOOL

Appellant first argues that the trial court abused its discretion in finding that Cumberland House is a school. He maintains that whether Cumberland House is a school is not a matter of common knowledge, and therefore, is not capable of judicial

---

[2]   The court later granted appellant's demurrer to recklessly endangering another person.

[3]   Appellant concedes that his actions constituted simple assault, 18 Pa. C.S.A. § 2701(a). Accordingly, he seeks a reversal of the adjudication of aggravated assault; he does not seek a reversal of adjudication of delinquency, which is still grounded upon the simple assault.

notice. Moreover, appellant argues, there is no evidence of record to support a finding that Cumberland House is a school for purposes of 18 Pa. C.S.A. § 2702(a)(5).

The Commonwealth argues that the trial court could have taken judicial notice of a fact which is not common knowledge, as long as the fact is *capable* of accurate and ready verification. The Commonwealth additionally contends that appellant had ample opportunity to rebut the evidence consisting of judicial notice. We cannot agree.

A court may take judicial notice of an indisputable adjudicative fact. *Commonwealth ex rel. Duff v. Keenan*, 347 Pa. 574, 33 A.2d 244 (1943). A fact is considered indisputable if it "is so well established as to be a matter of common knowledge." *Albert Appeal*, 372 Pa. 13, 20, 92 A.2d 663, 666 (1952). *See also Haber v. Monroe County Vo-Tech. School*, 296 Pa. Super. 54, 60, 442 A.2d 292, 295-96 (1982), *quoting Petro v. Kennedy Tp. Bd. Commissioners*, 49 Pa. Cmwlth. 305, 311, 411 A.2d 849, 852 (1980) (judicial notice is appropriate if fact is so well-known as not to require supporting evidence). Conversely, a court cannot take judicial notice of a disputed question of fact. *Haber, supra.* By taking judicial notice of a fact so commonly known, the court avoids the needless formality of introducing evidence to prove an incontestable issue. *Sheppard v. Old Heritage Mutual Ins. Co.*, 492 Pa. 581, 425 A.2d 304 (1980); *Haber, supra.*

Judicial notice itself does not necessarily establish a fact. Judicial notice of a fact, when correctly taken, constitutes evidence, which like any evidence, may be rebutted. *See Commonwealth v. Covert*, 322 Pa. Super. 192, 198, 469 A.2d 248, 251 (1983) ("judicial notice should not serve to deny the opposing party the chance to disprove the fact sought to be judicially noticed"). If the evidence derived from judicial notice remains unrebutted, it may support a finding of fact.

The careful use of judicial notice is especially important in criminal cases. A court may judicially notice an indisputable fact even though it establishes an element of a crime. *See, e.g., Commonwealth v. Bigelow*, 250 Pa. Super. 330, 333 n.2, 378 A.2d 961, 963 n.2 (1977), *aff'd*, 484 Pa. 476, 399 A.2d 392 (1979) (court could have taken judicial notice that Philadelphia is a city of the first class in prosecution for carrying a firearm on a public street in a city of the first class); *Commonwealth v. Morgan*, 265 Pa. Super. 225, 401 A.2d 1182 (1979) (*dicta*) (in determining whether an element of possessing an instrument of crime existed, court may take judicial notice that a gun is commonly used for criminal purposes, but may not be able to take judicial notice that certain other instruments are commonly used for criminal purposes). However, when the "fact" is not so well-known within the community as to be indisputable, the court cannot judicially notice it to satisfy an element of a crime. *See*

Commonwealth v. Brose, 412 Pa. 276, 194 A.2d 322 (1963) (whether radar signs were posted on side of road on date appellant was speeding was a fact question to be supported by evidence adduced by the Commonwealth; judicial notice was improper); *see also Commonwealth v. Brown*, 312 Pa. Super. 383, 458 A.2d 1012 (1983) (judicial notice of situs of milepost 290 on Route 22 was improper because it was not a matter of common knowledge).

Some jurisdictions apply a second basis for allowing judicial notice. For example, Rule 201(b) of the Federal Rules of Evidence provides:

> (b) **Kinds of Facts**. A judicially noticed fact must be one not subject to reasonable dispute in that it is either (1) generally known within the territorial jurisdiction of the trial court or (2) capable of accurate and ready determination by resort to sources whose accuracy cannot reasonably be called in question.

See also Fortunata Giudice and C. William Kraft, *The Presently Expanding Concept of Judicial Notice, supra* at 532-33 n.22, *quoting Uniform Rule of Evidence* 9 ("Facts Which Must or May Be Judicially Noticed"); *McCormick on Evidence, supra* § 330 ("Facts Capable of Certain Verification"). Pennsylvania courts have not yet officially adopted this second approach. *Commonwealth v. Brown, supra* at 385 n.2., 458 A.2d at 1013 n.2.

Although Pennsylvania courts have not applied a "capable of verification" standard, judicial notice may be employed in somewhat similar, limited circumstances. By statute, a trial court shall treat as evidence a factual proposition that *is supported by reference to an appropriate governmental publication. See* 45 Pa. C.S.A. § 506 ("The contents of the code, of the permanent supplement thereto, and of the bulletin, shall be judicially noticed."); *Commonwealth v. Denny*, 372 Pa. Super. 317, 322-23, 539 A.2d 814, 816 (1987) (to prosecute for speeding violation, Commonwealth must show not only certification of accuracy, but also that the testing facility has been granted official testing status by the Department of Transportation; proof of official testing status may be shown by a letter under seal from the D.O.T. or by "a citation to the Pennsylvania Bulletin which lists the station as an official testing station"). *Cf. Commonwealth v. McGinnis*, 511 Pa. 520, 515 A.2d 847 (1986) (error for court to take judicial notice that *modified* breathalizer had been approved by Department of Health where uncontroverted evidence was that instrument had *not* been approved).

In *Commonwealth v. Kittleberger*, 420 Pa. Super. 104, 616 A.2d 1 (1992), we recently held that, for the trial court to take judicial notice that a certain type of radar gun was approved by the Pennsylvania Department of Transportation, the Commonwealth must refer to the published approval in the Pennsylvania Bulletin. We explained:

> In sustaining its burden of proof, the Commonwealth need not produce a certificate from PennDOT which expressly indicates approval of a particular speed timing device. Rather, the legislature has considerably lessened the Commonwealth's evidentiary burden of enabling the courts to take judicial notice of the fact that the device has been approved by PennDOT, provided that the approval has been published in the Pennsylvania Bulletin. *See* 45 Pa. C.S.A. § 506 (providing for judicial notice) and §§ 724-725 (requiring Commonwealth agency regulations to be published in the Pennsylvania Bulletin); 75 Pa. C.S.A. § 3368(d) (requiring PennDOT to classify and approve speed timing devices by regulation).
>
> As applied here, the certified record identified the radar gun used to measure appellant's speed as a Falcon. N.T. 7/1/91 at 4-5. PennDOT has approved Falcon radar guns for use by the Pennsylvania State Police. 19 Pa. Bull. No. 50, Part I, at 5346 (December 16, 1989). Consequently, the Commonwealth could have established the requisite element of approval in this case merely by asking the lower court to take judicial notice of the fact that the department's approval of the Falcon radar gun was published in the Pennsylvania Bulletin. 45 Pa. C.S.A. § 506.

Id. at ___, 616 A.2d at 3. In *Kittleberger*, because the Commonwealth did not request the trial court to take judicial notice of the fact that the approval appeared in the Pennsylvania Bulletin, an element of the offense was not established, even though the approval was *actually* published. *Id.* at ___, ___, 616 A.2d at 3, 6. Moreover, this Court was constrained from taking judicial notice of something that was neither noticed below nor supported by evidence. *Id.* at ___, 616 A.2d at 6.

The mere capability of ready and accurate verification is an insufficient basis for judicial notice. The record must disclose at least some reference to the authoritative source for a court to take judicial notice pursuant to 45 Pa. C.S.A. § 506. *Commonwealth v. Kittleberger, supra; Commonwealth v. Denny, supra.*

"A court may not support an adjudication of guilt with evidence not part of the trial record." *Commonwealth v. Wasiuta*, 280 Pa. Super. 256, 259, 421 A.2d 710, 711 (1980). *See also Commonwealth v. Martell*, 307 Pa. Super. 1, 5, 452 A.2d 873, 875 (1982), *citing id.* Accordingly, in reviewing a trial court decision for sufficient evidence, an appellate court must be provided adequate indicia of what evidence the fact finder considered. *See Alko Exp. Lines v. Pennsylvania Public Utility Com.*, 152 Pa. Super. 27, 36, 30 A.2d 440, 444 (1943). *See also Wells v. Pittsburgh, Board of Ed.*, 31 Pa. Cmwlth. 1, 374 A.2d 1009. Therefore, a criminal conviction cannot stand based upon judicial notice of a *disputable* fact which otherwise lacks evidentiary support. *Commonwealth v. Brose, supra; Commonwealth v. Brown, supra.* Of course, the prosecutor's mere recitation of the Commonwealth's version of the facts does not constitute competent evidence. *Commonwealth v. Royster*, 524 Pa. 333, 339, 572 A.2d 683, 686 (1990).

Thus, in deciding whether a trial court erred in taking judicial notice, we must determine whether the notice was of an indisputable fact, *i.e.*, one which is so commonly known that it need not be supported with evidence, or one which, according to statute, is noticeable because there is recorded reference to an appropriate governmental publication, such as the Pennsylvania Bulletin. If the finding of fact is wrongly based upon judicial notice, the appellate court must then determine whether the finding was otherwise supported by evidence of record.

Pursuant to such review, we must determine whether the "fact" that Cumberland House is a school was common knowledge, whether the record includes reference to a government publication which shows that Cumberland House is certified as a school, or whether there was sufficient evidence of record to support a finding that it was a school. At trial, the court detoured the discussion of whether appellant was guilty of aggravated assault pursuant to 18 Pa. C.S.A. § 2702(a)(1) to whether appellant committed an assault under subsection (a)(5). The prosecutor readily requested the court to take judicial notice that Cumberland House was a school. This discussion followed:

> THE COURT: I don't know that it is.
>
> If you can get me some indication that it is, I'll certainly take notice to the fact.
>
> Is Cumberland House a licensed school, do you know, a CBS?
>
> MS. NUROFF: I don't know, Your Honor.
>
> THE COURT: What?
>
> MS. NUROFF: I don't know, Your Honor.
>
> THE COURT: I don't know, either.
>
> MS. NUROFF: I know that Lower Kensington is, so I would assume that they all operate the same way.
>
> THE COURT: Well, I can't take judicial notice of an assumption, but I'll take a short recess.
>
> MS. HARLEY: Thank you.
>
> THE COURT: And, if it is, of course, I will overrule the demurrer on that basis.
>
> We won't get into the one-punch situation.

* * *

(A short recess was taken.)

* * *

THE COURT: Alright. My understanding is that the Commonwealth has ascertained that Cumberland House is an accredited school.

I grant the Commonwealth leave to open its case, request [t]he Court to take judicial notice of the fact.

MS. McCARTNEY: Judge, I'm going to object to that.

THE COURT: Well, you can object all you want.

MS. HARLEY: Your Honor, I would request that you take judicial notice that the school is accredited, and, therefore, it comes under the meaning of the statute under Subsection 5.

THE COURT: Notice is taken.

MS. McCARTNEY: I want my objection noted, for the record.

THE COURT: It is.

What do you think she's doing there?

Alright. Your demurrer's overruled, on that basis.

MS. McCARTNEY: Your Honor, the defense would rest.

N.T. January 7, 1992 at 8-10.

The foregoing discourse indicates that Cumberland House was not so obviously a school. None of the attorneys even knew whether it was a school. Nor did the trial court know. Therefore, whether it was a school was not common knowledge. Accordingly, judicial notice could not be based upon common knowledge.

Moreover, the Commonwealth opened its case and moved the court to take judicial notice that Cumberland House was a school, without ever referring to an authoritative governmental publication which indicated such certification. Similarly, the trial court judicially noticed the "fact" without mentioning an authoritative source.

Without some reference to a publication which confirmed a governmental agency's certification of Cumberland House as a "school," the trial court was not empowered to take judicial notice pursuant to 45 Pa. C.S.A. § 506. *Commonwealth v. Kittleberger, supra; Commonwealth v. Denny, supra.* Therefore, the trial court erred in taking judicial notice on this basis as well.

Finally, the record does not disclose the basis on which the court found that Cumberland House was a school. Absent some evidentiary foundation, the court erred in finding that it was a school. In our review for sufficient evidence, therefore, we cannot treat as a fact that the assault took place in a school.

> SUFFICIENCY OF THE EVIDENCE: 18 Pa. C.S.A. § 2702(a)(5)
> (AGGRAVATED ASSAULT FOR ASSAULTING TEACHER, SCHOOL EMPLOYEE, OR STUDENT ACTING IN SPECIFIED ROLE)

Appellant also argues that there was insufficient evidence for the trial court to find him guilty under 18 Pa. C.S.A. § 2702(a)(5). We agree.

Our standard of reviewing a verdict for sufficient evidence is as follows. "On appeal, we must examine the evidence in the light most favorable to the Commonwealth, drawing all reasonable inferences therefrom." *Commonwealth v. Gerulis*, 420 Pa. Super. 266, ___, 616 A.2d 686, 689 (1992), *quoting Commonwealth v. Berkowitz*, 415 Pa. Super. 505, 515, 609 A.2d 1338, 1343 (1992), *allocatur granted*, 531 Pa. 650, 613 A.2d 556 (1992). The evidence is sufficient to support a verdict if the fact finder "could have reasonably determined from the evidence that all of the necessary elements of the crime were established." *Gerulis, supra, quoting Berkowitz, supra.*

The criminal provision at issue is 18 Pa. C.S.A. § 2702(a)(5):

§ 2702. Aggravated Assault

(a) **Offense defined.**—A person is guilty of aggravated assault if he:

* * *

(5) attempts to cause or intentionally or knowingly causes bodily injury to a teaching staff member, school board member, other employee or student of any elementary or secondary publicly-funded educational institution, any elementary or secondary private school licensed by the Department of Education or any elementary or secondary parochial school while acting in the scope of his or her employment or because of his or her employment relationship to the school.

This Court has appended the words "or while acting in his or her role as a student" to the end of this provision to effectuate the statutory purpose. *Commonwealth v. Scott*, 376 Pa. Super. 416, 546 A.2d 96 (1988), *allocatur denied*, 522 Pa. 612, 563 A.2d 497 (1989). Therefore, to be convicted under this subsection, a defendant must have assaulted a victim while that victim was acting in the scope of his or her employment relationship to the school, 18 Pa. C.S.A. § 2702(a)(5), or "in his or her role as a student." *Scott, supra.*

In *Commonwealth v. Scott, supra*, we did not reach the question of whether an assault must occur on school grounds for it to constitute an aggravated assault under section 2702(a)(5). The issue is now ripe for our disposition.

Section 2702(a)(5) focuses on the status of the victim. The only reference to schools is part of a description of the status of the victim, who must be an employee acting in the scope of his or her employment, 18 Pa. C.S.A. § 2702(a)(5), or a student while acting in his or her role as a student, *Commonwealth v. Scott, supra* at 424, 546 A.2d at 100. The statute itself provides no geographical limit.

In addition to the language of section 2702(a)(5), the texts of the two other statutes which were enacted along with the instant statute further indicate that no geographical limitation was contemplated for the aggravated assault offense. For example, in one companion statute, the same legislature expressly made location an element of the crime of possession of weapons on school property:

§ 912. Possession of weapon on school property.

* * *

(b) **Offense defined.**—A person commits a misdemeanor of the first degree if he possesses a weapon in the buildings of, on the grounds of, or in any conveyance providing transportation to or from any elementary or secondary publicly-funded educational institution, any elementary or secondary private school licensed by the Department of Education or any elementary or secondary parochial school.

18 Pa. C.S.A. § 912(b). Moreover, in another part of the Act of October 16, 1980, P.L. 978 (the "1980 Act"), the legislature added to the anti-obscenity statute, making illegal the display of any obscene explicit sexual materials " . . . in any business or commercial establishment where minors, as a part of the general public or otherwise, are or will probably be exposed to view all or any part of such materials." 18 Pa. C.S.A. § 5903(a)(1).

While the companion portions of the 1980 Act each specified geographical location as an element of the offense, the aggravated assault provision did not. This distinction among simultaneously enacted statutes further evidences the legislative intent to protect certain citizens while acting in specific roles, regardless of the situs of an assault. Therefore, the location of the assault is not an element of 18 Pa. C.S.A. § 2702(a)(5).

Although the situs of an assault is not an element of this statute, the location of an assault is probative to the dispositive issue of whether the victim was acting in his or her role as an employee or student. The fact finder should consider all relevant circumstances, including the situs of an attack, in determining whether the victim of an assault was acting in one of the specific roles which our General Assembly has granted special protection. Because the situs of the assault is so interwoven with the status of the victim, the finding of fact that a person was assaulted at a school must be properly supported.

As we held above, the trial court erred in finding that the situs of the assault, Cumberland House, was a school. We must now review the entire trial transcript for any other evidence which may support a finding of guilt under section 2702(a)(5). At appellant's trial for simple assault, aggravated assault, and recklessly endangering another person, the Commonwealth and appellant stipulated as follows:

> MS. HARLEY: Your Honor, if I may, if the Commonwealth were to proceed with live testimony today, the Commonwealth would first call [T.T.], fifteen years old.
>
> Mr. [T.] would state that, back on December 10 of 1991, he was living at Cumberland House, C-U-M-B-E-R-L-A-N-D, which is located at 248 West Girard Avenue, here in the city and county of Philadelphia.
>
> He would state that, at that time, defendant, Mr. [S.], was, also, living at Cumberland House.
>
> He would state that, at, approximately, 7:30 p.m., while he was in the living room, watching television, the defendant, Mr. [S.] came into the room. The lights were turned off.
>
> The defendant approached the complaining witness, Mr. [T.], and punched him, one time, with the defendant's right fist in the complaining witness' jaw, knocking the complaining witness to the ground.
>
> At that time, assistants came and separated the defendant from the complaining witness.
>
> Mr. [T.] would state that he was taken to Girard Medical Center, the following day; that being, December 11 of 1991.
>
> THE COURT: Taken where?
>
> MS. HARLEY: Girard Medical Center, located at 8th and Girard Streets.
>
> THE COURT: Girard Avenue.
>
> MS. HARLEY: Girard Avenue—excuse me, Your Honor—because, when he awakened, on December 11, his face was swollen and sore, and he could not open his mouth.
>
> He would state that he, then, had an operation when he awakened from that. His jaw and entire mouth [were] wired closed.
>
> He would state that the—his—jaw was wired closed for, approximately, four weeks, at which point, he returned to a private doctor, who removed the wires.
>
> Your Honor, additionally, the complaining witness would state that he made no attempt to strike the defendant and said nothing to him.

Additionally, Your Honor, there would have been a stipulation, by and between counsel, as to the medical records.

I would ask that they be marked, Commonwealth Exhibit, C-1, and moved into evidence.

I'd just, if I can.

Counsel has seen them.

* * *

(Medical records were marked for identification as, Commonwealth's Exhibit, C-1).

* * *

MS. HARLEY: And, Your Honor, I'd mark—

THE COURT: Pass them up.

MS. HARLEY: —off for you, in which it states that the complaint—

THE COURT: I'll read it.

MS. HARLEY: Thanks.

* * *

(Handed to The Court.)

* * *

MS. HARLEY: And, Your Honor, I'll just note, for the record, that the treating physician was a Dr. Branconaro, B-R-A-N-C-O-N-A-R-O.

THE COURT: Alright. I'm being referred to the Operating Room Record Chart, copy, dated, 12/13/91.

MS. HARLEY: Your Honor, is that accepted in evidence?

THE COURT: You can keep that.

MS. HARLEY: Thank you.

* * *

(Commonwealth's Exhibit, C-1, was admitted into evidence.)

* * *

MS. HARLEY: Your Honor, with that testimony, Commonwealth would rest.

MS. McCARTNEY: Judge, the defense would demur to the charges of Aggravated Assault and REAP.

N.T. January 7, 1992 at 3-6.

The trial evidence did not address whether the victim was acting in his role as a student. There was no valid evidence that T.T. was participating in any school related event or that he was even in a school. To the contrary, the stipulation merely established that T.T. was watching television at 7:30 p.m. in the living quarters of Cumberland House. The

Commonwealth did not prove that the recipient of the punch was acting in his role as a student. Therefore, appellant is not guilty of aggravated assault under 18 Pa. C.S.A. § 2702(a)(5). *Commonwealth v. Scott, supra.*

* * *

CONCLUSION

The trial court in this case abused its discretion in concluding that Cumberland House is a school. Cumberland House's status as a school was not common knowledge, and neither the Commonwealth, as proponent of judicial notice, nor the court, placed on the record reference to an authoritative governmental publication showing state certification of Cumberland House as a school. 45 Pa. C.S.A. § 506. Accordingly, judicial notice was inappropriate. Moreover, there was no trial evidence to support such a finding.

The trial court further erred in concluding that appellant is guilty of aggravated assault pursuant to 18 Pa. C.S.A. § 2702(a)(5). There was no evidence that the recipient of appellant's punch was acting in his role as a student.

Finally, the Commonwealth's failure to request an adjudication under 18 Pa. C.S.A. § 2702(a)(1) constituted waiver. Accordingly, we can neither sit as a trial court and determine whether appellant committed aggravated assault pursuant to section 2702(a)(1) nor remand for a retrial.

We must reverse the adjudication of delinquency for aggravated assault, and appellant's record should so reflect our ruling. However, there was sufficient evidence to find appellant delinquent for simple assault. Accordingly, we reverse the adjudication of delinquency based upon a violation of section 2702(a)(5) and affirm the adjudication of delinquency based upon a violation of section 2701(a)(1) for simple assault.

Order reversed in part and affirmed in part. Jurisdiction relinquished.

COMMONWEALTH of Pennsylvania
v.
Darrell SCOTT, Appellant
Superior Court of Pennsylvania
369 A.2d 809 (Pa. Super. Ct. 1976)

[Some footnotes may have been omitted.]

CIRILLO, President Judge:

This is an appeal from a judgment of sentence entered in the Court of Common Pleas of Dauphin County following Darrell Scott's conviction for aggravated assault. We affirm.

During the 1985-86 school year, Rawn Marshall was a student completing his eighth grade semester at the Scott Intermediate School in Harrisburg, Pennsylvania. On April 18, 1986, the appellant, Darrell Scott, decided to visit his brother at the intermediate school with his two nephews. Prior to his visit to the school, Scott had never met Rawn Marshall.

At approximately 12:00 noon, during physical education class, Marshall became involved in a argument with an unidentified student during a basketball game. The fray ended uneventfully, however, when Marshall was leaving school at approximately 4:00 p.m., the individual who argued with him during gym class, along with several other young men, approached him. Scott came forward from the group and proclaimed that "a friend of mine wants to fight you." Undaunted by Scott's provocations, Marshall continued walking without a response. Scott then lunged at Marshall, and struck him on the side of his head. Marshall temporarily lost his balance from the blow, but then recovered and sprinted to the principal's office. There, he related the course of events to the principal as well as to his mother. The principal then summoned the police.

Following an investigation of the events at the intermediate school, Scott was arrested and charged with aggravated assault, 18 Pa. C.S. § 2702(a)(5). On February 17, 1986, Scott was tried before a jury in the Court of Common Pleas Dauphin County and convicted. Post-verdict motions were filed and denied by the court. On September 22, 1987, Scott was sentenced to serve not less than two months nor more than twenty-three months incarceration. This appeal followed.

Scott advances the following two issues for our review: (1) whether the evidence adduced at trial was sufficient to sustain his conviction of aggravated assault pursuant to 18 Pa. C.S. § 2702(a)(5); and (2) whether the trial court erred in refusing to instruct the jury that an employment relationship must be found between the victim and the school before § 2702(a)(5) is applicable.

Scott initially contends that the evidence adduced at trial was insufficient as a matter of law in establishing that he committed aggravated assault pursuant to section 2702(a)(5). Specifically, Scott maintains that the Commonwealth failed to prove that his conduct was perpetrated against Marshall *inside* the school building or classroom, or that the act was committed against an individual *acting within the scope of his employment*. Both of these criteria, he avows, are requisite elements to sustain a conviction under § 2702(a)(5).

Generally, the following test is applied when this court reviews the sufficiency of evidence sustaining a conviction:

> The test of sufficiency of the evidence—irrespective of whether it is direct or circumstantial, or both—is whether, accepting as true all the evidence and all reasonable inferences therefrom, upon which if believed the [trier of fact] could properly have based [the] verdict, it is sufficient in law to prove beyond a reasonable doubt that the defendant is guilty of the crime or crimes of which he has been convicted. In reviewing the evidence, we must consider it in the light most favorable to the Commonwealth, which won the verdict at the trial court.

Commonwealth v. Dunlap, 351 Pa. Super. 43, 45, 505 A.2d 255, 256 (1985) (citations omitted). Here, Scott was convicted of aggravated assault. Section 2702 of our Crimes Code defines aggravated assault under subsection (a)(5) as follows:

> (a) **Offense defined**.—A person is guilty of aggravated assault if he:

> (5) attempts to cause or intentionally or knowingly causes bodily injury to a teaching staff member, school board member, other employee or student of any elementary or secondary publicly-funded educational institution, any elementary or secondary private school licensed by the Department of Education or any elementary or secondary parochial school while acting in the scope of his or her employment or because of his or her employment relationship to the school.

18 Pa. C.S. § 2702(a)(5).

Scott submits that a reading of the legislative debate surrounding section (a)(5) undeniably discloses that our lawmakers intended to limit criminal responsibility under subsection (a)(5) to those who perpetrate aggravated assaults inside school buildings. We note however, that Scott failed to promote this claim before the trial court in his post-verdict motions.

It is now axiomatic that issues which are not raised in the trial court, or preserved for review in post-trial motions, cannot be raised for the first time on appeal. *Commonwealth v. Monarch*, 510 Pa. 138, 507 A.2d 74 (1986); Pa. R.A.P. 302(a); Pa. R. Crim. P. 1123. In *Monarch*, our supreme court stated:

> The post-verdict motions court serves as the initial step in the appellate review of trial proceedings. Our law requires that all assignments of error, whether pre-trial or at trial, must be raised in post-verdict motions. The failure of a

defendant to raise assignments of error in post-verdict motions results in the preclusion of later review of those issues
by an appellate court. One of the purposes for this rule is to
afford trial courts the first opportunity to correct error or
grant new trials where necessary and, thus, obviate the
need for appellate review.

510 Pa. at 146, 507 A.2d at 78 (citations omitted) (emphasis
added). Scott failed to include this claim in his post-verdict
motions, and it is therefore waived.

Scott also maintains that subsection (a)(5) "clearly states that
the assault must be perpetrated on an individual acting in the
scope of his or her employment or because of his or her employment relationship to the school." He asserts that since
Rawn Marshall was merely a student, and not engaged in an
employment capacity with the school, his conviction under
section 2702(a)(5) cannot stand.

Essentially, Scott asks this court to read section 2702, as it applies to this case, in the following manner:

> A person is guilty of aggravated assault if he . . . attempts to
> cause or intentionally or knowingly causes bodily injury to
> a . . . *student of any elementary or secondary publicly
> funded educational institution,* . . . *while acting in the scope
> of his or her employment* or because of his or her employ-
> ment relationship with the school.

18 Pa. C.S. § 2702(a)(5) (emphasis added). In other words,
Scott contends that this language mandates that an *elementary school student,* who is the victim of an assault, must
stand in an *employment relationship with the school* in order
for his or her assailant to be criminally liable for an aggravated assault.

In addressing this claim, we consider it elucidating to undertake a cursory review of the legislative history surrounding
section 2702. While we are cognizant of the tenet of law that
the discussions of our lawmakers during floor debate is not
widely recognized as authoritative in gleaning the legislative
intent of an enactment, our rules of statutory construction
nonetheless permit us to consider the contemporaneous legislative history where the words of the statute are not explicit.
1 Pa. C.S. § 1921(c)(7). In the instant case, we believe that the
legislative debate sheds light upon the reason underpinning
our General Assembly's apparently untenable directive that
an elementary school student must be employed by his or her
school in order for the child's assailant to be criminally liable
for aggravated assault under section 2702(a)(5).

The legislative history of Senate Bill 544 discloses that, in
its original form, the bill did not include the word "student."
It was not until the third consideration of the bill by the
House of Representatives that it was amended by adding
the word "student". *See generally* Pa. Legislative Journal,
House, 422 (Feb. 13, 1980). The sponsor of the amendment,

Representative Richardson of Philadelphia County, offered the following remarks in support of the added language:

> Mr. Speaker, this is a very simple amendment. What it does is it adds the word "student." In the school district of Philadelphia in the sixth district where I live and where my legislative district encompasses, we have a serious problem concerning the fact that a number of people who come from outside the school into the school may not only inflict harm upon any school board employee or a teacher or someone who works for the board [but] would also inflict that same harm upon a student who enters inside the building who is a student of the school. We feel there needs to be some protection to protect the student inside the classroom who attends that school so that he is protected from being beaten up also inside the school, and I, therefore, Mr. Speaker, ask for an affirmative vote on this amendment.

Pa. Legislative Journal, House, 422 (Feb. 13, 1980). It appears, therefore, that our General Assembly added the word "student," but failed to realize that the phrase "while acting in the scope of his or her employment or because of his or her employment relationship to the school" could be read to modify the word student. We cannot believe that our General Assembly, by any stretch of the imagination, meant that a seven-year-old elementary student must be employed by his or her school in order to be afforded protection under the statute. As the trial court aptly observed, "common sense and justice both dictate that the addition of the word student was not solely to protect students working in their schools. It is doubtful that any elementary school employs elementary students in any capacity. It would be unlawful . . . ."

We firmly believe that our lawmaking body enacted this specific provision to deter roving groups of youths from disrupting the scholastic environment and committing assaults on teachers *and all students* seeking to secure an education. Buttressing this conclusion are the comments of Senator O'Pake during floor debate of the proposed bill:

> Senate Bill No. 544 will serve notice to those who would willfully destroy the educational environment with an act of violence or terrorism, that they will be held responsible for their acts. There is no reason for our children to be intimidated and abused in our schools. A school is a place for learning—not a combat zone . . . . This tough legislation is needed if we hope to protect our children and teachers from the tidal wave of violence which is engulfing our schools.

Pa. Legislative Journal, Senate, 2081-2082, 2082 (Sept. 30, 1980). This noble purpose applies regardless of the student's employment relationship with the school.

Additionally, it is well-established that our Statutory Construction Act disfavors surplusage. We have consistently upheld the supposition that our lawmaking body is presumed to have intended to avoid mere surplusage in the words, sentences and provisions of its laws. *Commonwealth v. Saul,* 346 Pa. Super. 155, 499 A.2d 358 (1985); 1 Pa. C.S. § 1921(a), 1922(2). Accordingly, we must construe a statute, if possible, so as to give effect to every word. *Commonwealth v. Mlinarich,* 345 Pa. Super. 269, 498 A.2d 395 (1985) *alloc. den.* 512 Pa. 115, 516 A.2d 299 (1986). Pursuant to section 2702, our parliamentarians sought to impose criminal liability for aggravated assault upon an individual who attempts to cause or intentionally or knowingly causes bodily injury to an *"employee or student* of any elementary or secondary publicly-funded educational institution." 18 Pa. C.S. § 2702(a)(5) (emphasis added). If our General Assembly only sought to impose liability for aggravated assaults perpetrated against students acting in the scope of their employment relationship with the school, as Scott advocates, then the addition of the word "student" would have been unnecessary and mere surplusage. Anybody working for the school district would be afforded protection under the statutory scheme merely by their designation as an "employee." Giving effect to each and every word of the statute, we therefore assume that our legislature intended to protect all employees of the school district *as well as* all students.

Moreover, we cannot, as a matter of statutory construction, assume that our legislature intended such an absurd or unreasonable result in their enactment. 1 Pa. C.S. § 1922; *Commonwealth v. Westcott,* 362 Pa. Super. 176, 523 A.2d 1140 (1987) *alloc. den.* 516 Pa. 640, 533 A.2d 712 (1987). Although we are constrained by the principle that penal provisions must be strictly construed, our supreme court has stated that "[a] phrase necessary to the construction of a statute may be added if it does not conflict with the obvious purpose and intent of the statute, nor in any way affects its scope." *Commonwealth v. Fisher,* 485 Pa. 8, 13, 400 A.2d 1284, 1287 (1979) (footnote omitted); 1 Pa. C.S. § 1923(c) ("Words and phrases which may be necessary to the proper interpretation of a statute and which do not conflict with its obvious purpose and intent, nor in any way affect its scope and operation, may be added in the construction thereof.")

Since the statute in question is susceptible to varying interpretations, with one being absurd and the other complying with the obvious legislative intent, we will construe subsection (a)(5) as if it contained the language "or while acting in his or her role as a student" following the last word of the subsection. We believe that this interpretation will serve to effectuate the purpose of the statute until our legislature deems it appropriate to address its apparent omission. Furthermore, we do not believe that this judicially interposed language either conflicts with the obvious purport of the statute or in any way affects its scope and operation. In sum, we have reviewed all the evidence proffered at trial in the light most favorable to the Commonwealth, and accepting as true all the evidence and all reasonable inferences from that evidence, conclude that the trier of fact could reasonably have found that Scott was guilty beyond a reasonable doubt of aggravated assault under section (a)(5). Consequently, we reject Scott's strained interpretation of section 2702, and find that "student employment" is not a requisite element to sustain a conviction under section 2702(a)(5).

Scott next claims that Judge Natale erred in refusing to instruct the jury that in order to sustain a conviction under section 2702(a)(5), he must have assaulted a person who had an employment relationship with the school. Since we were unable to accept Scott's claim that subsection (a)(5) requires that the victim be in an employment relationship with the school, we similarly reject the notion that the jury should have been instructed on such an element. Having found no error in Judge Natale's jury instruction, we therefore affirm the judgment of sentence.

Judgment of sentence affirmed.

DEL SOLE, J., files dissenting opinion.

DEL SOLE, Judge, dissenting:

I must dissent from the majority's rewriting of 18 Pa. C.S.A. § 2702(a)(5). While I agree with the majority that what the General Assembly intended was to prevent persons from entering on school premises, engaging in altercations and disrupting the educational process, I cannot subscribe to the majority's interpretation of the subject statute.

The majority's interpretation of the statute would mean that anyone who assaults an employee of a school district or a student of the school district, *at any time*, would be subject to a charge of aggravated assault. Rather, it is my belief that the General Assembly sought to limit the upgrading the assault to the aggravated range only when the assault occurred to someone who was in a specific relationship with the school.

The majority's interpretation would mean that students who engage in an altercation on a weekend that may have been precipitated by a school sponsored sporting event the previous week would be subjected to aggravated assault charges under this Section.

I do not find Appellant's view of the statute strained. Rather, I find the majority's attempt to justify their statutory construction as strained.

Since the statute is not clearly drawn I think the best thing that this court can do is suggest that the General Assembly redraft it in order that it might serve the laudable purpose which its sponsors intended.

COMMONWEALTH of Pennsylvania
v.
Terrance Lorenzo BRYANT, Appellant
Superior Court of Pennsylvania
423 A.2d 407 (Pa. Super. Ct. 1980)

[Some footnotes may have been omitted.]

PER CURIAM:

Terrance Lorenzo Bryant, the appellant, was indicted on five counts of robbery, four counts of theft by unlawful taking, five counts of aggravated assault and one count of criminal conspiracy. Appellant pleaded not guilty and waived jury trial. In a non-jury trial before Honorable Samuel Strauss, he was found guilty of four counts of robbery, three counts of theft by unlawful taking, four counts of aggravated assault, and the one count of conspiracy. Appellant was sentenced to not less than two and not more than four years for each of the four counts of robbery; these sentences were to run consecutively. Sentence was suspended on the remaining counts.

The relevant facts of the crimes are as follows:

On the evening of March 6, 1978, two armed, black males forcibly entered an apartment located in the North Side section of the City of Pittsburgh. At that time, the apartment was occupied by five individuals, Richard Sayers, Kevin McCallister, John Piatrantonia, the three lessees—as well as Karen Steffy, and Jean Daley, visitors. The intruders demanded drugs and money, threatened the occupants with harm if neither were forthcoming, and emphasized their intent by physically assaulting the victims. Money and other valuables belonging to four of the five persons present were taken, the exception being Ms. Steffy.

At trial, Ms. Daley, Ms. Steffy, Mr. Sayers and Mr. McCallister identified Mr. Bryant as one of the assailants. They all described him as a black man with platted hair, wearing a navy blue pea coat and a blue denim hat. Three of them testified to being put through a photographic identification procedure and having picked Mr. Bryant's picture from police files. Two of them had picked appellant out of a line-up. Mr. Piatrantonia did not testify at trial, resulting in the counts against Mr. Bryant involving him being dropped. The defense presented was an alibi, several witnesses testifying that appellant was at home at the time of the robbery.

Initially, appellant argues that the evidence presented at trial was insufficient to prove his identity as one of the perpetrators of the offenses for which he was convicted. In evaluating the sufficiency of this evidence, all evidence, direct or circumstantial, must be read in a light most favorable to the Commonwealth, and the Commonwealth must be given the benefit of all reasonable inferences arising therefrom. *Commonwealth v. Burns*, 409 Pa. 619, 187 A.2d 552 (1963), *Commonwealth v. Chasten*, 443 Pa. 29, 275 A.2d 305 (1971).

The evidence compiled by the Commonwealth to establish Mr. Bryant's identity as one of the perpetrators is more than sufficient. The crimes in question took place over a twenty to thirty minute period, and during this time, the perpetrators were in close proximity to the victims, often under good lighting. The four victims who were present as witnesses at trial made in-court identifications of the appellant as one of the robbers; each remained positive of their identification following cross-examination. The Pennsylvania Supreme Court in *Commonwealth v. Kloiber*, 378 Pa. 412, 106 A.2d 820, *cert. denied* 348 U.S. 875, 75 S. Ct. 112, 99 L. Ed. 688, stated:

> "Where the opportunity for positive identification is good and the witness is positive in his identification and his identification is not weakened by prior failure to identify but remains, even after cross-examination, positive and unqualified, the testimony as to identification need not be reviewed with caution-indeed the cases say that 'his (positive) testimony as to identity may be treated as the statement of a fact.'" Citations omitted. *Id.* at 424, 106 A.2d at 826.

As the victims had a good opportunity to observe the perpetrators and each remained steadfast in his courtroom identification, the in-court identifications must be taken as statements of fact under the rule of *Commonwealth v. Kloiber, supra*. The previous opportunities to identify were offered in the forms of the description given to the police, a photographic identification, and a line-up. The descriptions given to the police were of a fairly detailed nature, with little diversion between them except for the fact that each witness was more cognizant of certain details than were his fellows; these descriptions, then, are not such as would contradict and weaken the in-court identification. Three of the victims, Sayers, Daley, and McCallister, made pre-trial photographic identification, and each picked the photograph of the appellant and identified him as one of the robbers. Two of the witnesses at trial, Daley and McCallister, also picked the appellant out of a line-up while the other two victims who testified at trial did not participate. These facts sufficiently substantiate the Commonwealth's case.[1]

Secondly, appellant argues that the evidence was insufficient to prove beyond a reasonable doubt that a robbery was perpetrated against Ms. Steffy. However, the evidence is more than sufficient to sustain the conviction under the robbery statute.

---

[1]   We do not reach appellant's contention that the pre-trial photographic identification session was overly suggestive, and, consequently, tainted the in-court identification as appellant failed to properly preserve the issue for appellate review by specifically including it in the post-verdict motions. See Pa. R. Crim. P. 1123(a); *Commonwealth v. Hustler*, 243 Pa. Super. 200, 364 A.2d 940 (1976).

Appellant was convicted under 18 Pa. C.S.A. § 3701(a)(1)(ii) which states that a person is guilty of robbery if, "in the course of committing a theft, he . . . threatens another with or intentionally puts him in fear of serious bodily injury." "An act shall be deemed in the course of committing a theft if it occurs in an attempt to commit theft . . ." 18 Pa. C.S.A. § 3701(a)(2). A criminal attempt exists when a person with intent to commit a crime does any act which constitutes a substantial step toward the commission of that crime. 18 Pa. C.S.A. § 901(a). See also *Commonwealth v. Fierst*, 257 Pa. Super. 440, 390 A.2d 1318 (1978).

Appellant does not dispute the trial court's finding of an explicit or implicit threat of serious bodily injury made to Ms. Steffy; he contends only that he did not attempt a theft of her property. Hence, the issue on appeal is whether or not the evidence was sufficient to prove an intent to commit a theft of Ms. Steffy's property and a substantial step toward achieving that end. We believe the facts of the case reveal each of those elements.

The necessary intent is shown in the appellant's words and actions during the events in question. Following appellant's forced entry to the apartment, and the corralling of its occupants into one of the bedrooms, appellant stated that if he and his accomplice didn't "get some stuff out of this place . . . [there would be] some dead honkies laying around." He then proceeded to search the apartment and collected several items without regard to whom the owner of the property was. As Ms. Steffy was present in the apartment at the time of the robbery, appellant might reasonably have expected that some of the articles present in the apartment might belong to her. One may reasonably infer from these words and actions appellant's intent to take any attractive property belonging to Ms. Steffy which he might happen upon.

The requirement of a substantial step is satisfied by the forcible entry to the apartment and the subsequent search. As each of the requisite elements of an attempt to commit theft is present, and the trial court's finding of a threat of serious bodily harm unchallenged, we find that the Commonwealth has met its burden of proof under the statute and the conviction for robbery must stand.

Finally, appellant advances the argument that the evidence was insufficient as a matter of law to sustain convictions for aggravated assault against Richard Sayers, Karen Steffy, and Jean Daley. Aggravated assault occurs when a person:

> "attempts to cause serious bodily injury to another, or causes such injury intentionally, knowingly, or recklessly under circumstances manifesting extreme indifference to the value of human life." 18 Pa. C.S.A. § 2702(a)(1).

As the record contains no evidence whatsoever of serious bodily injury to any of the victims, to sustain the convictions, we would have to find sufficient evidence of an attempt to cause such harm.

We must agree with the appellant that the evidence falls short of supporting his convictions of aggravated assault. An examination of the record for proof of an attempt to cause serious bodily injury is likewise unsuccessful. The nature of harm which appellant must have attempted to cause in an aggravated assault has been defined in 18 Pa. C.S.A. § 2301 as:

> (b)odily injury which creates a substantial risk of death or which causes serious permanent disfigurement, or protracted loss or impairment of the function of any bodily member or organ.

The testimony reveals that Richard Sayers was handcuffed, poked in the side of his head with a gun, laid on the ground, and kicked once. Karen Steffy was forced at gunpoint into a room and thrown to the ground. Jean Daley was sitting in a chair throughout the robbery with a gun aimed at her head.

After reviewing the record, we are led to the conclusion that appellant's actions do not even evidence an attempt to inflict serious bodily injuries upon any of the victims. One isolated kick does not reflect an intent to cause permanent disfigurement nor does it create a substantial risk of death. *Commonwealth v. Alexander*, 477 Pa. 190, 383 A.2d 887 (1978). Likewise, the act of throwing someone to the ground is insufficient evidence of an intent to commit serious bodily injury as defined above. As to the charge of aggravated assault against Jean Daley, the Commonwealth concedes the charge is baseless, and an examination of the record corroborates this.

This is not to say that appellant's actions against the victims are without legal consequence. A person is guilty of assault if he

> "(1) attempts to cause or intentionally, knowingly or recklessly causes bodily injury to another.
>
> (2) negligently causes bodily injury to another with a deadly weapon, or
>
> (3) attempts by physical menace to put another in fear of imminent serious bodily injury." 18 Pa. C.S.A. § 2701.

Clearly, kicking and pointing at Richard Sayers with a firearm, was sufficient evidence of an attempt by the appellant to cause bodily harm and to put the victim in fear of imminent serious bodily injury. Likewise, the crime of assault was completed as to Karen Steffy when she was thrown to the ground by the appellant. We therefore modify appellant's convictions of aggravated assault upon Richard Sayers and Karen Steffy to simple assaults. See *Commonwealth v. Alexander, supra.* Since sentence was suspended on these counts of aggravated assault, we see no need to remand for resentencing on the lesser crime. See *Commonwealth v. Guenzer*, 255 Pa. Super. 587, 389 A.2d 133 (1978), *Commonwealth v. Portalatin*, 223 Pa. Super. 33, 297 A.2d 144 (1972).

Appellant also committed an assault upon Jean Daley by threatening her with a firearm. However, for sentencing purposes, we are compelled to consider this count merged with the robbery charge against this victim. The two victims above were not only threatened in the course of the robbery, but they were also subject to additional attacks by appellant when they were kicked or thrown to the ground. Consequently, the criminal acts with respect to those victims, were separate and distinct acts, warranting separate punishments. *Commonwealth ex rel. Moszczynski v. Ashe*, 343 Pa. 102, 21 A.2d 920 (1941), *Commonwealth v. Olsen*, 247 Pa. Super. 513, 372 A.2d 1207 (1977). However, appellant did not touch or injure Ms. Daley; rather, she remained in the same chair where she sat when appellant burst into the apartment. There are no additional facts with which to support the assault charge other than those facts which substantiated the robbery charge as to this victim, i.e., threatening her with a gun in the course of committing a theft. *Commonwealth v. Guenzer*, supra.

While one unlawful act may constitute more than one crime, appellant cannot be punished twice for the same act. *Commonwealth v. Cox*, 209 Pa. Super. 457, 228 A.2d 30 (1967). Thus, although we can sustain appellant's convictions on both robbery and simple assault, we can only sentence appellant on one count. We therefore modify appellant's conviction of aggravated assault upon Jean Daley to simple assault and vacate the suspended sentence as to that conviction.

Three counts of aggravated assault, specifically count three (3), count six (6), and count fourteen (14), are modified to simple assault, with sentence vacated as to count three. All other convictions and sentences affirmed.

✓ Matching Exercise

Please match the terms on the left with the definitions on the right. Write the term number in the blank.

Terms

1. Compensation
2. Negligence
3. Uniform Commercial Code (UCC)
4. Federal Rules of Civil Procedure
5. Model Penal Code
6. Proscenium
7. Intestate
8. Testate
9. Lawsuit
10. Administrator
11. Hypo (hypothetical)
12. Legalisms
13. Law Review
14. Cite checking
15. Shepardizing
16. Judicial clerkship
17. Note
18. Legalese   ·

Definitions:

A. ___ Conduct which falls below the standard established by law for the protection of others against unreasonable risk of harm.

B. ___ Criminal statute drafted in the '60s by the American Law Institute (ALI), a group of legal scholars, and since adopted by a number of states.

C. ___ One who has made a will.

D. ___ Researching to determine if a case has been overruled.

E. ___ Body of procedural rules which govern all civil actions in U.S. District Courts.

F. ___ A scenario which never occurred but could.

G. ___ A periodic publication of law schools containing lead articles on topical subjects by law professors, judges or attorneys, and case summaries by law review member-students. Staff is made up of honor or top law students.

H. ___ Payment of damages; making whole.

I. ___ Stage in the front of the classroom.

J. ___ Laws drafted by the National Conference of Commissioners on Uniform State Laws and the ALI governing commercial transactions. Parts have been adopted by all states.

K. ___ A case before a court.

L. ___ Doing research to confirm that the legal references are correct.

M. ___ Dying without a will.

N. ___ Working for a judge as a researcher and writer.

O. ___ A person appointed by the court to manage the assets and liabilities of a decedent.

P. ___ Strict, literal, or excessive conformity to the law.

Q. ___ Specialized language of the legal profession that has since been replaced by plain talk.

R. ___ An abstract; a memorandum.

CHAPTER 6—SYNTHESIZING CASES

Synthesizing Cases

To analyze a legal problem, you need to understand which law governs your problem, how that law has been applied in prior cases, and how that law applies to the facts of your situation. First, examine each case individually. To do this, read and brief each case to determine the facts, issues, legal theories, holding, rule, and reasoning. Once you understand the individual cases, look at the cases as a group and try to summarize the body of law these cases represent. To summarize or "synthesize" cases, look for similarities and differences and try to determine patterns among your cases. Look for common ideas. The following questions may help with your synthesis. A worksheet or chart or grouping cases and listing them on a large piece of paper may also help you to see patterns and organize the material.

Consider

- **the situation:**

    1. What law or laws will apply to your case?

    2. What are the elements or parts of that law?

    3. Which element will the court probably deal with first?

- **the cases which have dealt with a similar situation:**

    4. What cases discuss this element?

    5. Do these cases use the same rule or has the rule been varied at all?

    6. If they use the same rule, are the results consistent?

    7. If they do not use the same rule, are the inconsistencies explained by:

        a. the date of the decision?

        b. the court that decided the case? What is the case's position in the hierarchy of authority? Is this the highest court? Intermediate appellate court?

        c. the facts of the case?

        d. other identifiable factors by which to characterize the differences?

• *the courts dealing with those cases:*

8. Did the courts reach consistent decisions in applying the rule to these cases?

9. If the decisions are consistent, what general ideas or principles (if any) might these cases represent?

10. If the decisions are inconsistent, can you see a pattern or any sort of general trend? Are the inconsistencies explained by:

    a. the date of the decision? Is there a chronological trend?

    b. the court that decided the case? What is the case's position in the hierarchy of authority?

    c. the facts of the case?

    d. other identifiable factors or trends which to characterize the differences?

• *the parties involved in the disputes:*

11. What theories did the plaintiffs and defendants use in these cases?

12. How did the plaintiffs/defendants support their assertions? Did they use:

    a. plain language?

    b. analogous cases?

    c. factual distinctions?

    d. policy?

13. Do the cases that found for the plaintiffs/defendants have anything in common?

• *your theory:*

14. When you look at the whole group of cases or look at these cases in small groups, can you see a general principle or idea which they represent? Can you account for any inconsistencies in your theory?

You may want to make a chart for your cases or you may want to group cases together by name and a short summary according to what each case says about an element or part of a rule of law. For example, if you wanted to analyze whether a person had a duty to aid, you might find that generally a person has not duty, but that there are limited exceptions to this duty rule. One case dealing with the exceptions might tell you that if a party has a special relationship with a person that party might have a duty to aid. Other cases may help you to define a special relationship and if any other exceptions exist. Hence, you might decide to organize your material according to the general rule and the exceptions.

Rule of Law and Synthesis Charts

These charts may help you to detect patterns in cases. You could make charts to compare how different cases have interpreted the elements of a rule or a rule and its exception. You may also want to compare the facts, holdings, and rationales of cases dealing with similar issues. The charts are simply a tool to help you visualize similarities and differences in cases and organize the large bodies of information you will often have to deal with in addressing a legal problem.

Rule of Law Chart

		CASES		
		Yania	Rankin	Estate of Dennis
R U L E *O F* *L A W*	No general duty			
	Exception: if put person in peril			
	Exception: if person begins to aid			

Synthesis Chart

CASES			
	Yania	Rankin	Estate of Dennis
Facts			
Issues			
Theories			
Holding			
Rule			
Reasoning			
Notes			

✓ Exercise: Is There a Duty to Aid?

Consider the following hypothetical:

> Ms. Molly Nice works as a crossing guard at the corner of Forbes and Murray Avenues in Pittsburgh, Pennsylvania. As a crossing guard, Ms. Nice helps pedestrians cross the street, when the light permits it. Wearing bright and reflective clothing, she stands in the center of the intersection to stop any approaching traffic. All drivers know to stop when a crossing guard steps into the intersection. Ms. Nice is not authorized to stop traffic when the traffic light would otherwise permit traffic in the intersection.

> On many occasions, Ms. Nice has observed Jay Walker crossing the street against the traffic light and, in Ms. Nice's opinion, risking injury. Ms. Nice has sternly reprimanded Mr. Walker and instructed him to only cross the street when the light permits it. On April 5, Mr. Walker was at the corner of Forbes and Murray Avenues, running to catch a bus. He ran across the street against the light. As usual, Ms. Nice called out to Mr. Walker not to cross the street. Ms. Nice saw a car about to turn the corner, risking injury to Mr. Walker; however, Ms. Nice did not stop the car. The car hit Mr. Walker and knocked him to the ground.

> Marlon Kramer, the driver of the car was upset and shaken but managed to call 911 on his cellular phone. The crossing guard walked over and reminded Mr. Walker that this was the risk that Ms. Nice warned him about every day. Dr. Shady, a pedestrian, stopped to view the scene of the accident but offered no assistance, even though he carried his medical bag with him. In a nearby coffee shop, two police officers saw a crowd gathering but decided to finish their coffee and donuts before looking into the disturbance.

Using the *Yania*, *Rankin*, and the *City of Philadelphia* cases and the Restatement sections which follow, determine the prevailing rule of law in this jurisdiction. Then, apply the rule to determine who has a duty to aid Mr. Walker.

Be prepared to discuss the following questions:

1. What is the law?

2. How does the law apply here?

3. What should the law be?

4. What is the law on the duty to aid in your country?

Anna YANIA, Administratrix of the Estate of Joseph Yania, Deceased, Anna Yania, in her own right, and Anna Yania, Trustee ad litem, Appellant,

v.

John E. BIGAN

Supreme Court of Pennsylvania

155 A.2d 343 (Pa. 1959)

[Some footnotes may have been omitted.]

BENJAMIN R. JONES, Justice.

A bizarre and most unusual circumstance provides the background of this appeal.

On September 25, 1957 John E. Bigan was engaged in a coal strip-mining operation in Shade Township, Somerset County. On the property being stripped were large cuts or trenches created by Bigan when he removed the earthen overburden for the purpose of removing the coal underneath. One cut contained water 8 to 10 feet in depth with side walls or embankments 16 to 18 feet in height; at this cut Bigan had installed a pump to remove the water.

At approximately 4 p.m. on that date, Joseph F. Yania, the operator of another coal strip-mining operation, and one Boyd M. Ross went upon Bigan's property for the purpose of discussing a business matter with Bigan, and, while there, were asked by Bigan to aid him in starting the pump. Ross and Bigan entered the cut and stood at the point where the pump was located. Yania stood at the top of one of the cut's side walls and then jumped from the side wall—a height of 16 to 18 feet—into the water and was drowned.

Yania's widow, in her own right and on behalf of her three children, instituted wrongful death and survival actions against Bigan contending Bigan was responsible for Yania's death. Preliminary objections, in the nature of demurrers, to the complaint were filed on behalf of Bigan. The court below sustained the preliminary objections; from the entry of that order this appeal was taken.

Since Bigan has chosen to file preliminary objections, in the nature of demurrers, every material and relevant fact well pleaded in the complaint and every inference fairly deducible therefrom are to be taken as true. *Commonwealth v. Musser Forests, Inc.*, 394 Pa. 205, 209, 146 A.2d 714; *Byers v. Ward*, 368 Pa. 416, 420, 84 A.2d 307.

The complaint avers negligence in the following manner: (1) "The death by drowning of * * * [Yania] was caused entirely by the acts of [Bigan] * * * in *urging, enticing, taunting and inveigling* [Yania] to jump into the water, which [Bigan] knew or ought to have known was of a depth of 8 to 10 feet and dangerous to the life of anyone who would jump therein" (emphasis supplied); (2) "* * * [Bigan] violated his obligations to a business invitee in not having his premises reasonably safe, and not warning his business invitee of a dangerous condition and to the contrary urged, induced and inveigled [Yania] into a dangerous position and a dangerous act, whereby [Yania] came to his death"; (3) "After [Yania] was in the water, a highly dangerous position, having been induced and inveigled therein by [Bigan], [Bigan] failed and neglected to take reasonable steps and action to protect or assist [Yania], or extradite [Yania] from the dangerous position in which [Bigan] had placed him." Summarized, Bigan stands charged with three-fold negligence: (1) by urging, enticing, taunting and inveigling Yania to jump into the water; (2) by failing to warn Yania of a dangerous condition on the land, i.e. the cut wherein lay 8 to 10 feet of water; (3) by failing to go to Yania's rescue after he had jumped into the water.[1]

The Wrongful Death Act (Act of April 15, 1851, P.L. 669, § 19, 12 P.S. § 1601) and the Survival Act (Act of April 18, 1949, P.L. 512, art. VI, § 603, 20 P.S. § 320.603) "* * * really confer no more than rights to recover damages growing out of a single cause of action, namely, *the negligence of the defendant* which caused the damages suffered." (Emphasis supplied.) *Fisher v. Hill*, 368 Pa. 53, 58, 81 A.2d 860, 863. While the law presumes that Yania was not negligent, such presumption affords no basis for an inference that Bigan was negligent (*Wenhold v. O'Dea*, 338 Pa. 33, 35, 12 A.2d 115). Our inquiry must be to ascertain whether the well-pleaded facts in the complaint, assumedly true, would, if shown, suffice to prove negligent conduct on the part of Bigan.

Appellant initially contends that Yania's descent from the high embankment into the water and the resulting death were caused "entirely" by the spoken words and blandishments of Bigan delivered at a distance from Yania. The complaint does not allege that Yania slipped or that he was pushed or that Bigan made any *physical* impact upon Yania. On the contrary, the only inference deducible from the facts alleged in the complaint is that Bigan, by the employment of cajolery and inveiglement, caused such a *mental* impact on Yania that the latter was deprived of his volition and freedom of choice and placed under a compulsion to jump into the water. Had Yania been a child of tender years or a person mentally deficient then it is conceivable that taunting and enticement could constitute actionable negligence if it resulted in harm. However, to contend that such conduct directed to an adult in full possession of all his mental faculties constitutes actionable negligence is not only without precedent but completely

---

[1] So far as the record is concerned we must treat the 33 year old Yania as in full possession of his mental faculties at the time he jumped.

without merit. *McGrew v. Stone*, 53 Pa. 436; *Rugart v. Keebler-Weyl Baking Co.*, 277 Pa. 408, 121 A. 198, and *Bisson v. John B. Kelly Inc.*, 314 Pa. 99, 170 A. 139, relied upon by appellant, are clearly inapposite.

Appellant next urges that Bigan, as the possessor of the land, violated a duty owed to Yania in that his land contained a dangerous condition, i.e. the water-filled cut or trench, and he failed to warn Yania of such condition. Yania was a business invitee in that he entered upon the land for a common business purpose for the mutual benefit of Bigan and himself (Restatement, Torts, § 332; *Parsons v. Drake*, 347 Pa. 247, 250, 32 A.2d 27). As possessor of the land, Bigan would become subject to liability to Yania for any physical harm caused by any artificial or natural condition upon the land (1) if, and only if, Bigan knew or could have discovered the condition which, if known to him he should have realized involved an unreasonable risk of harm to Yania, (2) if Bigan had to reason to believe Yania would discover the condition or realize the risk of harm and (3) if he invited or permitted Yania to enter upon the land without exercising reasonable care to make the condition reasonably safe or give adequate warning to enable him to avoid the harm. *Schon v. Scranton-Springbrook Water Service Co.*, 381 Pa. 148, 152, 112 A.2d 89, and cases therein cited; *Engle v. Reider*, 366 Pa. 411, 77 A.2d 621; *Johnson v. Rulon*, 363 Pa. 585, 70 A.2d 325. The inapplicability of this rule of liability to the instant facts is readily apparent.

The *only* condition on Bigan's land which could possibly have contributed in any manner to Yania's death was the water-filled cut with its high embankment. Of this condition there was neither concealment nor failure to warn, but, on the contrary, the complaint specifically avers that Bigan not only requested Yania and Boyd to assist him in starting the pump to remove the water from the cut but "led" them to the cut itself. If this cut possessed any potentiality of danger, such a condition was as obvious and apparent to Yania as to Bigan, both coal strip-mine operators. Under the circumstances herein depicted Bigan could not be held liable in this respect.

Lastly, it is urged that Bigan failed to take the necessary steps to rescue Yania from the water. The mere fact that Bigan saw Yania in a position of peril in the water imposed upon him no legal, although a moral, obligation or duty to go to his rescue unless Bigan was legally responsible, in whole or in part, for placing Yania in the perilous position. Restatement, Torts, § 314. *Cf.* Restatement, Torts, § 322. The language of this Court in *Brown v. French*, 104 Pa. 604, 607, 608, is apt: "If it appeared that the deceased, by his own carelessness, contributed in any degree to the accident which caused the loss of his life, the defendants ought not to have been held to answer for the consequences resulting from that accident. * * * He voluntarily placed himself in the way of danger, and his death was the result of his own act. * * * That his undertaking was an exceedingly reckless and dangerous one, the event proves, but there was no one to blame for it but himself. He had the right to try the experiment, obviously dangerous as it was, but then also upon him rested the consequences of that experiment, and upon no one else; he may have been, and probably was, ignorant of the risk which he was taking upon himself, or knowing it, and trusting to his own skill, he may have regarded it as easily superable. But in either case, the result of his ignorance, or of his mistake, must rest with himself—and cannot be charged to the defendants." The complaint does not aver any facts which impose upon Bigan legal responsibility for placing Yania in the dangerous position in the water and, absent such legal responsibility, the law imposes on Bigan no duty of rescue.

Recognizing that the deceased Yania is entitled to the benefit of the presumption that he was exercising due care and extending to appellant the benefit of every well pleaded fact in this complaint and the fair inferences arising therefrom, yet we can reach but one conclusion: that Yania, a reasonable and prudent adult in full possession of all his mental faculties, undertook to perform an act which he knew or should have known was attended with more or less peril and it was the performance of that act and not any conduct upon Bigan's part which caused his unfortunate death.

Order affirmed.

Restatement (Second) of Torts § 314[1]

§ 314. Duty to Act for Protection of Others

The fact that the actor realizes or should realize that action on his part is necessary for another's aid or protection does not of itself impose upon him a duty to take such action.

§ 314 A. Special Relations Giving Rise to Duty to Aid or Protect

(1) A common carrier is under a duty to its passengers to take reasonable action

(a) to protect them against unreasonable risk of physical harm, and

(b) to give them first aid after it knows or has reason to know that they are ill or injured, and to care for them until they can be cared for by others.

(2) An innkeeper is under a similar duty to his guests.

(3) A possessor of land who holds it open to the public is under a similar duty to members of the public who enter in response to his invitation.

(4) One who is required by law to take or who voluntarily takes the custody of another under circumstances such as to deprive the other of his normal opportunities for protection is under a similar duty to the other.

§ 314 B. Duty to Protect Endangered or Hurt Employee

(1) If a servant, while acting within the scope of his employment, comes into a position of imminent danger of serious harm and this is known to the master or to a person who has duties of management, the master is subject to liability for a failure by himself or by such person to exercise reasonable care to avert the threatened harm.

(2) If a servant is hurt and thereby becomes helpless when acting within the scope of his employment and this is known to the master or to a person having duties of management, the master is subject to liability for his negligent failure or that of such person to give first aid to the servant and to care for him until he can be cared for by others.

§ 315. General Principle

There is no duty so to control the conduct of a third person as to prevent him from causing physical harm to another unless

(a) a special relation exists between the actor and the third person which imposes a duty upon the actor to control the third person's conduct, or

(b) a special relation exists between the actor and the other which gives to the other a right to protection.

---

1   Restatement (Second) of Torts (1965).

CITY OF PHILADELPHIA, Appellant,
v.
ESTATE OF Mary DENNIS, by her Administrator, Terry DENNIS, Appellee.
Commonwealth Court of Pennsylvania
636 A.2d 240 (Pa. Commw. Ct. 1993)

[Some footnotes may have been omitted.]

DOYLE, Judge.

The City of Philadelphia appeals by permission an interlocutory order of the Court of Common Pleas of Philadelphia County which overruled the City's preliminary objections in the nature of a demurrer to the complaint in trespass filed by Terry Dennis (Dennis), the administrator of the estate of Mary Dennis (decedent).

The case began on December 16, 1989, when the Philadelphia Police received various calls reporting that an individual, the decedent, was sitting on a bench in cold weather and appeared to be sick and in need of assistance. A police officer was dispatched to the scene and found decedent sitting on a bench near Broad and Spring Garden Streets, but erroneously concluded the decedent was drunk. The officer reported that conclusion to the dispatcher and left without taking any further action. Later, a passing police patrol car was stopped by bystanders and the police officers found decedent dead of what was subsequently determined to be hypothermia.

Dennis filed a complaint against the City, alleging that the City was negligent, *inter alia*, in failing to: (1) immediately respond to the phone calls made on decedent's behalf; (2) properly summon medical authorities to accurately determine decedent's condition; and (3) take decedent to the nearest hospital. The City filed preliminary objections in the form of a demurrer which alleged that Dennis's complaint failed to state a cause of action because it failed to establish a special relationship between decedent and the police, which is necessary to impose a duty upon the police to assist an individual; without such a duty a cause of action could not exist.[1]

By order of December 2, 1991, the trial court overruled the City's preliminary objections. The City subsequently petitioned the trial court to amend its interlocutory order to include the certification required by Section 702(b) of the Judicial Code to allow the City to seek permission to appeal the interlocutory order to this Court. The trial court amended its order on July 24, 1992. On September 28, 1992, we granted the City's petition for permission to appeal and this appeal followed.

---

[1] The elements of a cause of action in negligence are: (1) a duty recognized by law, requiring the actor to conform to a certain standard of conduct; (2) a failure of the actor to conform to that standard; (3) a causal connection between the conduct and the resulting injury; and (4) actual loss or damage to the interests of another. *Morena v. South Hills Health System*, 501 Pa. 634, 462 A.2d 680 (1983).

Initially, we note that:

> When reviewing preliminary objections in the nature of a demurrer, we accept as true all well-pleaded material facts in the complaint as well as all reasonable inferences that may be drawn from those facts. . . . Preliminary objections should be sustained and a complaint dismissed only in cases that are clear and free from doubt that the law will not permit recovery by the plaintiff.

Capital City Lodge 12 v. Harrisburg, 138 Pa. Commonwealth Ct. 475, 480, 588 A.2d 584, 586-87 (citations omitted), *petition for allowance of appeal denied*, 528 Pa. 614, 596 A.2d 159 (1991). The test is whether, from all the facts pled, the pleader will be able to prove facts legally sufficient to establish his or her right to relief. *Bower v. Bower*, 531 Pa. 54, 611 A.2d 181 (1992).

In *Thomas v. City of Philadelphia*, 133 Pa. Commonwealth Ct. 121, 574 A.2d 1205, *petition for allowance of appeal denied*, 527 Pa. 659, 593 A.2d 429 (1990), this Court summarized the duty of care owed by a municipality to the general public. We held that:

> There is generally 'no duty resting on a municipality or other governmental body to provide police protection to any particular person.'
>
> . . . .
>
> A very narrow exception to this no-duty rule exists, but only where there are circumstances establishing a special relationship between the police and the crime victim. In claiming a special relationship, the individual:
>
>> must demonstrate that the police were: 1) aware of the *individual's* particular situation or unique status, 2) had knowledge of the potential for the particular harm which the *individual* suffered, and 3) voluntarily assumed, in light of that knowledge, to protect the *individual* from the precise harm which was occasioned.

Id., 124-25, 574 A.2d at 1206 (quoting *Melendez v. City of Philadelphia*, 320 Pa. Superior Ct. 59, 64, 65, 466 A.2d 1060, 1064 (1983) (emphasis in original)).

Dennis's complaint made the following factual allegations:

> 5. Various telephone calls were made by persons unknown at this time to the Defendant's police department by dialing 911 and reporting that the decedent was sick and in need of assistance from the Defendant.
>
> 6. When a police officer from the Defendant's police department finally appeared at Broad and Spring Garden Streets sometime subsequent to all of the aforementioned telephone calls, said police officer, instead of taking her to the nearest hospital, instead radioed police dispatchers to tell them that the assignment was nothing more then [sic] a

drunken person sitting on the bench and thus did not take her to the nearest hospital.

7. Much later on December 16, 1989, and after all the aforesaid telephone calls had been made, a patrol car belonging to the Defendant was stopped by people in the area where decedent was sitting and the officer in the said patrol car determined at that time that decedent was deceased.

8. Plaintiff's decedent died of hypothermia as a result of *inter alia*, sitting outside in the weather as it then was.

Based on the above allegations, the trial court found that Dennis had pled sufficient facts to establish a special relationship between decedent and the police. However, even assuming that the first two criteria of the special relationship test are met,[2] nowhere does Dennis plead facts which satisfy the third requirement that the police voluntarily assumed the protection of decedent from the precise harm suffered, here hypothermia. Dennis apparently contends that because the initial officer's interaction with the decedent was sufficient to convince him that she was drunk, that this interaction in and of itself was sufficient to fulfill the third requirement. We disagree. Absent an express promise to render care or protection, no special relationship is created. *Rankin v. Southeastern Pennsylvania Transit Authority*, 146 Pa. Commonwealth Ct. 429, 606 A.2d 536 (1992); *Morris v. Musser*, 84 Pa. Commonwealth Ct. 170, 478 A.2d 937 (1984).

The trial court in its opinion relied primarily on *Socarras v. City of Philadelphia*, 123 Pa. Commonwealth Ct. 197, 552 A.2d 1171, *petitions for allowance of appeal denied*, 522 Pa. 605, 562 A.2d 828, and 522 Pa. 608, 562 A.2d 829 (1989); *City of Philadelphia v. Middleton*, 89 Pa. Commonwealth Ct. 362, 492 A.2d 763 (1985), and *Capanna v. City of Philadelphia*, 89 Pa. Commonwealth Ct. 349, 492 A.2d 761 (1985), to support its conclusion that a special relationship had been established. However, all of these cases are distinguishable from the case now before us.

In *Middleton*, the plaintiff, Middleton, was having a diabetic attack when he was approached by the police and accused of being drunk. Although Middleton attempted to explain his predicament to the police, he was incarcerated for eight hours without medical care. Similarly in *Capanna*, the police

---

[2] There is no factual allegation that the police were aware of either decedent's particular or unique situation or that she was potentially at risk of hypothermia. With regard to the first criterion, the police had merely been informed that decedent was "sick." Secondly, nothing indicates that the police were aware that decedent was at risk of hypothermia and furthermore, decedent's situation was hardly unique in that anyone outside in the winter is potentially at risk of hypothermia. Dennis did not even plead that the weather was *cold*, or that decedent was particularly underdressed for cold weather or that it should have been obvious to the police that prolonged exposure to cold may result in hypothermia.

responded to a call for a "hospital case." Instead of taking the plaintiff to the hospital, the officer arrested him and placed him in a cell where he died three hours later. In both these cases, the police met the third requirement by taking the respective plaintiffs into custody.

In *Socarras*, the plaintiff was injured when he struck a disabled vehicle. The vehicle's occupants had signalled to a passing police officer for assistance, but had been ignored by the officer. In that case, the Court found an express promise to care for the plaintiffs in a directive issued by the Philadelphia police ordering police officers to render assistance to motorists. *Socarras*, 123 Pa. Commonwealth Ct. at 201, 552 A.2d at 1173. Here, Dennis has not alleged that either the decedent was taken into custody or that the police had been expressly directed to care for individuals in Dennis's circumstances.

Dennis has only pled that the police responded to a call for assistance. A mere response by the police to a call for assistance or aid does not create a special relationship between the police and the person in need of aid. *Yates v. City of Philadelphia*, 134 Pa. Commonwealth Ct. 282, 578 A.2d 609 (1990), *petition for allowance of appeal denied*, 527 Pa. 660, 593 A.2d 430 (1991). In *Yates*, the Yates family called the police to break up a gang fight behind their home. The police arrived, but instead of stopping the fight, they remained in their car. After the police departed, a shot was fired at the rear of the Yates' house which struck and killed their daughter. This Court refused to find a special relationship where the police "did not assure the Yates family that they would protect them from the dangers caused by a gang fight. The focus of *Melendez* is on the individual and any danger unique to the individual from which the police specifically promise protection." *Yates*, 134 Pa. Commonwealth Ct. at 286, 578 A.2d at 611.

In *Rankin*, the plaintiff was stabbed on a local Philadelphia train. The plaintiff alleged that a police officer witnessed the stabbing and failed to prevent it. He further alleged that the officer escorted him from the train, told him to sit down on a bench, and told him he would be "alright." The plaintiff subsequently passed out and was left on the bench without medical attention for some four hours. *Rankin*, 146 Pa. Commonwealth Ct. at 432, 606 A.2d at 537. This court concluded that a special relationship existed because the three elements of the *Thomas* test were met. We inferred that the third element was met by the allegation that the police escorted the plaintiff from the train, seated him, and reassured him. In the case now before us, there are simply no facts pled from which we may make such an inference. Without the third element of a voluntary assumption by the officer in this case to protect the decedent, there can be no special relationship, no duty, and hence no liability.

Because Dennis failed to plead sufficient facts to allow recovery, we reverse the trial court's order. Therefore, we remand this case to the trial court for the entry of an order sustaining the City's preliminary objections and dismissing Dennis's complaint.

Hugh P. RANKIN, Jr., Appellant,

v.

SOUTHEASTERN PENNSYLVANIA TRANSPORTATION AUTHORITY and City of Philadelphia and Officer George Diamond and Chalmers Massey, Appellees

Commonwealth Court of Pennsylvania

606 A.2d 536 (Pa. Commw. Ct. 1992)

[Some footnotes may have been omitted.]

PALLADINO, Judge.

Hugh P. Rankin, Jr. (Rankin) appeals an order of the Court of Common Pleas of Philadelphia County granting summary judgment in favor of the City of Philadelphia (City) and Officer George Diamond (Diamond).

Rankin filed a complaint against the Southeastern Pennsylvania Transportation Authority (SEPTA), the City, Diamond and Chalmers Massey (Massey) to recover damages for injuries sustained by Rankin when he was traveling as a passenger on the Broad Street Subway on October 25, 1986. The relevant factual allegations of the complaint were as follows:

> 12. On or about October 25, 1986 in the early morning hours, at approximately 2:30 a.m., the plaintiff [Rankin] was a passenger and business invitee on the Broad Street Subway traveling North from City Hall.

> 13. Between City Hall and the Spring Garden stop of the Broad Street Subway Northbound, defendant, Chalmers Massey, for no reason whatsoever and without provocation, assaulted plaintiff and stabbed plaintiff in the back causing serious and permanent injuries as more particularly set forth hereinafter.

> 14. At the same time, defendant, George Diamond, who was employed as an agent, servant and employee of both defendant, SEPTA, and defendant, City of Philadelphia, and was a police officer was on board the Broad Street Subway train and witnessed the stabbing and the events leading up to the stabbing. However, said defendant did not prevent the stabbing or take any measures to prevent the assault upon the plaintiff.

> 15. After the stabbing, defendant, Diamond escorted defendant, Massey, and plaintiff from the Broad Street Subway train exiting onto the platform at the Spring Garden stop.

> 16. Plaintiff told defendant, Diamond, that he had been stabbed by defendant, Massey, in the back. However, defendant, Diamond, said that the Plaintiff would be alright [sic] and told him to sit down on the bench at the platform.

> 17. While the plaintiff was sitting down, he passed out and collapsed onto the platform itself and was allowed to lie on the platform with a stab wound in his back from 2:30 a.m. until approximately 6:45 a.m.

18. Plaintiff was unconscious and taken to Hahnemann University Hospital where he was diagnosed as suffering from a stab wound of the thoracic spine, particularly, a stab wound at T6 and T7.

Complaint at paragraphs 12-18.

Rankin alleged that the acts of commission or omission of Diamond, acting as the agent, employee and servant of SEPTA and the City as well as the acts of commission or omission of the City and SEPTA, who own operate and maintain the subway, amounted to a failure to exercise due care for the protection of Rankin who was a business invitee. Rankin sought monetary damages for his injuries and demanded a jury trial.

SEPTA, the City and Diamond filed preliminary objections to Rankin's complaint which were overruled. Answers and new matter were then filed by SEPTA, the City and Diamond, and answers to the new matter were filed by Rankin, SEPTA, the City and Diamond.

The City and Diamond filed a motion for summary judgment which was granted by the trial court on the ground that the City and Diamond owed Rankin no duty of care and that they were immune from suit on the basis of governmental immunity.

On appeal,[1] Rankin raises the following issues: (1) whether the City has waived the defense of governmental immunity in this case because the City has generally waived the defense of governmental immunity in actions commenced to recover damages for bodily injury or death caused by the negligent or unlawful conduct of a police officer while the police officer is acting within the scope of his employment; (2) whether the trial court erred by granting summary judgment to the City and Diamond because they had a duty to obtain medical care for Rankin; (3) whether the trial court erred by granting summary judgment to the City and Diamond because they had a duty to prevent the stabbing.

Summary judgment is only appropriate when, after examining the record in the light most favorable to the non-moving party, there is no genuine issue of material fact, and the movant clearly establishes entitlement to judgment as a matter of law. Summary judgment should be granted only where the pleadings, answers to interrogatories, depositions, admissions and affidavits establish that the movant's right to relief is clear and free from doubt. Pa. R.C.P. No. 1035(a). In this case the facts are not in dispute. We are concerned with whether the City and Diamond were entitled to summary judgment as a matter of law.

---

[1]   Our scope of review of an appeal of the entry of summary judgment is to determine whether an error of law has been committed or an abuse of discretion has occurred. *Peters Township School Authority v. United States Fidelity & Guaranty Co.*, 78 Pa. Commonwealth Ct. 365, 467 A.2d 904 (1983).

As to the first issue, Rankin argues that the City waived the defense of governmental immunity in this case when it enacted section 21-701 of the Philadelphia Code which states in pertinent part as follows:

WAIVER OF GOVERNMENTAL IMMUNITY

§ 21-701. Police Officers.

(a) The City shall not plead governmental immunity as a defense in any civil action commenced by any person sustaining bodily injury or death caused by negligent or unlawful conduct of any police officer while the latter is acting within the scope of his office or employment.

This court has held that the City acted within its home rule charter powers in enacting section 21-701 and that it effectively waived its immunity under the governmental immunity provisions of 42 Pa. C.S. §§ 8541-8564. *City of Philadelphia v. Gray*, 133 Pa. Commonwealth Ct. 396, 576 A.2d 411 (1990), *petition for allowance of appeal granted*, 526 Pa. 654, 586 A.2d 923 (1991). Rankin submits that the waiver of the immunity defense requires this court to reverse the trial court's grant of summary judgment in favor of the City and Diamond.

The City concedes that section 21-701 operates as a waiver of immunity, but argues that despite the waiver of immunity, it is entitled to summary judgment because Rankin has failed to establish that Diamond acted negligently. The elements of a cause of action in negligence are (1) a duty, recognized by law, requiring the actor to conform to a certain standard of conduct; (2) a failure to conform to that standard; (3) a causal connection between the conduct and the resulting injury; and (4) actual loss or damage to the interests of another. *Morena v. South Hills Health System*, 501 Pa. 634, 462 A.2d 680 (1983). In *Morris v. Musser*, 84 Pa. Commonwealth Ct. 170, 478 A.2d 937 (1984), this court held plaintiff from establishing what duty, if any, a police officer owed to him.

This brings us to the second issue raised by Rankin which is whether the trial court erred by granting summary judgment to the City and Diamond on the ground that the City and Diamond lacked a duty to obtain medical care for Rankin. The City argues that Rankin has not established that there was a duty on the part of Diamond to recognize a need for aid, or to render aid, to a member of the public for harm done by others absent a special relationship. The City relies on this court's decision in *Morris* in which this court adopted the no-duty rule which provides that "a police officer's obligation to protect the citizenry is a general duty owing to the public at large, and not a specific duty owing to particular persons." *Id.* at 174, 478 A.2d at 939.

This court has also adopted the special relationship exception to the no-duty rule which provides that "if the police enter into a special relationship with an individual, . . . the general duty owing to the public is narrowed into a specific duty owing to that person, the breach of which can give rise to a cause of action for damages." *Id.* at 174, 478 A.2d at 939-940.

The narrow special relationship exception to the no-duty rule exists only where there are circumstances establishing a special relationship between the police and the crime victim. A plaintiff must demonstrate that the police were:

> 1) aware of the *individual's* particular situation or unique status,
>
> 2) had knowledge of the potential for the particular harm which the *individual* suffered, and
>
> 3) voluntarily assumed, in light of the knowledge, to protect the *individual* from the precise harm which was occasioned.

Thomas v. City of Philadelphia, 133 Pa. Commonwealth Ct. 121, 125, 574 A.2d 1205, 1206, *petition for allowance of appeal denied*, 527 Pa. 659, 593 A.2d 429 (1990) (quoting *Melendez v. City of Philadelphia*, 320 Pa. Superior Ct. 59, 65, 466 A.2d 1060, 1064 (1983)) (emphasis in original).

The City argues that Rankin has not demonstrated that he fits within the special relationship exception; therefore, the no-duty rule applies and Diamond had no duty towards Rankin, the breach of which would give rise to a cause of action.

The no-duty rule did not relieve Diamond of the duty to protect Rankin after the stabbing when Diamond had witnessed the stabbing, was aware that Rankin was injured, and assisted Rankin out of the train and onto the platform. These factors demonstrate that 1) Diamond was aware of Rankin's particular situation or unique status, i.e., the fact that Rankin had been stabbed; 2) Diamond had knowledge of the potential for the particular harm which Rankin suffered, i.e., medically untreated injuries from the stabbing and inability to summon medical help; 3) Diamond voluntarily assumed, in light of that knowledge, to protect Rankin from the precise harm to which Rankin was subject when Diamond assisted Rankin from the train, seated him and assured him that he would be all right.

Therefore, we conclude that a special relationship existed between Diamond and Rankin which resulted in a duty on the part of Diamond to continue to assist Rankin and to summon medical aid for him.

Having determined that a duty existed, the breach of which forms a basis for Rankin's cause of action, we vacate the order of the trial court granting summary judgment and we remand for further proceedings consistent with this opinion.

Yania & Rankin Vocabulary

Instructions: To better understand this material, be sure you know the definitions of the following terms. Be prepared to define these terms for your classmates, using the techniques described in "Defining/Explaining a Term or Concept." (pg. 14)

1. Wrongful death
2. Survival action
3. Demurrer
4. Complaint
5. Negligence
6. Invitee
7. Duty
8. Liability
9. Actionable
10. Sustain
11. Appeal
12. Aver
13. Motion for summary judgment
14. Governmental immunity
15. Relinquish
16. Causal connection
17. Elements

✓ Refining Your Skills: Article Exercise

Please fill in the blank with the appropriate article ("a," "an," or "the") or leave it blank to indicate that no article is necessary.

"Dennis has only pled that _____ police responded to _____ call for assistance. _____ mere response to _____ call for assistance or aid does not create _____ special relationship between _____ police and _____ person in need of _____ aid. . . . In *Yates*, _____ Yates family called _____ police to break up _____ gang fight behind their home. _____ police arrived, but instead of stopping _____ fight, they remained in their car. After _____ car departed, _____ shot was fired at _____ rear of _____ Yates' house which struck and killed their daughter. This court refused to find _____ special relationship where _____ police 'did not assure _____ Yates family that they would protect them from _____ dangers caused by _____ gang fight. _____ focus of *Melendez* is on _____ individual and any danger unique to _____ individual from which _____ police specifically promise protection.'. . .

In *Rankin*, _____ plaintiff was stabbed on _____ local Philadelphia train. _____ plaintiff alleged that _____ police officer witnessed _____ stabbing and failed to prevent it. He further alleged that _____ officer escorted him from _____ train, told him to sit down on _____ bench, and told him he would be 'alright.' _____ plaintiff subsequently passed out and was left on _____ bench without _____ medical attention for some four hours. . . . This court concluded that _____ special relationship existed because _____ three elements of _____ *Thomas* test were met. We inferred that _____ third element was met by _____ allegation that _____ police escorted _____ plaintiff from _____ train, seated him, and reassured him. In _____ case now before us, there are simply no facts pled from which we can make such _____ inference. Without _____ third element of _____ voluntary assumption by _____ officer in this case to protect _____ decedent, there can be no special relationship, no duty, and hence no liability."

Excerpt from City of Philadelphia v. Estate of Dennis, 636 A.2d 240 (Pa. Commw. Ct. 1993).

✓ Matching Exercise

Please match the terms on the left with the definitions on the right. Write the term number in the blank.

Terms:

1. Bench trial
2. Jury trial
3. En banc decision
4. Civil action
5. Criminal action
6. Auditing class
7. Time management
8. Arguments
9. Opening statements
10. Core classes
11. Review session
12. Grade scale
13. Used textbook
14. New textbook
15. Civil procedure
16. Constitutional law
17. Orientation
18. Law School Admissions Text (LSAT)
19. Hornbooks

Definitions:

A. ____ Organizing time to fit in many activities.

B. ____ Test necessary for entrance to Law School; measures analytical and logic skills.

C. ____ Classes required for graduation; first year classes.

D. ____ Session when the entire membership of the court will participate in the decision rather than the regular quorum.

E. ____ Week before classes officially start in which first years become acquainted with the school.

F. ____ Case decided before a judge instead of a jury.

G. ____ Textbook that has never been used; brand new.

H. ____ Action brought to enforce, redress, or protect private rights.

I. ____ Taking a class but not receiving a grade for it.

J. ____ Going over the term's or year's material.

K. ____ Class that discusses the Federal Rules of Civil Procedure.

L. ____ Remarks addressed by attorney judge or jury on the merits of case or on points of law.

M. ____ Textbook that had been used before; not brand new.

N. ____ Outline or summary of nature of case and of anticipated proof presented by attorney to jury at start of trial, before any evidence is submitted.

O. ____ Commercial outline of textbooks.

P. ____ Law based on the United States Constitution and violations of rights granted by it.

Q. ____ Trial held before a jury.

R. ____ An action, suit, or cause instituted to punish an infraction of the criminal laws.

S. ____ A mark indicating a degree of accomplishment in school, ranging from A to F.

CHAPTER 7—ORAL ARGUMENTS

Oral Arguments

You will remember that when a case is on appeal, the court does not retry the case. Rather, it will address alleged legal errors from the lower court. When attorneys present a case to an appellate court, they present their legal arguments to the court in a brief. A brief is a formal written document that familiarizes the court with the case and explains and advocates the merits of the party's legal position on the issues in the case. Courts primarily consider the briefs of the parties when deciding the case. However, most appellate courts allow attorneys in some or all cases to present an argument orally to the court. An oral argument is not a speech to the court; rather, it is a dialogue between the attorney and the court on the merits of that party's legal argument. The attorney will attempt to persuade the court that it should rule in a particular way. Each attorney in the case will have a chance to present his or her legal issues to the court.

During the oral argument, the court may and usually does ask the attorney questions about the merits of the legal argument. This often appears to be hostile or heated questioning by the court. The court may also ask questions about the facts of the case. In addition, a judge who agrees with a party's legal position may try to bring out the merits of that position by asking the attorney "friendly" questions designed to showcase the party's best and strongest arguments. Judges may ask friendly questions to try to persuade their colleagues on the court to resolve the case in a particular way. Attorneys presenting oral arguments should be prepared to answer any type of question asked, but it is helpful if the attorney recognizes whether the judge is asking a hostile or friendly question.

✓ *Checklist for Preparing for Oral Argument:*

☐ 1. Keep in mind the purpose of oral argument is to persuade the court to adopt your legal position. You will do this by educating the court to the law in this area and by answering the court's questions.

☐ 2. Know everything in the record.[1]

☐ 3. Know the law. You should be familiar with every case upon which you or your opposing counsel relies. You should also be familiar with other cases addressing similar legal issues, even if you choose not to bring them to the court's attention. The court may wish to discuss them.

☐ 4. Prepare an outline of the oral argument you will present. You should be prepared for a hot or cold court.[2] Your argument should list the points you wish to discuss with the court. You should also have some notes to help you recall the important precedent cases. Remember that oral argument is not a speech, but is a dialogue with the court.

☐ 5. Bring with you to court:

   a. Your outline

   b. Both briefs

   c. The record or some portion of the record.[3]

   d. The law-copies of the important cases or notes about the important precedent cases.

   e. Pen and paper for taking notes while opposing counsel is presenting his or her argument.

☐ 6. Practice, practice, practice. In order to present a polished oral argument to the court, you should practice as much as possible. If you practice with friends and colleagues, be sure to have them ask you questions intermittently throughout your presentation. You could also practice in front of a mirror to assess your courtroom demeanor. While most students and attorneys feel a bit nervous when going before an appellate court, practicing will help you to feel more confident about your presentation.

1　The record is the collection of all documents filed in the case thus far. The record tells the court the factual and legal history of the case. All facts that you use on appeal must be found in the record.

2　A hot court is one that asks frequent questions of the attorneys. A cold court asks fewer questions and is apt to sit and let the attorneys present their arguments to the court uninterrupted.

3　Many times, attorneys in a civil case will prepare a reproduced record or record appendix. This is an abbreviated, photocopied version of the record, complete with an index for easy reference.

✓ Checklist for Giving the Oral Argument:

☐ 1. Arrive at the courtroom on time, dressed in a dark, conservative suit or dress.

☐ 2. The bailiff or tipstaff will instruct you on where to sit and stand.

☐ 3. When it is your turn to argue, approach the podium and stand still and straight. Then, introduce yourself to the court. A typical introduction is as follows:

> "Good morning, your honors. May it please the court, my name is _____ and I represent _____ in this case before the court. I have ____ issue(s) to discuss with the court today. . . . ." The appellant or petitioner can request rebuttal time of one or two minutes during the introduction. The appellee gets no rebuttal time. The appellee must respond to appellant's argument points during his or her argument.

☐ 4. The appellant should offer to give the court a brief statement of the facts of the case. If the court asks for the facts—BE PREPARED! Give a very short account of the critical facts of the case.

☐ 5. Present your argument to the court in an orderly way. Speak clearly and distinctly, using formal standard English. State your issues clearly and number them if you have more than one. Support each argument by relying on the precedent cases. Fully explain the reasoning that you would like to court to adopt on each issue.

☐ 6. The court is likely to ask questions interrupting the flow of your argument. Try to think positively about the court's questions. Questions indicate that the court is interested and involved with the legal issues you are presenting. In answering the court's questions, you have an opportunity to personally answer the concerns of the judges who will be deciding your case. You should welcome the court's questions.

When a judge asks a question, **you should**:

    a. **Stop immediately**. Do not even finish your sentence or your word.

    b. **Listen carefully**. Try to discern what type of question the judge is asking you.

    c. **Think about your answer**. You may take a few moments to collect your thoughts. It is fine to have a moment of silence before you answer. The court will appreciate that you are taking time to consider the question thoughtfully.

    d. **Answer the question**. Try to be definitive. If you can, tell the court "yes" or "no" and then explain why. If part of your prepared argument fits into the answer to a question, use it.

When a judge asks you a question, **you should not**:

a. **Tell the judge to wait** and be patient because you will get to that point in your argument soon. Answer the question immediately. Keep in mind that your purpose in oral argument is satisfy the court's concerns and questions about ruling in favor of your client.

b. **Argue with the judge**. While oral argument is a dialogue with the court, you must show the utmost deference and respect for the court. Even if you are not pleased with the judge's questions, this should never show in your tone of voice or your facial expression. Remember you are there to present your best case for your client.

c. **Answer the question you wish you had been asked**. Answer the court's questions directly. You should anticipate and prepare for questions directly testing the merits of your argument. Do not try to avoid them.

d. **Use rhetorical questions or ask the court a question**. You are in the courtroom to answer the court's questions. Maintain proper decorum by refraining from phrasing your responses as questions. You may, however, ask the court to rephrase an unclear question and most judges will gladly do so.

e. **Wait for the court to instruct you to return to your argument**. When you have finished answering the question return to a logical place in your argument.

¤ 7. During the argument you will be timed by a bailiff or clerk of court. As your time ends with the court, be prepared to give a succinct statement of the relief you request from the court and then sit down. Do not exceed your allotted time, unless the court is continuing to ask you questions. If that is the case, call the court's attention to the fact that your time has expired and ask the court's permission to continue.

¤ 8. Try to relax and enjoy the time you spend before the court. If you are well-prepared the time will pass quickly and you will know you have given your best effort to persuade the court on behalf of your client.[4]

---

4   To learn more about a judge's view of oral advocacy, see RUGGERO J. ALDISERT, WINNING ON APPEAL 293-341 (1996).

✓ Exercise: Giving Your Oral Argument

In order to fully understand how to prepare and give an oral argument to an appellate court, you will give a mock oral argument in class. You will argue about "search and seizure" in the criminal law. This will be a complex argument because you must understand two different standards to answer the question, "when is a person seized under the law." You will present your argument to the Supreme Court of Pennsylvania, a state supreme court. The Court will be deciding whether to adopt the United States Supreme Court standard for seizure under the Fourth Amendment to the United States Constitution, or whether to maintain the more protective standards afforded to criminal defendants under Pennsylvania Constitution. While all courts in the country must adopt the United States Supreme Court's standards to interpret the United States Constitution, states are free to offer greater protection to their citizens under their own constitutions.[5]

Half the class will argue for the prosecution that the court should explicitly accept the United States Supreme Court standard as the Pennsylvania standard. The other half of the class will argue for the defense that Pennsylvania should continue to offer its citizens great protection under Article 1, Section 8 of the Pennsylvania Constitution. Your professors will select judges for the court. You will argue the case of *Commonwealth v. Carroll* to the Pennsylvania Supreme Court. To begin to prepare for your argument become familiar with this case by reading the opinion of the Pennsylvania Superior Court. Next read the case articulating the United States Supreme Court Standard, *California v. Hodari D.* In order to further understand this case, read the cases of *Commonwealth v. Jones* and *Commonwealth v. Edmunds*.

After reading and briefing the cases, begin to formulate the argument you will make on behalf of your client. Practice your argument alone, with your classmates, or with your professor to be fully prepared to meet opposing counsel before your mock United States Supreme Court.

---

5   *See* William J. Brennan, *State Constitutions and the Protection of Individual Rights*, 90 HARV. L. REV. 489 (1977); William J. Brennan, *Symposium on the Revolution in State Constitutional Law*, 13 VT. L. REV. 11 (1988).

COMMONWEALTH of Pennsylvania, Appellant,
v.
Thomas Carl JONES a/k/a Thomas Carl Friday
Supreme Court of Pennsylvania
378 A.2d 835 (Pa. 1977)

[Some footnotes may have been omitted.]

EAGEN, Chief Justice.

Thomas Carl Jones was charged with murder and numerous related offenses in Montgomery County. He filed motions to suppress evidence of certain statements given by him to police and certain physical evidence seized by the police. Following a hearing on these motions, the Court of Common Pleas by order dated November 6, 1975 suppressed evidence of a .38 caliber gun taken by the police from Jones' possession and evidence of statements made by Jones to the police on April 6, 1975. The Commonwealth filed this appeal from that order. We now affirm.

The relevant facts as established at the suppression hearing are as follows:

On April 3, 1975, at approximately 1:11 p.m., the Norristown police, in response to a phone call, went to 1002 Sterigere Street, Norristown, where the dead body of Eleanor Friday reportedly had been discovered by Jones, her nephew. She had apparently been beaten with a blunt instrument. The police interviewed Jones on April 3rd.

On April 4, 1975, when the police sought Jones at his residence for further questioning, they discovered he had fled the area. The police also learned various facts which resulted in the issuance of a warrant for Jones' arrest for theft of movable property, 18 Pa. C.S.A. § 3125, namely, a .38 caliber revolver. Notice that an arrest warrant was outstanding against Jones was transmitted to the National Crime Information Center [NCIC].

On April 6, 1975, shortly after 7:00 a.m., Corporal Herbert Hoffman of the Missouri State Highway Patrol saw Jones apparently hitchhiking west on Interstate Highway 44 in Rolla, Missouri. Hoffman proceeded to the police station without encountering Jones. At about 8:30 a.m. on same day, Hoffman again observed Jones; but, in this instance, Jones was walking south about three miles from where he was first observed, on United States Route Number 63 which intersects Interstate 44. During both observations, Jones was without luggage. Hoffman, in uniform, stopped his vehicle, a marked police car, and asked Jones for identification. Jones handed Hoffman an identification card and Hoffman then "asked [Jones] to have a seat in the patrol car." Hoffman radioed to have a check on Jones run through the NCIC. While the check was being made, Hoffman and Jones engaged in "general conversation." Hoffman testified that Jones was free to leave before the results of the NCIC check were obtained. From the check, Hoffman learned of the outstanding arrest warrant.

Hoffman then asked Jones to step out of the car and Jones complied. As Jones did so, he held his hand up and informed Hoffman he had a weapon. Hoffman then searched Jones and obtained a .38 caliber gun. Hoffman advised Jones he was under arrest for carrying a concealed weapon and also advised him of his constitutional rights. Hoffman then transported Jones to a police station.

At 1:30 p.m. the same day, Hoffman, after having a conversation with a detective in Pennsylvania, spoke with Jones. During this conversation, Jones made various statements relating his activities on April 2nd and 3rd.

Hoffman testified that he approached Jones because his curiosity was aroused by Jones' general appearance, unshaven and unkempt, by his change of direction, by his not having luggage, and because he was not a local resident and had changed his route of travel from an Interstate Highway to a route which was not a "main artery." Additionally, Hoffman testified Jones was not violating any law when observed. Finally, Hoffman testified it was common practice to stop pedestrians on highways in Missouri to their identity and destination and to run computer checks on them.

The Court of Common Pleas ordered the gun and evidence of the statements made to Hoffman suppressed reasoning that the initial detention of Jones was illegal and that the gun and the statements of April 6th were the products of that illegal detention.

The Commonwealth urges the suppression court erred and contends: 1) the initial confrontation of Jones by Hoffman was not a seizure within the purview of the fourth amendment; and/or, 2) the confrontation, if within the purview of the fourth amendment, was justified under the circumstances as a limited investigatory stop.

As to its first contention, the Commonwealth argues that Hoffman merely approached Jones and questioned him, and that

> "[t]here is nothing in the Constitution which prevents a policeman from addressing questions to anyone on the streets."

Terry v. Ohio, 392 U.S. 1, 34, 88 S. Ct. 1868, 1886, 20 L. Ed. 2d 889 (1968) (White, J., concurring) [Hereinafter: Terry].

The Supreme Court of the United States has said:

> "not all personal intercourse between policemen and citizens involves 'seizures' of persons."

Terry, supra at 19, n.16, 88 S. Ct. at 1879, n.16. Similarly, we have said that:

> "A policeman may legally stop a person and question him. But he may not without a warrant restrain that person from

walking away . . ., unless he has 'probable cause' to arrest that person or he observes such unusual and suspicious conduct on the part of the person who is stopped . . . that the policeman may reasonably conclude that criminal activity may be afoot . . . ." [Footnote omitted.]

Commonwealth v. Berrios, 437 Pa. 338, 340, 263 A.2d 342, 343 (1970).

The line of distinction between merely "approaching a person and addressing questions to him" or "legally stopping" him, *Commonwealth v. Berrios, supra* at 340, 263 A.2d at 343, [Hereinafter: contact], and restraining him or making a "forcible stop," *Terry, supra*, 392 U.S. at 32, 88 S. Ct. at 1885 (Harlan, J., concurring) [Hereinafter: stop], is not subject to precise definition because of "the myriad daily situations in which policemen and citizens confront each other on the street." *Terry, supra* at 12, 88 S. Ct. at 1875. Each factual situation must be examined to determine if force was used to restrain the citizen in some way. Such force may include "physical force or [a] show of authority." *Terry, supra* at 19, n.16, 88 S. Ct. at 1879, n.16.

If a citizen approached by a police officer is ordered to stop or is physically restrained, obviously a "stop" occurs. Equally obvious is a situation where a police officer approaches a citizen and addresses questions to him, the citizen attempts to leave, and the officer orders him to remain or physically restrains him; here too a "stop" occurs. A more difficult situation arises where no order or physical restraint is involved and the citizen does not attempt to walk away. This situation is more difficult because a police officer in uniform must be considered as showing authority and thus exercising some force simply because he is in uniform, a symbol of authority, when he approaches a citizen and addresses questions to him.

But this is not to say that the force inherent in a uniform is sufficient in itself to warrant a conclusion that a restraint on liberty or a "stop" occurs when the citizen is approached and questioned. Indeed, *Terry, supra*, clearly indicates a uniform, as a symbol of authority, is not in itself a sufficient exercise of force to conclude a "stop" occurs when a citizen is approached and questioned.

Since an officer in uniform approaching a citizen and questioning him involves an exercise of force, i.e., a show of some authority, and since that force is insufficient to conclude a "stop" occurs, it follows that whether a "stop" occurs is not dependent on the presence or absence of any force; rather, it is dependent on the amount of force exercised.

Thus, to determine when a "stop" has occurred in the more difficult situation all of the circumstances which may in any way evidence a show of authority or exercise of force including such subtle factors as the demeanor of the police officer, the location of the confrontation, the manner of expression used by the officer in addressing the citizen, and the content of the interrogatories or statements must be examined. Once this factual examination has been made, the pivotal inquiry is whether, considering all of the facts and circumstances evidencing an exercise of force, "a reasonable man, innocent of any crime, would have thought [he was being restrained] had he been in the defendant's shoes." *United States v. McKethan*, 247 F. Supp. 324, 328 (D.D.C. 1965), *aff'd* by order No. 20,059 (D.C. Cir. 1966).

Instantly, we believe the totality of the circumstances would have led a reasonable man to conclude he was being restrained or stopped for investigatory purposes by Hoffman's initial exercise of force when confronting Jones. While the situation presents a close question, an examination of the entire situation shows not only an exercise of force but also an escalation in that exercise. Hoffman approached Jones on a highway in a marked car and in uniform and addressed questions to him. In doing so, he did not merely ask Jones his name; rather, he immediately sought identification from Jones, and, when Jones complied he escalated the exercise of force by asking Jones to be seated in the car. This latter request was not merely an attempt to obtain information; rather, while stated as a question, it sought control of Jones' movement.[1] Thus, we believe the Court of Common Pleas was correct in ruling the initial confrontation of Jones by Hoffman constituted a seizure within the purview of the fourth amendment, specifically a "stop for investigatory purposes."

As to the Commonwealth's second contention, that the initial seizure was justified as a limited investigatory stop, little discussion is required. A stop for investigatory purposes in this context is justified only if the "police officer observes unusual conduct which leads him reasonably to conclude in light of his experience that criminal activity may be afoot . . . ." *Terry, supra* 392 U.S. at 30, 88 S. Ct. at 1884. Hoffman testified his observations aroused his curiosity and suspicion about Jones; but, he also testified Jones was violating no law when observed and the record is devoid of any facts to support a reasonable conclusion that criminal activity may have been afoot. Thus, under the circumstances presented, the seizure lacked justification.

The order of the Court of Common Pleas is affirmed.

---

[1] We note that Hoffman's questions did not focus on a general investigation of crime; rather, they focused on Jones. Considering the nature of the questions and their focus on Jones, we believe a reasonable man would conclude Hoffman was displaying authority in order to restrain him. Compare *Commonwealth v. Fisher*, 466 Pa. 216, 352 A.2d 26 (1976), wherein we reiterated the requirement that *Miranda* warnings be given in a situation where a person reasonably believes his freedom of movement is restricted by interrogation which focuses on him.

Jones Vocabulary

Instructions: To better understand this material, be sure you know the definitions of the following terms. Be prepared to define these terms for your classmates, using the techniques described in "Defining/Explaining a Term or Concept." (pg. 14)

1. Motions
2. Evidence
3. Suppression hearing
4. Arrest warrant
5. Theft
6. Outstanding (warrant)
7. Seizure
8. Investigatory stop
9. Probable cause
10. Force
11. Authority
12. Restraint
13. Totality of the circumstances
14. To charge
15. To file
16. To suppress
17. To seize
18. To stop
19. To testify
20. To search
21. To err
22. To restrain

COMMONWEALTH of Pennsylvania, Appellee,
v.
Louis R. EDMUNDS, Appellant
Supreme Court of Pennsylvania
586 A.2d 887 (Pa. 1991)

[Some footnotes may have been omitted.]

CAPPY, Justice.

I. HISTORY OF THE CASE

The issue presented to this court is whether Pennsylvania should adopt the "good faith" exception to the exclusionary rule as articulated by the United States Supreme Court in the case of *United States v. Leon*, 468 U.S. 897, 104 S. Ct. 3405, 82 L. Ed. 2d 677 (1984). We conclude that a "good faith" exception to the exclusionary rule would frustrate the guarantees embodied in Article I, Section 8, of the Pennsylvania Constitution. Accordingly, the decision of the Superior Court is reversed.

The defendant in the instant case was found guilty after a non-jury trial on August 18, 1987 of criminal conspiracy, 18 Pa. C.S. Section 903(a)(1), simple possession, possession with intent to deliver, possession with intent to manufacture and manufacture of a controlled substance, in violation of the Controlled Substance, Drug, Device and Cosmetic Act, 35 P.S. § 780-101 *et seq.* The conviction was premised upon the admission into evidence of marijuana seized at the defendant's property pursuant to a search warrant, after information was received from two anonymous informants.

The trial court held that the search warrant failed to establish probable cause that the marijuana would be at the location to be searched on the date it was issued. The trial court found that the warrant failed to set forth with specificity the date upon which the anonymous informants observed the marijuana. *See Commonwealth v. Conner*, Pa. 333, 305 A.2d 341 (1973). However, the trial court went on to deny the defendant's motion to suppress the marijuana. Applying the rationale of *Leon*, the trial court looked beyond the four corners of the affidavit, in order to establish that the officers executing the warrant acted in "good faith" in relying upon the warrant to conduct the search. In reaching this conclusion the trial court also decided that *Leon* permitted the court to undercut the language of Pa. R. Crim. P. 2003,[1] which

---

[1] Pa. R. of Crim. P. 2003 provides in relevant part:

(a) No search warrant shall issue but upon probable cause supported by one or more affidavits sworn to before the issuing authority. The issuing authority, in determining whether probable cause has been established, may not consider any evidence outside the affidavits.

(b) At any hearing on a motion for the return or suppression of evidence, or for the suppression of the fruits of the evidence obtained pursuant to a search warrant, no evidence shall be admissible to establish probable cause other than the affidavits provided for in paragraph (a).

Rule 2003 was adopted following this Court's decision in *Commonwealth v. Milliken*, 450 Pa. 310, 300 A.2d 78 (1973). A fuller discussion of Rule 2003 and the *Milliken* case follows at pages 901-02, *infra*.

prohibits oral testimony outside the four corners of the written affidavit to supplement the finding of probable cause.

The Superior Court in a divided panel decision, opinion by Wieand J., dissent by Popovich J., affirmed the judgment of the trial court, specifically relying upon the decision of the United States Supreme Court in *Leon. Commonwealth v. Edmunds*, 373 Pa. Super. 384, 541 A.2d 368 (1988). Allocatur was granted by this Court.

The pertinent facts can be briefly summarized as follows. On August 5, 1985 State Police Trooper Michael Deise obtained a warrant from a district magistrate to search a white corrugated building and curtilage on the property of the defendant. The warrant on its face also included the defendant's residence as part of the property to be searched; however, the Commonwealth now concedes that probable cause did not properly exist for the search of the residence. As the affidavit of probable cause is central to our decision, we will set it forth in full:

> On the date of August 4, 1985, this affiant Michael D. Deise, Penna. State Police, was in contact by telephone with two anonymous Males who were and are members of the community where Louis R. Edmunds resides. Both anonymous males advised the affiant that while checking out familiar hunting areas off Rte. 31, east of Jones Mills and along the south side of Rte. 31. (sic) These men observed growing marijuana near a white corrugated building approximately 20 x 40 feet in a cleared off area. These men looked into the building and observed several plants that appeared to be marijuana. This affiant questioned both of these men as to their knowledge of marijuana. This affiant learned that one of these men saw growing marijuana numerous times while he was stationed in Viet Nam. The other male saw growing marijuana while at a police station. This affiant described a growing marijuana plant and its characteristics and they agreed that what they had viewed agreed with the description and also that it appeared to them to be marijuana as fully described by the affiant. The two males wish to remain anonymous for fear of retaliation or bodily harm. An anonymous male advised this affiant that Louis R. Edmunds lived there. Edmund's description being that of a white male in his middle thirties and he lived at the aforementioned location.
>
> On the 5th of August, 1985, this affiant with the use of a State Police helicopter, flew over the described location and observed the white corrugated building in the mountain area and located as described by the two males. Also on this date this affiant drove past the Rte. 31 entrance and observed a mail box with "Edmunds 228" printed on it.

After obtaining the warrant from the local magistrate, Trooper Deise, accompanied by three other troopers, served the warrant upon the defendant at his residence. Though he did not place the defendant under arrest at this time, the trooper did advise him of his Miranda rights, and had him read the warrant. The trooper also explained to the defendant that the warrant was not for his residence, although the warrant itself included the residence. Rather, the trooper stated that the warrant was meant to relate to the white corrugated building, and that they were searching for marijuana in that building.

The defendant acknowledged that he owned the land in question, but stated that he leased the white corrugated building to a Thomas Beacon. The defendant, followed by the trooper, went to the second floor of his residence to obtain a copy of the lease to demonstrate that the building was in fact leased to Mr. Beacon. Trooper Deise followed the defendant to ensure that he did not obtain a weapon or otherwise endanger the officers. While accompanying the defendant to the second floor, the trooper noticed near the top of the stairs four (4) large transparent plastic bags containing what appeared to be marijuana. Based upon this discovery the trooper placed the defendant under arrest.

After producing the lease which indicated that the white corrugated building was in fact leased to Thomas Beacon, the defendant accompanied the troopers to the building, which was approximately one-quarter of a mile away, up a steep mountainous terrain, on a separate parcel of property owned by Edmunds. The record is devoid of evidence that there was marijuana growing outside the corrugated building. The defendant unlocked the door of the white building and entered with the troopers. Inside the building the troopers discovered seventeen (17) growing marijuana plants, along with gardening implements, high-wattage lights, and a watering system. The marijuana was seized and the charges as recited above were brought against the defendant.

Prior to trial the defendant moved to suppress the marijuana seized in his residence, the marijuana found growing in the white corrugated building, as well as statements made by defendant Edmunds. A suppression hearing held by the trial court on January 27, 1986, at which time Trooper Deise testified concerning the information set forth in the affidavit of probable cause. Counsel for defendant moved to suppress all of the above evidence, on the ground that the warrant was constitutionally defective, and probable cause was lacking, because the warrant failed to set forth a time frame in which the informants had observed the marijuana.

Recognizing that the affidavit of probable cause was deficient on its face, the trial court granted the request of the district attorney to convene a supplemental suppression hearing, which occurred on April 21, 1986. The express purpose of this hearing was to allow the district attorney to provide oral supplementation of the facts set forth in the written affidavit and warrant, in order to establish a "good faith" exception to the exclusionary rule under the auspices of *Leon*. The Commonwealth thus introduced evidence that the two informants had observed the marijuana on August 4, 1986, and that such date had been related to District Justice Tlumac prior to the issuance of the warrant, although it was not contained in the affidavit of probable cause or the warrant itself.

Trooper Deise and District Justice Tlumac each offered testimony consistent with that position. However, the testimony of District Justice Tlumac was somewhat ambivalent. She testified that Trooper Deise appeared in her office on August 5, 1986, and related his conversation with the two anonymous informants. She stated that Trooper Deise thereafter dictated the affidavit, which she typed verbatim. She then prepared and issued the search warrant. When asked whether Trooper Deise had indicated that the events in question had occurred the preceding day, District Justice Tlumac testified as follows: "And I felt with knowing Officer Deise over a period of fifteen, twenty years and had countless search warrants, and they were always fresh, that apparently he wouldn't (sic) bring information that just occurred, that was so fresh. The question wouldn't even arose (sic) in my mind. And at that time I was under the impression this all occurred the day before."

Upon the close of the supplemental suppression hearing, the trial court found that, strictly adhering to Rule 2003 of the Pennsylvania Rules of Criminal Procedure, this warrant would be incapable of establishing probable cause to justify the search of defendant's property. The warrant failed to set forth a time frame from which a neutral and detached magistrate could reasonably infer that the criminal conduct observed was recent and would most likely still be in progress at the time the warrant was requested. *Conner, supra.*

The trial court went on to reason, however, that the facial invalidity of the warrant did not necessitate the exclusion of the evidence. On the basis of testimony offered by the district attorney at the supplemental suppression hearing, the trial court applied the federal test of *Leon*, and held that where the officer acts in "good faith" reliance upon the District Justice's determination of probable cause, the evidence seized will not be excluded at trial, regardless of the warrant's defects.

The trial court further concluded that the trooper, being reasonably well trained, believed the warrant to be valid because it had been issued by a neutral magistrate. Therefore, the trial court concluded that the trooper acted in "good faith" in executing the warrant, and determined that the federal *Leon* rule permitted the evidence to be introduced, despite the fact that the affidavit was defective and failed to establish probable cause under Pennsylvania law.

The Superior Court adopted the reasoning of the trial court, and went on to hold that Article I Section 8 of the Pennsylvania Constitution afforded no greater protection to its citizens than that provided under the 4th Amendment to the United States Constitution. The Superior Court panel found no compelling reason to deviate from the decision of the United States Supreme Court in *Leon*, and likewise endorsed the federal "good faith" exception to the exclusionary rule as a matter of Pennsylvania jurisprudence.

As a preliminary matter, we concur with the inevitable conclusion of the trial court and the Superior Court, that probable cause did not exist on the face of the warrant. In *Conner*, this Court made clear that a search warrant is defective if it is issued without reference to the time when the informant obtained his or her information. *Id.* 452 Pa. at 339, 305 A.2d at 345. Coupled with *Pa. R. Crim. P.* 2003, which mandates that courts in Pennsylvania shall not consider oral testimony outside the four corners of the written affidavit to supplement the finding of probable cause for a search warrant, we are compelled to conclude that the affidavit of probable cause and warrant were facially invalid. *Commonwealth v. Simmons*, 450 Pa. 624, 626, 301 A.2d 819, 820 (1973). As the Superior Court candidly stated, the affidavit in question "did not contain facts from which the date of the hunters' observations could be determined." 373 Pa. Super. at 390, 541 A.2d at 371. Indeed, the dissenting opinion of Mr. Justice McDermott concedes that probable cause was lacking.

We are not at liberty to ignore the *Leon* issue as it has been injected into the case by the trial court, and expressly affirmed by the Superior Court. Both lower courts have acknowledged, correctly, that Rule 2003 and our decision in *Conner* render the warrant invalid on its face under Pennsylvania law. The only way to salvage the warrant from facial invalidity is to disregard Rule 2003 and consider oral testimony outside the four corners of the affidavit to establish probable cause, which we are not free to do; or to consider the same oral testimony to establish a "good faith" exception under the federal *Leon* test, which is precisely what the trial court sought to accomplish. The trial judge conducted a supplemental suppression hearing for the express purpose of bringing the *Leon* issue four-square into this case, and the Superior Court affirmed explicitly on that basis. The "good faith" exception issue having thus been joined by both courts below, we are now constrained to address it.

The sole question in this case, therefore, is whether the Constitution of Pennsylvania incorporates a "good faith" exception to the exclusionary rule, which permits the introduction of evidence seized where probable cause is lacking on the face of the warrant.

Put in other terms, the question is whether the federal *Leon* test circumvents the acknowledged deficiencies under Pennsylvania law, and prevents the suppression of evidence seized pursuant to an *invalid search warrant*. For the reasons that follow, we conclude that it does not.

II. UNITED STATES v. LEON

Our starting point must be the decision of the United States Supreme Court in *Leon*. In *Leon*, the Supreme Court in 1984 departed from a long history of exclusionary rule jurisprudence dating back to *Weeks v. United States*, 232 U.S. 383, 34 S. Ct. 341, 58 L. Ed. 652 (1914) and *Mapp v. Ohio*, 367 U.S. 643, 81 S. Ct. 1684, 6 L. Ed. 2d 1081 (1961). The Court in *Leon* concluded that the 4th Amendment does not mandate suppression of illegally seized evidence obtained pursuant to a constitutionally defective warrant, so long as the police officer acted in good faith reliance upon the warrant issued by a neutral and detached magistrate.

In *Leon*, police officers in Burbank, California, had initiated a drug investigation after receiving a tip from a confidential informant that large quantities of cocaine and methaqualone were being sold from a residence. The informant had indicated that he witnessed a sale of methaqualone approximately five months earlier. The Burbank police set up a surveillance of three residences, and observed known drug offenders, including Leon, arriving in automobiles and leaving with small packages. *Leon*, 468 U.S. at 901-902, 104 S. Ct. at 3409-3410. The officers also observed certain of the suspects boarding separate flights for Miami. *Id.* at 902, 104 S. Ct. at 3409.

Based upon these and other observations, the Burbank police prepared an affidavit and obtained a search warrant from a Superior Court judge. A search of the suspects' residences and automobiles uncovered large quantities of cocaine and methaqualone. *Id.* at 902, 104 S. Ct. at 3409.

After being indicted in federal court, the respondents moved to suppress the evidence. The district court agreed that the affidavit was insufficient to establish probable cause. First, the observations of the informant had been made six months earlier, creating a staleness problem. Second, there was no basis for establishing the reliability or credibility of the informant, who had no track-record with respect to providing reliable information. Moreover, the police investigation "neither cured the staleness nor the details of the informant's declarations," *Id.* at 904, 104 S. Ct. at 3411. The information gathered by the police officers was "as consistent with innocence as it is with guilt." *Id.* at 903 n.2, 104 S. Ct. at 3410 n.2. Thus, the then-existing test for probable cause under *Aguilar-Spinelli* had not been met. *Id.* at 902 n.2, 104 S. Ct. at 3410 n.2.

The Court of Appeals in *Leon* affirmed, rejecting the government's invitation to recognize a good faith exception to the exclusionary rule. The United States Supreme Court reversed, in a 6-3 decision.

Justice White, writing for the majority in *Leon*, first indicated that the exclusionary rule was not a "necessary corollary of the Fourth Amendment." 468 U.S. at 905, 104 S. Ct. at 3411. Although *Olmstead v. United States*, 277 U.S. 438, 48 S. Ct. 564, 72 L. Ed. 944 (1928) and *Mapp v. Ohio, supra*, had suggested that the exclusion of illegally seized evidence was part-and-parcel of the 4th Amendment's guaranty, the *Leon* Court took the position that the exclusionary rule operates as "a judicially created remedy designed to safeguard Fourth Amendment rights generally through its deterrent effect, rather than a personal constitutional right of the party aggrieved." *Id.*, quoting *United States v. Calandra*, 414 U.S. 338, 348, 94 S. Ct. 613, 620, 38 L. Ed. 2d 561 (1974).

Justice White went on to conclude that the issue of whether the exclusionary rule should be imposed in a particular case "must be resolved by weighing the costs and benefits" of precluding such evidence from the prosecution's case. *Leon*, 468 U.S. at 906-907, 104 S. Ct. at 3411-3412. On the costs side of the analysis, Justice White declared that the exclusionary rule incurs "substantial social costs" in terms of "imped(ing) unacceptably the truth-finding functions of judge and jury." *Id.* at 907, 104 S. Ct. at 3412 *quoting United States v. Payner*, 447 U.S. 727, 734, 100 S. Ct. 2439, 2445, 65 L. Ed. 2d 468 (1980). As a result, Justice White noted that "some guilty defendants may free or receive reduced sentences as a result of favorable plea bargains." *Leon*, 468 U.S. at 907, 104 S. Ct. at 3412.

On the benefits side of the analysis, Justice White indicated that the *sole purpose* of the exclusionary rule under the 4th Amendment was to "deter police misconduct rather than to punish the errors of judges and magistrates." *Id.* at 916, 104 S. Ct. at 3417. Given this goal, Justice White concluded that there was no reason to presume that judges or magistrates would be more inclined to "ignore or subvert" the 4th Amendment if evidence seized pursuant to a defective warrant were admissible. The majority wrote: "Although there are assertions that some magistrates become rubber stamps for the police and others may be unable effectively to screen police conduct . . . we are not convinced that this is a problem of major proportions." 468 U.S. at 916 n.14, 104 S. Ct. at 3417 n.14 (citations omitted).

The Court in *Leon* found that the argument that the exclusionary rule "deters future inadequate presentations" by police officers or prevents "magistrate shopping" was "speculative." *Id.* at 918, 104 S. Ct. at 3418. Consequently, the Fourth Amendment was not served by excluding improperly seized evidence, except on rare occasions. Wrote the Court:

> In most such cases, there is no police illegality and thus nothing to deter. It is the magistrate's responsibility to

determine whether the officer's allegations establish probable cause and, if so, to issue a warrant comporting in form with requirements of the Fourth Amendment. In the ordinary case, an officer cannot be expected to question the magistrate's probable cause determination or his judgment that the form of the warrant is technically sufficient. . . . Penalizing the officer for the magistrate's error, rather than his own, cannot logically contribute to the deterrence of Fourth Amendment violations. 468 U.S. at 920-921, 104 S. Ct. at 3419.

The *Leon* majority therefore concluded that, where a police officer is acting in objective good faith, based upon a search warrant duly issued by a neutral magistrate judge, the 4th Amendment does not require exclusion of such evidence, even where it is later determined that probable cause was lacking for the warrant. Unless the police officer acted "knowingly" or "recklessly" in providing false information to the magistrate, or the affidavit of probable cause is "so lacking in indicia of probable cause as to render official belief in its existence unreasonable," the evidence is admissible. *Leon*, at 923, 104 S. Ct. at 3421, *quoting*, *Brown v. Illinois*, 422 U.S. 590, 610-611, 95 S. Ct. 2254, 2265, 45 L. Ed. 2d 416 (1975).

Thus, the *Leon* Court concluded that the drugs obtained through a defective search warrant, unsupported by probable cause, were nonetheless admissible as evidence without controverting the 4th Amendment. *Leon*, 468 U.S. at 925-926, 104 S. Ct. at 3421-3422.

The U.S. Supreme Court subsequently broadened the good-faith exception to the exclusionary rule, in the recent case of *Illinois v. Krull*, 480 U.S. 340, 107 S. Ct. 1160, 94 L. Ed. 2d 364 (1987). In *Krull*, the Court held that a good-faith exception to the exclusionary rule permits the introduction of evidence obtained by an officer in reliance upon a statute, even where that statute is thereafter determined to be unconstitutional. *Cf. Ybarra v. Illinois*, 444 U.S. 85, 100 S. Ct. 338, 62 L. Ed. 2d 238 (1979), and *Berger v. New York*, 388 U.S. 41, 87 S. Ct. 1873, 18 L. Ed. 2d 1040 (1967) (previously indicating that the use of such evidence violated the 4th Amendment).

We must now determine whether the good-faith exception to the exclusionary rule is properly part of the jurisprudence of this Commonwealth, by virtue of Article 1, Section 8 of the Pennsylvania Constitution. In concluding that it is not, we set forth a methodology to be followed in future state constitutional issues which arise under our own Constitution.

III. FACTORS TO CONSIDER IN UNDERTAKING PENNSYLVANIA CONSTITUTIONAL ANALYSIS

This Court has long emphasized that, in interpreting a provision of the Pennsylvania Constitution, we are not bound by the decisions of the United States Supreme Court which interpret similar (yet distinct) federal constitutional provisions. *See Commonwealth v. Sell*, 504 Pa. 46, 470 A.2d 457 (1983); *Commonwealth v. Melilli*, 521 Pa. 405, 555 A.2d 1254 (1989); *Commonwealth v. Bussey*, 486 Pa. 221, 404 A.2d 1309 (1979); *Commonwealth v. DeJohn*, 486 Pa. 32, 403 A.2d 1283 (1979), *cert. denied*, 444 U.S. 1032, 100 S. Ct. 704, 62 L. Ed. 2d 668 (1980). *Commonwealth v. Triplett*, 462 Pa. 244, 341 A.2d 62 (1975); *Commonwealth v. Richman*, 458 Pa. 167, 320 A.2d 351 (1974); *Commonwealth v. Campana*, 452 Pa. 233, 304 A.2d 432, *vacated*, 414 U.S. 808, 94 S. Ct. 73, 38 L. Ed. 2d 44 *on remand*, 455 Pa. 622, 314 A.2d 854, *cert. denied*, 417 U.S. 969, 94 S. Ct. 3172, 41 L. Ed. 2d 1139 (1974).

As Mr. Chief Justice Nix aptly stated in *Sell*, the federal constitution establishes certain minimum levels which are "equally applicable to the [analogous] state constitutional provision." *Id.* 504 Pa. at 63, 470 A.2d at 466, *quoting, Commonwealth v. Platou*, 455 Pa. 258, 260 n.2, 312 A.2d 29, 31 n.2 (1973). However, each state has the power to provide broader standards, and go beyond the minimum floor which is established by the federal Constitution. *Sell*, 504 Pa. at 63, 470 A.2d at 467.

The United States Supreme Court has repeatedly affirmed that the states are not only free to, but also to engage in independent analysis in drawing meaning from their own state constitutions. *See PruneYard Shopping Center v. Robins*, 447 U.S. 74, 80-82, 100 S. Ct. 2035, 2040-41, 64 L. Ed. 2d 741 (1980) (Rehnquist, J.). Indeed, this is a positive expression of the jurisprudence which has existed in the United States since the founding of the nation. Alexander Hamilton, lobbying for the ratification of the U.S. Constitution in the Federalist Papers over two hundred years ago, made clear that the Supremacy Clause of the Federal Constitution was never designed to overshadow the states, or prevent them from maintaining their own pockets of autonomy. *See* The Federalist No. 33 (A. Hamilton), in *The Federalist Papers* (The New American Library ed.) 204.

The past two decades have witnessed a strong resurgence of independent state constitutional analysis, in Pennsylvania and elsewhere. *See* Brennan, *State Constitutions and the Protection of Individual Rights*, 90 Harv. L. Rev. 489 (1977); *Developments in the Law—The Interpretation of State Constitutional Rights*, 95 Harv. L. Rev. 1324 (1982); Linde, *E Pluribus-Constitutional Theory and State Courts*, 18 Ga. L. Rev. 165 (1984); Abrahamson, *Criminal Law and State Constitutions: The Emergence of State Constitutional Law*, 63 Tex. L. Rev. 1141 (1985); Mosk, *State Constitutionalism: Both Liberal and Conservative*, 63 Tex. L. Rev. 1081 (1985); Brennan, *Symposium on the Revolution in State Constitutional Law*, 13 Vt. L. Rev. 11 (1988).

Here in Pennsylvania, we have stated with increasing frequency that it is both important and necessary that we

,undertake an independent analysis of the Pennsylvania Constitution, each time a provision of that fundamental document is implicated. Although we may accord weight to federal decisions where they "are found to be logically persuasive and well reasoned, paying due regard to precedent and the policies underlying specific constitutional guarantees," *Commonwealth v. Tarbert*, 517 Pa. 277, 283, 535 A.2d 1035, 1038 (1987), *quoting*, Brennan, *State Constitutions and the Protection of Individual Rights*, 90 Harv. L. Rev. 489, 502 (1977), we are free to reject the conclusions of the United States Supreme Court so long as we remain faithful to the minimum guarantees established by the United States Constitution.

The recent focus on the "New Federalism"[2] has emphasized the importance of state constitutions with respect to individual rights and criminal procedure. As such, we find it important to set forth certain factors to be briefed and analyzed by litigants in each case hereafter implicating a provision of the Pennsylvania constitution. The decision of the United States Supreme Court in *Michigan v. Long*, 463 U.S. 1032, 103 S. Ct. 3469, 77 L. Ed. 2d 1201 (1983), now requires us to make a "plain statement" of the adequate and independent state grounds upon which we rely, in order to avoid any doubt that we have rested our decision squarely upon Pennsylvania jurisprudence. Accordingly, as a general rule it is important that litigants brief and analyze at least the following four factors:

1) text of the Pennsylvania constitutional provision;

2) history of the provision, including Pennsylvania case-law;

3) related case-law from other states;

4) policy considerations, including unique issues of state and local concern, and applicability within modern Pennsylvania jurisprudence.

Depending upon the particular issue presented, an examination of related federal precedent may be useful as part of the state constitutional analysis, not as binding but as one form of guidance. However, it is essential that courts in Pennsylvania undertake an independent analysis under the Pennsylvania Constitution. Utilizing the above four factors, and having reviewed *Leon*, we conclude that a "good faith" exception to the exclusionary rule would frustrate the guarantees embodied in Article I, Section 8 of our Commonwealth's constitution.

---

[2]   The term "New Federalism" has been used increasingly to define the recent emphasis on independent state constitutional analysis. "Federalism in the Twenty-First Century," in *Federalism—The Shifting Balance* (J. Griffith ed., 1989); Abrahamson & Gutmann, *The New Federalism: State Constitutions and State Courts*, 71 Judicature 88 (1987); *See, e.g.*, Peters, *State Constitutional Law: Federalism in the Common Law Tradition*, 84 MICH. L. REV. 583 (1986); and, Douglas, *Federalism and State Constitutions*, 13 VT. L. REV. 127 (1988).

IV. ANALYSIS

A. *Text*

The text of Article 1, Section 8 of the Pennsylvania Constitution provides as follows:

Security from Searches and Seizures

Section 8. The people shall be secure in their persons, houses, papers and possessions from unreasonable searches and seizures, and no warrant to search any place or to seize any person or things shall issue without describing them as nearly as may be, nor without probable cause, supported by oath or affirmation subscribed to by the affiant.

Although the wording of the Pennsylvania Constitution is similar in language to the Fourth Amendment of the United States Constitution, we are not bound to interpret the two provisions as if they were mirror images, even where the text is similar or identical. *See, e.g., Tarbert,* 517 Pa. at 283, 535 A.2d at 1038. Thus, we must next examine history of Article I, Section 8, in order to draw meaning from that provision and consider the appropriateness of a "good faith" exception to the exclusionary rule in the Pennsylvania constitutional scheme.

B. *History*

We have made reference, on repeated occasions, to the unique history of Article 1, Section 8, as well as other provisions of the Pennsylvania Constitution. As we noted in *Sell*: "constitutional protection against unreasonable searches and seizures existed in Pennsylvania more than a decade before the adoption of the federal Constitution, and fifteen years prior to the promulgation of the Fourth Amendment." *Id.* 504 Pa. at 63, 470 A.2d at 466.

Perhaps the extent of the untapped history of the Pennsylvania Constitution should be underscored. Pennsylvania's Constitution was adopted on September 28, 1776, a full ten years prior to the ratification of the U.S. Constitution. Like the constitutions of Virginia, New Jersey, Maryland, and most of the original 13 Colonies, Pennsylvania's Constitution was drafted in the midst of the American Revolution, as the first overt expression of independence from the British Crown. *See* W. Adams, *The First American Constitutions* at 61 (1980). The Pennsylvania Constitution was therefore meant to reduce to writing a deep history of unwritten legal and moral codes which had guided the colonists from the beginning of William Penn's charter in 1681. *See* White, *Commentaries on the Constitution of Pennsylvania* (1907). Unlike the Bill of Rights of the United States Constitution which emerged as a later addendum in 1791, the Declaration of Rights in the Pennsylvania Constitution was an organic part of the state's original constitution of 1776, and appeared (not coincidentally) first in that document.

Thus, contrary to the popular misconception that state constitutions are somehow patterned after the United States Constitution, the reverse is true. The federal Bill of Rights borrowed heavily from the Declarations of contained in the constitutions of Pennsylvania and other colonies. *See* Brennan, *The Bill of Rights and the States*, in *The Great Rights* 67 (E. Cahn ed. 1963). For instance, the Pennsylvania Declaration of Rights was the "direct precursor" of the freedom of speech and press. See 1 B. Schwartz, *The Bill of Rights: A Documentary History* 262 (1971). The Delaware Declaration of Rights prohibited quartering of soldiers and ex-post facto laws. *Id.* at 276-78. North Carolina's Declaration of Rights provided a number of protections to the criminally accused—the right to trial by jury, the privilege against self-incrimination, and others—which later appeared in the United States Constitution. *Id.* at 286-88.

With respect to Article 1, Section 8 of the present Pennsylvania Constitution, which relates to freedom from unreasonable searches and seizures, that provision had its origin prior to the 4th Amendment, in Clause 10 of the original Constitution of 1776. *See Sell*, 504 Pa. at 63, 470 A.2d at 466. Specifically, the original version of the search and seizure provision reads as follows:

> The people have a right to hold themselves, their houses, papers and possessions free from search and seizure, and therefore warrants without oaths or affirmations first made, affording sufficient foundation for them, and whereby any officer or messenger may be commanded or required to search suspected places, or to seize any person or persons, his or their property, not particularly described, are contrary to that right and ought not be granted.

See Buckalew, *An Examination of the Constitution of Pennsylvania* at 13 (1883). The above provision was reworded at the time the Pennsylvania Constitution was revised extensively in 1790, and reappeared as Article 1, Section 8. The modern version of that provision has remained untouched for two hundred years, with the exception of the words "subscribed to by the affiant," which were added by the Constitutional Convention of 1873. *Id.*

The requirement of probable cause in this Commonwealth thus traces its origin to its original Constitution of 1776, drafted by the first convention of delegates chaired by Benjamin Franklin. *See* White, *supra*, at xxiii. The primary purpose of the warrant requirement was to abolish "general warrants," which had been used by the British to conduct sweeping searches of residences and businesses, based upon generalized suspicions. *See* White, *supra*, at 158; *Wakely v. Hart*, 6 Binn. 316 (1814). Therefore, at the time the Pennsylvania Constitution was drafted in 1776, the issue of searches and seizures unsupported by probable cause was of utmost concern to the constitutional draftsmen. *Id.*

Moreover, as this Court has stated repeatedly in interpreting Article 1, Section 8, that provision is meant to embody a strong notion of privacy, carefully safeguarded in this Commonwealth for the past two centuries. As we stated in *Sell*: "the survival of the language now employed in Article 1, Section 8 through over 200 years of profound change in other areas demonstrates that the paramount concern for privacy first adopted as part of our organic law in 1776 continues to enjoy the mandate of the people of this Commonwealth." *Id.* 504 Pa. at 65, 470 A.2d at 467. *See also Commonwealth v. Melilli; Commonwealth v. Bussey; Commonwealth v. DeJohn; Commonwealth v. Triplett; Commonwealth v. Richman; Commonwealth v. Campana; Commonwealth v. Platou*, 455 Pa. 258, 312 A.2d 29 (1973), *cert. denied, Pennsylvania v. Platou*, 417 U.S. 976, 94 S. Ct. 3183, 41 L. Ed. 2d 1146 (1974); *Denoncourt v. Com., State Ethics Com.*, 504 Pa. 191, 470 A.2d 945 (1983); *Commonwealth v. Miller*, 513 Pa. 118, 518 A.2d 1187 (1986); *Commonwealth v. Blystone*, 519 Pa. 450, 549 A.2d 81 (1988).

The history of Article I, Section 8, thus indicates that the purpose underlying the exclusionary rule in this Commonwealth is quite distinct from the purpose underlying the exclusionary rule under the 4th Amendment, as articulated by the majority in *Leon*.

The United States Supreme Court in *Leon* made clear that, in its view, the *sole purpose* for the exclusionary rule under the 4th Amendment was to deter police misconduct. *Id.* 468 U.S. at 916, 104 S. Ct. at 3417. The *Leon* majority also made clear that, under the Federal Constitution, the exclusionary rule operated as "a judicially created remedy designed to safeguard Fourth Amendment rights generally through its deterrent effect, rather than a personal constitutional right of the party aggrieved." *Id.* 468 U.S. at 906, 104 S. Ct. at 3412, 82 L. Ed. 2d at 687 *quoting, United States v. Calandra, supra*, 414 U.S. at 348, 94 S. Ct. at 620.

This reinterpretation differs from the way the exclusionary rule has evolved in Pennsylvania since the decision of *Mapp v. Ohio* in 1961 and represents a shift in judicial philosophy from the decisions of the United States Supreme Court dating back to *Weeks v. United States*.

Like many of its sister states, Pennsylvania did not adopt an exclusionary rule until the United States Supreme Court's decision in *Mapp* required it to do so. *See Elkins v. U.S.*, 364 U.S. 206, 225, 80 S. Ct. 1437, 1448, 4 L. Ed. 2d 1669 (1960). However, at the time the exclusionary rule was embraced in Pennsylvania, we clearly viewed it as a constitutional mandate. *Commonwealth v. Bosurgi*, 411 Pa. 56, 190 A.2d 304 (1963) (interpreting *Mapp* to require the exclusion of illegally seized evidence as "an essential part of both the 4th and

14th Amendments,") *Id.* at 64, 190 A.2d at 309, *quoting,* *Mapp,* 367 U.S. at 657, 81 S. Ct. at 1693. This interpretation was in keeping with a long line of federal cases, beginning with *Weeks* in 1914, which viewed the exclusionary rule as a necessary corrolary the prohibition against unreasonable searches and seizures.

As one commentator noted in piecing together the history of the exclusionary rule: "'Deterrence,' now claimed to be the primary ground for exclusion, seems to have had no substantial place in any of these conceptions of the practice." *See* White, *Forgotten Points in the Exclusionary Rule Debate,* 81 Mich. L. Rev. 1273, 1279 (1983).

During the first decade after *Mapp,* our decisions in Pennsylvania tended to parallel the cases interpreting the 4th Amendment. However, beginning in 1973, our case-law began to reflect a clear divergence from federal precedent. The United States Supreme Court at this time began moving towards a metamorphosed view, suggesting that the purpose of the exclusionary rule "is not to redress the injury to the *privacy* of the search victim (but, rather) to deter future *unlawful police conduct.*" *Calandra,* 414 U.S. at 347, 94 S. Ct. at 619 (emphasis added); *see also U.S. v. Peltier,* 422 U.S. 531, 536, 95 S. Ct. 2313, 2317, 45 L. Ed. 2d 374 (1975). At the same time this Court began to forge its own path under Article I, Section 8 of the Pennsylvania Constitution, declaring with increasing frequency that Article I, Section 8 of the Pennsylvania Constitution embodied a strong notion of privacy, notwithstanding federal cases to the contrary. In *Commonwealth v. Platou* and *Commonwealth v. DeJohn,* we made explicit that right to be free from unreasonable searches and seizures contained in Article I, Section 8 of the Pennsylvania Constitution is tied into the implicit right to privacy in this Commonwealth." *DeJohn,* 486 Pa. at 49, 403 A.2d at 1291. In *DeJohn,* we specifically refused to follow the U.S. Supreme Court's decision in *U.S. v. Miller,* 425 U.S. 435, 96 S. Ct. 1619, 48 L. Ed. 2d 71 (1976), which had held that a citizen had no standing to object to the seizure of his or her bank records.

From *DeJohn* forward, a steady line of case-law has evolved under the Pennsylvania Constitution, making clear that Article I, Section 8 is unshakably linked to a right of privacy in this Commonwealth. *See Commonwealth v. Platou,* (1973); *Commonwealth v. DeJohn,* (1979); *Commonwealth v. Sell,* (1983); *Commonwealth v. Miller,* (1986); *Commonwealth v. Blystone,* (1988); and *Commonwealth v. Melilli,* (1989).

As Mr. Justice Flaherty noted in *Denoncourt, supra,* in echoing the wisdom of Justice Brandeis over 60 years ago: "The makers of our Constitution undertook to secure conditions favorable to the pursuit of happiness . . . They conferred, as against the government, the right to be let alone—the most comprehensive of rights and the right most valued by civilized men." *Id.* 504 Pa. at 199, 470 A.2d at 948-49, *quoting Olmstead v. United States*, 277 U.S. 438, 478, 48 S. Ct. 564, 572, 72 L. Ed. 944 (1928) (Brandeis, J., dissenting).

Most recently, in *Melilli*, this Court cited with approval the decision of the Superior Court in *Commonwealth v. Beauford*, 327 Pa. Super. 253, 475 A.2d 783 (1984), *allocatur denied*, 508 Pa. 319, 496 A.2d 1143 (1985), holding that Article I, Section 8 of the Pennsylvania Constitution was offended by the installation of a pen register device without probable cause. Mr. Justice Papadakos, in rejecting the holding of the United States Supreme Court in *Smith v. Maryland*, 442 U.S. 735, 99 S. Ct. 2577, 61 L. Ed. 2d 220 (1979), emphasized that "Article I, Section 8 of the Pennsylvania Constitution . . . may be employed to guard *individual privacy* rights against unreasonable searches and seizures more zealously than the federal government does under the Constitution of the United States by serving as an independent source of supplemental rights." *Id.* 521 Pa. at 412, 555 A.2d at 1258. Mr. Justice Papadakos went on to conclude that, because a pen register "is the equivalent of a search warrant in its operative effect where the intrusion involves a violation of a privacy interest," the affidavit and order "must comply with the requirements of probable cause required under Pa. Rules of Criminal Procedure Chapter 2000, Search Warrants." *Id.* at 414, 555 A.2d 1259.

Thus, the exclusionary rule in Pennsylvania has consistently served to bolster the twin aims of Article I, Section 8; to-wit, the safeguarding of privacy and the fundamental requirement that warrants shall only be issued upon probable cause. *Melilli, supra.* As this Court explained in *Commonwealth v. Miller*:

> The linch-pin that has been developed to determine whether it is appropriate to issue a search warrant is the test of probable cause. *Commonwealth v. Chandler* [505 Pa. 113, 477 A.2d 851], *supra.* It is designed to protect us from unwarranted and even vindictive incursions upon our privacy. It insulates from dictatorial and tyrannical rule by the state, and preserves the concept of democracy that assures the freedom of its citizens. This concept is second to none in its importance in delineating the dignity of the individual living in a free society. *Id.* 513 Pa. at 127, 518 A.2d at 1191-92.

Whether the United States Supreme Court has determined that the exclusionary rule does not advance the 4th Amendment purpose of deterring police conduct is irrelevant. Indeed, we disagree with that Court's suggestion in *Leon* that we in Pennsylvania have been employing the exclusionary rule all these years to deter police corruption. We flatly reject this notion. We have no reason to believe that police officers or district justices in the Commonwealth of Pennsylvania do not engage in "good faith" in carrying out their duties. What

is significant, however, is that our Constitution has historically been interpreted to incorporate a strong right of privacy,
and an equally strong adherence to the requirement of probable cause under Article 1, Section 8. Citizens in this Commonwealth possess such rights, even where a police officer in
"good faith" carrying out his or her duties inadvertently invades the privacy or circumvents the strictures of probable
cause. To adopt a "good faith" exception to the exclusionary
rule, we believe, would virtually emasculate those clear safeguards which have been carefully developed under the Pennsylvania Constitution over the past 200 years.

C. *Related Case-Law From Other States*

A number of states other than Pennsylvania have confronted
the issue of whether to apply a "good faith" exception to the
exclusionary rule, under their own constitutions, in the wake
of *Leon*.

The highest courts of at least two states—Arkansas and Missouri—have seemingly embraced the good faith exception
under their own constitutions. *See Jackson v. State*, 291 Ark.
98, 722 S.W.2d 831 (1987); *State v. Brown*, 708 S.W.2d 140
(Mo. 1986) (en banc). Intermediary appellate courts in at
least four other states—Indiana, Kansas, Maryland and Louisiana—have indicated their acceptance of the "good faith"
exception. *See Mers v. State*, 482 N.E.2d 778 (Ind. Ct. App.
1985); *State v. Huber*, 10 Kan. App. 2d 560, 704 P.2d 1004
(1985); *Howell v. State*, 60 Md. App. 463, 483 A.2d 780
(1984). *State v. Martin*, 487 So. 2d 1295 (La. App. 3d Cir.),
writ denied 491 So. 2d 25 (La. 1986). In virtually all of
those states embracing the "good-faith" exception under
their own constitutions, however, the reasoning is a simple
affirmation of the logic of *Leon*, with little additional state
constitutional analysis.

On the other hand, the highest courts of at least four
states—New Jersey, New York, North Carolina and Connecticut—have chosen to reject the "good-faith" exception
under their own constitutions, with more detailed analysis of
state constitutional principles. See *State v. Marsala*, 216
Conn. 150, 579 A.2d 58 (1990), *State v. Novembrino*, 105
N.J. 95, 519 A.2d 820 (N.J. 1987); *People v. Bigelow*, 66
N.Y.2d 417, 497 N.Y.S.2d 630, 488 N.E.2d 451 (1985); *State
v. Carter*, 322 N.C. 709, 370 S.E.2d 553 (1988). *See also Mason v. State*, 534 A.2d 242 (Del. 1987) (rejecting good-faith
exception as statutory matter); *Commonwealth v. Upton*, 394
Mass. 363, 476 N.E.2d 548 (1985) (same); *Stringer v. State*,
491 So. 2d 837 (Miss. 1986) (Robertson, J., concurring). The
intermediate appellate courts of at least four additional
states—Tennessee, Wisconsin, Michigan, and Minnesota—have likewise eschewed the logic of *Leon* under their
own state constitutions. *See State v. Taylor*, 763 S.W.2d 756

(Tenn. Crim. App. 1987); *State v. Grawein*, 123 Wis. 2d 428, 367 N.W.2d 816 (Ct. App. 1985); *People v. Sundling*, 153 Mich. App. 277, 395 N.W.2d 308 (1986); *State v. Herbst*, 395 N.W.2d 399, 404 (Minn. App. 1986).

A mere scorecard of those states which have accepted and rejected *Leon* is certainly not dispositive of the issue in Pennsylvania. However, the logic of certain of those opinions bears upon our analysis under the Pennsylvania Constitution, particularly given the unique history of Article 1, Section 8.

In this respect, we draw support from other states which have declined to adopt a "good faith" exception, particularly New Jersey, Connecticut and North Carolina. In *State v. Novembrino, supra*, the New Jersey Supreme Court found that the "good faith" exception to the exclusionary rule was inconsistent with the New Jersey Constitution, because it would undermine the requirement of probable cause. Although New Jersey, like Pennsylvania, had no exclusionary rule in place prior to *Mapp v. Ohio* in 1961, the New Court found that it had become "imbedded" in the jurisprudence under that state's constitution. As the New Jersey court wrote in *Novembrino*:

> The exclusionary rule, by virtue of its consistent application over the past twenty-five years, has become an integral element of our state-constitutional guarantee that search warrants will not issue without probable cause. Its function is not merely to deter police misconduct. The rule also serves as the indispensable mechanism for vindicating the constitutional right to be free from unreasonable searches. *Id.* 519 A.2d at 856.

Similarly, the Connecticut Supreme Court—which most recently rejected the good faith exception on August 7, 1990—concluded that the purpose of the exclusionary rule under Article I, Section 7 of the Connecticut Constitution, was to "preserve the integrity of the warrant issuing process as a whole." *State v. Marsala*, 216 Conn. at 169, 579 A.2d at 67, *quoting*, S. Wasserstrom & W. Mertens, *The Exclusionary Rule on the Scaffold: But was it a Fair Trial?* 22 AM. Crim. L. Rev. 85,111. Thus, when evidence was suppressed under this provision due to a defective warrant, "the issuing authority . . . is not being 'punished' for a mistake, but is, rather, being informed that a constitutional violation has taken place and is also being instructed in how to avoid such violations in the future." *Marsala*, at 168, 579 A.2d at 67.

More directly on point, the North Carolina Supreme Court in *State v. Carter, supra*, rejected the "good faith" exception to the exclusionary rule, noting the importance of the *privacy rights* flowing from the search and seizure provision in the North Carolina Constitution. The court in *Carter* emphasized the need to preserve the integrity of the judiciary in

North Carolina, in excluding illegally seized evidence when such important rights of the citizenry were at stake. Wrote the North Carolina Supreme Court:

> The exclusionary sanction is indispensable to give effect to the constitutional principles prohibiting unreasonable search and seizure. We are persuaded that exclusionary rule is the only effective bulwark against governmental disregard for constitutionally protected privacy rights. Equally of importance in our reasoning, we adhere to the rule for the sake of maintaining the integrity of the judicial branch of government. *Id.* 370 S.E.2d at 559.

We similarly conclude that, given the strong right of privacy which inheres in Article 1, Section 8, as well as the clear prohibition against the issuance of warrants without probable cause, or based upon defective warrants, the good faith exception to the exclusionary rule would directly clash with those rights of citizens as developed in our Commonwealth over the past 200 years. To allow the judicial branch to participate, directly or indirectly, in the use of the fruits of illegal searches would only serve to undermine the integrity of the judiciary in this Commonwealth. *See Carter, supra, Marsala, supra.* From the perspective of the citizen whose rights are at stake, an invasion of privacy, in good faith or bad, is equally as intrusive. This is true whether it occurs through the actions of the legislative, executive or the judicial branch of government.

D. *Policy Considerations*

We recognize that, in analyzing any state constitutional provision, it is necessary to go beyond the bare text and history of that provision as it was drafted 200 years ago, and consider its application within the modern scheme of Pennsylvania jurisprudence. An assessment of various policy considerations, however, only supports our conclusion that the good faith exception to the exclusionary rule would be inconsistent with the jurisprudence surrounding Article 1, Section 8.

First, such a rule would effectively negate the judicially created mandate reflected in the Pennsylvania Rules of Criminal Procedure, in Rules 2003, 2005 and 2006. Specifically, Rule 2003 relates to the requirements for the issuance of a warrant, and provides in relevant part:

> (a) No search warrant shall issue but upon probable cause supported by one or more affidavits sworn to before the issuing authority. The issuing authority, in determining whether probable cause has been established, may not consider any evidence outside the affidavits.

> (b) At any hearing on a motion for the return or suppression of evidence, or for suppression of the fruits of evidence, obtained pursuant to a search warrant, no evidence shall be

admissible to establish probable cause other than the affidavits provided for in paragraph (a).

Rule 2003 thus adopts a "four corners" requirement, and
provides that only evidence contained within the four corners of the affidavit may be considered to establish probable
cause. This Rule, along with Rules 2005 and 2006 which re-
iterate that probable cause must exist on the face of the affidavit, were promulgated by this Court following this Court's
decision in *Commonwealth v. Milliken*, 450 Pa. 310, 300
A.2d 78 (1973). The decision in *Milliken* is significant, because it makes clear that the "four corners" requirement of
Rule 2003 was carefully and deliberately established in this
Commonwealth.

In *Milliken*, a police officer had obtained a warrant to search
the defendant's home for evidence relating to a murder,
based upon an informant's tip. The affidavit of probable
cause failed to set forth sufficient facts to establish the
"reliability" of the informant, under the prevailing
Aguilar-Spinelli test, rendering the warrant defective. At the
suppression hearing, however, the police officer testified
that he had given additional sworn oral testimony to the
magistrate at the time the warrant was issued, not reduced to
writing, which established the informant's reliability. The
magistrate admitted that his memory was "dimmed" by the
fact the proceeding was "some time ago," but essentially
corroborated the officer's story.

This Court in *Milliken* rejected the contention that Article I,
Section 8 of the Pennsylvania Constitution itself mandated
that all facts relied upon to establish probable cause be reduced to writing; the constitutional language itself contained
no such requirement. *Id.* 450 Pa. at 314, 300 A.2d at 81. We
therefore held that the sworn oral testimony of police officer
in that case could be used to supplement the affidavit. *Id.*
However, we went on to express deep concern for the fact
that "the 'passage of time' inevitably causes 'memories . . .
(to) fade.'" *Id.* at 313, 300 A.2d at 80, *quoting, Dickey v.
Florida*, 398 U.S. 30, 42, 90 S. Ct. 1564, 1571, 26 L. Ed. 2d
26 (1970) (Brennan, J., concurring). We stated that without a
transcribed record made contemporaneously with the issuance of the warrant, "subsequent review of the partially
unwritten proceeding may become tainted by possible addi-
tions of relevant information initially omitted but later supplied by hindsight." *Id.* 450 Pa. at 313, 300 A.2d at 80.

Recognizing this "troublesome" dilemma, this Court in a
thoughtful opinion written by the late Mr. Justice Roberts
(later Chief Justice Roberts) and joined by then Mr. Justice,
now Chief Justice Nix, announced in *Milliken* that we would
exercise our supervisory powers to formulate a rule of procedure mandating that "a sufficient written record (be) made

contemporaneously with the issuance of search warrants." *Id.* at 315, 300 A.2d at 81. We held that since this rule was procedural in nature, it could not be applied retroactively to invalidate the warrant in Milliken's case. However, we made clear that: "After the effective date of the rule the determination of probable cause by a suppression hearing court and an appellate court upon review will be made *only* from the written record prepared contemporaneously with the issuance of the search warrant." *Id.* at 315 n.3, 300 A.2d at 81 n.3 (emphasis in original). The result was the adoption of Pa. R. Crim. P. 2003 on March 28, 1973, effective in 60 days, which made explicit that probable cause for search warrants in Pennsylvania may be based only upon materials contained within the four corners of the written affidavit.

Rule 2003 thus serves to underscore the incongruity of adopting a good faith exception to the exclusionary rule in Pennsylvania. Although Rule 2003 is not constitutionally mandated by Article 1, Section 8, as *Milliken* correctly explains, it reflects yet another expression of this Court's unwavering insistence that probable cause exist before a warrant is issued, and only those facts memorialized in the written affidavit may be considered in establishing probable cause, in order to eliminate any chance of incomplete or reconstructed hindsight. It is true, as *Milliken* summarizes, that the history of Article 1, Section 8 does not itself prohibit the use of oral testimony to establish probable cause, outside the four corners of the warrant. Nonetheless, we have chosen to adopt that Rule as an administrative matter, *id.* at 315, 300 A.2d at 81, and that Rule has now stood in Pennsylvania for 17 years.

In the instant case, probable cause—as defined under Pennsylvania law—is lacking. Two lower courts have so held; we concur. Applying the federal *Leon* test would not only frustrate the procedural safeguards embodied in Rule 2003, but would permit the admission of illegally seized evidence in a variety of contexts where probable cause is lacking, so long as the police officer acted in "good faith." In *Leon* itself probable cause was absent entirely, yet illegally seized evidence was admitted into evidence. 468 U.S. at 905, 104 S. Ct. at 3411.

We cannot countenance such a wide departure from the text and history of Article 1, Section 8, nor can we permit the use of a "good faith" exception to effectively nullify Pa. R. Crim. P. 2003. Our Constitution requires that warrants shall not be issued except upon probable cause. We have specifically adopted Rule 2003 for the purpose of confining the probable cause inquiry to the written affidavit and warrant, in order to avoid any doubt as to the basis probable cause. We decline to undermine the clear mandate of these provisions by slavishly adhering to federal precedent where it diverges from two hundred years of our own constitutional jurisprudence.

A second policy consideration which bolsters our conclusion is that the underlying premise of *Leon* is still open to serious debate. Although it is clear that the exclusionary rule presents some cost to society, in allowing "some guilty defendants (to) . . . go free," *Leon*, 468 U.S. at 907, 104 S. Ct. at 3412, the extent of the costs are far from clear. A number of recent studies have indicated that the exclusion of illegally seized evidence has had a marginal effect in allowing guilty criminals to avoid successful prosecution. Indeed, the *Leon* decision itself indicates relatively low statistics with respect to the impact of the exclusionary rule in thwarting legitimate prosecutions. Equally as important, the alternative to the exclusionary rule most commonly advanced—i.e., allowing victims of improper searches to sue police officers directly—has raised serious concern among police officers.

A third policy consideration which compels our decisions is that, given the recent decision of the United States Supreme Court in *U.S. v. Gates, supra*, adopting a "totality of the circumstances test" in assessing probable cause, there is far less reason to adopt a "good faith" exception to the exclusionary rule. We have adopted *Gates* as a matter of Pennsylvania law in the recent case of *Commonwealth v. Gray, supra*. As a number of jurists have pointed out, the flexible *Gates* standard now eliminates much of the prior concern which existed with respect to an overly rigid application of the exclusionary rule.

Finally, the dangers of allowing magistrates to serve as "rubber stamps" and of fostering "magistrate-shopping," are evident under *Leon*. As the instant case illustrates, police officers and magistrates have historically worked closely together in this Commonwealth. Trooper Deise and District Justice Tlumac prepared the warrant and affidavit with Trooper Deise dictating the affidavit while the magistrate typed it verbatim.

There is no suggestion here that Trooper Deise and District Justice Tlumac acted other than in utmost "good faith" when preparing the warrant. Nevertheless, we are mindful of the fact that both state and federal interpretations of the 4th Amendment require a warrant to be issued by a "neutral and detached magistrate," because as Mr. Justice Papadakos noted, there is a requirement of "an independent determination of probable cause." *Commonwealth v. Smith*, 511 Pa. 36, 41, 511 A.2d 796, 798, *cert. den.*, 479 U.S. 1006, 107 S. Ct. 643, 93 L. Ed. 2d 700 (1986), *citing, Coolidge v. New Hampshire*, 403 U.S. 443, 91 S. Ct. 2022, 29 L. Ed. 2d 564 (1971). The reason for this requirement is evident. Would the District Justice act as nothing more than an adjunct of the police department, there would be no opportunity for *review* of the warrant prior to its issuance, and hence, a search warrant would be nothing more than the police's own determination of whether probable cause exists. We cannot countenance such a policy as it clearly runs afoul of our historically based system of government; which requires three *independent* branches.

It must be remembered that a District Justice is not a member of the executive branch—the police—but a member of the judiciary. By falling within the judicial branch of government, the District Justice is thus charged with the responsibility of being the *disinterested* arbiter of disputes and is charged further with acting as the bulwark between the police and the rights of citizens. Unless and until a magistrate *independently* determines there is probable cause, no warrant shall issue.

This is not to say that we distrust our police or district justices; far from it. We, in fact, have no doubt that police officers and district justices in Pennsylvania are intelligent, committed and independent enough to carry out their duties under the scheme which has evolved over the past thirty years, in order to safeguard the rights of our citizens.

However, requiring "neutral and detached magistrates" furthers the twin aims of safeguarding privacy and assuring that no warrant shall issue but upon probable cause. As such, we see no reason to eliminate this requirement, for if we did, we would eviscerate the purpose of requiring warrants prior to searches. As one member of the Mississippi Supreme Court noted in a similar vein: "If it ain't broke, don't fix it." *Stringer v. State, supra,* 491 So. 2d at 850.

CONCLUSION

Thirty years ago, when the exclusionary rule was first introduced, police officers were perhaps plagued with ill-defined, unarticulated rules governing their conduct. However, the past thirty years have seen a gradual sharpening of the process, with police officers adapting well to the exclusionary rule. *See* Note, *The Exclusionary Rule and Deterrence: An Empirical Study of Chicago Narcotics Officers,* 54 U. Chi. L. Rev. 1016 (1987).

The purpose of Rule 2003 is not to exclude *bona fide* evidence based upon technical errors and omissions by police officers or magistrates. Rather, Rule 2003 is meant to provide support for the probable cause requirement of Article I, Section 8, by assuring that there is an objective method for determining when probable cause exists, and when it does not.

In the instant case, the evidence seized from defendant Edmunds was the product of a constitutionally defective search warrant. Article I, Section 8 of the Pennsylvania Constitution does not incorporate a "good faith" exception to the exclusionary rule. Therefore, the marijuana seized from the white corrugated building, the marijuana seized from Edmund's home, and the written and oral statements obtained from Edmunds by the troopers, must be suppressed. We base our decision strictly upon the Pennsylvania Constitution; any reference to the United States Constitution is merely for guidance and does not compel our decision. *See Michigan v. Long, supra,* 463 U.S. at 1040-41, 103 S. Ct. at 3476-77.

Justice Brandeis, in his eloquent dissent in *Olmstead v. United States,* 277 U.S. 438, 48 S. Ct. 564, 72 L. Ed. 944 (1928), reminded us over a half-century ago:

> In a government of laws, existence of the government will be imperiled if it fails to observe the law scrupulously. Our government is the potent, the omnipresent teacher. For good or for ill, it teaches the whole people by its example. Crime is contagious. If the Government becomes a law-breaker, it breeds contempt for law; it invites every man to become a law unto himself; it invites anarchy. *Id.* at 485, 48 S. Ct. at 575.

Although the exclusionary rule may place a duty of thoroughness and care upon police officers and district justices in this Commonwealth, in order to safeguard the rights of citizens under Article I, Section 8, that is a small price to pay, we believe, for a democracy.

JUDGMENT OF SENTENCE REVERSED. Jurisdiction relinquished.

Edmunds Vocabulary

Instructions: To better understand this material, be sure you know the definitions of the following terms. Be prepared to define these terms for your classmates, using the techniques described in "Defining/Explaining a Term or Concept." (pg. 14)

1. Possession
2. Search warrant
3. Affidavit
4. Probable cause
5. Good faith exception
6. Conviction
7. Informant
8. District magistrate
9. Lease
10. Motion to suppress
11. Dissent
12. Jurisprudence
13. Exclusionary rule
14. Supremacy Clause
15. Pen register
16. Bona fide

California v. Hodari D.
Supreme Court of the United States
499 U.S. 621 (1991)

[Some footnotes may have been omitted.]

JUSTICE SCALIA delivered the opinion of the Court.

Late one evening in April 1988, Officers Brian McColgin and Jerry Pertoso were on patrol in a high-crime area of Oakland, California. They were dressed in street clothes but wearing jackets with "Police" embossed on both front and back. Their unmarked car proceeded west on Foothill Boulevard, and turned south onto 63rd Avenue. As they rounded the corner, they saw four or five youths huddled around a small red car parked at the curb. When the youths saw the officers' car approaching they apparently panicked, and took flight. The respondent here, Hodari D., and one companion ran west through an alley; the others fled south. The red car also headed south, at a high rate of speed.

The officers were suspicious and gave chase. McColgin remained in the car and continued south on 63rd Avenue; Pertoso left the car, ran back north along 63rd, then west on Foothill Boulevard, and turned south on 62nd Avenue. Hodari, meanwhile, emerged from the alley onto 62nd and ran north. Looking behind as he ran, he did not turn and see Pertoso until the officer was almost upon him, whereupon he tossed away what appeared to be a small rock. A moment later, Pertoso tackled Hodari, handcuffed him, and radioed for assistance. Hodari was found to be carrying $130 in cash and a pager; and the rock he had discarded was found to be crack cocaine.

In the juvenile proceeding brought against him, Hodari moved to suppress the evidence relating to the cocaine. The court denied the motion without opinion. The California Court of Appeal reversed, holding that Hodari had been "seized" when he saw Officer Pertoso running towards him, that this seizure was unreasonable under the Fourth Amendment, and that the evidence of cocaine had to be suppressed as the fruit of that illegal seizure. The California Supreme Court denied the State's application for review. We granted certiorari. 498 U.S. 807 (1990).

As this case comes to us, the only issue presented is whether, at the time he dropped the drugs, Hodari had been "seized" within the meaning of the Fourth Amendment.[1] If so, respondent argues, the drugs were the fruit of that seizure

---

[1] California conceded below that Officer Pertoso did not have the "reasonable suspicion" required to justify stopping Hodari, see *Terry v. Ohio*, 392 U.S. 1 (1968). That it would be unreasonable to stop, for brief inquiry, young men who scatter in panic upon the mere sighting of the police is not self-evident, and arguably contradicts proverbial common sense. See Proverbs 28:1 ("The wicked flee when no man pursueth"). We do not decide that point here, but rely entirely upon the State's concession.

and the evidence concerning them was properly excluded. If not, the drugs were abandoned by Hodari and lawfully recovered by the police, and the evidence should have been admitted. (In addition, of course, Pertoso's seeing the rock of cocaine, at least if he recognized it as such, would provide reasonable suspicion for the unquestioned seizure that occurred when he tackled Hodari. *Cf. Rios v. United States*, 364 U.S. 253 (1960).)

We have long understood that the Fourth Amendment's protection against "unreasonable . . . seizures" includes seizure of the person, see *Henry v. United States*, 361 U.S. 98, 100 (1959). From the time of the founding to the present, the word "seizure" has meant a "taking possession," 2 N. Webster, *An American Dictionary of the English Language* 67 (1828); 2 J. Bouvier, *A Law Dictionary* 510 (6th ed. 1856); *Webster's Third New International Dictionary* 2057 (1981). For most purposes at common law, the word connoted not merely grasping, or applying physical force to, the animate or inanimate object question, but actually bringing it within physical control. A ship still fleeing, even though under attack, would not be considered to have been seized as a war prize. *Cf. The Josefa Segunda*, 10 Wheat. 312, 325-326, 6 L. Ed. 320 (1825). A res capable of manual delivery was not seized until "tak[en] into custody." *Pelham v. Rose*, 9 Wall. 103, 106 (1870). To constitute an arrest, however—the quintessential "seizure of the person" under our Fourth Amendment jurisprudence—the mere grasping or application of physical force with lawful authority, whether or not it succeeded in subduing the arrestee, was sufficient. *See, e.g.*, *Whitehead v. Keyes*, 85 Mass. 495, 501 (1862) ("[A]n officer effects an arrest of a person whom he has authority to arrest, by laying his hand on him for the purpose of arresting him, though he may not succeed in stopping and holding him"); 1 *Restatement of Torts* § 41, Comment *h* (1934). As one commentator has described it:

> "There can be constructive detention, which will constitute an arrest, although the party is never actually brought within the physical control of the party making an arrest. This is accomplished by merely touching, however slightly, the body of the accused, by the party making the arrest and for that purpose, although he does not succeed in stopping or holding him even for an instant; as where the bailiff had tried to arrest one who fought him off by a fork, the court said, 'If the bailiff had touched him, that had been an arrest . . . .'" A. Cornelius, *Search and Seizure* 163-164 (2d ed. 1930) (footnote omitted).

To say that an arrest is effected by the slightest application of physical force, despite the arrestee's escape, is not to say that for Fourth Amendment purposes there is a *continuing* arrest during the period of fugitivity. If, for example, Pertoso had laid his hands upon Hodari to arrest him, but Hodari had broken away and had *then* cast away the cocaine, it would hardly be realistic to say that that disclosure had been made during the course of an arrest. *Cf. Thompson v. Whitman*, 18 Wall. 457, 471 (1874) ("A seizure is a single act, and not a continuous fact"). The present case, however, is even one step further removed. It does not involve the application of any physical force; Hodari was untouched by Officer Pertoso at the time he discarded the cocaine. His defense relies instead upon the proposition that a seizure occurs "when the officer, by means of physical force *or show of authority*, has in some way restrained the liberty of a citizen." *Terry v. Ohio*, 392 U.S. 1, 19 n.16 (1968) (emphasis added). Hodari contends (and we accept as true for purposes of this decision) that Pertoso's pursuit qualified as a "show of authority" calling upon Hodari to halt. The narrow question before us is whether, with respect to a show of authority as with respect to application of physical force, a seizure occurs even though the subject does not yield. We hold that it does not.

The language of the Fourth Amendment, of course, cannot sustain respondent's contention. The word "seizure" readily bears the meaning of a laying on of hands or application of physical force to restrain movement, even when it is ultimately unsuccessful. ("She seized the purse-snatcher, but he broke out of her grasp.") It does not remotely apply, however, to the prospect of a policeman yelling "Stop, in the name of the law!" at a fleeing form that continues to flee. That is no seizure.[2] Nor can the result respondent wishes to achieve be indirectly, as it were—by suggesting that Pertoso's uncomplied-with show of authority was a common-law arrest, and then appealing to the principle that all common-law arrests are seizures. An arrest requires *either* physical force (as described above) *or*, where that is absent, *submission* to the assertion of authority.

> "Mere words will not constitute an arrest, while, on the other hand, no actual, physical touching is essential. The apparent inconsistency in the two parts of this statement is explained by the fact that an assertion of authority and purpose to arrest followed by submission of the arrestee constitutes an arrest. There can be no arrest without either touching or submission." Perkins, *The Law of Arrest*, 25 Iowa L. Rev. 201, 206 (1940) (footnotes omitted).

---

[2] For this simple reason—which involves neither "logic-chopping," *post*, at 646, nor any arcane knowledge of legal history—it is irrelevant that English law proscribed "an unlawful *attempt* to take a presumptively innocent person into custody." *Post*, at 631. We have consulted the common-law to explain the meaning of seizure—and, contrary to the dissent's portrayal, to expand rather than contract that meaning (since one would not normally think that the mere touching of a person would suffice). But neither usage nor common-law tradition makes an *attempted* seizure a seizure. The common law may have made an attempted seizure unlawful in certain circumstances; but it made many things unlawful, very few of which were elevated to constitutional proscriptions.

We do not think it desirable, even as a policy matter, to stretch the Fourth Amendment beyond its words and beyond the meaning of arrest, as respondent urges.[3] Street pursuits always place the public at some risk, and compliance with police orders to stop should therefore be encouraged. Only a few of those orders, we must presume, will be without adequate basis, and since the addressee has no ready means of identifying the deficient ones it almost invariably is the responsible course to comply. Unlawful orders will not be deterred, moreover, by sanctioning through the exclusionary rule those of them that are *not* obeyed. Since policemen do not command "Stop!" expecting to be ignored, or give chase hoping to be outrun, it fully suffices to apply the deterrent to their genuine, successful seizures.

Respondent contends that his position is sustained by the so-called *Mendenhall* test, formulated by Justice Stewart's opinion in *United States v. Mendenhall*, 446 U.S. 544, 554 (1980), and adopted by the Court in later cases, see *Michigan v. Chesternut*, 486 U.S. 567, 573 (1988); *INS v. Delgado*, 466 U.S. 210, 215 (1984): "[A] person has been 'seized' within the meaning of the Fourth Amendment only if, in view of all the circumstances surrounding the incident, a reasonable person would have believed that he was not free to leave." 446 U.S. at 554. *See also Florida v. Royer*, 460 U.S. 491, 502 (1983) (opinion of White, J.). In seeking to rely upon that test here, respondent fails to read it carefully. It says that a person has been seized "only if," not that he has been seized "whenever"; it states a *necessary*, but not a *sufficient*, condition for seizure—or, more precisely, for seizure effected through a "show of authority." *Mendenhall* establishes that the test for existence of a "show of authority" is an objective one: not whether the citizen perceived that he was being ordered to restrict his movement, but whether the officer's words and actions would have conveyed that to a reasonable person. Application of this objective test was the basis for our decision in the other case relied upon by respondent, *Chesternut*, *supra*, where we concluded that the police cruiser's slow

---

[3] Nor have we ever done so. The dissent is wrong in saying that *Terry v. Ohio*, 392 U.S. 1 (1968), "broadened the range of encounters . . . encompassed within the term 'seizure,'" *post*, at 635. *Terry* unquestionably involved conduct that would constitute a common-law seizure; its novelty (if any) was in expanding the acceptable *justification* for such a seizure, beyond probable cause. The dissent is correct that *Katz v. United States*, 389 U.S. 347 (1967), "unequivocally reject[s] the notion that the common law of arrest defines the limits of the term 'seizure' in the Fourth Amendment," *post*, at 637. But we do not assert that it defines the limits of the term "seizure"; only that it defines the limits of a *seizure of the person*. What *Katz* stands for is the proposition that items which could not be subject to seizure at common law (*e.g.*, telephone conversations) can be seized under the Fourth Amendment. That is quite different from saying that what constitutes an arrest (a seizure of the person) has changed.

following of the defendant did not convey the message that he was not free to disregard the police and go about his business. We did not address in *Chesternut*, however, the question whether, if the *Mendenhall* test was met—if the message that the defendant was not free to leave *had* been conveyed—a Fourth Amendment seizure would have occurred. See 486 U.S. at 577 (Kennedy, J., concurring).

Quite relevant to the present case, however, was our decision in *Brower v. Inyo County*, 489 U.S. 593, 596 (1989). In that case, police cars with flashing lights had chased the decedent for 20 miles—surely an adequate "show of authority"—but he did not stop until his fatal crash into a police-erected blockade. The issue was whether his death could be held to be the consequence of an unreasonable seizure in violation of the Fourth Amendment. We did not even consider the possibility that a seizure could have occurred during the course of the chase because, as we explained, that "show of authority" did not produce his stop. *Id.* at 597. And we discussed, *ibid.*, an opinion of Justice Holmes, involving a situation not much different from the present case, where revenue agents had picked up containers dropped by moonshiners whom they were pursuing without adequate warrant. The containers were not excluded as the product of an unlawful seizure because "[t]he defendant's own acts, and those of his associates, disclosed the jug, the jar and the bottle—and there was no seizure in the sense of the law when the officers examined the contents of each after they had been abandoned." *Hester v. United States*, 265 U.S. 57, 58 (1924). The same is true here.

In sum, assuming that Pertoso's pursuit in the present case constituted a "show of authority" enjoining Hodari to halt, since Hodari did not comply with that injunction he was not seized until he was tackled. The cocaine abandoned while he was running was in this case not the fruit of a seizure, and his motion to exclude evidence of it was properly denied. We reverse the decision of the California Court of Appeal, and remand for further proceedings not inconsistent with this opinion.

It is so ordered.

JUSTICE STEVENS, with whom JUSTICE MARSHALL joins, dissenting.

The Court's narrow construction of the word "seizure" represents a significant, and in my view, unfortunate, departure from prior case law construing the Fourth Amendment.[1] Almost a quarter of a century ago, in two landmark cases—one

---

[1]   The Fourth Amendment to the Constitution protects "[t]he right of the people to be secure in their persons, houses, papers, and effects, against unreasonable searches and seizures . . . ."

broadening the protection of individual privacy,[2] and the other broadening the powers of law enforcement officers[3]—we rejected the method of Fourth Amendment analysis that today's majority endorses. In particular, the Court now adopts a definition of "seizure" that is unfaithful to a long line of Fourth Amendment cases. Even if the Court were defining seizure for the first time, which it is not, the definition that it chooses today is profoundly unwise. In its decision, the Court assumes, without acknowledging, that a police officer may now fire his weapon at an innocent citizen and not implicate the Fourth Amendment—as long as he misses his target.

For the purposes of decision, the following propositions are not in dispute. First, when Officer Pertoso began his pursuit of respondent,[4] the officer did not have a lawful basis for either stopping or arresting respondent. See App. 138-140; *ante*, at 623 n.1. Second, the officer's chase amounted to a "show of authority" as soon as respondent saw the officer nearly upon him. See *ante*, at 625-626, 629. Third, the act of discarding the rock of cocaine was the direct consequence of the show of authority. See Pet. for Cert. 48-49, 52. Fourth, as the Court correctly demonstrates, no common-law arrest occurred until the officer tackled respondent. See *ante*, at 624-625. Thus, the Court is quite right in concluding that the abandonment of the rock was not the fruit of a common-law arrest.

It is equally clear, however, that if the officer had succeeded in touching respondent before he dropped the rock—even if he did not subdue him—an arrest would have occurred.[5] See *ante*, at 624-625, 626. In that event (assuming the touching precipitated the abandonment), the evidence would have

---

[2] *Katz v. United States*, 389 U.S. 347 (1967).

[3] *Terry v. Ohio*, 392 U.S. 1 (1968).

[4] The Court's gratuitous quotation from Proverbs 28:1, see *ante*, at 623 n.1, mistakenly assumes that innocent residents have no reason to fear the sudden approach of strangers. We have previously considered, and rejected, this ivory-towered analysis of the real world for it fails to describe the experience of many residents, particularly if they are members of a minority. *See generally* Johnson, *Race and the Decision To Detain a Suspect*, 93 Yale L.J. 214 (1983). It has long been "a matter of common knowledge that men who are entirely innocent do sometimes fly from the scene of a crime through fear of being apprehended as the guilty parties, or from an unwillingness to appear as witnesses. Nor is it true as an accepted axiom of criminal law that 'the wicked flee when no man pursueth, but the righteous are as bold as a lion.'" *Alberty v. United States*, 162 U.S. 499, 511 (1896).

[5] "[I]f the officer pronounces words of arrest without an actual touching and the other immediately runs away, there is no escape (in the technical sense) because there was no arrest. It would be otherwise had the officer touched the arrestee for the purpose of apprehending him, because touching for the manifested purpose of arrest by one having lawful authority completes the apprehension, 'although he does not succeed in stopping or holding him even for an instant.'" Perkins, *The Law of Arrest*, 25 Iowa L. Rev. 201, 206 (1940) (footnotes omitted).

---

been the fruit of an unlawful common-law arrest. The distinction between the actual case and the hypothetical case is the same as the distinction between the common-law torts of assault and battery—a touching converts the former into the latter.[6] Although the distinction between assault and battery was important for pleading purposes, see 2 J. Chitty, Pleading *372-*376, the distinction should not take on constitutional dimensions. The Court mistakenly allows this common-law distinction to define its interpretation of the Fourth Amendment.

At the same time, the Court fails to recognize the existence of another, more telling, common-law distinction—the distinction between an arrest and an attempted arrest. As the Court teaches us, the distinction between battery and assault was critical to a correct understanding of the common law of arrest. See *ante*, at 626 ("An arrest requires *either* physical force . . . *or*, where that is absent, *submission* to the assertion of authority"). However, the facts of this case do not describe an actual arrest, but rather an unlawful *attempt* to take a presumptively innocent person into custody. Such an attempt was unlawful at common law.[7] Thus, if the Court wants to define the scope of the Fourth Amendment based on the common law, it should look, not to the common law of arrest, but to the common law of attempted arrest, according to the facts of this case.

The first question, then, is whether the common law should define the scope of the outer boundaries of the constitutional protection against unreasonable seizures. Even if, contrary to settled precedent, traditional common-law analysis were controlling, it would still be necessary to decide whether the unlawful attempt to make an arrest should be considered a seizure within the meaning of the Fourth Amendment, and whether the exclusionary rule should apply to unlawful attempts.

---

[6] "One who undertakes to make an arrest without lawful authority, or who attempts to do so in an unlawful manner, is guilty of an assault if the other is ordered to submit to the asserted authority, is guilty of battery if he lays hands on the other for this unlawful purpose . . . ." *Id.* at 263 (footnotes omitted).

[7] "[E]ven without touching the other, the officer may subject himself to liability if he undertakes to make an arrest without being privileged by law to do so.[3]

[3]"For example, an officer might be guilty of an assault because of an attempted arrest, without privilege, even if he did not succeed in touching the other. Furthermore, if the other submitted to such an arrest without physical contact, the officer is liable for false imprisonment. *Gold v. Bissell*, 1 Wend. 210 (N.Y. Sup. Ct. 1828)." *Id.* at 201.

the Court considered whether electronic surveillance conducted "without any trespass and without the seizure of any
material object fell outside the ambit of the Constitution." *Id.*
at 353. Over Justice Black's powerful dissent, we rejected
that "narrow view" of the Fourth Amendment and held that
electronic eavesdropping is a "search and seizure" within the
meaning of the Amendment. *Id.* at 353-354. We thus endorsed the position expounded by two of the dissenting Justices in *Olmstead v. United States*, 277 U.S. 438 (1928):

> "Time and again, this Court in giving effect to the principle
> underlying the Fourth Amendment, has refused to place an
> unduly literal construction upon it." *Id.* at 476 (Brandeis, J.,
> dissenting).

> "The direct operation or literal meaning of the words used
> do not measure the purpose or scope of its provisions. Un-
> der the principles established and applied by this Court, the
> Fourth Amendment safeguards against all evils that are like
> and equivalent to those embraced within the ordinary
> meaning of its words." *Id.* at 488 (Butler, J., dissenting).

Writing for the Court in *Katz*, Justice Stewart explained:

> "Thus, although a closely divided Court supposed in
> *Olmstead* that surveillance without any trespass and with-
> out the seizure of any material object fell outside the ambit
> of the Constitution, we have since departed from the nar-
> row view on which that decision rested. Indeed, we have
> expressly held that the Fourth Amendment governs not
> only the seizure of tangible items, but extends as well to
> the recording of oral statements, overheard without any
> 'technical trespass under . . . local property law.' *Silverman
> v. United States*, 365 U.S. 505, 511. Once this much
> is acknowledged, and once it is recognized that the
> Fourth Amendment protects people—and not simply 'ar-
> eas'—against unreasonable searches and seizures, it be-
> comes clear that the reach of that Amendment cannot turn
> upon the presence or absence of a physical intrusion into
> any given enclosure.

> "We conclude that the underpinnings of *Olmstead* and
> *Goldman* have been so eroded by our subsequent decisions
> that the 'trespass' doctrine there enunciated can no longer
> be regarded as controlling. The Government's activities in
> electronically listening to and recording the petitioner's
> words violated the privacy upon which he justifiably relied
> while using the telephone booth and thus constituted a
> 'search and seizure' within the meaning of the Fourth
> Amendment. The fact that the electronic device employed
> to achieve that end did not happen to penetrate the wall of
> the booth can have no constitutional significance.

> "The question remaining for decision, then, is whether the
> search and seizure conducted in this case complied with
> constitutional standards." 389 U.S. at 353-354.

Significantly, in the *Katz* opinion, the Court repeatedly used the word "seizure" to describe the process of recording sounds that could not possibly have been the subject of a common-law seizure. See *id.* at 356, 357.

Justice Black's reasoning, which was rejected by the Court in 1967, is remarkably similar to the reasoning adopted by the Court today. After criticizing "language-stretching judges," *id.* at 366, Justice Black wrote:

> "I do not deny that common sense requires and that this Court often has said that the Bill of Rights' safeguards should be given a liberal construction. This principle, however, does not justify construing the search and seizure amendment as applying to eavesdropping or the 'seizure' of conversations." *Id.* at 366-367.

> "Since I see no way in which the words of the Fourth Amendment can be construed to apply to eavesdropping, that closes the matter for me. In interpreting the Bill of Rights, I willingly go as far as a liberal construction of the language takes me, but I simply cannot in good conscience give a meaning to words which they have never before been thought to have and which they certainly do not have in common ordinary usage. I will not distort the words of the Amendment in order to 'keep the Constitution up to date' or 'to bring it into harmony with the times.' It was never meant that this Court have such power, which in effect would make us a continuously functioning constitutional convention." *Id.* at 373.

The expansive construction of the word "seizure" in the *Katz* case provided an appropriate predicate for the Court's holding in *Terry v. Ohio*, 392 U.S. 1 (1968), the following year.[8] Prior to *Terry*, the Fourth Amendment proscribed any seizure of the person that was not supported by the same probable-cause showing that would justify a custodial arrest.[9] See *Dunaway v. New York*, 442 U.S. 200, 207-209 (1979). Given

---

[8]   "We have recently held that 'the Fourth Amendment protects people, not places,' *Katz v. United States*, 389 U.S. 347, 351 (1967), and wherever an individual may harbor a reasonable 'expectation of privacy,' *id.* at 361 (Mr. Justice Harlan, concurring), he is entitled to be free from unreasonable governmental intrusion. Of course, the specific content and incidents of this right must be shaped by the context in which it is asserted. For 'what the Constitution forbids is not all searches and seizures, but unreasonable searches and seizures.' *Elkins v. United States*, 364 U.S. 206, 222 (1960)." *Terry v. Ohio*, 392 U.S. at 9.

[9]   *Hester v. United States*, 265 U.S. 57 (1924), the case on which the majority largely relies, was decided over 40 years before *Terry*. In that case, the defendant did not even argue that there was a seizure of his person. The Court's holding in *Hester* that the abandoned moonshine whiskey had not been seized simply did not address the question whether it would have been the fruit of a constitutional violation if there had been a seizure of the person before the whiskey was abandoned.

---

the fact that street encounters between citizens and police officers "are incredibly rich in diversity." *Terry*, 392 U.S. at 13, the Court recognized the need for flexibility and held that "reasonable" suspicion—a quantum of proof less demanding than probable cause—was adequate to justify a stop for investigatory purposes. *Id.* at 21-22. As a corollary to the lesser justification for the stop, the Court necessarily concluded that the word "seizure" in the Fourth Amendment encompasses official restraints on individual freedom that fall short of a common-law arrest. Thus, *Terry* broadened the range of encounters between the police and the citizen encompassed within the term "seizure," while at the same time, lowering the standard of proof necessary to justify a "stop" in the newly expanded category of seizures now covered by the Fourth Amendment.[10] The Court explained:

> "Our first task is to establish at what point in this encounter the Fourth Amendment becomes relevant. That is, we must decide whether and when Officer McFadden 'seized' Terry and whether and when he conducted a 'search.' There is some suggestion in the use of such terms as 'stop' and 'frisk' that such police conduct is outside the purview of the Fourth Amendment because neither action rises to the level of a 'search' or 'seizure' within the meaning of the Constitution. We emphatically reject this notion. It is quite plain that the Fourth Amendment governs 'seizures' of the person which do not eventuate in a trip to the station house and prosecution for crime—'arrests' in traditional terminology. It must be recognized that whenever a police officer accosts an individual and restrains his freedom to walk away, he has 'seized' that person." *Id.* at 16 (footnote omitted).

> "The distinctions of classical 'stop-and-frisk' theory thus serve to divert attention from the central inquiry under the Fourth Amendment—the reasonableness in all the circumstances of the particular governmental invasion of a citizen's personal security. 'Search' and 'seizure' are not talismans. We therefore reject the notions that the Fourth Amendment does not come into play at all as a limitation upon police conduct if the officers stop short of something called a 'technical arrest' or a 'full-blown search.'" *Id.* at 19.

The decisions in *Katz* and *Terry* unequivocally reject the notion that the common law of arrest defines the limits of the term "seizure" in the Fourth Amendment. In *Katz*, the Court abandoned the narrow view that would have limited a seizure to a material object, and, instead, held that the Fourth

---

[10] The Court applied this principle in *Brown v. Texas*, 443 U.S. 47 (1979):

> "We have recognized that in some circumstances an officer may detain a suspect briefly for questioning, although he does not have 'probable cause' to believe that the suspect is involved in criminal activity, as is required for a traditional arrest. However, we have required the officers to have a reasonable suspicion, based on objective facts, that the individual is involved in criminal activity." *Id.* at 51 (citations omitted).

Amendment extended to the recording of oral statements. And in *Terry*, the Court abandoned its traditional view that a seizure under the Fourth Amendment required probable cause, and, instead, expanded the definition of a seizure to include an investigative stop made on less than probable cause. Thus, the major premise underpinning the majority's entire analysis today—that the common law of arrest should define the term "seizure" for Fourth Amendment purposes, see *ante*, at 624-625—is seriously flawed. The Court mistakenly hearkens back to common law, while ignoring the expansive approach that the Court has taken in Fourth Amendment analysis since *Katz* and *Terry*.[11]

II

The Court fares no better when it tries to explain why the proper definition of the term "seizure" has been an open question until today. In *Terry*, in addition to stating that a seizure occurs "whenever a police officer accosts an individual and restrains his freedom to walk away," 392 U.S. at 16, the Court noted that a seizure occurs "when the officer, by means of physical force or show of authority, has in some way restrained the liberty of a citizen . . . ." *Id.* at 19 n.16. The touchstone of a seizure is the restraint of an individual's personal liberty "*in some way*." *Ibid.* (emphasis added).[12] Today the Court's reaction to respondent's reliance on *Terry* is to demonstrate that in "show of force" cases no common-law arrest occurs unless the arrestee *submits*. See *ante*, at 626-627. That answer, however, is plainly insufficient given the holding in *Terry* that the Fourth Amendment applies to stops that need not be justified by probable cause in the absence of a full-blown arrest.

In *United States v. Mendenhall*, 446 U.S. 544 (1980), the Court "adhere[d] to the view that a person is 'seized' only when, by means of physical force or a show of authority, his freedom of movement is restrained." *Id.* at 553. The Court looked to whether the citizen who is questioned "remains free to disregard the questions and walk away," and if he or she is able to do so, then "there has been no intrusion upon that person's liberty or privacy" that would require some "particularized and objective justification" under the Constitution. *Id.* at 554. The test for a "seizure," as formulated by the Court in *Mendenhall*, was whether, "in view of

---

[11]   It is noteworthy that the Court has relied so heavily on cases and commentary that antedated *Katz* and *Terry*.

[12]   "The essential teaching of the Court's decision in *Terry*—that an individual's right to personal security and freedom must be respected even in encounters with the police that fall short of full arrest—has been consistently reaffirmed." *INS v. Delgado*, 466 U.S. 210, 227 (1984) (Brennan, J., concurring in part and dissenting in part).

all of the circumstances surrounding the incident, a reasonable person would have believed that he was not free to leave." *Ibid.* Examples of seizures include "the threatening presence of several officers, the display of a weapon by an officer, some physical touching of the person of the citizen, or the use of language or tone of voice indicating that compliance with the officer's request might be compelled." *Ibid.* The Court's unwillingness today to adhere to the "reasonable person" standard, as formulated by Justice Stewart in *Mendenhall*, marks an unnecessary departure from Fourth Amendment case law.

The Court today draws the novel conclusion that even though no seizure can occur *unless* the *Mendenhall* reasonable person standard is met, see *ante*, at 628, the fact that the standard has been met does not necessarily mean that a seizure has occurred. See *ibid.* (*Mendenhall* "states a *necessary*, but not a *sufficient* condition for seizure . . . effected through a 'show of authority'"). If it were true that a seizure requires more than whether a reasonable person felt free to leave, then the following passage from the Court's opinion in *INS v. Delgado*, 466 U.S. 210 (1984), is at best, seriously misleading:

> "As we have noted elsewhere: 'Obviously, not all personal intercourse between policemen and citizens involves "seizures" of persons. Only when the officer, by means of physical force or show of authority, has restrained the liberty of a citizen may we conclude that a "seizure" has occurred.' *Terry v. Ohio, supra*, at 19 n.16. While applying such a test is relatively straightforward in a situation resembling a traditional arrest, see *Dunaway v. New York*, 442 U.S. 200, 212-216 (1979), the protection against unreasonable seizures also extends to 'seizures that involve only a brief detention short of traditional arrest.' *United States v. Brignoni-Ponce*, 422 U.S. 873, 878 (1975). What has evolved from our cases is a determination that an initially consensual encounter between a police officer and a citizen can be transformed into a seizure or detention within the meaning of the Fourth Amendment, 'if, in view of all the circumstances surrounding the incident, a reasonable person would have believed that he was not free to leave.' *Mendenhall, supra*, at 554 (footnote omitted); see *Florida v. Royer*, 460 U.S. 491, 502 (1983) (plurality opinion)." *Id.* at 215.

More importantly, in *Florida v. Royer*, 460 U.S. 491 (1983), a plurality of the Court adopted Justice Stewart's formulation in *Mendenhall* as the appropriate standard for determining when police questioning crosses the threshold from a consensual encounter to a forcible stop. In *Royer*, the Court held that an illegal seizure had occurred. As a predicate for that holding, Justice White, in his opinion for the plurality, explained that the citizen "may not be detained *even momentarily* without reasonable, objective grounds for doing so; and his refusal to listen or answer does not, without more, furnish those grounds. *United States v. Mendenhall, supra,* at 556 (opinion of Stewart, J.)." 460 U.S. at 498 (emphasis added). The rule looks, not to the subjective perceptions of the person questioned, but rather, to the objective characteristics of the encounter that may suggest whether a reasonable person would have felt free to leave.

Even though momentary, a seizure occurs whenever an objective evaluation of a police officer's show of force conveys the message that the citizen is not entirely free to leave—in other words, that his or her liberty is being restrained in a significant way. That the Court understood the *Mendenhall* definition as both necessary and sufficient to describe a Fourth Amendment seizure is evident from this passage in our opinion in *United States v. Jacobsen,* 466 U.S. 109 (1984):

> "A 'seizure' of property occurs when there is some meaningful interference with an individual's possessory interests in that property.[13]

Finally, it is noteworthy that in *Michigan v. Chesternut,* 486 U.S. 567 (1988), the State asked us to repudiate the reasonable person standard developed in *Terry, Mendenhall, Delgado,* and *Royer.*[14] We decided, however, to "adhere to our traditional contextual approach," 486 U.S. at 573. In our opinion, we described Justice Stewart's analysis in *Mendenhall* as "a test to be applied in determining whether 'a person has been "seized" within the meaning of the Fourth Amendment'" and noted that "[t]he Court has since embraced this test." 486 U.S. at 573. Moreover, in commenting on the virtues of the test, we explained that it focused on the police officer's conduct:

> "The test's objective standard—looking to the reasonable man's interpretation of the conduct in question—allows the police to determine in advance whether the conduct contemplated will implicate the Fourth Amendment." *Id.* at 574.

---

[13] "See *United States v. Place,* 462 U.S. 696 (1983); *id.* at 716 (BRENNAN, J., concurring in result); *Texas v. Brown,* 460 U.S. 730, 747-748 (1983) (STEVENS, J., concurring in judgment); *see also United States v. Chadwick,* 433 U.S. 1, 13-14 n.8 (1977); *Hale v. Henkel,* 201 U.S. 43, 76 (1906). While the concept of a 'seizure' of property is not much discussed in our cases, this definition follows from our oft-repeated definition of the 'seizure' of a person within the meaning of the Fourth Amendment—meaningful interference, however brief, with an individual's freedom of movement. See *Michigan v. Summers,* 452 U.S. 692, 696 (1981); *Reid v. Georgia,* 448 U.S. 438, 440 n. (1980) *(per curiam); United States v. Mendenhall,* 446 U.S. 544, 551-554 (1980) (opinion of Stewart, J.); *Brown v. Texas,* 443 U.S. 47, 50 (1979); *United States v. Brignoni-Ponce,* 422 U.S. 873, 878 (1975); *Cupp v. Murphy,* 412 U.S. 291, 294-295 (1973); *Davis v. Mississippi,* 394 U.S. 721, 726-727 (1969); *Terry v. Ohio,* 392 U.S. at 16, 19 n.16." *Id.* at 113, and n.5.

[14] "Petitioner argues that the Fourth Amendment is never implicated until an individual stops in response to the police's show of authority. Thus, petitioner would have us rule that a lack of objective and particularized suspicion would not poison police conduct, no matter how coercive, as long as the police did not succeed in actually apprehending the individual." *Michigan v. Chesternut,* 486 U.S. at 572.

Expressing his approval of the Court's rejection of Michigan's argument in *Chesternut*, Professor LaFave observed:

> "The 'free to leave' concept, in other words, has nothing to do with a particular suspect's choice to flee rather than submit or with his assessment of the probability of successful flight. Were it otherwise, police would be encouraged to utilize a very threatening but sufficiently slow chase as an evidence-gathering technique whenever they lack even the reasonable suspicion needed for a *Terry* stop." 3 W. LaFave, *Search and Seizure* § 9.2, p. 61 (2d ed. 1987, Supp. 1991).

Whatever else one may think of today's decision, it unquestionably represents a departure from earlier Fourth Amendment case law. The notion that our prior cases contemplated a distinction between seizures effected by a touching on the one hand, and those effected by a show of force on the other hand, and that all of our repeated descriptions of the *Mendenhall* test stated only a necessary, but not a sufficient, condition for finding seizures in the latter category, is nothing if not creative lawmaking. Moreover, by narrowing the definition of the term seizure, instead of enlarging the scope of reasonable justifications for seizures, the Court has significantly limited the protection provided to the ordinary citizen by the Fourth Amendment. As we explained in *Terry*:

> "The danger in the logic which proceeds upon distinctions between a 'stop' and an 'arrest,' or 'seizure' of the person, and between a 'frisk' and a 'search' is twofold. It seeks to isolate from constitutional scrutiny the initial stages of the contact between the policeman and the citizen. And by suggesting a rigid all-or-nothing model of justification and regulation under the Amendment, it obscures the utility of limitations upon the scope, as well as the initiation, of police action as a means of constitutional regulation." *Terry v. Ohio*, 392 U.S. at 17.

III

In this case the officer's show of force—taking the form of a head-on chase—adequately conveyed the message that respondent was not free to leave.[15] Whereas in *Mendenhall*, there was "nothing in the record [to] sugges[t] that the respondent had any objective reason to believe that she was not free to end the conversation in the concourse and proceed on her way," 446 U.S. at 555, here, respondent attempted to

---

[15]   The California Court of Appeal noted:

> "This case involves more than a pursuit, as Officer Pertoso did not pursue [respondent], but ran in such a fashion as to cut him off and confront him head on. Under the rationale of *Chesternut*, this action is reasonably perceived as an intrusion upon one's freedom of movement and as a maneuver intended to block or 'otherwise control the direction or speed' of one's movement." App. A to Pet. for Cert. 9.

end "the conversation" before it began and soon found himself literally "not free to leave" when confronted by an officer running toward him head-on who eventually tackled him to the ground. There was an interval of time between the moment that respondent saw the officer fast approaching and the moment when he was tackled, and thus brought under the control of the officer. The question is whether the Fourth Amendment was implicated at the earlier or the later moment.

Because the facts of this case are somewhat unusual, it is appropriate to note that the same issue would arise if the show of force took the form of a command to "freeze," a warning shot, or the sound of sirens accompanied by a patrol car's flashing lights. In any of these situations, there may be a significant time interval between the initiation of the officer's show of force and the complete submission by the citizen. At least on the facts of this case, the Court concludes that the timing of the seizure is governed by the citizen's reaction, rather than by the officer's conduct. See *ante* at 626-627. One consequence of this conclusion is that the point at which the interaction between citizen and police officer becomes a seizure occurs, not when a reasonable citizen believes he or she is no longer free to go, but, rather, only after the officer exercises control over the citizen.

In my view, our interests in effective law enforcement and in personal liberty[16] would be better served by adhering to a standard that "allows the police to determine in advance whether the conduct contemplated will implicate the Fourth Amendment." *Chesternut*, 486 U.S. at 574. The range of possible responses to a police show of force, and the multitude of problems that may arise in determining whether, and at which moment, there has been "submission," can only create uncertainty and generate litigation.

In some cases, of course, it is immediately apparent at which moment the suspect submitted to an officer's show of force. For example, if the victim is killed by an officer's gunshot,[17] as in *Tennessee v. Garner*, 471 U.S. 1, 11 (1985) ("A police officer may not seize an unarmed, nondangerous suspect by

---

[16] "To determine the constitutionality of a seizure '[w]e must balance the nature and quality of the intrusion on the individual's Fourth Amendment interests against the importance of the governmental interests alleged to justify the intrusion.'" *Tennessee v. Garner*, 471 U.S. 1, 8 (1985) (citation omitted).

[17] Even under the common law, "If an officer shoots at an arrestee when he is not privileged to do so, he is guilty of an aggravated assault. And if death results from an arrest, or attempted arrest, which was not authorized at all, . . . the arrester is guilty of manslaughter or, in extreme cases, of murder." Perkins, 25 Iowa L. Rev. at 263-264.

shooting him dead"),[18] or by a hidden roadblock, as in *Brower v. Inyo County*, 489 U.S. 593 (1989), the submission is unquestionably complete. But what if, for example, William James Caldwell (Brower) had just been wounded before being apprehended? Would it be correct to say that no seizure had occurred and therefore the Fourth Amendment was not implicated even if the pursuing officer had no justification whatsoever for initiating the chase? The Court's opinion in *Brower* suggests that the officer's responsibility should not depend on the character of the victim's evasive action. The Court wrote:

> "Brower's independent decision to continue the chase can no more eliminate respondents' responsibility for the termination of his movement effected by the roadblock than Garner's independent decision to flee eliminated the Memphis police officer's responsibility for the termination of his movement effected by the bullet." *Id.* at 595.

It seems equally clear to me that the constitutionality of a police officer's show of force should be measured by the conditions that exist at the time of the officer's action. A search must be justified on the basis of the facts available at the time it is initiated; the subsequent discovery of evidence does not retroactively validate an unconstitutional search. The same approach should apply to seizures; the character of the citizen's response should not govern the constitutionality of the officer's conduct.

If an officer effects an arrest by touching a citizen, apparently the Court would accept the fact that a seizure occurred, even if the arrestee should thereafter break loose and flee. In such a case, the constitutionality of the seizure would be evaluated as of the time the officer acted. That category of seizures would then be analyzed in the same way as searches, namely, was the police action justified when it took place? It is anomalous, at best, to fashion a different rule for the subcategory of "show of force" arrests.

In cases within this new subcategory, there will be a period of time during which the citizen's liberty has been restrained, but he or she has not yet completely submitted to the show of force. A motorist pulled over by a highway patrol car cannot come to an immediate stop, even if the motorist intends to obey the patrol car's signal. If an officer decides to make the kind of random stop forbidden by *Delaware v. Prouse*, 440 U.S. 648 (1979), and, after flashing his lights, but before the vehicle comes to a complete stop, sees that the license plate has expired, can he justify his action on the ground that the

---

[18]   In *Tennessee v. Garner*, even the dissent agreed with the majority that the police officer who shot at a fleeing suspect had "'seized' [the suspect] by shooting him." 471 U.S. at 25 (O'CONNOR, J., dissenting).

seizure became lawful after it was initiated but before it was completed? In an airport setting, may a drug enforcement agent now approach a group of passengers with his gun drawn, announce a "baggage search," and rely on the passengers' reactions to justify his investigative stops? The holding of today's majority fails to recognize the coercive and intimidating nature of such behavior and creates a rule that may allow such behavior to go unchecked.

The deterrent purposes of the exclusionary rule focus on the conduct of law enforcement officers and on discouraging improper behavior on their part,[19] and not on the reaction of the citizen to the show of force. In the present case, if Officer Pertoso had succeeded in tackling respondent before he dropped the rock of cocaine, the rock unquestionably would have been excluded as the fruit of the officer's unlawful seizure. Instead, under the Court's logic-chopping analysis, the exclusionary rule has no application because an attempt to make an unconstitutional seizure is beyond the coverage of the Fourth Amendment, no matter how outrageous or unreasonable the officer's conduct may be.

It is too early to know the consequences of the Court's holding. If carried to its logical conclusion, it will encourage unlawful displays of force that will frighten countless innocent citizens into surrendering whatever privacy rights they may still have. It is not too soon, however, to note the irony in the fact that the Court's own justification for its result is its analysis of the rules of the common law of arrest that antedated our decisions in *Katz* and *Terry*. Yet, even in those days the common law provided the citizen with protection against an attempt to make an unlawful arrest. See nn.5 and 7, *supra*.

---

[19] The purpose of the Fourth Amendment is "'to prevent arbitrary and oppressive interference by enforcement officials with the privacy and personal security of individuals.'" *INS v. Delgado*, 466 U.S. at 215 (quoting *United States v. Martinez-Fuerte*, 428 U.S. 543, 554 (1976)); see *Mendenhall*, 446 U.S. at 553-554 (same); *Terry v. Ohio*, 392 U.S. at 12 ("Ever since its inception, the rule excluding evidence seized in violation of the Fourth Amendment has been recognized as a principal mode of discouraging lawless police conduct"); 4 W. LaFave, *Search and Seizure* § 11.4(j), pp. 459-460 (2d ed. 1987) ("Incriminating admissions and attempts to dispose of incriminating evidence are common and predictable consequences of illegal arrests and searches, and thus to admit such evidence would encourage such Fourth Amendment violations in future cases").

Justice Brandeis wrote eloquently about the overarching purpose of the Fourth Amendment:

"The makers of our Constitution . . . sought to protect Americans in their beliefs, their thoughts, their emotions and their sensations. They conferred, as against the Government, the right to be let alone—the most comprehensive of rights and the right most valued by civilized men. To protect that right, every unjustifiable intrusion by the Government upon the privacy of the individual, whatever the means employed, must be deemed a violation of the Fourth Amendment." *Olmstead v. United States*, 277 U.S. 438, 478 (1928) (dissenting opinion).

Today's opinion has lost sight of these purposes.

The central message of *Katz* and *Terry* was that the protection the Fourth Amendment provides to the average citizen is not rigidly confined by ancient common-law precept. The message that today's literal-minded majority conveys is that the common law, rather than our understanding of the Fourth Amendment as it has developed over the last quarter of a century, defines, and limits, the scope of a seizure. The Court today defines a seizure as commencing, not with egregious police conduct, but rather with submission by the citizen. Thus, it both delays the point at which "the Fourth Amendment becomes relevant"[20] to an encounter and limits the range of encounters that will come under the heading of "seizure." Today's qualification of the Fourth Amendment means that innocent citizens may remain "secure in their persons . . . against unreasonable searches and seizures" only at the discretion of the police.[21]

Some sacrifice of freedom always accompanies an expansion in the Executive's unreviewable[22] law enforcement powers. A court more sensitive to the purposes of the Fourth Amendment would insist on greater rewards to society before decreeing the sacrifice it makes today. Alexander Bickel presciently wrote that "many actions of government have two aspects: their immediate, necessarily intended, practical effects, and their perhaps unintended or unappreciated bearing on values we hold to have more general and permanent interest."[23] The Court's immediate concern with containing criminal activity poses a substantial, though unintended, threat to values that are fundamental and enduring.

I respectfully dissent.

———————————

[20] *Terry v. Ohio*, 392 U.S. at 16.

[21] Justice Jackson presaged this development when he wrote:

"[A]n illegal search and seizure usually is a single incident, perpetrated by surprise, conducted in haste, kept purposely beyond the court's supervision and limited only by the judgment and moderation of officers whose own interests and records are often at stake in the search. . . . The citizen's choice is quietly to submit to whatever the officers undertake or to resist at risk of arrest or immediate violence." *Brinegar v. United States*, 338 U.S. 160, 182 (1949) (dissenting opinion).

[22] "[T]he right to be secure against searches and seizures is one of the most difficult to protect. Since the officers are themselves the chief invaders, there is no enforcement outside of court. . . . There may be, and I am convinced that there are, many unlawful searches of homes and automobiles of innocent people which turn up nothing incriminating, in which no arrest is made, about which courts do nothing, and about which we never hear." *Id.* at 181(Jackson, J., dissenting).

[23] *The Least Dangerous Branch* 24 (1962).

Hodari D. Vocabulary

Instructions: To better understand this material, be sure you know the definitions of the following terms. Be prepared to define these terms for your classmates, using the techniques described in "Defining/Explaining a Term or Concept." (pg. 14)

1. Seizure
2. Fourth Amendment
3. Fruit of the poisonous tree
4. Respondent
5. Reasonable suspicion
6. Res
7. Custody
8. Constructive
9. Bailiff
10. Force
11. Fugitive
12. Liberty
13. Show of authority
14. Common law
15. To grant certiorari

Commonwealth of Pennsylvania, Appellant
v.
Richard Carroll
Superior Court of Pennsylvania.
268 A.2d 398 (Pa. Super. Ct. 1993)

[Some footnotes may have been omitted.]

CIRILLO, Judge.

This is an appeal by the Commonwealth from a pre-trial order of the Court of Common Pleas of Philadelphia County suppressing the introduction of 47 packets of narcotics at the trial of Richard Carroll. We reverse.

Carroll was arrested, without a warrant, on November 22, 1989, and charged with possession of a controlled substance and possession of a controlled substance with the intent to deliver.

At 11:21 a.m. on November 22, two uniformed police officers, Joseph Milligan and John Reinecker, while on routine patrol in a marked police vehicle, saw two men standing on the sidewalk of Olive Street, Philadelphia. Officer Reinecker told Officer Milligan he wanted to investigate one of the men, and gave no reason.

Both officers left the patrol car and Officer Reinecker spoke to the man he had suggested investigating. The second man, Carroll, stood with his hands in the pockets of his jacket. Officer Milligan, with his hand over his gun, approached Carroll and started to ask him to take his hands out of his pockets.

Carroll turned and fled into an alley on the west side of Olive Street, slipped and fell in the debris. Officer Milligan followed Carroll and at a distance of a 10 to 15 feet saw two brown tinted, heat-sealed packets containing a white substance fall from Carroll's pocket into the debris in the alley.

Officer Milligan approached Carroll who was still face down in the debris in the alley, drew his gun, and told Carroll to stay on the ground with his hands behind his back. Officer Milligan put handcuffs on the still prone Carroll, arrested him, and searched his coat pockets, finding 45 additional brown tinted packets. Officer Milligan patted Carroll down a second time in a search for weapons and then retrieved the two dropped brown tinted packets from the debris. After Carroll was taken to the police station, a custodial search revealed $404.00 in cash.

The Commonwealth disputes several of the suppression court's findings. The Commonwealth argues Officer Milligan did not have his hand on his gun, that he did not pursue Carroll, and that he did not approach Carroll until after he had fallen and dropped the drugs.

When we review a suppression ruling, we are bound by the reasonable factual findings of the suppression court,

Commonwealth v. Hamlin, 503 Pa. 210, 469 A.2d 137 (1983), unless we find an abuse of discretion or an error of law. *Commonwealth v. Cortez*, 507 Pa. 529, 491 A.2d 111 (1985). Credibility determinations may not be disturbed on appeal. *Commonwealth v. Whitney*, 511 Pa. 232, 512 A.2d 1152 (1986). We are, therefore, despite the Commonwealth's vigorous argument to the contrary, bound to accept the reasonable factual findings of the suppression court. *Hamlin, supra*; *Whitney, supra.*

Under questioning by the assistant district attorney at the suppression hearing Officer Milligan testified that he had his hand on his gun when he approached Carroll.

> Q: [A]t what point in what happened did you draw your gun specifically in relationship to where you saw the packets go to the ground?

> A: Well, when he started to run, actually I had my hand on the gun because he had his hands in his pockets. But, it happened so fast and I drew my gun as he was laying on the ground and after the packets were on the ground.

When we look at the testimony we are persuaded that the suppression court's finding of fact that Officer Milligan had his hand on his holstered gun when he chased Carroll is reasonable. *Hamlin, supra*; *Whitney, supra.*

The question before this court is whether the police officer's pursuit of Carroll was a seizure. If it was not a seizure then the drugs were lawfully found and finding the drugs in these circumstances gave rise to the probable cause to arrest and search Carroll. If the pursuit was a seizure, then when Carroll dropped or discarded the drug packets the abandonment was impermissibly coerced. If the drugs were abandoned after seizure, then the officer must demonstrate that he had either probable cause to make the seizure reasonable or a reasonable suspicion for a *Terry* stop and frisk.

This case raises the question of whether Pennsylvania will follow the federal constitutional definition of seizure recently adopted in *California v. Hodari D.*, 499 U.S. 621, 111 S. Ct. 1547, 113 L. Ed. 2d 690 (1991), or will continue to follow a line of Pennsylvania cases which afford a suspect a greater degree of protection under the state constitution.

Seizure under the Fourth Amendment to the U.S. Constitution

Seizure was defined by Justice Stewart in *United States v. Mendenhall*, 446 U.S. 544, 100 S. Ct. 1870, 64 L. Ed. 2d 497 (1980) (plurality opinion) and adopted by the U.S. Supreme Court in *Michigan v. Chesternut*, 486 U.S. 567, 573, 108 S. Ct. 1975, 1979, 100 L. Ed. 2d 565 (1988): "A person has been seized within the meaning of the Fourth Amendment only if, in view of all the circumstances surrounding the incident, a reasonable person would have believed that he was not free to leave." This has become known as the *Mendenhall* reasonable person test for when a seizure occurs.

The definition adopted in *Chesternut* followed from the formulation in *Terry v. Ohio*, 392 U.S. 1, 19 n.16, 88 S. Ct. 1868, 1879 n.16, 20 L. Ed. 2d 889 (1968), that a seizure occurs "when the officer, by means of physical force or show of authority, has in some way restrained the liberty of a citizen."

In *Hodari D.*, *supra*, the Supreme Court held that pursuing a fleeing suspect is not a seizure for Fourth Amendment purposes; therefore, a rock of cocaine discarded during the pursuit was not the fruit of an illegal seizure and need not be suppressed as evidence at trial.

The more narrow question in *Hodari D.* was whether a "show of authority" without more is a seizure. The court held that it was not. An arrest requires either physical force or submission to the assertion of authority. *Id.* 499 U.S. at ___, 111 S. Ct. at 1551. There is no seizure based on show of authority unless it is complied with. *Id.*, citing *Brower v. Inyo County*, 489 U.S. 593, 109 S. Ct. 1378, 103 L. Ed. 2d 628 (1989). No search or seizure occurs when a police officer examines abandoned materials, even if the act of abandonment occurs during a police chase. *Hodari D.*, citing *Hester v. United States*, 265 U.S. 57, 44 S. Ct. 445, 68 L. Ed. 898 (1924).

In *Hodari D.*, when the officers began their pursuit they did not have a lawful basis for either stopping or arresting the suspects. *Hodari D.* holds that a show of authority alone is not seizure; only if the subject submits to the show of authority or if the police officer makes contact with the subject is there a seizure. *Id.* 499 U.S. at ___, 111 S. Ct. at 1548.

Thus, *Hodari D.* modifies the *Mendenhall* reasonable person test, a person is seized when he reasonably believes he is not free to leave, to hold that seizure is not effected until an officer has used physical restraint or the citizen has submitted to a show of authority. Since *Hodari D.*, for Fourth Amendment purposes, a show of authority alone is not a seizure.

In the case at hand, under the criteria of *Hodari D.* there was no seizure at the time the packets of cocaine fell out of Carroll's pockets. There was a "show of authority" without the requisite submission to create a seizure. *Hodari D.*, *supra*.

Seizure under Art. I, Section 8 of the Pennsylvania Constitution

Finding as we do that the pursuit of Carroll was not a seizure in terms of the Fourth Amendment, *Hodari D.*, *supra*, we turn now to the question of whether Carroll or the drugs were seized in violation of the Pennsylvania Constitution. The Pennsylvania Constitution may afford greater protections than the U.S. Constitution. *Commonwealth v. Edmunds*, 526 Pa. 374, 586 A.2d 887 (1991) (declining to the adopt the "good faith" exception to the exclusionary rule). It is "important and necessary to undertake an independent analysis of the Pennsylvania Constitution each time a provision of that fundamental document is implicated." *Id.* at 389, 586 A.2d at 894-95.

The *Edmunds* court outlined the steps to an independent analysis of state constitutional grounds which are: an examination of the text of the constitutional article, the history of its application, the jurisprudence of the question in other states, and the policy considerations behind the constitutional provision. *Id.*

Article I, section 8 of the Pennsylvania Constitution provides:

Security from Searches and Seizures

Section 8. The people shall be secure in their persons, houses, papers and possessions from unreasonable searches and seizures, and no warrant to search any place or to seize any person or thing shall issue without describing them as nearly as may be, nor without probable cause, supported by oath or affirmation subscribed to by the affiant.

Const. Art. I, § 8.

One of the first Pennsylvania cases to consider the exclusionary rule after *Mapp v. Ohio*, 367 U.S. 643, 81 S. Ct. 1684, 6 L. Ed. 2d 1081 (1961) made it applicable to the states was *Commonwealth v. Bosurgi*, 411 Pa. 56, 190 A.2d 304 (1963). In *Bosurgi*, the Pennsylvania Supreme Court adopted *Mapp* which prohibits use of evidence which is the product of an unreasonable search or seizure. *Id.* 411 Pa. at 65, 190 A.2d at 309. The *Bosurgi* court read *Mapp* as allowing each state to make an independent assessment of what was a "reasonable search and seizure." *Id.* 411 Pa. at 65, 190 A.2d at 309. The issue in *Bosurgi* was whether a warrantless search based on a vague description was reasonable. The court found that it was because the subject acquiesced or submitted to the search. *Bosurgi* suggests that the state jurisprudence of search and seizure has been co-extensive with the jurisprudence of the Fourth Amendment; but *Bosurgi* reserved to the state the right to define what is a reasonable search or seizure.

Pennsylvania courts have not hesitated to articulate separate state constitutional grounds for their holdings. *See Edmunds, supra; see also Commonwealth v. Zettlemoyer*, 500 Pa. 16, 454 A.2d 937 (1982) (death penalty jurisprudence co-extensive); *Commonwealth v. Henderson*, 496 Pa. 349, 437 A.2d 387 (1981) (interested-adult rule protecting minors from self-incrimination has its foundation in state law); *Commonwealth v. Triplett*, 462 Pa. 244, 341 A.2d 62 (1975) (separate Pennsylvania constitutional grounds for *Miranda*). When confronted with a federal precedent which appears to alter state precedent, the state court must re-examine the source of the Pennsylvania precedent. *Edmunds, supra.*

The Pennsylvania Supreme Court considered the question of whether police pursuit created forced or coerced abandonment in *Commonwealth v. Jeffries*, 454 Pa. 320, 311 A.2d 914 (1973). Jeffries "quickened his pace" walking on the sidewalk when a police car pulled along side. Police observation quickly turned to pursuit when Jeffries ran. He discarded a jacket during the chase which, it was found, had foil packets of heroin in the pocket. *Id.* at 322, 311 A.2d at 916. The court held that flight alone is neither probable cause for arrest, nor is it alone reasonable suspicion to justify a *Terry* stop and frisk. *Id.* 454 Pa. at 325, 311 A.2d at 917. The court held without probable cause or articulable suspicion, the police have unlawfully coerced the abandonment of the incriminating property. *Id.* at 326, 311 A.2d at 918.

The Pennsylvania Supreme Court found in *Commonwealth v. Jones*, 474 Pa. 364, 378 A.2d 835 (1977), that when the police order a citizen to stop a seizure has occurred. *Id.* at 371, 378 A.2d at 839. The court found that seizure is judged in the totality of the circumstances, including the demeanor and the words of the police officer and the location of the encounter. *Id.* The standard is objective: would a reasonable person, innocent of any crime, believe he was being restrained. *Id.* at 372-73, 378 A.2d at 839-40; *see also Commonwealth v. Williams*, 287 Pa. Super. 19, 429 A.2d 698 (1981). In *Commonwealth v. Barnett*, 484 Pa. 211, 398 A.2d 1019 (1979), the court distinguished between approaching a suspect, which is not a seizure, and attempting to stop him, which is. The court held that when the officers pursued a fleeing suspect, they coerced the abandonment of the contraband. *Id.* at 215-16, 398 A.2d at 1021.

Each of the Pennsylvania cases in the *Jeffries* line, which Carroll argues establishes a greater and distinguishable protection under the Pennsylvania constitution, defines the right protected in terms of the Fourth Amendment. The holding in *Jeffries*, for instance, is that "it is clear the police had no right to 'arrest' or 'seize' Jeffries and the action of the police in chasing him and subsequently arresting him was a violation of his Fourth Amendment right." *Id.* 454 Pa. at 325-26, 311 A.2d at 917. Likewise in *Jones*, "the initial confrontation of Jones . . . constituted a seizure within the purview of the fourth amendment." 474 Pa. at 374, 378 A.2d at 840. Consequently, while Pennsylvania has read *Mapp v. Ohio* as commanding that the states establish their own definitions of what is a reasonable and what is an unreasonable search or seizure, *Bosurgi, supra*, Pennsylvania has relied on the jurisprudence of the Fourth Amendment to inform the state's definition of seizure. *Jeffries, supra; Jones, supra*. As a result, Pennsylvania jurisprudence of search and seizure closely parallels that of the Fourth Amendment. *Hodari D.* may represent a departure from traditional Fourth Amendment jurisprudence, as Justice Stevens characterized it in his dissent to

Hodari D. and Judge Ford Elliott characterized it in her dissent to *Peterfield, supra,* but there is nothing in Pennsylvania law which prevents us from following its logic.

The fourth prong of the *Edmunds* test to determine if we should find greater protections for the individual under Pennsylvania's constitution than those afforded under the U.S. Constitution requires that we look at the jurisprudence of the question in other states. Twenty-three states have found the reasoning of *Hodari D.* applicable. Five states have found that their constitutions afford greater protection than does the Fourth Amendment following *Hodari D.*

The final prong of the *Edmunds* test is public policy. Two public policy considerations guide our thinking: the first and most fundamental is the right of a citizen to be free of unwarranted privacy invasions by the police. The second and less compelling argument, although it is one advanced in *Hodari D.,* is the public benefit in curtailing the number of police chases.

A violation of the constitutional right to be free from unreasonable searches and seizures occurs at the moment of search, not at the moment that any contraband found in an unreasonable search is admitted at trial. *Katz v. United States,* 389 U.S. 347, 88 S. Ct. 507, 19 L. Ed. 2d 576 (1967); *Mapp, supra; Bosurgi, supra.* Therefore, public policy demands that our rule of law be designed to reduce the number of impermissible searches; suppression of the "fruit of the poisonous tree" is a remedy, not an end in itself. *Mapp, supra; Commonwealth v. Rodriguez,* 532 Pa. 62, 614 A.2d 1378 (1992). If we are to reduce the number of impermissible searches, we can best accomplish that by giving police and citizens alike clear guidance to govern their interactions. *Chesternut, supra.* And, we must reserve to the citizen the control over any encounter with authority which is not based on probable cause or reasonable suspicion. *Commonwealth v. Metz,* 412 Pa. Super. 100, 117-118, 602 A.2d 1328, 1337 (1991), *appeal granted,* 531 Pa. 652, 613 A.2d 558 (1992), (Kelly, J., concurring).

If a police officer approaches a citizen without probable cause to arrest, *Commonwealth v. Duncan,* 514 Pa. 395, 525 A.2d 1177 (1987), or reasonable suspicion to detain and interrogate, *Terry v. Ohio, supra; Commonwealth v. Hicks,* 434 Pa. 153, 253 A.2d 276 (1969), then that citizen is not seized unless he or she is physically restrained or submits to the assertion of authority. *Hodari D., supra.* A citizen may demonstrate his or her objectively reasonable belief that he is free to leave, *Mendenhall, supra,* by leaving, as did both Hodari D. and, in the case at hand, Carroll. Flight alone cannot create either probable cause to arrest nor reasonable suspicion to detain. *In the Interest of Barry W.,* 423 Pa. Super. 549, 621 A.2d 669 (1993). Under the reasoning of *Hodari D.,* it is only the actions of the citizen, the act of discarding contraband or exposing it to view, not the action of the police officer in pursuit, which can give rise to probable cause or reasonable suspicion. Carroll always had his own legal protections in his own hands, and so long as he carefully exercised his right to privacy, that is did not throw away or drop contraband within sight of a police officer, he would not have created the probable cause necessary to justify his arrest.

When we follow the reasoning of *Hodari D.*, we have not changed the equation of police/citizen encounters, we have only made clearer the standard by which we evaluate the permissibility of the police intrusion. Not every encounter between police and the citizenry is a seizure. *Terry, supra.* Police may approach a citizen to give or get information. *Mendenhall, supra*, 446 U.S. at 553, 100 S. Ct. at 1876. If the citizen chooses to end or avoid an encounter with a police officer, he is free to do so. *See Metz, supra* ("[t]he free citizen in a free country such as ours of course retains the discretion to run, walk, crawl or stop at that moment . . .") (Kelly, J., concurring). If the officer chooses to pursue the retreating or fleeing suspect, in a slowly moving car, *Jeffries, supra*, by chasing, *Jones, supra*, or as here, chasing with a hand on a holstered gun, the action of the officer cannot transform the encounter from one without probable cause or reasonable suspicion to one with probable cause or reasonable suspicion. Only the actions of the citizen can change the nature of the encounter, or, more accurately, create a new encounter. The choice to provide probable cause for an arrest or reasonable suspicion for a detention lies with the citizen, not with the officer. Only when a citizen exposes contraband to the officer's view will the nature of the encounter between the two change. If the citizen provides an officer with probable cause or reasonable suspicion, then seizure is reasonable. Therefore, control over the fundamental right to be secure in our persons resides where it constitutionally belongs, in the hands of the citizen.

Following the reasoning of *Hodari D.* should result in fewer rather than more police chases of otherwise not suspected citizens. Since flight alone cannot create reasonable suspicion or probable cause, *Barry W., supra*, only the additional actions of a citizen, i.e., dropping contraband in front of an officer, can create the requisite probable cause or reasonable suspicion for seizure. This is a clearer and brighter line than is the jurisprudence of coerced abandonment because the nature of an encounter between a police officer and a citizen is measured at the time of the approach. Under *Hodari D.* a police officer no longer has to make a curbside evaluation of just how far he can go without creating coerced abandonment. Both the officer and citizen now know that only the citizen can create probable cause or reasonable suspicion by abandoning contraband and that the police officer no longer has a grey area of conduct before his pursuit becomes a seizure. Under *Hodari D.*, seizure is either physical restraint or the submission to the assertion of authority. If a citizen exercises his right to end an encounter with a police officer, he is free to do so and remains free to do so unless he, the citizen, gives the officer probable cause or reasonable suspicion to arrest him. Flight alone does not do that. *Barry W., supra.*

Using the concept of coerced abandonment to describe a situation of quasi-seizure is a slippery slope on which neither the police officer nor the citizen has clear guidance. What is coercion? Following in the car? Chasing at a walk? Chasing at a run? Chasing with a hand on a holstered gun? The gradation of possibility between an officer and a retreating citizen left an officer unclear at what time his or her actions crossed the line from approach to pursuit. Following the reasoning of *Hodari D.* removes that calculation from the equation which delineates permissible from impermissible police contacts. An officer may approach a citizen, may question a citizen, may even detain a citizen, but an officer may not search or seize a citizen unless he or she has probable cause or reasonable suspicion. *Terry, supra.* Thus, an officer will know at all times during an interaction with a citizen whether he or she has the right to seize that citizen. The answer will always be no unless the officer has probable cause or reasonable suspicion.

Contrary to Carroll's argument and that of the dissent in *Hodari D.*, the holding of *Hodari D.* does not shield a wide range of police conduct from constitutional scrutiny. Indeed, *Hodari D.* places greater emphasis on the constitutional permissibility of the original encounter by returning to the citizen the control over his own constitutional rights. A citizen approached by a police officer who is *arguendo* without probable cause or reasonable suspicion may choose to converse with, comply with and submit to all that the police officer asks. Any search which ensues is an impermissible invasion of Fourth Amendment expectations of privacy and any fruit of the poisonous tree will be suppressed as such because we have a show of authority and submission as required by *Hodari D.* If the citizen chooses to end the encounter with the police officer, he or she is free to go without arousing reasonable suspicion or probable cause. *Barry W.* And, he or she may go in any fashion which suits him or her, walking, running, crawling. Whether or not the police officer follows, the encounter will not be infused with probable cause or reasonable suspicion unless the citizen chooses to so infuse it. When and only when the citizen exposes something private, i.e. contraband, to the view of the officer would the nature of the encounter change. At all times, the citizen has the control over the encounter; this is all the state and federal constitutions demand. *Katz, supra; Rodriguez, supra.* All of the choices are those of the citizen and all of the control lies in the hands of the citizen.

Thus, when we examine the source of Pennsylvania's law of search and seizure as we must under *Edmunds, supra,* to decide whether to follow state or federal precedent regarding the moment at which seizure occurs, we find that the history of the state jurisprudence is couched in terms of the federal decisions, *Jeffries, supra; Jones, supra; Barnett, supra.* Only five states have found greater protections in their state constitutions than that afforded by the Fourth Amendment after *Hodari D.* and twenty-three states have not distinguished their constitutional protections from those afforded by the Fourth Amendment after *Hodari D.* And, finally, the public policy considerations of preventing unreasonable searches and seizures and limiting police chases, are better served by a bright line test in which the citizen controls the nature of an encounter with the police. Nor is there any overriding state public policy command which would justify a departure from federal jurisprudence.

Therefore, when we apply the reasoning of *Hodari D.* to the case at hand, we find that when the officer approached Carroll there was no seizure because Carroll was neither physically restrained nor did he submit to the officer's assertion of authority. When the pursuing officer saw the dropped or discarded drugs, he then had the requisite probable cause to arrest and search Carroll. Since neither the officer's approach to or pursuit of Carroll was a seizure, the cocaine packets dropped in the alley are not "fruit of the poisonous tree" and should not have been suppressed.

Order reversed.

WIEAND, TAMILIA and HUDOCK, JJ., join.

CAVANAUGH, J., files a CONCURRING OPINION, in which TAMILIA and HUDOCK, JJ., join.

JOHNSON, J., files a DISSENTING OPINION, in which McEWEN, DEL SOLE and BECK, JJ., join.

CAVANAUGH, Judge, concurring.

* * *

TAMILIA and HUDOCK, JJ., join.

JOHNSON, Judge, dissenting.

In the present case, we are requested to determine a single issue of law: whether this Court will follow the United State's Supreme Court's decision in *California v. Hodari D.,* 499 U.S. ___, 111 S. Ct. 1547, 113 L. Ed. 2d 690 (1991), in deciding whether a person who abandons contraband while being chased by police was "seized" and thus entitled to invoke the protection of Article 1, Section 8, of the Pennsylvania Constitution to suppress the contraband. Because I understand the holding in *Hodari D.* to be contrary to settled Pennsylvania precedent regarding seizures of persons and the doctrine of coerced abandonment, I must dissent.

Our supreme court defined the standard under which we are to review an appeal from the grant of a motion to suppress in *Commonwealth v. DeWitt*, 530 Pa. 299, 301, 608 A.2d 1030, 1031 (1992) (citations omitted):

> We begin by noting that where a motion to suppress has been filed, the burden is on the Commonwealth to establish that the challenged evidence is admissible. In reviewing the ruling of a suppression court, our task is to determine whether the factual findings are supported by the record. If so, we are bound by those findings. Where, as here, it is the Commonwealth who is appealing the decision of the suppression court, we must consider only the evidence of the defendant's witnesses and so much of the evidence for the prosecution as read in the context of the record as a whole remains uncontradicted.

The facts of this case, when viewed in light of the above standard, reveal that on October 22, 1989, uniformed police officers Joseph Milligan and John Reinecker were on patrol in a marked police car when they observed Richard Carroll and another individual standing on the corner of Olive Street in Philadelphia. Officer Reinecker stated to Officer Milligan, without reason, that he wanted to investigate the individual standing with Carroll. Both officers exited the vehicle and approached the two men. While Officer Reinecker was speaking to Carroll's companion, Officer Milligan approached Carroll with his hand on his gun and started to tell him to remove his hands from his pockets. Before the officer could finish his statement, Carroll turned and fled down an alley. Officer Milligan pursued Carroll, who then slipped and fell. During his fall, two brown-tinted heat-sealed packages containing a white substance dropped from Carroll's pocket. Upon reaching Carroll, Officer Milligan drew his gun and instructed Carroll to remain face down on the ground, with his hands behind his back. Carroll was then handcuffed, arrested and searched. The search of Carroll's pocket revealed 45 additional brown-tinted packets containing a white substance.

Following his arrest, Carroll litigated a motion to suppress the material seized by the police, claiming that the packets were dropped as the result of an illegal stop and seizure by Officer Milligan. The trial court, following a full hearing, granted Carroll's Motion to Suppress, finding that Carroll's loss of the packets from his pockets was the product of the coercive acts on the part of the police, who had neither reasonable suspicion nor probable cause to stop Carroll. The Commonwealth appealed to this Court, which certified this case for *en banc* review.

The Commonwealth contends, and the Majority holds, that we must follow the recent decision of the United States Supreme Court in *California v. Hodari, D., supra*, in the present case to conclude that there was no seizure of Carroll under either the Fourth Amendment of the United States Constitution or under Article 1, Section 8, of the Pennsylvania Constitution, and therefore, no constitutional principle supports suppression. In *Hodari D.*, the police, without probable cause or reasonable suspicion, approached a group of youths who immediately fled. One of the youths was *Hodari D.*, who upon close pursuit by one of the police officers, discarded what appeared to be a rock but was later discovered to be crack cocaine. Hodari D. was then arrested. Hodari D. moved to suppress the crack as the product of his illegal seizure by police. The trial court denied the petition but the California Court of Appeals reversed, holding that the police seizure of Hodari D. was unreasonable and requiring that the crack be suppressed. The California Supreme Court denied appellate review. The United States Supreme Court granted *certiorari*, reversed the California Court of Appeals and held that Hodari D. was not seized within the meaning of the Fourth Amendment and therefore, the cocaine was not a product of an illegal seizure subject to suppression.

In *Hodari D.*, Justice Scalia speaking for the Court, conceded that the police officers had neither probable cause nor reasonable suspicion to stop Hodari D. The Court concluded, however, relying on archaic common-law theories of arrest and the dictionary definition of seizure, that where an individual does not yield to a show of police authority, that person is not seized and therefore Fourth Amendment guarantees are simply not implicated in such an interaction. The Court in *Hodari D.*, specifically rejected the long-held legal definition of seizure that, "[o]nly when the officer, by means of physical force or show of authority has restrained the liberty of a citizen may we conclude that a 'seizure' has occurred." *Terry v. Ohio*, 392 U.S. 1, 20, 88 S. Ct. 1868, 1879, 20 L. Ed. 2d 889, 905 (1968). The Court also redefined the test for seizure as articulated in *United States v. Mendenhall*, 446 U.S. 544, 553, 100 S. Ct. 1870, 1877, 64 L. Ed. 2d 497, 509 (1980) which stated: "that a person is 'seized' only when, by means of physical force or show of authority, his freedom of movement is restrained." The *Mendenhall* Court stated that the test for courts to apply to determine whether a seizure had occurred was whether "in view of all of the circumstances surrounding the incident, a reasonable person would have believed he was not free to leave." *Id.* at 554, 100 S. Ct. at 1877, 64 L. Ed. 2d at 509. The Court in *Mendenhall* then gave examples of what would constitute a show of authority by the police including, "the threatening presence of several officers, the display of a weapon by an officer, some physical touching of the person of the citizen, or the use of language or tone of voice indicating that compliance with the officer's request would be compelled." *Id.*

In what the *Hodari D.* dissent interpreted as "nothing if not creative lawmaking," (*Hodari D.*, 499 U.S. at ___, 111 S. Ct.

at 1559, 113 L. Ed. 2d at 707), Justice Scalia interpreted *Mendenhall* to require the police show of force as a "necessary, but not a sufficient condition" for a seizure. *Hodari D.* at ___, 111 S. Ct. at 1551, 113 L. Ed. 2d at 698. In order for the seizure to be effectuated under the new *Hodari D.* standard, the police show of force must now be coupled with submission to police authority. *Hodari D.* at ___, 111 S. Ct. at 1552, 113 L. Ed. 2d at 699. No longer does the "free to leave" standard apply in determining whether a seizure has occurred. Now, whether a seizure has occurred, absent physical restraint by the police, depends upon the individual's reaction to the show of authority by the police. *Hodari D.* at ___, 111 S. Ct. at 1559, 113 L. Ed. 2d at 707 (dissenting opinion by Stevens, J.). The Court reasoned that since despite a show of force by the police, Hodari D. did not submit to police authority, he was not seized. Seizure under the new standard did not occur until Hodari D. was tackled by police officers. Therefore, Hodari D. had voluntarily abandoned the crack cocaine, and as such, the crack was lawfully recovered by police and was properly admissible as evidence.

The facts of *Hodari D.* are similar to the facts of the present case. Here, the police officer approached Carroll with his hand on his gun, using an authoritative tone of voice. Carroll, however, did not submit to the authority of the police but chose to flee. Under *Hodari D.*, whether the officer had reasonable suspicion or probable cause to stop Carroll or whether a reasonable person would have felt not free to leave the scene must be ignored. In determining whether Carroll was seized, we must now only look to the individual's response to the police show of authority. Where, as here, a person decides to flee and is pursued, no seizure has occurred, regardless of the police show of force. It is only when the police actually physically restrained Carroll, with his face to the ground, at gunpoint, will *Hodari D.* permit a court to find, under the Fourth Amendment, that Carroll was seized.

I will concede, as do all parties to this litigation, that we are bound to apply *Hodari D.* in cases arising solely under the federal constitution. *Commonwealth v. Harper*, 416 Pa. Super. 608, 611 A.2d 1211 (1992). However, I disagree with the Commonwealth's contention that we are bound to apply *Hodari D.* to claims arising under Article 1, Section 8, absent a statement to this effect by our supreme court.

In *Commonwealth v. Edmunds*, 526 Pa. 374, 586 A.2d 887 (1991), our supreme court articulated the process through which the courts should consider claims arising under the Pennsylvania Constitution, especially addressing concerns arising under Article 1, Section 8. There, the court stated that when interpreting provisions of the Pennsylvania Constitution, courts of this Commonwealth are not bound by the decisions of the United States Supreme Court which interpret similar provisions of the federal constitution. *Id.* at 388, 586

A.2d at 894. While the federal constitution establishes certain minimum levels applicable to the states, each state has the power to implement broader standards under the provisions of its state constitution. *Id.* at 388, 586 A.2d 894. The court, there, cited to Brennan, *State Constitutions and the Protection of Individual Rights*, 90 Harv. L. Rev. 489 (1977), stating:

> Although we may accord weight to federal decisions where they are found to be logical and well reasoned, paying due regard to precedent and the policies underlying specific constitutional guarantees, we are free to reject the conclusions of the United States Supreme Court so long as we remain faithful to the minimal guarantees established by the United States Constitution.

Id. at 389, 586 A.2d at 895.

Edmunds requires that four factors be briefed and analyzed by the parties in any case which implicates a provision of the Pennsylvania constitution. *Id.* at 390, 586 A.2d at 895 *citing Michigan v. Long*, 463 U.S. 1032, 103 S. Ct. 3469, 77 L. Ed. 2d 1201 (1983). Those factors are:

> 1. the text of the Pennsylvania constitutional provisions;
>
> 2. the history of the provision, including Pennsylvania case law;
>
> 3. related case-law from other states; and
>
> 4. policy considerations, including issues of state and local concern, and applicability with modern Pennsylvania jurisprudence.

Id.

Since both Carroll and the Commonwealth have fully complied with this briefing and analysis requirement under *Edmunds*, this Court has the responsibility to undertake an independent analysis of the question presented under the Pennsylvania Constitution. I will now proceed with that required analysis.

First, the text of Article 1, Section 8 of the Pennsylvania Constitution provides:

> Security from Searches and Seizures
>
> Section 8. The people shall be secure in their persons, houses, papers and possessions from unreasonable searches and seizures, and no warrant to search any place or to seize any person or things shall issue without describing them as nearly as may be, nor without probable cause, supported by oath or affirmation subscribed to by the affiant.

The provisions of the Pennsylvania Constitution, while similar to the federal provisions in the Fourth Amendment, have been interpreted independently by our supreme court to afford greater protection to criminal defendants than those provided under the federal constitution. *See, e.g., Commonwealth v. Edmunds, supra; Commonwealth v. Melilli,* 521 Pa. 405, 555 A.2d 1254 (1989); *Commonwealth v. Sell,* 504 Pa. 46, 470 A.2d 457 (1983); *Commonwealth v. Bussey,* 486 Pa. 221, 404 A.2d 1309 (1979).

Second, the history of the Pennsylvania Constitution provides insight into the independent development of the law regarding search and seizure in this Commonwealth. Article 1, Section 8 predated the drafting of the Fourth Amendment by more than a decade. *Commonwealth v. Sell,* 504 Pa. at 63, 470 A.2d at 466. Our supreme court indicated the significance of this provision of our constitution throughout the history of this Commonwealth in *Sell* when it stated:

> In construing Article 1, Section 8, we find it highly significant that the language employed in that provision does not vary in any significant respect from the words of its counterpart in our first constitution. The test of Article 1, Section 8 thus provides no basis for the conclusion that the philosophy and purpose it embodies today differs from those which first prompted the Commonwealth to guarantee protection from unreasonable government intrusion. Rather, the survival of the language now employed in Article 1, Section 8 through over 200 years of profound change in other areas demonstrates that the paramount concern for privacy first adopted as a part of our organic law in 1776 continues to enjoy the mandate of the people of this Commonwealth.

Commonwealth v. Sell at 65, 470 A.2d at 457.

In *Edmunds,* the supreme court further clarified that while safeguarding personal privacy is the underlying purpose for the protection of the exclusionary rule afforded to Pennsylvania citizens under Article 1, Section 8, the purpose of the protection of the exclusionary rule afforded under the Fourth Amendment is very different. There, the court indicated that:

> The history of Article 1, Section 8, thus indicates that the purpose underlying the exclusionary rule in this Commonwealth is quite distinct from the purpose underlying the exclusionary rule under the 4th Amendment, as articulated in [*United States v.*] *Leon* [468 U.S. 897, 104 S. Ct. 3405, 82 L. Ed. 2d 677 (1984)].

> The United Stated Supreme Court in *Leon* made clear that, in its view, the sole purpose for the exclusionary rule was to deter police misconduct. The *Leon* majority also made clear that, under the Federal Constitution, the exclusionary rule operated as "a judicially created remedy designed to safeguard Fourth Amendment rights generally through its deterrent effect, rather than a personal constitutional right of the party aggrieved."

Edmunds, 526 Pa. at 394-395, 586 A.2d at 897 (citations omitted) (emphasis in original).

With these historical differences in mind, I now turn to the law of seizure and coerced abandonment as it has evolved in this Commonwealth.

In *Commonwealth v. Hicks*, 434 Pa. 153, 253 A.2d 276 (1969), our supreme court first adopted the United States Supreme Court's decision in *Terry v. Ohio*, 392 U.S. 1, 88 S. Ct. 1868, 20 L. Ed. 2d 889 (1968). There, the court specifically articulated the reasonable suspicion standard, under which the police may seize an individual without probable cause. In *Hicks*, the court stated that, for such a precautionary seizure and search to be legitimate, there must first exist on the part of the police a reasonable belief that criminal activity is afoot and that the seized person is armed and dangerous. *Id.* 434 Pa. at 158-159, 253 A.2d at 279-280. This test for whether a "*Terry* stop" is legitimate remains the standard in this Commonwealth today and has been specifically adopted under Article 1, Section 8, of the Pennsylvania Constitution in *Commonwealth v. Rodriguez*, 532 Pa. 62, 614 A.2d 1378 (1992).

Our supreme court addressed the issue of coerced abandonment in *Commonwealth v. Jeffries*, 454 Pa. 320, 311 A.2d 914 (1973). The facts of that case, as stated by the *Jeffries* court are:

> On the afternoon of November 6, 1970, four police officers in an unmarked police automobile observed Jeffries walking along a public street in Pittsburgh. One officer testified that when Jeffries saw the officers, he 'quickened his pace.' Upon seeing him do so, the officer left the police vehicle and started to pursue Jeffries, who then began to run. While giving chase, the officer observed Jeffries throw a cigarette package under an automobile parked along the street. Shortly thereafter, the officer overtook Jeffries and directed him to stand against a wall. At that moment the other officers arrived on the scene and they were told by the officer, who apprehended Jeffries, to "hold him one minute." The officer then recovered the cigarette package from underneath the parked vehicle, and it was found to contain several foil-wrapped packages of a substance later determined to be heroin.

Jeffries at 322, 311 A.2d at 916.

Jeffries contended that his abandonment of the contraband was the direct result of his illegal seizure by the police. Our supreme court agreed, holding that flight in and of itself does not constitute probable cause for arrest. The court also held that Jeffries' flight did not give officers reasonable suspicion to justify a seizure under *Terry, supra*, stating: "Thus, it is clear the police had no right to 'arrest' or 'seize' Jeffries and the action of the police in chasing him and subsequently arresting him was a violation of his Fourth Amendment right." *Jeffries*, 454 Pa. at 325-326, 311 A.2d at 917.

In *Commonwealth v. Jones*, 474 Pa. 364, 373, 378 A.2d 835, 840 (1977), our supreme court adopted the standard which Pennsylvania courts now apply in determining what amount of force constitutes a "seizure." The court put forth the test for whether an individual was seized as whether "a reasonable [person], innocent of any crime, would have thought he was being restrained had he been in the defendant's shoes." *Jones* at 373, 378 A.2d at 840.

The issue of coerced abandonment was again addressed by our supreme court in *Commonwealth v. Barnett*, 484 Pa. 211, 398 A.2d 1019 (1979). There, officers on patrol in an unmarked police car observed Barnett walking down the street with his hands in his pockets. When Barnett noticed the police officers, he ducked behind a parked car. The officers then stopped the car, whereupon Barnett ran. The officers chased Barnett, who discarded a pistol and ammunition during the pursuit. Barnett was subsequently apprehended, arrested, and charged with various firearms offenses and other crimes. The trial court suppressed the gun and the bullets as products of an unlawful seizure. Our supreme court upheld the suppression order stating:

> Under these circumstances, the suppression court was correct in finding that the officers did more than merely approach appellee for questioning. The police conduct here amounted to a coercive factor which was the main reason that appellee abandoned the weapon.

Barnett, 484 Pa. at 216, 398 A.2d 1019.

The Pennsylvania courts have consistently applied the tests articulated in *Hicks*, *Jeffries*, *Jones*, and *Barnett* when determining whether a police show of authority constitutes a seizure, whether the seizure was made with probable cause or reasonable suspicion and whether contraband abandoned while police were approaching or pursuing an individual was the product of an illegal seizure. *See, e.g., Commonwealth v. Lovette*, 498 Pa. 665, 450 A.2d 975 (1982), *cert. denied*, 459 U.S. 1178, 103 S. Ct. 830, 74 L. Ed. 2d 1025 (1983); *Commonwealth v. Hall*, 475 Pa. 482, 380 A.2d 1238 (1977); *Commonwealth v. Brown*, 388 Pa. Super. 187, 565 A.2d 177 (1989); *Commonwealth v. Bulling*, 331 Pa. Super. 84, 480 A.2d 254 (1984).

This Court has addressed *Hodari D.* in several cases in which individuals had abandoned contraband during an interaction with the police. In *Commonwealth v. Harper*, 416 Pa. Super. 608, 611 A.2d 1211 (1992), a panel of this Court was presented with the issue of whether a person who discarded items of clothing, in which contraband was found, while being pursued by police was "seized" for purposes of the Fourth Amendment. In *Harper*, we were constrained to follow the dictates of *Hodari D.* for Fourth Amendment purposes and concluded that no seizure had occurred during the police chase of the defendant. In that case, however, no claims were made under the Pennsylvania Constitution.

There, Judge Beck writing for our Court described the reasoning in *Hodari D.* to be a marked departure from the generally recognized principles used by the federal courts to determine whether a "seizure" under the Fourth Amendment has occurred. *Harper*, 416 Pa. Super. at 613, 611 A.2d at 1215-1216. In that case, we specifically examined the *Hodari D.* Court's rejection of the standard for determining whether a seizure has occurred, which was set forth by the United States Supreme Court in *Mendenhall, supra*, and *Michigan v. Chesternut*, 486 U.S. 567, 108 S. Ct. 1975, 100 L. Ed. 2d 565 (1988). This is the same standard adopted by our supreme court in *Jones, supra*. In *Harper*, the radical change made by *Hodari D.* in Fourth Amendment jurisprudence was illustrated by citation to a comment in 3 W. LaFave, *Search and Seizure* § 9.2, p. 89-90 (2d ed. 1987, Supp. 1992), which states:

> What the Court in *Hodari D.* ought to have recognized is that the "not free to leave" concept of *Mendenhall-Royer* has nothing to do with a particular suspect's choice to flee rather than submit or with his assessment of the probability of successful fight. But instead, as the dissenters lament, the majority "concludes that the timing of the seizure is governed by the citizen's reaction, rather than by the officer's conduct." In this sense as well, *Hodari D.* is inconsistent with established Fourth Amendment jurisprudence, including principles emphasized in the very cases relied upon by the majority. . . . in *Michigan v. Chesternut*, the Court reiterated that in determining whether a Terry stop has occurred, it is necessary to utilize a standard that "allows police to determine in advance whether the conduct contemplated will implicate the Fourth Amendment." Such is certainly not the case in *Hodari D.*, for what would otherwise be a groundless and thus illegal *Terry* seizure becomes conduct totally outside the Fourth Amendment merely because of the suspect's nonsubmission.

Harper, 416 Pa. Super. at 618, 611 A.2d at 1216.

In *Commonwealth v. Peterfield*, 415 Pa. Super. 313, 609 A.2d 540 (1992), *appeal denied*, ___ Pa. ___, 618 A.2d 400 (1992), Judge Kelly, without joinder, cited *Hodari D.* to hold that since Peterfield, the arrestee, did not submit to the police show of force, he could not be considered "seized" for purposes of the Fourth Amendment. *Id.* In that case, Peterfield made a claim that, under Article 1, Section 8, he had been illegally seized when he abandoned the contraband, and that all fruits of that seizure should be suppressed. Judge Kelly, however, refused to consider Peterfield's claim under the Pennsylvania Constitution because he had not complied with the briefing requirements put forth in *Edmunds, supra*, that would enable a court to separately analyze such a claim. *Id.* 415 Pa. Super. at 321, 609 A.2d at 543-544. In *Peterfield*, the second judge concurred in the result only, and the third judge dissented.

In *In the Interest of Barry W,* 423 Pa. Super. 549, 621 A.2d 669 (1993) (*en banc*), this Court again discussed *Hodari D.* and its divergence from established Pennsylvania precedent but found *Hodari D.* to be inapplicable to that case, as the issue before the court was not whether a seizure had occurred but whether flight alone could justify reasonable suspicion by the police to forcibly detain the appellant.

While *Hodari D.* has been discussed in other decisions by this Court, this is the first time the issue of whether *Hodari D.* should be applied in the context of a state constitutional claim has been placed squarely before us. Under the third requirement in *Edmunds,* a court interpreting a provision of the state constitution should inform itself of the decisions in sister states regarding the adoption of a newly promulgated rule under the United States Constitution with regard to similar provisions contained in the state constitutions of those jurisdictions. I will now undertake that inquiry.

There has not been uniform acceptance or rejection of *Hodari D.* in other jurisdictions which have faced the issue of whether *Hodari D.* should become the standard under the constitutions of those states.

In *State v. Doss,* 254 N.J. Super. 122, 603 A.2d 102, *cert. denied,* 130 N.J. 17, 611 A.2d 655 (1992), the New Jersey Superior Court was not faced directly with the issue of whether *Hodari D.* should be applied under the constitution of that state. However, the court clearly stated that the holding in *Hodari D.*, "that pursuit of a suspect by the police was neither a 'search' nor a 'seizure'" was not a permissible conclusion under New Jersey law, as police may only chase a suspect after they have formed "at least an 'articulable suspicion' that [the suspect] was or had been engaged in the commission of a criminal offense." *Id.* 254 N.J. Super. at 127-128, 603 A.2d at 104-105.

In *People v. Holmes,* 585 N.Y.S.2d 718, 181 A.D.2d 27 (1992), the New York Supreme Court Appellate Division considered whether that state should adopt the holding of *Hodari D.* as applicable to a claim under the New York State Constitution. The facts of *Holmes* are similar to the facts of the present case. There, police officers recognized the appellant as an individual who had previously been arrested on drug charges. The police officers, without reasonable suspicion that the appellant was armed or in the process of committing a crime, called to the appellant and gave chase when the appellant turned and fled. During his flight, Holmes discarded a bag containing narcotics, which was recovered by the police after Holmes' apprehension. Holmes moved to suppress the narcotics as the fruit of an illegal seizure.

In *Holmes*, the court held that *Hodari D.* overruled prior New York cases interpreting the Fourth Amendment. However, the court refused to follow *Hodari D.* under Article 1, Section 12, of the New York State Constitution, which provides protections against unreasonable searches and seizures similar to those provided for in Article 1, Section 8, of the Pennsylvania Constitution. There, the court held that the New York Constitution provides greater protection for the privacy of its citizens against unreasonable seizures than its federal counterpart. *Id.* 585 N.Y.S.2d at 719-720, 181 A.D.2d at 28-32.

Similarly, in *State v. Oquendo*, 223 Conn. 635, 613 A.2d 1300 (1992), the Supreme Court of Connecticut also considered the implications of *Hodari D.* upon a claim made under the section of the Connecticut Constitution protecting against unreasonable searches and seizures. In that case, a police officer stopped Oquendo and his companion because the officer suspected that they could possibly be involved with neighborhood burglaries since they were wearing coats on a warm night. The police officer summoned Oquendo and requested that he produce the duffle bag he was carrying. At that point, Oquendo fled and the police officer pursued. During the pursuit, Oquendo discarded the duffle bag, containing cocaine, which was recovered by the police. Oquendo was subsequently arrested, and moved for suppression of the contents of the duffle bag, as the products of an illegal seizure.

The Supreme Court of Connecticut held that the provisions of the constitution of that state provided greater protection for the privacy of its citizens than the federal constitution and refused to apply *Hodari D.* to the state constitutional claim. *Oquendo*, 223 Conn. at 652, 613 A.2d at 1310. The court rejected *Hodari D.* as providing too restrictive a definition of seizure that was inconsistent with the previous decisions of that court, despite that fact that the protections under the state constitution had always followed the path dictated by the Fourth Amendment jurisprudence of the United States Supreme Court. *Id.*

The Supreme Court of Hawaii has also had the opportunity to address the issue of whether *Hodari D.* should be followed when a claim arises implicating that state's constitutional protection against unreasonable searches and seizures. *State v. Quino*, 74 Haw. 161, 840 P.2d 358 (1992), *cert. denied*, ___ U.S. ___, 113 S. Ct. 1849, 123 L. Ed. 2d 472 (1993). There, the court rejected *Hodari D.* as inconsistent with the previous holdings of that court regarding seizures. The court stated that Hawaii has chosen to afford greater protection to its citizens by rejecting the United States Supreme Court's requirement that physical force or submission to an assertion of authority determines whether a person has been seized. *Id.* 840 P.2d at 359. In rejecting the public policy implications of *Hodari D.*, the court stated:

> We cannot allow the police to randomly "encounter" individuals without any objective basis for suspecting them of misconduct and then place them in a coercive environment in order to develop reasonable suspicion to justify their detention. This investigative technique is based on the proposition that an otherwise innocent person, who comes under police scrutiny for no good reason, is not innocent unless he or she convinces the police that he or she is.

Id. at 365.

In *State v. Holmes*, 311 Or. 400, 813 P.2d 28 (1991), the Oregon Supreme Court considered the question of what constitutes a seizure under both the Oregon Constitution and the federal constitution. While the court accepted the holding in *Hodari D.* for the purposes of Fourth Amendment analysis, it defined seizure for the purposes of state constitutional questions much differently than the definition put forth in *Hodari D.* In defining what constitutes a "seizure" under the Oregon Constitution, the court stated:

> We hold that a "seizure" of a person occurs under Article 1, section 9, of the Oregon Constitution (a) if a law enforcement officer intentionally and significantly restricts, interferes with, or otherwise deprives an individual of that individual's liberty or freedom of movement; or (b) whenever an individual believes that (a) above, has occurred and such belief is objectively reasonable in the circumstances.

Id. 311 Or. at 409, 813 P.2d at 34. This definition is similar to the standard articulated in *Mendenhall, supra,* and the definition of seizure which has until to the present time been followed under the Pennsylvania Constitution.

I find the reasoning of the New Jersey, New York, Connecticut, Hawaii, and Oregon courts to be both sound and persuasive. In each of these states the courts have chosen to remain with the *Mendenhall* "free to leave" analysis. In each of these states, as in Pennsylvania, analysis under state constitutional provisions relating to search and seizure had previously been co-extensive with the analysis provided by the United States Supreme Court in deciding Fourth Amendment issues relating to seizure and coerced abandonment. However due to the dramatic departure that the *Hodari D.* decision represents from the well-established meaning of seizure as it has developed, these state courts would not countenance such an infringement upon the privacy of their citizens.

The Commonwealth brief informs us that "other jurisdictions that have considered the *Hodari D.* rule that a suspect who decides to flee has not been 'seized,' have accepted and followed it." Brief for Appellant at 17. It is not until its reply brief that the Commonwealth admits that some other states have rejected *Hodari D.*, contending, without citation, that "[t]he majority of states to consider this issue have found the reasoning of *Hodari D.* to be persuasive." Reply Brief for Appellant at 14.

The Majority cites to the split of authority among our sister states regarding this issue as twenty three states accepting of the reasoning of *Hodari D.* and five states rejecting such reasoning. However, after a thorough review of the cases cited, my research reveals that many of the cited state court decisions apply the rationale of *Hodari D.* only in the context of claims made under the Fourth Amendment to the United States Constitution, rather than claims made specifically under similar provisions of the state constitution. As it is uncontested that the holding of *Hodari D.* must be applied to all claims arising solely under the Fourth Amendment to the United States Constitution, I will address only those decisions from other jurisdictions which have held that *Hodari D.* should become the standard for determining whether a seizure has occurred under a state constitutional analysis.

In *People v. Arangure*, 230 Cal. App. 3d 1302, 282 Cal. Rptr. 51 (1991), the California Court of Appeals adopted *Hodari D.* for the analysis of a state constitutional claim regarding seizure and coerced abandonment of contraband. The court, however, prefaced its discussion of state constitutional analysis by stating that courts in California are required to interpret state constitutional claims as controlled by Federal precedent due to the adoption of Proposition 8 in 1982, enacted as Article 1, Section 28 of the California Constitution. Otherwise known as the Truth in Evidence Clause, that section abrogates suppression of evidence seized in violation of the California Constitution but not the federal constitution. Hence, the court in California was required to accept *Hodari D.* for the purposes of a state constitutional claim.

The Louisiana Courts have apparently split on this issue with the Louisiana Court of Appeals accepting *Hodari D.* for the purposes of state constitutional analysis in *State v. Gainer*, 591 So. 2d 1328 (La. Ct. App. 4th Cir. 1991) and then rejecting the *Hodari D.* analysis for a similar claim under the state constitution in *State v. Tucker*, 604 So. 2d 600 (La. Ct. App. 2d Cir. 1992), *appeal granted*, 609 So. 2d 212 (La. 1992).

In *State v. Shahid*, 813 S.W.2d 38 (Mo. Ct. App. 1991), the Missouri Court of Appeals followed *Hodari D.* for purposes of its state constitution but engaged in no separate state constitutional analysis, thus providing little guidance to this court.

The Supreme Court of Idaho in *State v. Rawlings*, 121 Idaho 930, 829 P.2d 520 (1992), cited *Hodari D.* with approval but did not specifically adopt the *Hodari D.* rationale under the Idaho Constitution, as that issue had not been squarely placed before the court.

In *Henderson v. Maryland*, 89 Md. App. 19, 597 A.2d 486 (1991), the Maryland Court of Special Appeals, addressed a claim substantially similar to the claim in the case *sub judice*. There, the court adopted the reasoning of *Hodari D.* for the purposes of the Maryland Constitution, rejecting the appellant's claim that Article 26 of the Maryland Declaration of Rights provided greater protection than does the Fourth Amendment to the United States Constitution. *Id.* 597 A.2d at 488.

In *Welfare of E.D.J.*, 492 N.W.2d 829 (Minn. App. 1992), *appeal granted*, (January 15, 1993), the Minnesota Court of Appeals, an intermediate appellate court, also adopted the reasoning of *Hodari D.* in interpreting what constitutes a seizure under the constitution of that state. There, the court held that while "[t]here may be compelling reasons for interpreting Article 1, Section 10, of the Minnesota Constitution differently than the United States Supreme Court has interpreted the Fourth Amendment in *Hodari D.*," the appellant in *E.D.J.* presented the court with no historical basis or court precedent which would permit the court a departure from the federal standard. *Id.* at 830-831. The court also noted that the Minnesota Supreme Court has neither accepted nor rejected *Hodari D.*, for the purpose of determining whether there has been a seizure for purposes of the Minnesota Constitution.

Similarly, the Courts of Appeals in Ohio and Texas have adopted the standard articulated by *Hodari D.* under the Fourth Amendment for purposes of interpreting similar provisions under the constitutions of those states. See *Ohio v. Barnwell*, 1993 WL 135796 (No. 64297 Ohio App., filed April 29, 1993); *Texas v. Rose*, 844 S.W.2d 911 (Tex. App. 1992).

There appears to be no uniform acceptance or rejection of *Hodari D.* among our sister states. However, several other jurisdictions have rejected *Hodari D.* despite the fact that their state constitutional definitions of seizure had previously been coextensive with federal law. This reinforces the principle that Pennsylvania need not adopt *Hodari D.* merely because our supreme court has previously interpreted the term seizure, for purposes of the Pennsylvania Constitution, in a manner consistent with the decisions of the United States Supreme Court. To the contrary, this Court has the obligation, when presented with a claim pursuant to the Pennsylvania Constitution, to independently evaluate whether the protections provided to the citizens of this Commonwealth should exceed those dictated under federal law. *Edmunds, supra.*

The fourth requirement under *Edmunds*, requires that courts discuss the policy considerations involved in accepting federal precedent in the context of a claim made under the Pennsylvania Constitution. First, I view this Court's adoption of

Hodari D. as a drastic departure from the standard for what determines whether a "seizure" has occurred under the established law of this Commonwealth. *See, e.g., Hicks, supra, Jeffries, supra, Jones, supra. See also Harper, supra.*

Second, *Hodari D.* represents a standard under which police officers are unable to predict whether their actions will result in a seizure or will be outside the protection of Article 1, Section 8, or the Fourth Amendment entirely since whether or not a seizure occurs under *Hodari D.* depends not upon the actions of the police but upon the reactions of the individual involved. Justice Stevens, in describing the virtues of the *Mendenhall* test and the dangers of the approach now promulgated by the *Hodari D.* majority, cited to 3 W. LaFave, *Search and Seizure* § 9.2 at 61 (2d ed. 1987, Supp. 1991):

> The "free to leave" concept, in other words, has nothing to do with a particular suspect's choice to flee rather than submit or with his assessment of the probability of successful flight. Were it otherwise, police would be encouraged to utilize a very threatening but sufficiently slow chase as a evidence-gathering technique whenever they lack even the reasonable suspicion needed for a Terry stop.

Hodari D., 499 U.S. at ___, 111 S. Ct. at 1559, 113 L. Ed. 2d at 707 (Stevens, J., dissenting). Under *Hodari D.*, this second scenario put forth hypothetically by LaFave, *supra*, has been sanctioned under federal law. No longer will law enforcement authorities be required to assess the impact of their actions prior to pursuing individuals despite the lack of any reasonable suspicion that those individual may be armed or engaged in criminal activity.

Finally, in Pennsylvania, prior to the majority's adoption of the *Hodari D.* rule, the pedestrian had no obligation to comply with any detention upon merely being viewed by the police. *Commonwealth v. Metz*, 412 Pa. Super. 100, 119, 602 A.2d 1328, 1337 (1992), *appeal denied*, 531 Pa. 652, 613 A.2d 558 (1992) (Kelly, J., concurring). The free citizen in a country such as ours of course retains the discretion to run, walk, crawl or stop at that moment or any other under such circumstances, and accordingly, neither the police nor the courts can draw any adverse inferences from the exercise of any such discretion. *Id.; Commonwealth v. Martinez*, 403 Pa. Super. 125, 128, 588 A.2d 513, 514 (1991), *appeal denied*, 530 Pa. 653, 608 A.2d 29 (1992). However, with this Court's adoption of the *Hodari D.* standard, a citizen can enjoy the rights and protections of the Fourth Amendment and Article 1, Section 8, only if that citizen immediately complies with any police directive, regardless of whether the police officer is acting without reasonable suspicion. At least one commentator has predicted that in *Hodari D.*, the Supreme Court is on the verge of preventing citizens from walking away from police encounters. Note, *California v. Hodari, D.: The*

Demise of the Reasonable Person Test in Fourth Amendment Analysis, 12 N. Ill. L. Rev. 463, 494 (1992).

I am unwilling to participate in adopting *Hodari D.* as the law under the Pennsylvania Constitution. I share the fears of Justices Stevens and Marshall that, "[i]f carried to its logical conclusion, it will encourage unlawful displays of force that will frighten countless innocent citizens into surrendering whatever privacy rights they may still have." *Hodari D.*, 499 U.S. at ___, 111 S. Ct. at 1561, 113 L. Ed. 2d at 710 (Stevens, J., dissenting).

After a full review of the four *Edmunds* factors, as well as a full review of *Hodari D.* and previous Pennsylvania and United Stated Supreme Court precedents, I can only conclude that to adopt *Hodari D.* as binding on the rights of the citizens of Pennsylvania under Article 1, Section 8, of our constitution would be to overrule all existing precedent on the law of seizure in Pennsylvania. I, therefore, will not join with the Majority in its decision in this case.

Returning to the present case, I would apply the traditional standard articulated in *Jeffries* and *Jones, supra,* to the actions of the police officer in order to determine whether Carroll was "seized" for purposes of Article 1, Section 8, of the Pennsylvania Constitution. I would conclude that a reasonable person would have believed that he was not free to leave when, after his attempted departure from a police officer, he was pursued. When an individual who exercises his right to walk away from a police show of authority is then pursued, a reasonable person would conclude that he or she was not free to leave. *See Jeffries, supra.*

If Carroll were "seized" at the time he fell and dropped the drugs from his pocket, under our traditional analysis, we would then inquire whether the police officer was acting with reasonable suspicion or probable cause. In the present case, the Commonwealth has offered no evidence that the officer who approached Carroll with his hand on his gun had a reasonable and articulable belief that Carroll might be armed or that criminal activity might be afoot. Any police detention, in the absence of such an articulable belief, renders the police actions illegal and requires suppression of all evidence which was the product of such a "seizure." *Jeffries, supra; Martinez, supra.*

As I conclude that the "abandonment" of the contraband by Carroll was the product of illegal police conduct, I would affirm the order of the suppression court. I, therefore, respectfully dissent.

McEWEN, DEL SOLE and BECK, JJ. join.

Carroll Vocabulary

Instructions: To better understand this material, be sure you know the definitions of the following terms. Be prepared to define these terms for your classmates, using the techniques described in "Defining/Explaining a Term or Concept." (pg. 14)

1. Fruit of the poisonous tree
2. Factual findings
3. Abuse of discretion
4. Error of law
5. Credibility
6. Pursuit
7. Abandonment
8. Reasonable suspicion
9. Plurality opinion
10. Physical force
11. Submission
12. Good faith exception (to the exclusionary rule)
13. Self-incrimination
14. Totality of the circumstances
15. Contraband

✓ Matching Exercise

Please match the terms on the left with the definitions on the right. Write the term number in the blank.

Terms:

1. Extemship
2. Internship
3. Policy issues
4. Consent
5. Inchoate crimes
6. Conversion
7. Black-letter law
8. Issue spotter test
9. Dropping the course (Add/Drop)
10. Talking law
11. Moot court competition
12. Study group
13. Pass/Fail
14. First draft
15. Final draft
16. Gift
17. Quid pro quo
18. Closed book exams
19. Open book exams

Definitions:

A. ___ An informal term indicating the basic principles of law generally accepted by the courts and/or embodied in the statutes.

B. ___ A voluntary transfer of property to another made gratuitously and without consideration.

C. ___ Agreement; approval.

D. ___ Working for credits at a legal facility.

E. ___ The first copy of a memo, brief, or other written material.

F. ___ An incipient, unfinished crime which generally leads to another crime.

G. ___ A competition in law school in which hypothetical cases are argued in a court.

H. ___ Working at a legal facility for money while still in school.

I. ___ Talking about cases, using legal sayings outside of the classroom in general conversation with fellow law students.

J. ___ Finished or complete memo, brief, or other written material after editing has been done.

K. ___ Giving something to obtain something.

L. ___ Depriving an owner of his or her property permanently or for an indefinite time.

M. ___ Tests in which the relevant questions of law must be found and explained.

N. ___ Issues directed at the concern for the welfare or prosperity of the state or community.

O. ___ Tests in which outside material, such as textbooks and outlines, can be consulted will the test is being taken.

P. ___ Getting credit for a class taken but not a grade.

Q. ___ Tests in which no material can be consulted while the test is being taken.

R. ___ Taking a class off of your schedule without consequence (or adding a class to your schedule.

S. ___ A small assembling of people to review class material and prepare for exams.

Oral Arguments in the Case of *Davis v. Monroe County Board of Education*

Attorneys use oral argument skills every day. The following is an excerpt from the actual oral arguments presented before the United States Supreme Court in the case of *Davis v. Monroe County Board of Education*. The facts of the case and the Court's opinion are found in Appendix E. When reading the oral arguments pay special attention to the different types of questions the justices ask. Knowing the difference between easy "friendly" questions and challenging "merit testing" questions is very important in arguing your case. Also note the deference the two attorneys give to the Court. Proper respect for the bench is nearly as important as a solid argument in persuading a court.

Verna L. Williams, Esq., Counsel for Petitioner
W. Warren Plowden, Esq., Counsel for Respondent

Chief Justice: We'll hear arguments first this morning in No. 97-843, *Aurelia Davis v. the Monroe County Board of Education*. Ms. Williams . . . .

Opening:

Ms. Williams: Mr. Chief Justice, and may it please the Court. At issue in this case is whether Title IX's broad prohibition against sex discrimination requires schools to remedy and address student-to-student sexual harassment.

Procedural posture from court below:

The Eleventh Circuit has decided that Title IX imposes no obligations on schools to remedy this type of discrimination, no matter how severe or pervasive the harassment, no matter how cognizant school officials are of it, no matter how capable officials were of remedying the harassment. Under this blanket rule, schools simply cannot be held accountable under Title IX either in court or in the administrative enforcement context for refusing to address this discrimination. This result cannot be squared with Title IX and with this Court's interpretations of the statute.

Friendly question:

Justice O'Conner: May I ask, Ms. Williams, how you propose to cabin this cause of action were we to agree with you? I'm sure that school children nationwide tease each other, and little boys tease little girls, and so forth throughout their years in school. And is every one of those incidents going to lead to some kind of a lawsuit?

Ms. Williams:	No, Your Honor. The legal framework that has developed in this area provides standards for determining what constitutes sexual harassment and what isn't sexual harassment.

Friendly question:

Justice O'Connor:	What standards would you think would govern to cabin this kind of cause of action?
Ms. Williams:	First, I would recommend looking at the Title VII standards. The Court said in *Gebser* that Title VII standards inform whether sexual harassment is sex discrimination under Title IX. And under those standards, a particular instance isn't sexual harassment unless it is severe. It's pervasive, unless it is sufficiently . . . unless it is objectively offensive to a reasonable person, unless it is offensive to the person who has experienced the sexual harassment.

Merit testing question:

Justice Scalia:	Gee, but little girls always tease little boys and little boys always tease little girls. That's pervasive.
Ms. Williams:	It's pervasive, but it is not severe.
Justice Scalia:	In my experience, it's severe.
Ms. Williams:	But it doesn't always . . . .

Question expressing concern:

Justice Scalia:	The concern is, I think, that if you simply take the same standards of Title VII, i.e., anything that would be sexual harassment in the work place, when done by a co-worker or a supervisor to a subordinate or a co-worker, that which is sexual harassment there is also sexual harassment for which the school district is liable when a seven year old does it to a six year old or a thirteen year old does it to a twelve year old. The concern is, as you've said, you take the same standards. You would remove what is a pervasive problem in the schools from the hands of educators and psychologists and give that problem to lawyers and judges. Now, I don't think the latter is the right group of people to solve it. Perhaps it is. Perhaps it isn't. But I want to bring out into the open what I think is the problem or a problem, and I know what I've said may not be the case.
Ms. Williams:	We understand the concern and we think that, first of all, the Title VII standards wouldn't apply wholesale in the education context. They would inform the analysis of sexual harassment in the first instance. And the second thing is that Title IX doesn't require schools to be successful in addressing student-to-student sexual harassment. In other

words, to avoid being held out of compliance with Title IX, the school would need to take reasonable steps to remedy and address the sexual harassment.

Question crucial to justice's thinking

Justice Kennedy:	I think then that every school district in the nation should adopt guidelines and codes, as we've suggested for employers. Do you think there was a suggestion in the congressional debates and in the text of this statute that there would be federal standards for school behavior in every classroom thinking in this country?

Merit testing question

Ms. Williams:	We're not suggesting that there are federal standards for school behavior. We are suggesting . . . .
Justice Kennedy:	I thought this was a federal statute we're talking about.
Ms. Williams:	Well, we are talking about a federal statute, but the federal statute imposes the obligation on educational institutions to ensure that no person is excluded from participation in, denied the benefits of, or subjected to discrimination under the education program or activity.
Justice Kennedy:	Now let's be very careful here. If you're going to have standards, they're federal standards, are they not?
Ms. Williams:	Yes.
Justice Kennedy:	Thank you.

Merit testing question

Justice Scalia:	Do you really think it imposes an obligation on these educational institutions to prevent anyone being denied the benefits of or excluded from participation in, that's what it requires every school district to do?
Ms. Williams:	The prohibition is broad.

CHAPTER 8—CLIENT INTERVIEWS AND NEGOTIATION

Client Interview

Interviewing a client is important for establishing a relationship with the client and for gathering information. A complete interview will allow you to communicate well with your client and allow you to collect the information you need to research the problem and advise your client correctly. The following are some things you should consider when preparing and conducting a client interview.

Before the Interview:

Begin by preparing carefully. Get all the information you can prior to the interview. Ask the client to bring all documents to the interview. Do preliminary research if possible.

Consider what the objectives are. Determine what your client wants or thinks he or she wants. Try to establish what the client needs or fears. Decide what can be done to help this client and if you can do it. If you decide to help the client, consider the nature of the attorney-client relationship and the scope of that relationship. Plan your short- and long-term goals.

Beginning the Interview:

Try to connect with the client. This means you should show empathy for the client. Begin with small talk focused on the client. Use active listening skills, eye contact, and indicate that you are following the conversation by nodding your head or otherwise indicating that you are actively listening. Select a comfortable physical location.

Try to establish your relationship by asking if the client has seen another attorney about this matter. Determine whether there are any conflicts of interest or if there is ex parte contact with a party represented by another attorney.

Be up-front about your fees. You should mention your fees early on in the meeting. Explain the fees generally and then explain that you can give an estimate or a "better idea" of the exact costs after you have talked further. Ask the client directly if he or she has any problem with the general information you have conveyed about your fees. In this way, you can open up lines of communication about the cost. When discussing fees, be sure to reassure the client that you will do everything you can to take care of the problem. You may also want to let the client know ways that you can work to keep costs down if the fees are an issue.

Start the interview by letting the client talk. Small talk at the beginning may help to identify why the client has come to see you. Rephrase what the client tells you to make sure you understand the client's view. Say something like, "So if I understand correctly, you are here because . . . ." If you have a client who is reluctant to talk, you will have to draw the client out. Try to use the open-ended style of questioning discussed earlier in this text rather than yes-no questions.

Once you have identified the reason for the client's visit, you want to gather as much information as possible. Again use open-ended questions to collect the facts. ("Can you tell me more about . . .?" "Could you tell me what happened next?") You want to learn about the client not just the legal problem. Allow the client to state the problem as they see it so that you can understand both the legal issues and the client's needs. Be patient and encourage the client to take his or her time. Try not to interrogate the client or ask questions too quickly. If you focus the interview too soon, you may loose information and end up with an incomplete understanding of the legal issues involved. Don't ignore the client's concerns even if you regard them as unimportant. If you focus only on the legal facts, you risk sending the message to the client that you don't really care. You may also miss essential information about the client's personality which will allow you to prepare an effective plan. Try not to take too many notes in the early stages of the interview or consider asking a secretary or another associate to take notes so that you can listen. You may want to ask the client if you can tape the interview.

Once you have an overview of the facts, try to get the details. Try to determine the chronological sequence of events. Fill in as many gaps as possible. Begin asking more focused or probing questions to determine "who, what, when, where, and why." If a client mentions something you view as a tangent, don't ignore it. Tell the client, for example, that you "will come back to that" or that you'd "like to hear more about that," but that you first would like to focus on the initial question. Then after the client has answered your question, return to the client's point.

After collecting the details, try to establish the counter-view. You want to be somewhat skeptical, at least in the sense that you want to be sure you have an accurate view of the situation. Try to expose for yourself the client's assumptions and beliefs. Try to get the client to reveal his or her biases by asking the client to explain certain statements. Try to get the client to assert the reason for his or her conclusions. Try to imagine the circumstances that your client is explaining. Try to view it from the client's prospective and then consider how the other side might view the situation. Find out what information client doesn't know and whether a statement is the client's belief or a verifiable fact.

Make sure to identify what remedy the client has in mind. You may have to refocus the client's goals and objectives but be sure to listen to what it is the client wants. Be careful not to give an opinion too early. If a client asks you for an opinion, don't ignore the question. Acknowledge what the client is asking but let the client know that you need to gather sufficient information to formulate an opinion.

In advising the client, don't rush to a judgement. Consider the situation and the ramifications of potential solutions carefully before offering advice. Try to summarize what the client has told you so that you can confirm what it is the client wants. Look at both the long-range and short-term goals or objectives. You may need to rank or prioritize these goals and objectives since some of them may conflict. You may want to explore solutions with your client. Present alternative courses of action and look at the legal and nonlegal consequences. You will need to evaluate what is practical and realistic for the client, both financially and socially.

Tell the client what the process will be. Outline the course of action, and tell him or her your immediate plans and overall steps. Often you will need some time to investigate the situation, so you may only be able to give a general plan. Don't rush to a definitive answer on the merits of the case. Be realistic about what you can provide. Try not to promise results. You will need to verify facts and research the issue so be sure to give yourself time for these tasks.

In wrapping-up the interview, you may want to leave the client with some assignment so that he or she feels involved in the process. For example, you may want the client to collect necessary documents and get them to you or find further information. Make sure the client knows how to reach you during the process and that the client understands what the next steps will be.

✓ *Exercise*:

You will be interviewing a client in the next class. The client is coming to you regarding a landlord-tenant dispute. Generally, the client will want to know about a landlord's duty to make repairs on a broken balcony door lock and the landlord's liability for third-party acts. You will be interviewing either the landlord or tenant according to your assignment in class. Your professor will assign some students to play the roles of the landlord and tenant. In preparation for this interview, please read the following cases, and try to consider the basic legal issues involved and what information you will need to know:

Pugh v. Holmes	239
Glickman Real Estate Development v. Korf	253
Feld v. Merriam	256
Reider v. Martin	262

If you are acting in the role of tenant read the memorandum for Claudia Perez (p. 233-34).

If you are acting in the role of landlord read the memorandum for Mr. or Mrs. Crusher (p. 236-38).

MEMORANDUM

To: The actors playing Claudia or Claudio Perez

From: Your Professor

Re: Your role as tenant

Your name is Claudia Perez. You recently graduated from law school and are an associate at the Philadelphia law firm of Marshall, Scalia, and O'Connor. Another associate in your firm has suggested that you contact the EFL law firm regarding a problem you are having with your landlords.

When you moved to Philadelphia, you knew you would be working very long hours, so you decided to live in center city Philadelphia. You selected an expensive apartment building called The Atrium. Mr. and Mrs. William and Wilma Crusher are the landlords, owners and managers of the building. The tenants at The Atrium consider it to be a very secure building. There have been no crimes reported from the building in the past eight years. The building has good lighting in the lobby, on every floor and in the underground garage. As additional security, the Crushers hired security guards to provide "around the clock" protection for the tenants and the building. Two security guards are on duty at all times. One guard patrols inside and outside the building. The other guard stays at the entrance to the building. When guests enter the building, the guard uses an elaborate intercommunication system to call tenants in their apartments to see if guests may enter.

You rented a beautiful one bedroom apartment on the second floor of The Atrium at a rental price of $2,000 per month. The apartment is equipped with every modern convenience and has a large balcony overlooking the city. The balconies to all apartments on the second floor are adjoining but are separated by brick walls that are about four feet high. You moved into your apartment on April 1 of this year and paid your first month's rent and a security deposit to Mr. Crusher.

You work long hours. However, because the spring has been unusually warm, you have been able to spend time on your balcony enjoying your view of the city. You could enter your balcony through a sliding glass door that opened with a special combination lock. On April 15, you found that the combination lock no longer worked. After experimenting with it for a few minutes, you found that the lock would open if you pushed "0."

That evening, you called to report the broken lock to Mr. Crusher and offered to get a locksmith to fix it immediately. Mr. Crusher reminded you that the lease stipulated that only the landlords could make repairs in the apartment. Mr. Crusher stated that the lock was custom-made and only the manufacturer could properly repair it. You asked how long it would take to repair the lock, but Mr. Crusher did not know.

One week later, the lock remained broken and you again notified Mr. Crusher who assured you that he would repair the lock soon. By May 1, Mr. Crusher still had not repaired the lock and the lock had deteriorated to where it opened without pushing any number. You felt upset and fearful for your safety. You sent the Crushers a letter stating that you would not pay the rent until they repaired the lock.

In addition, since mid-May, you have complained to Mr. Crusher about your next-door neighbor, Jack Shade. Shade always had his door open and stared at the residents and their visitors as they walked in the hallway. This made you nervous, as you had to walk by Shade's apartment to get to your own. You also observed Shade staring at you from his balcony. In addition, you would also hear loud voices coming from Shade's apartment during all hours of the day and night. You suspected that Shade was involved with something illegal. Pursuant to your complaints, Mr. Crusher asked Shade to keep his door closed. Shade apologized and complied with Mr. Crusher's request. While you no longer complained about Jack Shade, you didn't feel entirely comfortable about your neighbor.

The balcony door lock remained broken, so you did not pay your rent for June. On June 31, Mr. Crusher visited your apartment and demanded that you pay the two months' rent. He brought a large wooden dowel with him to secure your door until he could repair it. Mr. Crusher told you that he was sick of your constant complaining. You were annoyed and yelled back at him in a loud voice that your apartment was not safe and that you would pay only when your door lock was repaired. Then, regaining your composure, you offered to have the lock repaired yourself. However, Mr. Crusher reminded you that the manufacturer would have to repair the lock. Mr. Crusher said that your balcony door would be secure if you used the wooden dowel. He offered to place it in the balcony door. You refused, and said you could fit into the door by yourself.

You were exhausted from your encounter with Mr. Crusher and you spent part of the evening reclining on your balcony with a glass of wine. You were tired and went to bed early, forgetting to put the wooden dowel in the balcony door. One hour later, you heard a loud noise and the sound of the sliding glass door opening. Suddenly, someone wearing a Halloween mask rushed into your bedroom and assaulted you. You were unconscious for several minutes as a result of the beating. During that time, the intruder stole several valuable items and then escaped.

You suffered physical injuries and emotional distress that still required medical attention. Immediately after the attack, Mr. Crusher repaired the lock on the balcony door. The police have not arrested the perpetrator of the crime, but the prime suspect is Jack Shade.

You would like to ask the law firm to represent you in a civil suit against the Crushers. You would like to recover damages for the items stolen from your apartment and for your physical and emotional injuries. You feel that the Crushers are responsible for the attack and should compensate you for your losses and injuries. You are also concerned that the Crushers will counterclaim for the unpaid rent for May and June. You will pay the rent for July, but feel that you should not have to pay the rent for May or June. Do you have a claim in negligence against the Crushers for failing to protect you from the assailant's criminal acts? Do you have any potential defenses if the Crushers sue you for the unpaid rent?

Acting Tips

Familiarize yourself with the facts of this case. You may bring the script with you to the client interview. Feel free to add facts consistent with the character and the scenario in response to questions about minor facts not contained in this script. Try to make the attorney question you to find out the facts. However, if the attorney is having trouble, give enough facts for the attorney to question you further. If the attorney has not learned all the facts and the end of the interview is approaching, start giving the fact to him or her. The students will gather all the facts for their assignment from you during the client interview.

The legal issue the students will address in their memorandum is the implied warranty of habitability and the landlord's liability for third party acts.

Good luck and have fun!

MEMORANDUM

To: The actors playing Mr. or Mrs. Crusher

From: Your Professor

Re: Your role as landlord

Your name is William or Wilma Crusher. You and your spouse own and manage a luxury apartment building in center city Philadelphia known as The Atrium. You are coming to the EFL law firm today because your tenant, Ms. Claudia Perez, stopped paying her rent in May and now owes you $4,000 for two months' rent.

Ms. Perez moved into her one bedroom apartment on April 1 of this year. The problem began almost immediately after that time. Perez paid her first month's rent and her security deposit at the proper time. On April 15, Perez called you to complain about the combination lock on the sliding glass balcony door. The weather had been unusually warm that day, so Perez had been enjoying a view of the city from her large balcony when she found that the lock no longer worked. After experimenting with the lock, she found that the lock would open if she pressed "0". Ms. Perez offered to get a locksmith to fix the lock immediately. You reminded her that the lease stipulated that only the landlord could make repairs in her apartment. You told Ms. Perez that the lock was custom-made and that only the manufacturer could properly repair it. Perez asked how long it would take to fix the lock and you said you didn't know but you would call the manufacturer as soon as possible.

The next day, April 16, you called the company and left a message with the answering service. One week later, the lock remained broken and Ms. Perez called you again about fixing the lock. You left another message with the manufacturer on April 23.

By May 1, the manufacturer had not returned your phone calls and the lock was still broken. Ms. Perez informed you that the lock had deteriorated to where it opened without pushing any number. She sent you a letter saying she feared for her safety and would not pay the May rent until you repaired the lock.

You, and you believe your tenants, consider The Atrium to be a very secure building. There have been no crimes reported in the building in the past eight years. The building has very good lighting in the lobby, on every floor, and in the underground parking garage. For additional security, you employ two security guards for "around the clock" protection of the tenants and the building. Two security guards are on duty at all times. One guard patrols inside and outside the building. The other guard stays at the entrance to the building. When guests enter the building, the guard uses an elaborate intercommunication system to call tenants in their apartments to see whether the guests may enter.

You believe Ms. Perez's apartment is very secure. Her apartment is a beautiful one bedroom unit on the second floor of The Atrium that rents for $2,000 per month. It is equipped with every modern convenience. Ms. Perez's apartment has a particularly large balcony with an exceptional view of downtown Philadelphia. The balconies to all the apartments on the second floor are adjoining but are separated by brick walls that are about four feet high.

On May 1, you wrote a letter to the lock manufacturer requesting that they repair the lock or that they send you a list of locksmiths authorized to make repairs. You and your spouse have been visiting your vacation home in the south of France for the last several weeks and were hoping to have some response upon your return. During your absence, you instructed your staff to act quickly should the manufacturer respond. However, you have had no response from the manufacturer and Ms. Perez refused to pay her June rent.

On May 15, Ms. Perez came to complain to you about her next-door neighbor, Jack Shade. Shade always had his door open and stared at the residents and their visitors as they went by. Ms. Perez said this made her nervous as she had to walk by Shade's apartment to get to her own. Ms. Perez would also hear loud voices coming from his apartment at all hours of the day and night. She suspected that Shade was involved in something illegal. Pursuant to Ms. Perez's complaints, you asked Shade to keep his door closed. Shade apologized and complied with your request.

Ms. Perez did not pay her rent for June. On June 31, you visited Ms. Perez's apartment and told her that you expected her to pay the two months' rent. You brought a large round wooden dowel with you to secure her door. You told her that you were sick of her constant complaining. Ms. Perez was annoyed and yelled back at you in a loud voice that her apartment was unsafe and that she would pay only when you fixed her balcony lock. Then, in a calmer and quieter voice, she asked if she could have the lock fixed herself. However, you once again refused, stating that the manufacturer had to repair the lock. You then offered to place the wood in the door; however, Ms. Perez told you she could fit the wood into the door herself.

The next morning, the Philadelphia police notified you that Ms. Perez had been attacked in her apartment. The masked assailant gained entry through the sliding glass balcony door. Ms. Perez apparently forgot to put the wood in the sliding door. Ms. Perez suffered physical and emotional injuries and the intruder stole several valuable items from her apartment while she was unconscious. The police have not arrested the perpetrator of the crime, but the prime suspect is Jack Shade.

The day after the attack, you repaired the lock on the sliding glass door.

You suspect that Ms. Perez will attempt to hold you liable for the criminal acts of the unknown third party. You suspect that she will try to recover damages for her injuries and her lost property. You do not believe you should be liable to Ms. Perez for any amount of damages. You also believe Ms. Perez should pay full rent for months of May and June.

Acting Tips

Familiarize yourself with these facts and try to assume your character for the client interview. You may bring the script with you to be sure you do not forget any important facts. Feel free to add facts that are consistent with this scenario and the character, if you are asked a question about a minor fact not mentioned in this script. Try to let the students gain the information they need through questioning. However, if the interview is nearing its end and they still do not have all the facts, start to give them important information that will lead to productive questions from them. If they still have not elicited all the facts after hints from you, tell them the important facts. The students need to get all their factual information for their assignment from you during the client interview.

The legal issue involved is the implied warranty of habitability and the landlord's liability for third party acts. While the subjective belief of the parties is not dispositive of the legal question, remember that the Crushers believe that they are acting in good faith and that Ms. Perez is a complainer who is trying to cheat them on the rent.

Good luck and have fun!

J. C. PUGH, Appellant,

v.

Eloise P. HOLMES, Appellee.
Supreme Court of Pennsylvania
405 A.2d 897 (Pa. 1979)

[Some footnotes may have been omitted.]

LARSEN, Justice.

Eloise Holmes, appellee, had been, pursuant to an oral month-to-month lease, renting a residential dwelling in Chambersburg in Franklin County at the rate of $60.00 per month from November, 1971 until recently. Her landlord, appellant J. C. Pugh, instituted two separate landlord-tenant actions against appellee before a justice of the peace, the first resulting in a judgment for unpaid rent (for the period from September, 1975 through June, 1976) and the second resulting in a judgment for unpaid rent (for the period from June, 1976 through August, 1976) and for possession of the premises. Following Mrs. Holmes' appeals to the Court of Common Pleas of Franklin County, appellant filed separate complaints, the first seeking unpaid rent and the second seeking both unpaid rent and possession. In both actions, appellee filed answers asserting a defense of the landlord's alleged breach of an implied warranty of habitability. Additionally, in the second action, appellee asserted a setoff due in an amount which she claimed she had spent to repair a broken lock after having given appellant notice and a reasonable opportunity to repair the lock. Appellee also filed a counterclaim for the cost of repairing other allegedly defective conditions of which she had given appellant notice. Appellant filed preliminary objections to the answer and counterclaim which the Court of Common Pleas sustained finding that appellee's answer failed to set forth a legal defense to the landlord's actions, and that the counterclaim failed to set forth a legal cause of action.

On appeal, the Superior Court, by opinion of President Judge Jacobs, reversed and remanded. The Superior Court abolished the doctrine of *caveat emptor* as applied to residential leases and held that a warranty of habitability by the landlord will be implied in all such leases, which implied warrant would be mutually dependent upon the tenant's obligation to pay rent. *Pugh v. Holmes*, 253 Pa. Super. 76, 384 A.2d 1234 (1978) (Price, J. dissenting). By order dated July 20, 1978, this Court granted appellant's petition for allowance of appeal.

I. DOCTRINE OF CAVEAT EMPTOR ABOLISHED/ IMPLIED WARRANTY OF HABITABILITY ADOPTED

The doctrine of *caveat emptor* comported with the needs of the society in which it developed. However, we find that the doctrine of *caveat emptor* has outlived its usefulness and must be abolished, and that, in order to keep in step with the realities of modern day leasing, it is appropriate to adopt an implied warranty of habitability in residential leases. The rule of *caveat emptor*, as applied to landlord-tenant relationships, developed in England in the sixteenth century and was adopted in the nineteenth century as the law of this Commonwealth in *Moore v. Weber*, 71 Pa. 429 (1872). *Moore* held "The rule here, as in other cases, is *caveat emptor*. The lessee's eyes are his bargain. He is bound to examine the premises he rents, and secure himself by covenants to repair." *Id.* at 432. In the primarily agrarian society in which the doctrine developed, the law viewed the lease transaction as a conveyance of land for a term, and the focal interest in the conveyance was the land—any shelters or structures existing on the land were "incidental" concerns. The rent was viewed as "coming out of the land" itself, not from the dwelling or the dweller. The feudal landlord

> "had no obligations to the tenant other than those made expressly, and the tenant's obligation to pay rent was independent of the landlord's [covenants] . . . The doctrine of *caveat emptor* was fully applicable. The tenant's only protections were to inspect the premises before taking possession or to extract express warranties from the landlord. It was assumed that landlords and tenants held equal bargaining power in arranging their rental agreements, and that the agrarian tenant had the ability to inspect the dwelling adequately and to make simple repairs in the buildings which possessed no modern conveniences such as indoor plumbing or electrical wiring.

> As agrarian society declined and population centers shifted from rural to urban areas, the common law concepts of landlord-tenant relationships did not change. Despite the facts that the primary purpose of the urban leasing arrangement was housing and not land and that the tenant could neither adequately inspect nor repair urban dwelling units, landlords still were not held to any implied warranties in the places they rented and tenants leased dwellings at their own risk."

Pugh v. Holmes, 384 A.2d at 1237-38.

As stated by appellee, "times have changed. So has the law." (Brief for appellee at 3). Today, the doctrine of the implied warranty of habitability has attained majority status in the United States, the doctrine having been embraced by the appellate courts and/or the legislatures of some 40 state jurisdictions and the District of Columbia. The warranty recognizes that the modern tenant is not interested in land, but rather bargains for a dwelling house suitable for habitation.

> "Functionally viewed, the modern apartment dweller is a consumer of housing services. The contemporary leasing of residences envisions one person (landlord) exchanging for periodic payments (rent) a bundle of goods and services, rights and obligations. The now classic description

of this economic reality appears in *Javins v. First National Realty Corp.*, 138 U.S. App. D.C. 369, 428 F.2d 1071, 1074, *cert. denied*, 400 U.S. 925, 91 S. Ct. 186, 27 L. Ed. 2d 185 (1970) (footnote omitted). When American city dwellers both rich and poor, seek 'shelter today, they seek a well known package of goods and services—a package which includes not merely walls and ceilings, but also adequate heat, light and ventilation, serviceable plumbing facilities, secure windows and doors, proper sanitation, and proper maintenance.' "

Commonwealth v. Monumental Properties, Inc., 459 Pa. 450, 467-68, 329 A.2d 812, 820-21 (1974) (holding Unfair Trade Practices and Consumer Protection Law applicable to residential leases.)

Moreover, prospective tenants today can have vastly inferior bargaining power compared with the landlord, as was recognized in *Reitmeyer v. Sprecher*, 431 Pa. 284, 243 A.2d 395 (1968). In *Reitmeyer* this Court stated:

> "Stark necessity very often forces a tenant into occupancy of premises far from desirable and in a defective state of repair. The acute housing shortage mandates that the average prospective tenant accede to the demands of the prospective landlord as to conditions of rental, which, under ordinary conditions with housing available, the average tenant would not and should not accept.

> No longer does the average prospective tenant occupy a free bargaining status and no longer do the average landlord-to-be and tenant-to-be negotiate a lease on an 'arm's length' basis."

Id. at 289-90, 243 A.2d at 398.

The Superior Court correctly observed that to join the trend toward an implied warranty of habitability would not be a complete and sudden break with the past, but would be the "next step in the law which has been developing in the Commonwealth for a number of years." 384 A.2d at 1239. Pennsylvania courts have held that a tenant's obligation to pay rent was mutually dependent on *express* covenants of a landlord to repair and that a material breach of the landlord's covenant to repair relieved a tenant from his obligation to pay rent. *McDanel v. Mack Realty Company*, 315 Pa. 174, 172 A. 97 (1934). In *Reitmeyer v. Sprecher, supra*, recognizing the contractual nature of modern leasing and the severe housing shortage resulting in unequal bargaining power, this Court adopted § 357 of the Restatement (Second) of Torts and imposed liability on a landlord who had breached a covenant to repair a dangerous condition on the premises, which breach resulted in injury to the tenant. In *Elderkin v. Gaster*, 447 Pa. 118, 288 A.2d 771 (1972), we abolished *caveat emptor* and adopted an implied warranty of habitability in sales of new homes to buyers by vendors/builders. In *Elderkin* we noted "*caveat emptor* developed when the buyer and seller were in an equal bargaining position and they could readily be expected to protect themselves in the deed. . . . 'The *caveat emptor* rule as applied to new houses is an anachronism patently out of harmony with modern home buying practices.' " *Id.* at 127-28, 288 A.2d at 776 (citations omitted).

In 1974, *Commonwealth v. Monumental Properties, Inc.*, *supra*, we held the Unfair Trade Practices and Consumer Protection Law, Act of December 17, 1968, P.L. 1224, §§ 1-9, 73 P.S. §§ 201-1 to 201-9 (1971), applicable to residential leases, primarily because of the functional, contractual view of modern leasing and the housing crises in the Commonwealth. *Id.* at 467, 474-77, 824, 329 A.2d at 820-21, 824. The inferior bargaining position of some tenants caused by the housing shortage made the protection of these consumer laws necessary. Similarly, consumers of goods have received the protections of the implied warranties of merchantability and fitness for a particular purpose since 1953. Uniform Commercial Code, Act of April 6, 1953 P.L. 3, §§ 2-314, 2-315, *as reenacted*, Act of October 2, 1959, P.L. 1023, § 2, 12A P.S. §§ 2-314, 2-315 (1970).

More recently we held that a lessee of commercial property is relieved from the obligation to pay rent when the leased premises are destroyed by fire. *Albert M. Greenfield & Co., Inc. v. Kolea*, 475 Pa. 351, 380 A.2d 758 (1977). This Court stated "In reaching a decision involving the landlord-tenant relationship, too often courts have relied on outdated common law property principles and presumptions and have refused to consider the factors necessary for an equitable and just conclusion. . . . Buildings are critical to the functioning of modern society. When the parties bargain for the use of a building, the soil beneath is generally of little consequence. Our laws should develop to reflect these changes." *Id.* at 356-57, 380 A.2d at 760.

Given the foregoing considerations and authority, we affirm the Superior Court's holding that a lease is in the nature of a contract and is to be controlled by principles of contract law. The covenants and warranties in the lease are mutually dependent; the tenant's obligation to pay rent and the landlord's obligation imposed by the implied warranty of habitability to provide and maintain habitable premises are, therefore, dependent and a material breach of one of these obligations will relieve the obligation of the other so long as the breach continues.

II. ADOPTION OF IMPLIED WARRANTY OF HABITABILITY: A PROPER JUDICIAL FUNCTION

Appellant does not argue that an implied warranty of habitability does not comport with current understanding of the landlord-tenant relationship. In light of the overwhelming authority in favor of the warrant, he would be hard pressed to do so. Rather, the thrust of appellant's argument is that the establishment of an implied warranty of habitability is the setting of social policy, which is a function of the legislature. Specifically, appellant maintains that, because the legislature has acted in the field via the Rent Withholding Act, Act of January 24, 1966, P.L. 1534, *as amended*, 35 P.S. § 1700-1 (1977), the courts are prohibited from further development of common law solutions to landlord-tenant/habitability problems. We cannot accept this position.

The Rent Withholding Act (hereinafter the Act) provides:

> "Notwithstanding any other provision of law, or of any agreement, whether oral or in writing, whenever the Department of Licenses and Inspections of any city of the first class, or the Department of Public Safety of any city of the second class, second class A, or third class as the case may be, or any Public Health Department of any such city, or of the county in which such city is located, certifies a dwelling as unfit for human habitation, the duty of any tenant of such dwelling to pay, and the right of the landlord to collect rent shall be suspended without affecting any other terms or conditions of the landlord-tenant relationship, until the dwelling is certified as fit for human habitation or until the tenancy is terminated for any reason other than nonpayment of rent. During any period when the duty to pay rent is suspended, and the tenant continues to occupy the dwelling, the rent withheld shall be deposited by the tenant in an escrow account in a bank or trust company approved by the city or county as the case may be and shall be paid to the landlord when the dwelling is certified as fit for human habitation at any time within six months from the date on which the dwelling was certified as unfit for human habitation. If, at the end of six months after the certification of a dwelling as unfit for human habitation, such dwelling has not been certified as fit for human habitation, any moneys deposited in escrow on account of continued occupancy shall be payable to the depositor, except that any funds deposited in escrow may be used, for the purpose of making such dwelling fit for human habitation and for the payment of utility services for which the landlord is obligated but which he refuses or is unable to pay. No tenant shall be evicted for any reason whatsoever while rent is deposited in escrow."

Initially we note the Act is applicable only to cities of the first three classes and so is, by its terms, not applicable to the case at bar. Nevertheless, we must consider appellant's contention that, by acting *at all*, the legislature has precluded the judiciary from common law development in the landlord-tenant/habitability area.

The Act does not purport to be the exclusive tenant remedy for unsavory housing, nor does it attempt to replace or alter certain limited and already existing tenant remedies such as constructive eviction. *Kelly v. Miller,* 249 Pa. 314, 94 A. 1055 (1915). The Act's silence as to constructive eviction could not be construed, without more, as a legislative abolition of that doctrine. Neither can mere enactment of the Rent Withholding Act signal a legislative intent to remove from the courts the authority to fashion new remedies where appropriate in the landlord-tenant field.

Caveat emptor was a creature of the common law. *Elderkin v. Gastner, supra* at 123, 288 A.2d at 774. Courts have a duty "to reappraise old doctrines in the light of the facts and values of contemporary life—particularly old common law doctrines which the courts themselves have created and developed." *Javins v. First National Realty Corp., supra* 138 U.S. App. D.C. at 372, 373, 428 F.2d, 1074 at 1074, quoted in *Albert M. Greenfield & Co., Inc. v. Kolea, supra* at 357, 380 A.2d at 760. And when a rule has been duly tested by experience and found inconsistent with the sense of justice or the social welfare there should be little hesitation in "frank avowal and full abandonment." Cardozo, *The Nature of the Judicial Process,* 150-51 (1921), cited in *Griffith v. United Airlines, Inc.,* 416 Pa. 1, 23, 203 A.2d 796, 806 (1964). We have followed these principles recently in several decisions which are clearly founded on a realization of, and adaption of the law to correspond to, changing social policy. *Ayala v. Philadelphia Board of Education,* 453 Pa. 584, 305 A.2d 877 (1973) (governmental immunity abolished) and *Flagiello v. Pennsylvania Hospital,* 417 Pa. 486, 208 A.2d 193 (1965) (immunity for charitable institutions abolished).

In reappraising antiquated laws, it is entirely proper to seek guidance from policies underlying related legislation.

> "[c]ourts, in assessing the continued vitality of precedents, rules and doctrines of the past, may give weight to the policies reflected in more recent, widespread legislation, though the statutes do not apply—treating the total body of the statutory law in the manner endorsed long ago by Mr. Justice Stone 'as both a declaration and a source of law, and as premise for legal reasoning' (*The Common Law in the United States,* 50 Harv. L. Rev. 4, 13 [1976])." Introduction to Restatement (Second) of Property, Landlord and Tenant.

The purpose of the Act is to restore substandard housing to a reasonable level of habitability as swiftly as possible and to deter landlords from allowing their property to deteriorate into a condition unfit for habitation. *Newland v. Newland,* 26 Pa. Cmwlth. 519, 364 A.2d 988 (1976) and *Palmer v. Allegheny County Health Department,* 21 Pa. Cmwlth. 246, 345 A.2d 317 (1975). The adoption of the implied warranty of habitability is consistent with this policy.

Appellate courts of other jurisdictions have considered and rejected the argument that a state's rent withholding act or other statutory remedies precluded judicial adoption of the implied warranty of habitability. In *Boston Housing v. Hemingway*, 363 Mass. 184, 293 N.E.2d 831 (1973), the Massachusetts Supreme Court reviewed the overwhelming support from other jurisdictions which have judicially sanctioned the implied warranty and stated "All of these decisions are predicated on the implied assumption that remedial legislation designed to promote safe and sanitary housing does not preclude the courts from fashioning new common law rights and remedies to facilitate the policy of safe and sanitary housing embodied in the withholding statutes." *Id.* at 293 N.E.2d 841. That court further reasoned that failure to adopt the warranty of habitability would render that state's statutory law and common law conceptually and functionally inconsistent. *See also Green v. Superior Court*, 10 Cal. 3d 616, 111 Cal. Rptr. 704, 517 P.2d 1168 (1974) (state statute authorizing tenants to repair defective conditions and deduct expenses from rent held not exclusive remedy and not preclusive of judicial adoption of common law implied warranty of habitability) and *Jack Springs, Inc. v. Little*, 50 Ill. 2d 351, 280 N.E.2d 208 (1972) (rent withholding statute not exclusive remedy and not preclusive of judicial adoption of common law implied warranty of habitability); *cf. Blackwell v. Del Bosco, Colo.*, 558 P.2d 563 (1976) (lone appellate decision deferring adoption of implied warranty of habitability to legislature, although not predicated on existing statutory tenant rights and remedies). We conclude, therefore, that the Rent Withholding Act is not the exclusive tenant remedy for a landlord's failure to maintain the leased premises in a habitable state nor does it preclude judicial development of common law landlord and tenant obligations, rights and remedies. To the contrary, the Act supports the adoption of the implied warranty of habitability.

III. BREACH OF THE IMPLIED WARRANTY OF HABITABILITY

Appellant also asserts that the Superior Court erred by failing to establish definite standards by which habitability can be measured and breach of the warranty ascertained. We disagree—the parameters of the warranty were adequately defined by the Superior Court.

"The implied warranty is designed to insure that a landlord will provide facilities and services vital to the life, health, and safety of the tenant and to the use of the premises for residential purposes. *King v. Moorehead*, at 495 S.W.2d 75." *Pugh v. Holmes*, 384 A.2d at 1240. This warranty is applicable both at the beginning of the lease and throughout its duration. *Id.* citing *Old Town Development Co. v. Langford*, 349 N.E.2d 744, 764 (Ind. App. 1976) and *Mease v. Fox*, 200 N.W.2d 791, 796 (Iowa 1972).

In order to constitute a breach of the warranty the defect must be of a nature and kind which will prevent the use of the dwelling for its intended purpose to provide premises fit for habitation by its dwellers. At a minimum, this means the premises must be safe and sanitary—of course, there is no obligation on the part of the landlord to supply a perfect or aesthetically pleasing dwelling. *Pugh v. Holmes*, 384 A.2d at 1240. "Materiality of the breach is a question of fact to be decided by the trier of fact on a case-by-case basis." *Id.* Several factors (not exclusive) are listed by the Superior Court as considerations in determining materiality, including the existence of housing code violations and the nature, seriousness and duration of the defect. *Id.*

We believe these standards fully capable of guiding the fact finder in his determination of materiality of the breach. Further, these standards are flexible enough to allow the gradual development of the habitability doctrine in the best common law tradition. This finds support in *Elderkin v. Gaster, supra,* wherein we declined to establish rigid standards for determining habitability and its breach in the builder/vendor-vendee context and, instead, defined habitability in terms of "contemporary community standards" and breach of the warranty as whether the defect prevented the use of the dwelling for the purposes intended—habitation. 447 Pa. at 128, 288 A.2d at 777. In that case, we held that lack of a potable water supply to the home prevented its use as habitation and, accordingly, found the implied warranty of habitability to have been breached.

Additionally, we agree with the Superior Court that, to assert a breach of the implied warranty of habitability, a tenant must prove he or she gave notice to the landlord of the defect or condition, that he (the landlord) had a reasonable opportunity to make the necessary repairs, and that he failed to do so. 384 A.2d at 1241.

Appellant would require that a determination of breach of the implied warranty be dependent upon proof of violations of the local housing codes. We decline to accept this argument as it would unnecessarily restrict the determination of breach. The Supreme Court of Massachusetts was asked to define their implied warranty of habitability by reference to a housing code of statewide applicability, but declined to do so. In *Boston Housing Authority v. Hemingway*, 293 N.E.2d 831 (Mass. 1973) that court stated:

> "The State Sanitary Code minimum standards of fitness for human habitation and any relevant local health regulations provide the trial court with the threshold requirements that all housing must meet. Proof of any violation of these regulations would usually constitute compelling evidence that the apartment was not in habitable condition, regardless of whether the evidence was sufficient proof of a constructive

eviction under our old case law. However, the protection afforded by the implied warranty or [sic] habitability does not necessarily coincide with the Code's requirements. There may be instances where conditions not covered by the Code regulations render the apartment uninhabitable. Although we have eliminated the defense of constructive eviction in favor of a warranty of habitability defense, a fact situation, which would have demonstrated a constructive eviction, would now be sufficient proof of a material breach of the warranty of habitability, regardless of whether a sanitary code violation existed or not. 293 N.E.2d at 844, n.16."

Other courts have likewise concluded that the existence of housing code violations is only one of several evidentiary considerations that enter into the materiality of the breach issue. E.g., *Foisy v. Wyman*, 83 Wash. 2d 22, 515 P.2d 160 (1973); *King v. Moorehead*, 495 S.W.2d 65 (Mo. App. 1973); *Mease v. Fox*, 200 N.W.2d 791 (Iowa 1972). This reasoning is even more persuasive in Pennsylvania where there is no statewide housing code and where many municipalities have not promulgated local housing regulations.

In this case, appellee alleged ten specific defective conditions including a leaky roof, lack of hot water, leaking toilet and pipes, cockroach infestation and hazardous floors and steps. If proven on remand, these conditions would substantially prevent the use of the premises as a habitable dwelling place and could justify a finding by the trier of fact that a breach of the implied warranty of habitability had occurred.

IV. REMEDIES FOR BREACH OF IMPLIED WARRANTY OF HABITABILITY

As the adoption today of the implied warranty of habitability creates new legal rights and obligations, it is essential for this Court to outline and clarify some of the available remedies and the manner in which these remedies are to be implemented. The tenant may vacate the premises where the landlord materially breaches the implied warranty of habitability—we have held analogously where the landlord materially breaches express covenants to repair or to maintain the leasehold in a habitable state. See *McDanel v. Mack Realty Co., supra*, 315 Pa. at 174, 172 A. 97. Surrender of possession by the tenant would terminate his obligation to pay rent under the lease. *Lemle v. Breeden*, 51 Haw. 426, 462 P.2d 470 (1969) *Murray, On Contracts—A Revision of Grismore on Contracts, § 183, Mutual Performances in Leases The Implied Warranty of Habitability* (1974) (hereinafter *Murray*).

Where the tenant remains in possession, and the landlord sues for possession for unpaid rent, the implied warranty of habitability may be asserted as a defense. Virtually all courts addressing the issue of breach of this warranty as a defense concur with this view. See *e.g.*, cases cited by the Superior

Court at 384 A.2d 1240 and *Rome v. Walker*, 38 Mich. App. 458, 196 N.W.2d 850 (1972); *Fritz v. Warthen*, 298 Minn. 54, 213 N.W.2d 339 (1973); see Restatement (Second) of Property, Landlord and Tenant, § 11.1 (Rent Abatement). If the landlord totally breached the implied warranty of habitability, the tenant's obligation to pay rent would be abated in full—the action for possession would fail because there would be no unpaid rent. *Pugh v. Holmes, supra*, 384 A.2d at 1241, *citing Javins v. First National Realty Corp., supra*, 138 U.S. App. D.C. at 380-81, 428 F.2d 1082-83. If the landlord had not breached the warranty at all, no part of the tenant's obligation to pay rent would be abated and the landlord would be entitled to a judgment for possession and for unpaid rent. *Id.* If there had been a partial breach of the warranty, the obligation to pay rent would be abated in part only. In such case, a judgment for possession must be denied if the tenant agrees to pay that portion of the rent not abated; if the tenant refuses to pay the partial rent due, a judgment granting possession would be ordered. *Id.*

Appellant urges that the failure of the Superior Court to require a method of escrowing unpaid rent monies is "the most glaring defect" in the Superior Court's decision below. This Court is in favor of an escrow procedure, but is not inclined to make such procedure mandatory. Rather, the decision whether a tenant should deposit all or some of the unpaid rents into escrow should lie in the sound discretion of the trial judge or magistrate. The tenant may retain his rent, subject to the court's discretionary power to order him, following a hearing on the petition of the landlord or tenant, to deposit all or some of the rent with the court or a receiver appointed by the court. This is the approach taken by a majority of the courts which permit the tenant to withhold rent pending the outcome of litigation in which the defense of the implied warranty of habitability is asserted. Restatement (Second) of Property, Landlord and Tenant § 11.3, Reporter's note 2 (1970) *citing, e.g., Javins v. First National Realty Corp., supra* and *Hinson v. Delis*, 26 Cal. App. 3d 62, 102 Cal. Rptr. 661 (1972). Factors to be considered include the seriousness and duration of the alleged defects, and the likelihood that the tenant will be able to successfully demonstrate the breach of warranty. *Id.*

Also at issue in this case is the availability of the "repair and deduct" remedy. Appellee, after allegedly giving notice to the landlord and a reasonable opportunity to repair, repaired a broken door lock and deducted $6.00 from her rent for the month of May, 1975. We have held that, where a landlord fails to perform a lease covenant, the tenant may perform it at his own expense (if reasonable) and deduct the cost of his performance from the amount of rent due and payable. *McDanel v. Mack Realty Co., supra*, 315 Pa. at 177, 172 A. 97 (landlord failed to perform covenant to supply heat—tenant could have provided heat and deducted reasonable costs from rent). Similarly, the repair and deduct remedy is appropriate for breaches of the implied warranty of habitability. This remedy has been approved in other jurisdictions, *Marini v. Ireland*, 56 N.J. 130, 265 A.2d 526 (1970); *Garcia v. Freeland Realty Co.*, 63 Misc. 2d 937, 314 N.Y.S.2d 215 (1970) and by the Restatement (Second) of Property, Landlord and Tenant § 11.2. Section 11.2 provides "[i]f a tenant is entitled to apply his rent to eliminate the landlord's default, the tenant, after proper notice to the landlord, may deduct from his rent reasonable costs incurred in eliminating the default." "Proper notice" in this instance is one that describes the default and specifies what steps will be taken by the tenant to correct it if the landlord has not eliminated the defective condition within a reasonable time. *See* Comment a. to § 11.2. The use of the repair and deduct remedy is not, of course, unlimited. Repairs must be reasonably priced and cannot exceed the amount of the rent available to apply against the cost, i.e. the amount of rent owed for the term of the lease. *Merilh v. Pan American Films*, 200 So. 2d 398 (La. App. 1967). See comment c. to § 11.2. Further the tenant runs the risk of an adverse court finding on the necessity of the repairs—if the court finds that the repairs were not needed to render the premises habitable, the court must find the rent deduction unreasonable. In such event, the landlord could obtain a judgment for the amount of rent deducted. Or if the repairs were needed but the cost was excessive, the landlord could recover the difference between the actual cost and what would have been the reasonable cost of repairs.

Appellant also asserted a counterclaim for $25.00 for repairs allegedly made at various times to the heating system, the bathroom floor and to replace a broken window pane. In principle, we see little difference between the counterclaim for repairs and the "repair and deduct" remedy. The counterclaim can be utilized to recover damages from already paid rents based upon expenses incurred in making repairs of defective conditions after failure of the landlord to repair within a reasonable time following proper notice. See *Marini v. Ireland, supra* and *Garcia v. Freeland Realty Co., supra, Pines v. Perssion*, 14 Wis. 2d 590, 111 N.W.2d 409 (1961). The limitations applicable to the repair and deduct remedy are applicable here as well—the cost of the repairs must be reasonable and the maximum amount which the tenant may expend is the amount of rent owed for the term of the lease. However the counterclaim is not available where the tenant has not paid his rent for the period in which the repairs are made and the cost of the repairs do not exceed the rent owed for that period. In that case, there are no damages as the tenant has already been compensated for the cost of repairs by not paying rent.

Finally, since the lease is a contract, other traditional contract remedies such as specific performance are available to enforce the implied warranty of habitability. *Javins, supra* 138 U.S. App. D.C. at 380, at 428 F.2d 1082, n.61; *see* Uniform Residential Landlord and Tenant Act § 4.101(b) (1972) *and* Blumberg and Robbins, *Beyond URLTA: A Program for Achieving Real Tenant Goals*, 11 Harv. Civ. Rts. Civ. Lib. L. Rev. 1 (1976). As with other contracts, however, specific performance is an equitable remedy not available as a matter of course but only in unique situations. 11 S. Williston, *Contracts* § 1418A (3d ed. 1968); *Murray, supra* at § 220.

V. MEASURE OF RENT ABATED

The Superior Court held, where the tenant claims the breach of warranty of habitability as a defense or counterclaim "the monthly rent past and future (until the dwelling is returned to a habitable state) may be reduced by the difference between the agreed upon rent and the fair rental value of the apartment in its present condition." It is urged that this Court adopt the "percentage reduction of use" method of calculating damages for breach of the implied warranty (This method would reduce the amount of rent owed by a percentage equal to the percentage by which the use of the premises has been decreased by the breach of warranty.) rather than the "fair rental value" approach suggested by the Superior Court. We hold that the "percentage reduction in use" method is the correct manner of determining the amount by which the obligation to pay rent is abated.

The "fair market value" approach suffers from two drawbacks. The first is that it assumes there is a *fair* market for the defective premises. This assumption is questionable given the housing crises which exists today. *Reitmeyer v. Sprecher, supra* 431 Pa. at 289-90, 243 A.2d at 398 (1968). Because of the housing shortage, "Premises which, under normal circumstances, would be completely unattractive for rental are now, by necessity, at a premium." *Id.* at 290, 243 A.2d at 398. As one author phrased it "it seems questionable whether in asserting damages in this situation cognizance should be taken of a 'fair' market value of noncomplying housing—such a market could be regarded as an illegal 'black market' existing only by violation of law." Note, 84 Harv. L. Rev. 729, 737 (1971).

The second flaw is a practical one. The determination of the fair market value of the defective dwelling would in all probability require some type of market survey, statistical evidence, or expert testimony from realtors or appraisers familiar with the local rental market. *See* Moskovitz, *"The Implied Warranty of Habitability: A New Doctrine Raising New Issues*: 62 Calif. L. Rev. 1444, 1467-68 (1974). "The cost of obtaining such evidence or testimony would simply be prohibitive to many litigants, especially low-income tenants." *Id.*

One court which initially adopted a "fair market value" approach in computing the amount of rent to be abated, *McKenna v. Begin*, 3 Mass. App. 168, 325 N.E.2d 587 (1975) (*McKenna I*), rejected that approach following appeal from the trial court on remand, and opted for the "percentage reduction in use" formula, *McKenna v. Begin*, 362 N.E.2d 548 (Mass. App. 1977) (*McKenna II*), in order to fashion a measure of damages "which more closely reflects the actual injury suffered by [the tenant]." 362 N.E.2d 552. Under this approach, the rent is to be abated "by a percentage reflecting the diminution the value of the use and enjoyment of leased premises by reason of the existence of defects which gave rise to the breach of habitability." *Id.* citing *Green v. Superior Court, supra, Academy Spires, Inc. v. Brown*, 111 N.J. Super. 477, 268 A.2d 556 (1970) and *Morbeth Realty Corp. v. Rosenshine*, 67 Misc. 2d 325, 323 N.Y.S.2d 363 (N.Y. Cir. Ct. 1971).

This method of evaluation better achieves the goal of returning the injured party (the tenant) to the position he would have been in if performance had been rendered as warranted. Corbin, *Contracts* § 992 (1964); *Murray, supra* at § 220. The tenant bargains for habitable premises and the rental price reflects the value placed on those premises by the parties. Therefore, where the premises are rendered uninhabitable, in whole or in part, the contract price (fixed by the lease) is to be reduced by the percentage which reflects the diminution in use for the intended purpose. Another advantage of the percentage reduction method is that the need for expert testimony is greatly reduced as the determination in "percentage of reduction in use" of a residential dwelling is a matter within the capabilities of the layman.

Finally, there should be no doubt that recovery will not be precluded simply because there is some uncertainty as to the precise amount of damages incurred. It is well established that mere uncertainty as to the amount of damages will not bar recovery where it is clear that damages were the certain result of the defendant's conduct. *Academy Spires, Inc., supra*, 111 N.J. Super. at 486, 268 A.2d 556. McCormick, *Damages* § 27, p. 101 (1935). The basis for this rule is that the breaching party should not be allowed to shift the loss to the injured party when damages, even if uncertain in amount, were certainly the responsibility of the party in breach. *Story Parchment Company v. Paterson Paper Company*, 282 U.S. 555, 563, 51 S. Ct. 248, 75 L. Ed. 544 (1931). As noted by the Supreme Court of California, damages in this case "do not differ significantly from a host of analogous situations, in both contract and tort law, in which damages cannot be computed with complete certainty." *Green v. Superior Court, supra*, 10 Cal. 3d at 638, 111 Cal. Rptr. at 719, 517 P.2d at 1183.

Accordingly, on remand, if breach of the implied warranty of habitability is proven, the trial court is to apply the "percentage reduction in use" formula to determine the percentage by which the use and enjoyment of the premises had been diminished.

For the foregoing reasons, we overrule all cases inconsistent with this opinion, affirm the order of the Superior Court with the aforementioned modifications, and remand to the Court of Common Pleas of Franklin County for proceedings consonant with this opinion.

GLICKMAN REAL ESTATE DEVELOPMENT, Appellee,
v.
Richard KORF, David Notkin, Robert Fitzgerald & Robert Linett, All Jointly and Severally Liable, Appellants.
Superior Court of Pennsylvania.
446 A.2d 300 (Pa. Super. Ct. 1982)

[Some footnotes may have been omitted.]

CIRILLO, Judge:

This is an appeal from an Order of the Court of Common Pleas of Allegheny County, whereby judgment in the amount of $804.00 was entered for the appellee, landlord.

The landlord filed a Complaint in Assumpsit, alleging that the appellants, tenants, breached their lease of April 24, 1978. The landlord claimed damages of $2490.00. The tenants filed an Answer and Counterclaim, alleging that the landlord failed to maintain the premises in habitable condition. The tenants sought damages of $1863.00, plus costs, interest, punitive damages and attorneys' fees. On September 7, 1979, following a hearing before a Board of Arbitrators, the tenants were awarded the sum of $800.00. The landlord appealed this award to the Court of Common Pleas. On July 15, 1980, this case was tried before the Honorable Robert A. Doyle, sitting without a jury. Judge Doyle found for the landlord in the amount of $804.00. Following an untimely appeal and remand, the tenants filed *Nunc Pro Tunc* Exceptions alleging, *inter alia*, that the verdict was illegal and against the weight of the evidence. After argument before a court en banc, on February 14, 1981, the Exceptions were dismissed, and this appeal followed.

The tenants allege, on appeal, that the findings of the trial court, in favor of the landlord, were against the weight of the evidence and contrary to the law.

In April, 1978, after having inspected the premises located at 5303 Beeler Street, Pittsburgh, Pennsylvania, the tenants entered into a fifteen month lease agreement with the landlord beginning June 1, 1978. The total rent was $6210.00, payable in installments of $415.00 per month, with a $15.00 rebate for timely payments. The tenants were also required to give the landlord a security deposit of $500.00. At the time the agreement was executed, the tenants incorporated into the lease their request that the thermostat on the stove and the gas space heaters in the bedrooms be repaired.

Throughout the term of the lease, the tenants made several other requests for repairs to the premises. In November, 1978, the Allegheny County Health Department made an inspection of the premises. Under department regulations, violations totaling 20 points renders a dwelling unfit for human habitation. Their inspection noted violations totaling 33 points and on November 21, 1978, the landlord was given notice that the premises were considered unfit for human habitation. The tenants were admitted into a rent withholding program and beginning on December 1, 1979, they made payments into an escrow account with the Mellon Bank.

By mid-December, 1978, the landlord had installed a new central heating system and had made numerous other repairs. In February, 1979, the county paid to the landlord the tenants' rent held in escrow. However, at an inspection which took place on February 21, 1979, new defects were found and the tenants were again entitled to begin rent withholding, starting on March 1, 1979. The tenants did not make these subsequent payments into escrow, rather, they stopped paying any rent whatsoever. The lower court found that the total repairs made by the landlord, in a residence which he bought for $22,500.00, amounted to over $8000.00 and included the installation of new electrical wiring, plumbing, a roof and a bathroom. The lower court also found that all of the matters noted by the Allegheny County Health Department on re-inspection were abated prior to the time that the tenants vacated the premises on May 31, 1979.

While it is true that an appellate court is not bound by a trial court's finding of fact which is flagrantly contrary to the evidence, we do not find such an abuse by the court below in this instance.

The Pennsylvania Supreme Court, in the case of *Pugh v. Holmes*, 486 Pa. 272, 405 A.2d 897 (1979), held that the doctrine of caveat emptor is no longer applicable to residential leases, but instead, all residential leases contain an implied warranty of habitability. The Court went on to say that at a minimum, the implied warranty of habitability means that the premises must be safe and sanitary; however, there is no obligation on the part of the landlord to supply a perfect or aesthetically pleasing dwelling. *Id.* at 289, 405 A.2d 897. To be a breach of the implied warranty of habitability, the defect must be of a kind and nature which prevents the use of the dwelling for its intended purpose to provide premises fit for habitation. *Id.* at 289, 405 A.2d 897. To establish a breach of the warranty of habitability, the defect must be of a kind and nature which prevents the use of the dwelling for its intended purpose to provide premises fit for habitation. *Id.* at 289, 405 A.2d 897. To establish a breach of the warranty of habitability, a tenant must prove that he or she gave notice to the landlord of the defect or condition, that the landlord had a reasonable opportunity to make the necessary repairs and that the landlord failed to do so. *Id.* at 290, 405 A.2d 897.

In this case, the tenants gave notice to the landlord of several defects in the leased premises. This was an old dwelling being leased to the tenants and the condition of the building was reflected in the moderate rent charged by the landlord. We find that the landlord made the necessary repairs to maintain the premises in a habitable condition and did so within a reasonable time. Specifically, the tenants claim that there was no heat on the second and third floors until the middle of December, 1978. The landlord had offered to either repair the broken space heaters, which could have been done promptly, or to put in a new central heating system, which would take a longer time to install. The tenants opted for the new heating system. In light of the time necessary to put in an entirely new heating system, as well as the availability of workmen to do the job, the delay in restoring heat to the premises was not unreasonable.

After an inspection of the premises, the Allegheny County Health Department gave notice to the landlord on November 21, 1978 that the premises were unfit for human habitation. Under the Rent Withholding Act, the tenants were entitled to pay rent into escrow if they wished to remain on the premises. The right of a tenant to pay rent into escrow under the Rent Withholding Act is a temporary measure to compel the owner to make the property fit for human habitation under the penalty of losing his rent for six months or having his property condemned as unsafe and unfit. *Klein v. Allegheny County Health Department*, 441 Pa. 1, 269 A.2d 647 (1969); *Newland v. Newland*, 26 Pa. Cmwlth. 519, 364 A.2d 988 (1976). Starting in December, 1978, the tenants made rent payments into escrow. By February, 1979 the County Health Department determined that the premises were fit for habitation and awarded the rent paid into escrow to the landlord. Later in February, 1979, after discovering new violations on the premises, the County Health Department again allowed the tenants to pay rent into escrow, thus starting anew the six-month withholding period provided for in the Rent Withholding Act.[1] The tenants, however, did not make these subsequent rent payments to the escrow account or to the landlord, even though they remained on the property until May 31, 1979. The Rent Withholding Act expressly states that "[d]uring any period when the duty to pay rent is suspended, and the tenant continues to occupy the dwelling, the rent withheld shall be deposited by the tenant into an escrow account . . ." This language makes it clear that a tenant may in no event remain in possession of premises determined to be "unfit for human habitation" without paying the required rent to the escrowee. *DePaul v. Kauffman*, 441 Pa. 386, 272 A.2d 500 (1971). Consequently the tenants clearly breached their obligation to make rental payments under the lease agreement.

Accordingly, we affirm the JUDGMENT of the court below.

---

[1] *Klein v. Allegheny County Health Department, supra*, interpreted the Rent Withholding Act to provide for as many six month withholding periods as are necessary until a dwelling is certified as fit for habitation. Thus, in the present case, after paying the funds in the escrow account to the landlord and then finding additional defects which made the premises unfit for habitation, the Health Department properly started a new six month period during which the tenants could pay rent into escrow.

Samuel FELD and Peggy Feld,
v.
John W. MERRIAM
Supreme Court of Pennsylvania
485 A.2d 742 (Pa. 1984)

[Some footnotes may have been omitted.]

OPINION

McDERMOTT, Justice.

Peggy and Samuel Feld were tenants in the large Cedarbrook Apartment complex, consisting of 150 acres and 1,000 apartments housed in three high rise buildings. For an extra rental fee the apartments are serviced by parking garages adjacent to the apartment buildings. On the evening of June 27, 1975, about 9:00 P.M., the Felds, returning from a social engagement, drove as usual to their allotted space in the parking garage. Then began the events that brings before us the question of a landlord's liability for the criminal acts of unknown third persons. We are not unaware of the social, economic and philosophic dimensions of the questions posed.

While the Felds were parking their car, they were set upon by three armed felons. At gun point, accompanied by two of the felons, they were forced to the back seat of their car. Followed by the third felon in an "old, blue broken down car," they were driven past the guard on duty at the gate, out into the night, to the ferine disposal of three criminals. To clear the car for their main criminal purpose, the felons started to force Mr. Feld into the trunk of the car. Mrs. Feld pled her husband's illness and to save him, offered herself for her husband's life. Thereupon the felons released Mr. Feld on a deserted street corner and drove Mrs. Feld to the lonely precincts of a country club. There is no need to recite the horrors that brave and loving woman suffered. Suffice it to say they extorted a terrible penalty from her defenseless innocence.

The Felds brought suit against the appellees, owners of the complex, alleging a duty of protection owed by the landlord, the breach of the duty, and injuries resulting therefrom. Named as defendants were John Merriam, Thomas Wynne, Inc., the Cedarbrook Joint Venture, and Globe Security Systems, Inc. Following an eight-day trial, the jury returned a plaintiff's verdict and a judgment totaling six million dollars against Merriam, Thomas Wynne, Inc., and the Cedarbrook Joint Venture. The jury absolved Globe Security of any liability. Common Pleas, per the Honorable Jacob Kalish, denied motions for a new trial, judgment N.O.V. and remittitur.

On appeal the Superior Court affirmed the lower court, with the exception that the award of punitive damages to Samuel Feld was reduced by one half. Both Cedarbrook and Mr. Feld filed petitions for allowance of appeal, which were granted. We now reverse.

I

The threshold question is whether a landlord has any duty to protect tenants from the foreseeable criminal acts of third persons, and if so, under what circumstances. Well settled law holds landlords to a duty to protect tenants from injury rising out of their negligent failure to maintain their premises in a safe condition. *See Smith v. M.P.W. Realty Co. Inc.*, 423 Pa. 536, 225 A.2d 227 (1967). *Lopez v. Gukenback*, 391 Pa. 359, 137 A.2d 771 (1958). That rule of law is addressed to their failure of reasonable care, a failure of care caused by their own negligence, a condition, the cause of which was either known or knowable by reasonable precaution. The criminal acts of a third person belong to a different category and can bear no analogy to the unfixed radiator, unlighted steps, falling ceiling, or the other myriad possibilities of one's personal negligence. To render one liable for the deliberate criminal acts of unknown third persons can only be a judicial rule for given limited circumstances.

The closest analogy is the duty of owners of land who hold their property open to the public for business purposes. *See Leary v. Lawrence Sales Corp.*, 442 Pa. 389, 275 A.2d 32 (1971). They are subject to liability for the accidental, negligent or intentionally harmful acts of third persons, as are common carriers, innkeepers and other owners of places of public resort. Section 344, comment (f) of the Restatement (Second) of Torts, adopted by this court in *Moran v. Valley Forge Drive-In Theater, Inc.*, 431 Pa. 432, 246 A.2d 875 (1968), requires that they take reasonable precaution against that which might be reasonably anticipated. The reason is clear; places to which the general public are invited might indeed anticipate, either from common experience or known fact, that places of general public resort are also places where what men can do, they might. One who invites all may reasonably expect that all might not behave, and bears responsibility for injury that follows the absence of reasonable precaution against that common expectation. The common areas of an apartment complex are not open to the public, nor are the general public expected or invited to gather there for other purposes than to visit tenants.

Tenants in a huge apartment complex, or a tenant on the second floor of a house converted to an apartment, do not live where the world is invited to come. Absent agreement, the landlord cannot be expected to protect them against the wiles of felonry any more than the society can always protect them upon the common streets and highways leading to their residence or indeed in their home itself.

An apartment building is not a place of public resort where one who profits from the very public it invites must bear what losses that public may create. It is of its nature private and only for those specifically invited. The criminal can be expected anywhere, any time, and has been a risk of life for a long time. He can be expected in the village, monastery and the castle keep.

In the present case the Superior Court departed from the traditional rule that a person cannot be liable for the criminal acts of third parties when it held "that in all areas of the leasehold, particularly in the area under his control, the landlord is under a duty to provide adequate security to protect his tenants from the foreseeable criminal actions of third persons." *Feld v. Merriam, et al.*, 314 Pa. Super. 414, 427, 461 A.2d 225, 231 (1983).

The Superior Court viewed the imposition of this new duty as merely an extension of the landlord's existing duty to maintain the common areas to be free from the risk of harm caused by physical defects. However, in so holding that court failed to recognize the crucial distinction between the risk of injury from a physical defect in the property, and the risk from the criminal act of a third person. In the former situation the landlord has effectively perpetuated the risk of injury by refusing to correct a known and verifiable defect. On the other hand, the risk of injury from the criminal acts of third persons arises not from the conduct of the landlord but from the conduct of an unpredictable independent agent. To impose a general duty in the latter case would effectively require landlords to be insurers of their tenants safety: a burden which could never be completely met given the unfortunate realities of modern society.

Our analysis however does not stop here, for although there is a general rule against holding a person liable for the criminal conduct of another absent a preexisting duty, there is also an exception to that rule, i.e., where a party assumes a duty, whether gratuitously or for consideration, and so negligently performs that duty that another suffers damage. *Pascarella v. Kelley*, 378 Pa. 18, 105 A.2d 70 (1954). See *Rehder v. Miller*, 35 Pa. Super. 344 (1908).

This exception has been capsulized in Section 323 of the Restatement (Second) of Torts, which provides:

> **§ 323. Negligent Performance of Undertaking to Render Services**
>
> One who undertakes, gratuitously or for consideration, to render services to another which he should recognize as necessary for the protection of the other's person or things, is subject to liability to the other for physical harm resulting from his failure to exercise reasonable care to perform his undertaking, if
>
> (a) his failure to exercise such care increases the risk of such harm, or

(b) the harm is suffered because of the other's reliance upon the undertaking.

Previously we adopted this section as an accurate statement of the law in this Commonwealth. *Gradel v. Inouye*, 491 Pa. 534, 421 A.2d 674 (1980); *DeJesus v. Liberty Mutual Insurance Co.*, 423 Pa. 198, 223 A.2d 849 (1966).

Expounding on the proper application of Section 323 the drafters indicated that

> [T]his Section applies to any undertaking to render services to another which the defendant should recognize as necessary for the protection of the other's person or things. It applies whether the harm to other or his things results from the defendant's negligent conduct in the manner of his performance of the undertaking, or from his failure to exercise reasonable care to complete it or to protect the other when he discontinues it.

Comment (a) § 323 Restatement (Second) of Torts. These comments are particularly relevant in a situation such as the present where a landlord undertakes to secure the areas within his control and possibly fosters a reliance by his tenants on his efforts.

Absent therefore an agreement wherein the landlord offers or voluntarily proffers a program, we find no general duty of a landlord to protect tenants against criminal intrusion. However, a landlord may, as indicated, incur a duty voluntarily or by specific agreement if to attract or keep tenants he provides a program of security. A program of security is not the usual and normal precautions that a reasonable home owner would employ to protect his property. It is, as in the case before us, an extra precaution, such as personnel specifically charged to patrol and protect the premises. Personnel charged with such protection may be expected to perform their duties with the usual reasonable care required under standard tort law for ordinary negligence. When a landlord by agreement or voluntarily offers a program to protect the premises, he must perform the task in a reasonable manner and where a harm follows a reasonable expectation of that harm, he is liable. The duty is one of reasonable care under the circumstances. It is not the duty of an insurer and a landlord is not liable unless his failure is the proximate cause of the harm.

A tenant may rely upon a program of protection only within the reasonable expectations of the program. He cannot expect that a landlord will defeat all the designs of felonry. He can expect, however, that the program will be reasonably pursued and not fail due to its negligent exercise. If a landlord offers protection during certain periods of the day or night a tenant can only expect reasonable protection during the periods offered. If, however, during the periods offered, the protection fails by a lack of reasonable care, and that lack is the proximate cause of the injury, the landlord can be held liable. A tenant may not expect more than is offered. If, for instance, one guard is offered, he cannot expect the same quality and type of protection that two guards would have provided, nor may he expect the benefits that a different program might have provided. He can only expect the benefits reasonably expected of the program as offered and that that program will be conducted with reasonable care.

In the present case the trial judge, when instructing the jury, was placed in the unenviable position of predicting how we would resolve this difficult question. Although we commend him on his endeavor, we are constrained to reverse the verdict, since the jury instructions which were given imposed upon the landlord a duty greater than that which we today hold to have existed.

II

Cedarbrook also argues that the evidence of negligence failed to support the jury's punitive damages award, and that the introduction of evidence concerning appellant's considerable wealth was so prejudicial as to taint the jury's compensatory damages award. In light of our grant of a new trial on the issue of liability, the issues regarding damages are moot. However, in anticipation of the same issues arising at retrial, we will address them.

A. Punitive Damages

This Court has embraced the guideline of Section 908(2) of the Restatement (Second) of Torts regarding the imposition of punitive damages: "Punitive damages may be awarded for conduct that is outrageous, because of the defendant's evil motive or his reckless indifference to the rights of others." *See Chambers v. Montgomery*, 411 Pa. 339, 192 A.2d 355 (1963). Punitive damages must be based on conduct which is " 'malicious,' 'wanton,' 'reckless,' willful,' or 'oppressive' . . ." *Id.* at 344-45, 192 A.2d at 358, *citing Hughes v. Babcock*, 349 Pa. 475, 37 A.2d 551 (1944).

Further, one must look to "the act itself together with all the circumstances including the motive of the wrongdoers and the relations between the parties . . ." *Chambers v. Montgomery, supra*, 411 Pa. at 345, 192 A.2d at 358. *See also Pittsburgh Outdoor Advertising Co. v. Virginia Manor Apartments Inc.*, 436 Pa. 350, 260 A.2d 801 (1970).

The state of mind of the actor is vital. The act, or the failure to act, must be intentional, reckless or malicious.

The danger here was not an easily perceptible one. While a jury might find that Cedarbrook failed to reasonably perform the duty it undertook, the evidence presented was insufficient to support a finding that they acted with the state of mind necessary to impose punitive damages. While the record indicates that the security systems might have been inadequate under the circumstances, there was no evidence of an evil motive or a reckless indifference to the safety of the tenants.

In deciding whether to impose punitive damages a court should not look to the third party's criminal conduct, which in this case was truly outrageous; a court should not look at the end result, which in this case also was outrageous; rather, the court should examine the actor's conduct. As a matter of law, on this record, a jury could not conclude that appellants' conduct was outrageous. Thus the trial court erred in submitting this issue to the jury.

B. Compensatory Damages

As a result of the trial judge's determination that the issue of punitive damages was a jury question, evidence was allowed concerning appellant's considerable wealth. Cedarbrook argues that this evidence had a prejudicial effect on the jury and thus the compensatory damage award of three million dollars should be vacated. We agree.

A jury may not consider a defendant's wealth in setting compensatory damages. It is "improper, irrelevant, prejudicial, and clearly beyond the legally established boundaries." *Trimble v. Merloe*, 413 Pa. 408, 410, 197 A.2d 457, 458 (1964). However, a defendant's wealth is relevant to set punitive damages. *Arye v. Dickstein*, 337 Pa. 471, 474, 12 A.2d 19, 20 (1940).

As we stated earlier, the outrageous conduct necessary to send the issue of punitive damages to the jury was not present in this case. Here, evidence showed that appellant's financial net worth was $40 million. The trial court resisted Cedarbrook's effort to try the issue of punitive damages separately, and refused to deliver Cedarbrook's suggested instruction that consideration of appellant's wealth was not relevant in fixing the amount of compensatory damages. Rather, a broader cautionary instruction was delivered which was inadequate to overcome any prejudice which might have resulted from the introduction of evidence regarding appellant's wealth.

Where the issue of punitive damages incorrectly goes to the jury, and where the trial court fails to sufficiently warn the jury that they may not look to a defendant's wealth in setting compensatory damages, evidence of the wealth of a defendant may improperly prejudice the jury and a compensatory damage award should be set aside.

For the reasons stated above, this case must be remanded to the lower court for a new trial, in accordance with the standards stated.

Lisa REIDER, Appellant,

v.

Frank A. MARTIN, John Brzyski and J.T.B. Associates, a partnership, Appellees.

Superior Court of Pennsylvania

519 A.2d 507 (Pa. Super. Ct. 1987)

[Some footnotes may have been omitted.]

DEL SOLE, Judge:

During the academic year of 1982-1983, Appellant, a Lehigh University senior, rented one of three apartments located at 28 East Third Street, Bethlehem, Pennsylvania, owned by Appellees. On or about February 4, 1983, Appellant was raped, beaten, and robbed in the stairway outside her apartment. The perpetrator, one Melvin Dean Smith, had entered the building through an unsecured front door and followed Appellant up the stairs as she entered her apartment building.[1]

Appellant commenced this civil action for damages, alleging that Appellees were negligent in failing to supply the apartment building with an operative front door lock. On numerous occasions prior to the February 4, 1983 incident, Appellees were informed by Appellant and other tenants that the front door lock of the building was inoperative and requested that the lock be repaired or replaced. In response, Appellees notified their tenants that the necessary repairs and/or replacements would be performed. Despite these repeated assurances, the lock remained in disrepair up to the night of the rape and assault. Appellant contends that, as a result of Appellees' negligence, she sustained severe psychological injuries, humiliation, pain and suffering, loss of income and deprivation of life's pleasures.

A jury trial commenced on April 22, 1985 in which Appellant was ordered to first present her case on liability. Two days of testimony were presented on Appellees' notice of the defective lock, their assurances that they would repair the lock, and their failure to do so. Following this testimony, Appellees presented before the trial court a Motion for Compulsory Nonsuit. Thereafter, the nonsuit was granted based upon the court's interpretation of the case of *Feld v. Merriam*, 506 Pa. 383, 485 A.2d 742 (1984). In *Feld*, our Supreme Court held that no general duty of a landlord exists to protect tenants against criminal intrusion; however, if a landlord agrees, or voluntarily proffers protection in order to attract or keep tenants, the landlord may incur such a duty. *Id.* at 485 A.2d 747.

Appellant filed a Motion for Post-Trial Relief on May 2, 1985 which requested the trial court to remove the nonsuit.

---

[1] Melvin Dean Smith was tried and convicted of rape, assault and armed robbery, and was sentenced to a prison term of 12-24 years.

Appellant's Motion for Post-Trial Relief was subsequently denied by Order of Court on January 13, 1986. This appeal follows.

Appellant advances before this Court two charges of error allegedly committed by the trial court. First, Appellant contends the trial judge improperly interpreted the applicability of *Feld v. Merriam, supra,* in relation to the facts of the instant case. Second, Appellant claims the trial judge abused his discretion in granting Appellees' various motions in limine.

Our scope of review for determining whether a compulsory nonsuit should have been granted is well established. A judgment of nonsuit may be entered only in clear cases and a plaintiff must be afforded the benefit of every fact and reasonable inference arising from the evidence. Likewise, all conflicts in the testimony must be resolved in the plaintiff's favor. *McNally v. Liebowitz,* 498 Pa. 163, 445 A.2d 716, 719 (1982). "Thus an order granting a nonsuit is proper only if the jury, viewing the evidence and all reasonable inferences arising from it, in the light most favorable to the plaintiff, could not reasonably conclude that the elements of the cause of action have been established." *Morena v. South Hills Health System,* 501 Pa. 634, 462 A.2d 680, 683 (1983) (citations omitted).

I. Application of *Feld v. Merriam*

Because this is the first time in which we are specifically called upon to interpret the impact of *Feld,* we shall synopsize both the procedural and substantive aspects of that case. The *Feld* case involved a married couple who were tenants in a large apartment complex owned by defendant-owners. One evening the Felds were parking their car in a garage adjacent to the apartment buildings when they were set upon by three armed felons. The felons forced the couple into a car, and, after releasing Mr. Feld on a deserted street corner, drove to the lonely precincts of a country club where they assaulted Mrs. Feld.

The Felds brought suit against the defendant-owners alleging a duty of protection owed by the landlord, the breach of such duty, and injuries resulting therefrom. Following an eight-day trial, the jury returned a verdict in favor of the Felds. The defendant-owners filed post-trial motions for a new trial, judgment n.o.v., and remittur, which were subsequently denied. On appeal, this court affirmed the trial court, with the exception that punitive damages awarded were reduced by one-half.

On review by our Supreme Court, it was noted that the issue presented in that case was one of first impression. The question addressed was "whether a landlord has any duty to protect tenants from the foreseeable criminal acts of third persons, and if so, under what circumstances." *Id.* at 485 A.2d 745. In arriving at its conclusions, the court noted a distinction between the risk of injury from a physical defect in the property, and the risk from the criminal act of a third person:

> In the former situation the landlord has effectively perpetuated the risk of injury by refusing to correct a known and verifiable defect. On the other hand, the risk of injury from the criminal acts of third persons arises not from the conduct of the landlord but from the conduct of an unpredictable independent agent. To impose a general duty in the latter case would effectively require landlords to be insurers of their tenants safety: a burden which could never be completely met given the unfortunate realities of modern society.

Id. at 485 A.2d 746.

The court, however, opined that this general rule is not without exception. Relying upon the Restatement (Second) of Torts § 323, the court stated that "where a party assumes a duty, whether gratuitously or for consideration, and so negligently performs that duty that another suffers damages," liability may be imposed.[2] *Ibid.*

The court next applied the newly-generated rule, and its exception, to the *Feld* circumstances and held that:

> [a]bsent therefore an agreement wherein the landlord offers or voluntarily proffers a program, we find no general duty of a landlord to protect tenants against criminal intrusion. However, a landlord may, as indicated, incur a duty voluntarily or by specific agreement if to attract or keep tenants he provides a program of security. A program of security is not the usual and normal precautions that a reasonable home owner would employ to protect his property. It is, as in the case before us, an extra precaution, such as personnel specifically charged to patrol and protect the premises.

Id. at 485 A.2d 747.

It is on this last excerpt of the *Feld* opinion which the trial judge based his decision to grant a compulsory nonsuit. By its opinion, the trial court found that no duty existed on the part of Appellees inasmuch as no "program of security," as defined in *Feld*, was promised:

> The installation of a front door lock is nothing more than a reasonable homeowner would do to protect his property. It

---

[2] § 323. Negligent Performance of Undertaking to Render Services.

One who undertakes, gratuitously or for consideration, to render services to another which he should recognize as necessary for the protection of the other's person or things, is subject to liability to the other for physical harm resulting from his failure to exercise reasonable care to perform his undertaking, if

(a) his failure to exercise such care increases the risk of such harm, or

(b) the harm is suffered because of the other's reliance upon the undertaking.

is not an extra precaution. . . . The Supreme Court did not intend to impose a duty on a landlord who negligently undertakes the performance of normal security precautions. The essence of the *Feld* case is that the landlord must somehow hold himself out as a provider of security to a prospective tenant through a program providing extra precautions. Only when a landlord holds himself out as such, and negligently fails in his undertaking, can he be found liable for criminal acts inflicted upon his tenants. (Trial Court Opinion, p. 5).

The trial court thereby concluded that Appellant merely alleged an unenforceable promise by Appellees to repair the front door, instead of an agreement between the parties calling for a "program of security."

We disagree and find the trial court rendered a too narrow interpretation of the phrase "program of security." The trial court mistakenly found Appellant had the burden of proving that Appellees held themselves out as "providers of security." Likewise, the trial court held that a landlord's duty does not rise to such status unless he/she undertakes extra precautions, "such as video monitors, security guards, or an alarm system." (Trial Court Opinion, p. 5). Although the Supreme Court commented that an *example* of an extra precaution would be "personnel specifically charged to patrol and protect the premises," it in no way indicated that all security systems must be of a complicated nature. Rather, the court recognized that a bona fide security systems could range from being the most rudimentary devices to being elaborate programs of safety:

> A tenant may rely upon a program of protection only within the reasonable expectations of the program. He can expect, however, that the program will be reasonably pursued and not fail due to its negligent exercise. . . . A tenant may not expect more than is offered. . . . He can only expect the benefits reasonably expected of the program as offered and that that program will be conducted with reasonable care.

Id. at 485 A.2d 747.

From our reading of *Feld*, we find that the touchstone in determining if a "program of security" exists is whether or not the program promises to provide an additional factor of safety. This is a *substantive* analysis. By comparison, the trial court's reasoning is awry insofar as it lends too much emphasis to the *form* of the security system and whether it involves hired security personnel or utilizes mechanical wizardry.

At first blush, a secured outside door seemingly does not amount to a "program of security." However, we find that the impact of safety resulting therefrom places this precaution squarely within the definition of a security program as enunciated by our Supreme Court. Initially we note that Appellees clearly had no preexisting duty to supply their tenants with a functional front door lock. Appellees, however, "assumed the duty" by consistently promising to remedy the situation, thereby fostering a possible "reliance by [their] tenants on [their] efforts." *Id.* at 485 A.2d 747. By agreeing to make the necessary repairs to the outside door, Appellees tacitly agreed to provide the tenants with a method by which they could have monitored those people who gained access to the interior of the apartment building. The locked front door would have been an assurance that those who knocked on the front door to gain ingress, and who were subsequently admitted, were indeed invited guests of the tenants.

Albeit there was no agreement to hire security personnel or to install an electronic alarm system, this does not detract from the fact that Appellees agreed to supply the additional protection of a locked exterior door which the locks installed on each apartment unit's door surely could not provide. It is evident that by failing to make the necessary adjustments to the lock, Appellees denied their tenants the greatly enhanced level of security that such an elementary undertaking would have provided.

In keeping within the mandates of *Feld*, we note that Appellant could only expect the same quality and type of protection that the second locked door would have provided and nothing more. However, Appellees did not supply these benefits which Appellant had a right to reasonably anticipate.

Accordingly, we hold the trial judge erred by granting Appellees' motion for compulsory nonsuit. Instead we find that the jury should have been allowed to determine whether Appellees undertook the duty to provide the locked door, whether Appellees breached this duty, and whether such failure was a substantial factor in bringing about the harm to Appellant.

Landlord/Tenant Vocabulary

(from *Pugh, Glickman, Feld,* and *Reider*)

Instructions: To better understand this material, be sure you know the definitions of the following terms. Be prepared to define these terms for your classmates, using the techniques described in "Defining/Explaining a Term or Concept." (pg. 14)

1. Month-to-month lease
2. Justice of the peace
3. Rent
4. Possession
5. Breach
6. Implied warranty of habitability
7. Set off
8. Counterclaim
9. Legal cause of action
10. Caveat emptor
11. Lease
12. Covenant
13. Conveyance
14. Obligation
15. Bargain
16. Arm's length (transaction)
17. Deed
18. Implied warranty of merchantability and fitness
19. Uniform Commercial Code (UCC)
20. Lessee
21. Warranty
22. Material breach
23. Escrow account
24. Constructive eviction
25. Specific performance
26. Equitable remedy
27. Fair rental value
28. To rent
29. To abate
30. To bargain
31. To preclude
32. Arbiter
33. Nunc pro tunc
34. Punitive damages
35. En banc
36. Rent Withholding Act
37. Liability
38. Leasehold
39. Compensatory damages
40. Felon
41. Motion for new trial
42. Remitter
43. Negligent
44. Foreseeable
45. Reasonable care
46. Proximate cause
47. Jury instructions
48. State of mind
49. Procedural posture
50. Sine qua non
51. Public policy
52. Concur
53. Compulsory nonsuit
54. Civil action
55. Testimony
56. Discretion
57. Motions in limine
58. Scope of review
59. Procedural
60. Substantive
61. Merits

✓ Negotiation Exercise

You have interviewed your client and have considered how the law applies to his or her case. Now, assume that the tenant has filed a complaint alleging damages for the assault the tenant suffered. Also assume that the landlord has counter-claimed for the unpaid rent. The court has set a date for trial but both clients would rather settle this dispute through negotiation.

Try to negotiate a settlement on behalf of your client. To prepare for this negotiation, you should review the landlord-tenant cases and read the following article on negotiation. Next, read the general negotiating information and the confidential information that follows. Only read your client's confidential information. Meet with any colleagues with whom you will be working and discuss your negotiation strategy. Next, you will meet with opposing counsel. Negotiate to reach a mutually agreeable settlement. When you have settled the dispute, draft your agreement. All parties to the negotiation should sign this agreement. Good luck.

Negotiation[1]

I. Introduction

Negotiation is a process intended to resolve disputes between contesting parties through discussion of facts, issues, and solutions.[2] Negotiation is a fundamental alternative dispute resolution ("ADR") method and its importance should never be underestimated. In most negotiations, the parties work to design solutions to their problems together without a neutral third party. Resolution through negotiation depends upon both parties' willingness to work together, make compromises, and reach an agreement.

II. Overview of Negotiation and Other Methods of Alternative Dispute Resolution[3]

ADR is a system of processes designed to assist parties in resolving their disputes economically and more quickly than the traditional court system. Its value lies in reducing the time, cost, and uncertainty of the civil justice system. There are many methods of ADR but they are not all appropriate for every dispute. An attorney must determine whether or not to use ADR and if so, which method is most appropriate. The three primary ADR methods are negotiation, mediation, and arbitration.

Negotiation is an ADR process intended to resolve disputes between contesting parties through meeting, discussing, and agreeing upon facts, issues, and solutions. The object of negotiation is the final disposition of differences between parties in a faster, less expensive, more expeditious, and perhaps less formal manner than is available in traditional judicial or administrative proceedings. The parties work by themselves to design solutions to their problems. Negotiation occurs in most other forms of dispute resolution, but in some cases it may be the only process available because the parties refuse to introduce an outside third party into their dispute. Resolution through negotiation depends upon both parties' desire to resolve their disputes quickly while compromising their positions

---

1   With special thanks to Michael J. Herzog for his help in preparing this text.

2   See ROGER FISHER & WILLIAM URY, GETTING TO YES (Bruce Patton ed., 2d ed. 1991), for further discussion of this form of ADR. *See also* WILLIAM URY, GETTING PAST NO (1993).

3   For more information about ADR, see 4 AM. JUR. 2d *Arbitration* §§ 8-13 (1995); EDWARD BRUNET & CHARLES B. CRAVER, ALTERNATIVE DISPUTE RESOLUTION: THE ADVOCATE'S PERSPECTIVE (1997); Richard Chernick, *Controlling the Process: The Scope of Arbitration, in* AMERICAN LAW INSTITUTE & AMERICAN BAR ASSOCIATION, ALI-ABA COURSE OF STUDY, ALTERNATIVE DISPUTE RESOLUTION (ADR): HOW TO USE IT TO YOUR ADVANTAGE! (1996); CHARLES B. CRAVER, EFFECTIVE LEGAL NEGOTIATE AND SETTLEMENT (1997); ROBERT M. SMITH, 2 ADR FOR FINANCIAL INSTITUTIONS, chs. 5-6 (1995); *ABCs of ADR: A Dispute Resolution Glossary*, ALTERNATIVES, Aug. 1992; Michael J. Herzog, *Arbitration Overview Memorandum*, FDIC Internal Memorandum (June 20, 1997) (on file with author).

---

to some extent. In those cases where the parties are unable to reach agreement, litigation often ensues.

Mediation is a private, voluntary process in which an impartial person, called a mediator, facilitates communication between the parties to promote a mutually agreeable settlement. The parties have the ability to select a mediator that has subject-matter expertise in the field of their dispute. During the process, the parties may present evidence, arguments, and interests similar to a trial. If a mutually-acceptable agreement is reached between the parties, the agreement is enforceable as a contract.

Arbitration is the most well known alternative dispute resolution process and is the ADR form with which most lawyers are familiar and comfortable because it is most like litigation. Arbitration is a process by which parties refer, usually voluntarily, their disputes to an arbitrator, often selected by the parties. Arbitration is attractive to disputants because parties have control over the time, place, procedures, and form of the award. Generally, arbitration can be categorized as binding, non-binding, or compulsory, and is often perceived to be a faster, more efficient means of dispute settlement than litigation.

Binding arbitration is a private adversarial process in which the disputing parties choose a neutral person, or a panel of three arbitrators, to hear their dispute and to render a final and binding decision or award. Binding arbitration awards are enforceable by courts and are not subject to judicial review. The process of non-binding arbitration is the same as binding arbitration except that the arbitrator's decision is only advisory. Compulsory arbitration is mandated by statute or rule, and is different from traditional arbitration in a number of ways. First, a judicial arbitrator's award is binding only if the parties make it binding. Otherwise, the parties have a right to a trial de novo. Also, parties to private arbitration limit the court's involvement to compelling arbitration or enforcing the award. In addition, unless otherwise provided, discovery in private arbitration is more limited, and evidentiary rules more relaxed, than in judicial arbitration.

III. Advantages of Using Negotiation as Opposed to Litigation

There are many reasons why parties believe negotiation is a more efficient means of dispute settlement than litigation. The perceived advantages of negotiation include reduced length of time for dispute resolution, reduced court congestion, cases settled earlier, increased involvement of parties, maintenance of privacy of the process, and a completely voluntary process. Most importantly, if an agreement is reached, it is enforceable as a contract.

A dispute processed through negotiation is often disposed of more quickly than if the parties had made their way through the court system to a final judgment. Negotiation tends to be a speedier process, in part, because negotiation is completely voluntary. Additionally, the parties control the proceedings. There is no third party facilitator and the process is informal and unstructured. The parties can negotiate as soon as they agree to engage in negotiation. In terms of time, a mutually acceptable settlement can be reached in less than an hour, as opposed to litigation which may take several years.

Another benefit is the privacy of the process. Taking the dispute out of the court-room and into the relative informality of negotiation may reduce hostility and confrontation between the parties. A negotiation hearing is not open to the pub-lic, and unless the result later becomes the subject of a court proceeding, it is not a matter of public record.

Additionally, if an agreement is reached, it is enforceable as a contract. Parties engaging in negotiation thus enjoy the benefit of reaching a binding agreement without stepping into a courtroom.

IV. Disadvantages of Using Negotiation as a Means of Dispute Resolution

Negotiation has some potential disadvantages. First, as a result of negotiation be-ing voluntary, one party cannot force another party to engage in the process. Con-sequently, the process may never begin if one party is hesitant to initiate negotiation. Second, negotiation may limit the parties' control over the outcome of the process. Since a third-party facilitator is not used, if the parties reach an impasse, the negotiation might never reach settlement. Third, in those cases where the parties are unable to reach agreement in solving their problems, litiga-tion often ensues. Fourth, negotiation alone might be considered a fairly weak form of dispute resolution, and might more be more valuable if coupled with an-other form of ADR.

V. Techniques for Negotiating

This section outlines techniques for conducting successful negotiations. These tips provide a logical and orderly approach to prepare for any negotiation ses-sion. Also, as you read through these tips, consider the following hypothetical: your client lives on the second floor of a luxury apartment complex in the center of Philadelphia. The door lock on your client's sliding glass balcony door breaks, and an unidentified assailant enters through the door and attacks the tenant. Can the landlord be held liable for the harm to your client?

1. Identify Issues

When identifying the issues, first, consider the legal issues. It is imperative to de-termine the underlying issue and any implications involved. For, example, in a landlord/tenant dispute, determine on what the underlying cause of action may be premised: negligence, respondeat superior, breach of fiduciary duty. Next, identify the factual issues. Was the landlord on notice due to his knowledge of the broken door lock? How many times did the landlord promise to call the lock-smith? Finally, identify the specific issues to your client and to the other party. Consider issues that are critical to your client. Also consider issues that are criti-cal to the other party.

2. Collect Information

Collect all information relevant to your client's position: how did the door lock break; which door lock required replacement; was the apartment on the first or second floor of the complex. In addition, gather information about the other party: how many times was the landlord notified of the broken lock; did the landlord contact the lock manufacturer. Consider the applicability of information gathered from other sources.

3. Identify Strengths and Weaknesses

Identify the strengths and weaknesses of your client's case. For instance, the fact that your client notified the landlord of the broken lock on three different occurrences is evidence that the landlord was on notice of the defect. If your client failed, however, to place a wooden dowel in the track of the door, your client's position may be weakened. When identifying your client's strengths and weaknesses, consider your client's alternatives to settlement. Is your client willing to take this case to a jury trial as opposed to settling out of court? Consider the implications if your client fails to reach a negotiated settlement. Is your client disclosing too much information during the negotiation so that the other party would rather go to trial?

Once you determine your client's strengths and weaknesses, identify the other party's strengths and weaknesses. What are the other party's alternatives to reaching settlement? Does the landlord have an interest in settling out of court to avoid negative publicity? What will happen if the other party fails to reach settlement? Does the landlord have any pressures to make sure this case is settled?

4. Determine Objectives for Negotiation

First, determine the goals for each negotiation session. Is the goal to settle the whole case now or is the goal to settle only part of the case? If there is more than one issue involved, your client may benefit by settling a particular issue during negotiation rather than risking a detrimental result in court. Is the goal of the negotiation to gather more information? Your client may use the negotiation to "test the waters" by identifying any unknown information, thereby determining the strength of the other party's position.

Next, determine the objectives of each party. What are your client's objectives? Is your client seeking monetary damages and/or looking to have the lock repaired? Is your client's objective to have the landlord publicly reprimanded in the hope of encouraging timely repairs in the future? After determining your client's objectives, consider the objectives for the other party. Is the landlord willing to take the case to trial in order to clear his name without having to admit any wrongdoing? Is the landlord setting precedent by taking the case to trial as opposed to settling out of court? Consider the public's interests. Does the public stand to benefit by having the case go to the jury?

Finally, determine the form of the agreement. What will an agreement look like (if there is one)? What provisions must be included in the agreement? For instance, a provision requiring the landlord to repair a broken lock within one day of notice might be suggested. Are there any provisions that your client wants excluded from the agreement? For example, your client may not want a provision mandating him or her to place a wooden dowel in the track of a sliding door in addition to securing the lock.

5. Evaluate Alternatives and Potential Outcomes

Is there a range (not necessarily a monetary range) where both parties might agree? Evaluate settlement alternatives available to your client and try to determine the other party's settlement range. As a result, a zone of agreement might be present in which the parties would be willing to reach agreement. Are there options that provide mutual benefit to both parties? For instance, both parties may be willing to save the expense and time of litigation and settle the case with negotiation.

Remember, you can always walk away from the negotiation without reaching an agreement. If the other party is unwilling to move from their demands, terminating the negotiation session might be in your client's best interest.

6. Clarify Client's Position

It is crucial to understand what your client wants to achieve from the negotiation. As an attorney, you represent your client and must be an advocate for his or her interests. Consider the minimum amount that your client is willing to accept from the other party. Determine the maximum your client is willing to pay. Remember, you have an ethical obligation to inform your client of any · settlement offers that the other party presents. In addition, it is imperative to define what your client must have. However, always remain cognizant of your client's position.

7. Estimate Other Party's Position

Before reaching the negotiation table, determine the other party's strongest argument. The landlord, for instance, might argue contributory negligence as a result of your client's failure to place to a wooden dowel in the track of the door. Anticipating the other party's position assists in preparing well reasoned counter-arguments. Also, estimate the other party's opening position. Will the other party make a reasonable opening offer or do you anticipate an inflated offer?

8. Develop Strategy

First, develop specific strategies and tactics with your client before the negotiation begins. Consider who is going to make the first offer. Next, decide the opening issue in a multi-issue case. You might decide to begin the negotiation with your strongest argument, move to a weaker position, and finish with your second best argument. On the other hand, you may decide to lead with your weakest argument and end with your strongest. There is no set formula for success. Your negotiation strategy varies depending upon the circumstances surrounding each session. Finally, establish your client's opening position. Are you planning to implement a hard strategy by using an inflated opening position, or will you employ a more subtle approach and begin with a more reasonable position?

Discuss with your client how to use any confidential information. Your client may not authorize you to disclose specific information. Make sure you understand the limits of your authority and make sure to never cross the line!

9. Prepare

Prepare thoroughly. Plan with your client. Begin preparing well before the negotiation so that you can accommodate your client's schedule.

Consider using a mock negotiation session in order to acquaint your client with the process. Try to replicate how the real negotiation session is going to take place. Contemplate using outsiders to play the other party.

10. Don't Rush

Do not have the misconception that a negotiation session will always result in a speedy resolution. Allow the negotiation to develop at a reasonable pace without rushing to reach a settlement. Be patient.

The negotiation may take abrupt turns. Be prepared in the event that you'll have to deviate from your original strategy. Be flexible, and keep an open mind. You may want to include the option of meeting again. Also, you may want to take a break so that the parties have time to think and reflect. Try not to reject ideas too quickly.

VII. Closing Remarks

To become an effective attorney, negotiation must be a part of your repertoire. Negotiation potentially offers numerous benefits. Your ethical obligation to inform your client of all forms of dispute resolution provides an excellent opportunity to introduce the process of negotiation. Strive to serve your clients well by making a concerted effort to improve your negotiating skills.

General Negotiating Information

Ms. Perez filed a complaint in negligence claiming damages of $2 million. Mr. Crusher has filed an answer denying responsibility for Ms. Perez's injuries. He has also filed a counter-claim for the unpaid rent for September and October, a total of $4000, plus interest. The trial is set for tomorrow, but the judge is furious that the parties have not yet reached a settlement.

1. Assume that the negotiation will take place in the office of defense counsel.

2. Each negotiating team should take ten minutes to review your strategy for this session. Then, each plaintiff team should proceed to the office of defense counsel. Defense counsel should hold up your team number so opposing counsel can find you.

3. Each team should negotiate in good faith to achieve a settlement.

4. Negotiating facilitators will be available if you have questions or need help continuing your negotiation.

5. Upon completing your negotiation, each team should submit your written proposed settlement agreement to your professor. Each attorney student should sign the settlement agreement.

6. Good luck.

Tenant's Confidential Information

Ms. Perez does not want to go to trial since she does not feel emotionally or financially able to cope with it. She is also worried that her failure to use the dowel could be a problem for her at trial. However, she is convinced that Crusher is responsible for her attack. She does not want you to reveal that she is unwilling to go to trial.

She believe that Crusher should compensate her for the items stolen from her apartment which include: a stereo worth $1000, a camera worth $500, and $500 in cash. She also feels she should be compensated for her physical and emotional injuries. Her medical expenses have so far reached $20,000 for the ambulance, emergency room, intensive care, specialists, and a one-week hospital stay. Ms. Perez belongs to a health maintenance organization (HMO), but is refusing to pay for some of the procedures.

Her doctors have said that she will require reconstructive surgery and months of physical therapy. Her doctors also say she is suffering from Post Traumatic Stress Disorder as a result of the attack. Therefore, she will require psychological counseling twice a week for the indefinite future.

She has taken a leave of absence from her job and is staying with her parents outside Philadelphia where she can receive constant attention. The doctors have indicted that she will not be able to return to work for several months.

Ms. Perez is willing to pay the rent in order to avoid being sued. She believes she should settle for $1 million since she is aware of a similar case in which the jury awarded $2 million. Nevertheless, she is willing to settle for $250,000 or less as long as she does not have to go to trial.

Landlord's Confidential Information

Mr. Crusher absolutely does not want to go to trial. He believes the publicity will be very bad for his business. Already several tenants have left The Atrium, and Crusher is having a difficult time finding new tenants. He has never had a problem renting apartments in the past so he is sure the incident is keeping people away.

He wants to settle, but he does not believe he is responsible for Ms. Perez's attack, especially since she forgot to use the dowel to secure the door. Furthermore, he wants Ms. Perez to pay the rent she owes for September and October. He might be willing to forget about the past-due rent as long as Ms. Perez will acknowledge that her premises were habitable.

He is extremely worried that anything he pays her towards her physical or emotional injuries will be construed as an admission of liability. He does have insurance, and the insurance company has authorized him to pay $500,000 if necessary to settle the claim. However, the insurance company is not willing to pay more. Crusher's personal assets total $10 million. He is ready to pay $500,000, the full amount of the policy, but he believes he should not have to pay more than $200,000. Above all, he definitely does not want to go to trial.

Negotiation Vocabulary

Instructions: To better understand this material, be sure you know the definitions of the following terms. Be prepared to define these terms for your classmates, using the techniques described in "Defining/Explaining a Term or Concept" (pg. 14).

1. Alternative	34. Pointless
2. Approach	35. Preconceived
3. Assess	36. Predetermined
4. Atmosphere	37. To presuppose
5. Attitude	38. Priority
6. Brushed aside	39. To reject
7. Concern	40. To sound out
8. To confront	41. To strive
9. Counterpart	42. Tightrope act
10. Deadlocked	43. To wear someone else
11. To document	44. To affront
12. Eventual	45. Applicability
13. To exploit	46. To alter
14. To expose	47. To assume
15. Good chemistry	48. Contradictory
16. Imprecise	49. Disconcerting
17. Inconsistency	50. Drawback
18. Initial	51. Etiquette
19. Interrogation	52. Failure
20. Leeway	53. To fish
21. Likelihood	54. To impact
22. Major	55. To infer
23. To misrepresent facts	56. Irreversible
24. Must	57. Prolonged
25. Mutual	58. Punctuality
26. Mutual gain	59. To stress
27. Mutually beneficial	60. Unanticipated
28. Optimal	61. Unbearable
29. Option	62. To achieve
30. Outset	63. To agree
31. Perception	64. Agreement
32. Outset	65. Balance of power
33. Perception	66. Bargaining power

67. Bottom line
68. Compensation
69. Concession
70. Condition
71. To confirm
72. To convince/persuade
73. To demand
74. Demands
75. Final offer
76. Flexibility
77. Flexible
78. Force majeure
79. Hardball, softball
80. To have connections
81. Inflexibility
82. Inflexible
83. Negotiations
84. Objective
85. Proposal
86. Counterproposal
87. To shy away
88. Trait
89. Strategy

90. Trading card/tradable
91. Ultimatum
92. Unyielding
93. Arbitration
94. Collective bargaining
95. Mediation
96. Musts
97. Benefits
98. To gravitate
99. Impact
100. Inquiry
101. Preliminary
102. To push for
103. Diversionary
104. Inadequate
105. Leverage
106. To turn a blind eye
107. Vulnerable
108. Adamant
109. Consensus decision making
110. Deference
111. Home court advantage

✓ Exercise: Negotiation Terms

Please decide which negotiation term best completes each sentence.

Negotiation Terms:

bargaining power	impasse
compromise	must have
disclosure	mutually beneficial

Sentences:

1. Mary _____ a public apology from her employer or else she will not make a deal.

2. Plaintiff passenger's ideal settlement figure was one million dollars, while defendant driver's ideal settlement figure was five hundred thousand dollars. Thus, the actual settlement figure of seven hundred fifty thousand dollars represented a _____.

3. The divorce settlement between Mr. and Mrs. Black is _____, since the terms of the agreement fall within each party's settlement range.

4. In order to avoid the expense and time associated with litigation, John had hoped to settle his breach of contract claim against Elizabeth. Following several intensive days of negotiating, the parties recognized that they had reached an _____, since John refused to accept anything less than $60,000 and Elizabeth refused to offer anything higher than $40,000.

5. Before the commencement of negotiations, Susan had determined that her client's settlement _____ included obtaining sole custody of her child and receiving a reasonable monthly child support.

6. Use of an inflated opening position evidenced plaintiff's pursuit of a _____ against her opponent.

7. The fact that plaintiff had a high likelihood of recovering damages at trial considerably strengthened his _____ over defendant during the negotiation process.

8. Defendant's attorney employed diversionary techniques as a means of avoiding _____ of his client's confidential information.

✓ Matching Exercise

Please read the terms and definitions listed below. In the blank next to each numbered term, please write the letter of the definition that best describes the term.

Vocabulary Term List

1. To resolve _____

2. Limits of authority _____

3. Settlement _____

4. Alternative _____

5. To exploit _____

6. To estimate _____

7. Optimal _____

8. To sound out _____

9. Priority _____

10. Soft ball _____

11. Perception _____

12. To affront _____

13. Tightrope act _____

14. Concession _____

15. Bottom line _____

16. Ultimatum _____

17. Arbitration _____

18. Hard ball _____

19. Mediation _____

20. To accept _____

Definition List

A. To ask questions to get an idea as to a person's feelings about a certain issue.

B. The furthest a party is willing to go to reach an agreement; minimum terms that a party would accept given his or her alternatives to a settlement.

C. To insult.

D. Process by which parties refer their disputes to an impartial third person, selected by them to render a decision. (need better definition).

E. To judge or determine generally but carefully; calculate approximately.

F. An inflexible approach to negotiation; an approach used to force the opposition to accept conditions.

G. A final proposal or terms whose rejection will result in the breaking off of negotiations.

H. To cause a person to decide. To reach as a decision or intention; determine.

I. To take what is offered or given; to receive favorably; approve.

J. To use for one's benefit or profit (this can be done at the expense of someone else).

K. A private, voluntary process in which an impartial person called a neutral facilitates communication between the parties to promote a mutually agreeable settlement.

L. A flexible approach to negotiation; an approach used to reach an acceptable compromise.

M. The best possible.

N. The way someone sees or regards something.

O. A difficult balance.

P. Power restrictions or boundaries; constraints on party's ability to negotiate.

Q. How you rate something in terms of its importance.

R. Act or process of adjusting or determining; an adjustment between persons concerning their dealings or difficulties; an agreement by which parties having disputed matters between them reach or ascertain what is coming from one to the other . . . . Agreement to terminate or forestall all or part of a lawsuit.

S. Other possible solution.

T. Compromise made by one side in order to reach an agreement.

SECTION III
Independent Writing and Research

CHAPTER 9—WORKING INDEPENDENTLY

At some point in your stay in the United States you will probably want to pursue independent research or will be asked to pursue independent research as part of a course. This last section is designed to help you pursue this research.

Writing a Seminar Paper

You will probably be asked to write a seminar paper during your law school studies. These papers are scholarly works which are typically between 15 and 50 pages and are to be of publishable quality which means they should be throughly researched, demonstrate creativity, and be well-written. You will probably also be asked to give a presentation about your seminar paper.

Seminar papers look much like the student written papers in law reviews and law journals. These student submissions are referred to as note papers or comments and often appear toward the end of the law review. These papers often focus on a weakness in the law, either a weakness in a specific law, a policy, or doctrine, or in the implementation. They might also focus on a circuit split where, for example, courts in different jurisdictions disagree about how to resolve a similar dispute. Some student written papers are critiques of a recent judicial opinion or are a prediction of how an upcoming case will be decided. Sometimes, they examine a current social problem, an emerging legal issue or a trend in the law. These papers, ideally, examine some problem or weakness in the law and propose a solution to this problem.

Seminar papers tend to adhere to a fairly standard format. They include approximately five subparts: an introduction which introduces the topic and indicates the structure of the paper, a detailed discussion of a legal situation or background, a detailed discussion of the problem or a detailed discussion of the facts and holding of the case which is being critiqued, a proposed solution and possibly an evaluation of that solution or a critique of the judicial reasoning in the case, and a conclusion. When you select a topic for your seminar paper, try to find a timely topic, something which is current. Try to find a topic which has not been written upon too often. The best seminar topics actually contribute to or influence the field of law in some manner.

A well-written seminar paper has several attributes or features.[1] The thesis is clear. The topic and the author's position is explicitly stated at the beginning. The author discretely and definitively defines the issue discussed in the paper. The problem is neither too broad nor too narrow. The author defines a research niche which fills a gap in the field. The relevance of the problem or issue is clearly stated. Readers understand why this is an important issue, why they should care about it, and how this research paper contributes to the field.

The author proposes an original solution which is supported by data. The solution is evaluated, weaknesses are addressed, and alternatives considered. The author also acknowledges when a source detracts from or weakens the proposed solution or argument. The author addresses the weaknesses of his or her argument and addresses alternative view points. The author approaches the problem or question from a number of different angles to gain a better understanding of the issues involved.

The author has thoroughly researched the topic and relies predominately on primary authority. The paper identifies and interprets evidence that is relevant to the author's position, and the author acknowledges contributions by others in the field. The author accurately interprets the sources used to support his or her view. The interpretation is accurate if the authority the author uses to support actually does support the idea. For example, if readers look to the cited authority, the readers would find the information the author suggests in his or her paper. The author takes a strong position and reaches conclusions which are supported by appropriate authority. The author explains how he or she reached conclusions and explains any underlying assumptions he or she is making. The author acknowledges when a source supports a position by using a proper citation to authority. For instance, the author places a footnote or endnote reference according the Bluebook, which is a uniform citation system.[2]

The argument is easy to follow because the author uses roadmaps to guide the reader through the paper. For example, the author states the framework of the paper in the introduction and organizes the paper according to this framework. Moreover, the readers understand the relationship between ideas; the author introduces the purpose of each section at the beginning of each section and recapitulates the main idea and tells the reader where the next section is going at the end of each section. The paper contains headings and subheadings which organizes main ideas and supporting ideas into small, easier to read parts. The author writes clearly, uses proper grammar, and eliminates all typographical errors.

Examine several student written articles in a law review or law journal. Identify a few which you think are well-written. See if your criteria is similar to the criteria

---

1   For more information on writing a seminar paper, see Eugene Volokh, *Writing a Student Article*, 48 J. LEGAL EDUC. 247 (1998).

2   THE BLUEBOOK (16th ed. 1996).

above. List any other criteria you used to evaluate these papers. Finally see if you can identify specific devices the authors have used to fulfill this criteria.

✓ *Exercise:*

Research potential seminar topics. Write up a summary of your proposed topic, prepare an outline for the potential seminar paper, and a list of sources you could use to write the paper. On the basis of this research, you should prepare a 5-10 minute presentation discussing your proposed topic. Explain the topic, describe why you think this topic is interesting, why others should find it important, and how you propose to carry out your research. Remember, do not write the seminar paper, only present a proposal. You may choose any topic but keep in mind that seminar papers are problem/solution-type papers so you should look for a current legal problem or issue and consider potential solutions. You should begin to re-search and evaluate existing solutions as well as proposing original ideas. Your presentation should discuss the preliminary results of your research and the re-search strategy you plan to pursue. In selecting a topic, consider an area of law you are interested in and actually may want to write about during the aca-demic year. Also, you should carry out a preemption check to make sure you can potentially contribute something to this area. If several people have written on your proposed topic, determine how your original approach can add to this subject area.

Analyzing and Researching a Legal Problem

To begin looking for a potential research topic or to investigate any research problem, keep the following suggestions in mind.

1. Begin your research problem by trying to **categorize the factual information** involved. You will need to consider who or what is involved in the problem. Examine what the parties did and why they acted in a particular manner. Look at whether their motives or state of mind is evident. Consider what important events occurred and when they happened and where. Be sure you understand the sequence of events and if there is anything significant about the location of the events.

2. Next try to **categorize the legal information**. Consider what legal theory applies to this situation. Consider what relief the parties are seeking and what defenses are available. Note the procedural history of the case.

3. **Brainstorm**. What terms might describe the situation. How might the legal system refer to this sort of situation. Try to think of a few terms, and then expand your list by adding broader or narrower terms, related terms, or synonyms and antonyms. You may want to look in a dictionary to see if you can generate more terms. Legal encyclopedias such as Corpus Juris Secundum (CJS) or annotations like American Law Reports (ALR) may also help you refine terms and will help you locate primary authority.

4. Prepare a **research strategy**. Keep track of what you plan to do and what you have done in a research notebook. Consider what information you have and consider how you can gather more. For example, if you are looking for more cases, shepardize the cases you have and look to other jurisdictions to see how the situation is handled or if they provide any clues to how your jurisdiction will handle the situation. Look for law review articles on related topics. These articles may help you locate cases or develop a theory. You can find law review articles by using Infotrac. You can find further articles by shepardizing.

5. **Evaluate your sources**. Consider the type of information or "authority" you have. Primary authority is produced by legislators, courts, or government agencies with the official capacity to make or determine law. Primary authority includes case decisions, statutes, constitutions, court rules, and regulations. Secondary authority is a descriptive summary of what a person or group believes the law to be. Secondary authority includes treatises, law reviews, books, restatements, commentaries. While primary authority may be mandatory or persuasive, secondary authority is always persuasive authority which means that a court is not bound to obey it. Primary authority which is mandatory, however, binds a court. This means that a court must obey the information. For example, a trial court must obey the decision of an appellate court in its jurisdiction, so an appellate court decision would be mandatory authority to that trial court. A decision by an appellate court in another jurisdiction would be primary persuasive authority.

6. Periodically **review** your facts and legal situation and reevaluate search terms so that you may refine your issue and fill in any gaps in your analysis and research.

✓ Exercise: Internet Scavenger Hunt

An important component of research in the United States is Internet research. Increasingly, professionals from all walks of life are using the Internet to fulfill day-to-day tasks. Lawyers are no exception. The Internet is full of legal information. By knowing where to search, the American lawyer can save himself or herself hours of research time. The following exercise is designed to help familiarize you with some of the legal information available to lawyers online.

Start at the University of Pittsburgh School of Law's Library web site, **http://www.law.pitt.edu/library/librhome.htm**, unless otherwise noted. In order to answer the following questions, use the internet links provided on this page. GOOD LUCK!

1. Describe the functions of the National Aeronautics and Space Administration, as codified in the Code of Federal Regulations? Which federal regulation gives you the answer?

2. Using JURIST, find the title of an article dealing with the Second Amendment of the U.S. Constitution. Include the author's name and the name of the scholarly journal in which the article was published.

3. What are the act and bill numbers of the 1998 Pennsylvania statute amending the Judicial Code to allow arraignments by audio-video communication? When was the bill signed by the Pennsylvania Senate? When was it signed by the Pennsylvania House of Representatives? When did the Governor receive the bill for approval? When did he approve the bill?

4. What is the street address of the U.S. Court of International Trade? How many judges sit on the court?

5. Go to the home page of the American Bar Association (http://www.abanet.org). Who would you contact for a lawyer referral in Pittsburgh, Pennsylvania? What is the phone number you would call?

6. What is the total cost of obtaining a marriage license in Allegheny County, Pennsylvania?

7. What is the name of the 1999 Cornell Law School International Law Journal Symposium? What is the volume and number of the corresponding symposium issue of the Cornell International Law Journal?

8. What are the functions of the Office of the Solicitor General? Within the U.S. Department of Justice, which positions are above the Solicitor General?

9. How much time does the U.S. Supreme Court allow each side to present oral arguments? Which Supreme Court rule tells you this?

10. Using LEXIS or Westlaw, find a case where the facts include the United States arresting and prosecuting the skin of an afghan urial (a type of sheep). Where does this case constitute binding precedent?

Legal Citation Form

The *Bluebook*

The *Bluebook* is the most commonly used citation or referencing system in law. It was created by the *Harvard Law Review* in an effort to standardize the method of referencing legal authority in legal documents and scholarly articles. The following provides a brief summary of the basic *Bluebook* rules. They should not replace the *Bluebook*.

Basic Citation Forms[3]

There are four main types of citations: 1) cases; 2) statutes; 3) periodicals; 4) books.

Case Citation (Rule 10)

Long Form

The standard long form case citation should be used the first time a case is cited. The long form case citation contains:

- An introductory signal, if necessary. (Rule 1.2). Signals indicate the purpose for which the citation is made and the degree of support the citation gives.
- The name of the case, either italicized or underlined. (Rule 10.2) Use the names of both parties, if mentioned. Abbreviate where appropriate. (Table 6, Table 10)
- The volume and reporter where you can find the case. For state cases, you will generally cite to the regional reporters. For federal cases, you will cite to one of the federal reporters. For U.S. Supreme Court cases, you will generally cite to the United States reporter. (Rule 10.3, Table 1)
- The first page of the case. (Rule 10.3.2)
- The pinpoint cite (when appropriate), that is, the exact page within the opinion to which you want to direct the reader's attention. (Rule 3.3)
- In parentheses, the name of the court issuing the opinion and the year in which the opinion was issued. (Rules 10.4 & 10.5) BUT: In U.S. Supreme Court cases, do not name the court—only include the year of the opinion in parentheses.

---

3   References are to THE BLUEBOOK (16th ed. 1996).

Examples:

State court opinions with two (or more) named parties:

> *See Niederman v. Brodsky*, 261 A.2d 84, 90 (Pa. 1970).
> *See Rankin v. Southeastern Pa. Transp. Auth.*, 606 A.2d 536, 536 (Pa. Commw. Ct. 1992).

State court opinions with one named party:

> *See In the Interest of D.S.*, 622 A.2d 954, 95 8 (Pa. Super. Ct. 1993).

Federal court opinions:

> *See Dellums v. Bush*, 752 F. Supp. 1141, 1143 (D.D.C. 1990).
> *Filartiga v. Pena-Irala*, 630 F.2d 876, 881 (2d Cir. 1980).

U.S. Supreme Court opinions:

> *See California v. Hodari D.*, 499 U.S. 621, 624 (1991).

Short Form (Rule 10.9, Practitioners' Note 4)

This form of citation is appropriate only after the long form has been used previously. This cite consists of:

- The name of the first party (if the first party is the name of a government or other common litigant then use the name of the second party). (Rule 10.9(a))
- The volume number and reporter
- The word "at," plus the specific page to which you are citing

Examples:

See Niederman, 261 A.2d at 91.
See Rankin, 606 A.2d at 537.
See Dellums, 752 F. Supp. at 1144.
Filartiga, 630 F.2d at 881.
See Hodari D., 499 U.S. at 626. NOT: *California*, 499 U.S. at 626.

"Super Short" Form (Rule 10. 9, Practitioners' Note 4)

This form of citation is only appropriate where the complete long cite, short cite, or super short cite of the case appears as the immediately preceding citation. This cite consists of:

- The abbreviation "id.", either italicized or underlined.
- The word "at."
- The specific page reference.
- ✓ If the citation refers to the same page or pages as the preceding citation, id. does not require a page reference.

Examples:

See Niederman, 261 A.2d at 91.

See id. at 92.

See id.

Id. at 93.

Law review footnote form differs from the citation form for court documents and legal memoranda. Use this form for cases:

California v. Hodari D., 499 U.S. 621, 624 (1991).

Hodari D., 499 U.S. at 626.

Statute and Restatement Citation (Rule 12, Table 1)

Statute

The standard citation of a statute contains:

- An introductory signal, if necessary. (Rule 1.2)
- The number of the code title.
- The abbreviation for the code. (Rule 12.3)
- The statutory section number.
- The date and edition and/or supplement. (Rule 12.3.2)

✓ Federal Statutes are cited either to the United States Code (U.S.C.), which is preferred, or to the Statutes at Large (Stat.).

✓ When citing state statutes, refer to Table 1. Each state has its own statutory compilations.

Examples:

See 28 U.S.C. § 1331 (1976).

29 U.S.C. § 1016 (1982 & Supp. 1997).

See 35 Pa. Cons. Stat. Ann. § 1700-1 (West 1997).

Restatement of the Law (Rule 12.8.5)

When citing to a Restatement of the Law, include:

- An introductory signal, if necessary. (Rule 1.2)
- The name of the Restatement.
- The section number.
- The date the Restatement was released, in parentheses.
- Include the comment or reporter's note number, if necessary.

Examples:

Restatement (Second) of Torts § 323 (1965).

See Restatement (Third) of Foreign Relations Law § 464 cmt. i (1986).

Law Review Footnote form:

Restatement (Second) of Torts §323 (1965).

Periodicals (Rule 16)

Periodicals are divided into three categories: 1) consecutively paginated journals, such as most law reviews (16.2); 2) nonconsecutively paginated journals, such as most magazines (16.3); 3) newspapers (16.4).

Consecutively Paginated Journals

A cite for a consecutively paginated journal contains:

- An introductory signal, if necessary. (Rule 1.2)
- The full name of the author.
- The full title of the article, either italicized or underlined.
- The volume number.
- The periodical's name, in ordinary roman type. (Table 13, Table 10, Practitioners' note P.1)
- The first page of the article.
- The pinpoint cite, if appropriate.
- The year of publication, in parentheses.

Example:

Pamela Samuelson, *Good Legal Writing: Of Orwell and Window Panes*, 46 U. Pitt. L. Rev. 149, 155 (1984).

✓ For short form citation, use the author's last name, the word "supra" (italicized or underlined), the word "at," and the specific page number containing the material cited.

Example:

See Samuelson, *supra*, at 157.

✓ The "super short" form, *id.*, may also be used, when appropriate.

Law Review Form:

Pamela Samuelson, *Good Legal Writing: Of Orwell and Window Panes*, 46 U. PITT. L. REV. 149, 155 (1984).

Nonconsecutively Paginated Journals

A cite for a nonconsecutively paginated journal contains:

- An introductory signal, if necessary. (Rule 1.2)
- The full name of the author.
- The full title of the article, either italicized or underlined.
- The periodical's name, in ordinary roman type. (Table 13, Table 10. P.1)
- The date of issue as it appears on the cover of the periodical.
- The word "at."
- The first page of the article.
- The pinpoint cite, if appropriate.

Examples:

Mark Seal, *Diamonds Aren't Forever*, Vanity Fair, December 1999, at 248, 256.
See Caren Marcus, *The Domestic Disease*, Pittsburgh, April 2000, at 62, 64.

✓ The short form citation is the same as for consecutively paginated journals.

✓ The "super short" form, id., may also be used, when appropriate.

Law Review Form:

See Caren Marcus, *The Domestic Disease*, PITTSBURGH, April 2000, at 62, 64.

Newspapers

A cite for a newspaper article contains:

- An introductory signal, if necessary.
- The name of the author.
- The title of the article, either italicized or underlined.
- The newspaper's name, in ordinary roman type. (Table 13, Table 10, P.1)
- The date the article was printed.
- The word "at."
- The first page on which the article is found.

Examples:

See Warren E. Leary, *Poor Management by NASA is blamed for Mars Failure*, N.Y. TIMES, March 29, 2000, at Al.

Patricia Sabatini, *Rand Corp. Plans First Project With Pitt*, Pittsburgh Post-Gazette, March 24, 2000, at D 1.

Law Review Form:

Patricia Sabatini, *Rand Corp. Plans First Project With Pitt*, PITTSBURGH POST-GAZETTE, March 24, 2000, at D 1.

Books (Rule 15)

The standard book citation contains:

- An introductory signal, if appropriate. (Rule 1.2)
- The volume number (if a multi-volume work).
- The author's name.
- The title of the book, either italicized or underlined (do not include any subtitles).
- The page, section number, or paragraph number you are citing.
- The edition number (if more than one) and the publication date, in parentheses.

✓ Include information about translators or editors where appropriate. (Rule 15.1.2)

Examples:

See 21 Charles Alan Wright & Kenneth A. Graham, Jr., *Federal Practice and Procedure* § 5023 (1977).

See Thomas M. Franck & Michael J. Glennon, *Foreign Relations and National Security Law* 821 (2d ed. 1987).

Josef Skvorecky, *The Engineer of Human Souls* 409 (Paul R. Wilson trans., Dalkey Archive Press 1999) (1977).

✓ The short form citation is the same as for consecutively paginated journals.

✓ The "super short" form, id., may also be used, when appropriate.

Examples:

Franck & Glennon, *supra*, at 245.
See id. at 253.

Law Review Form:

See 21 CHARLES ALAN WRIGHT & KENNETH A. GRAHAM, JR., FEDERAL PRACTICE AND PROCEDURE § 5023 (1977).

APPENDICES

APPENDIX A: GLOSSARY

Abandon	To desert, surrender, forsake, or cede.
Abandoned Pleadings	A pleading which is no longer sought to be used.
Abandonment	The surrender, relinquishment, disclaimer, or cession of property or of rights. Voluntary relinquishment of all right, title, claim and possession, with the intention of not reclaiming it.
Abate	To throw down, to beat down, destroy, quash. To do away with or nullify or lessen or diminish.
Abuse of discretion	A failure to exercise a sound, reasonable, and legal discretion. It is a strict legal term indicating that appellate court is of the opinion that there was commission of an error of law by the trial court.
Acceptance	A manifestation of assent to terms thereof made by offeree in a manner-invited or required by offer.
Ace	To perform exceptionally well on an exam or an assignment.
Achieve	To reach your goals.
Action	A lawsuit brought in court.
Actionable	That for which an action will be; furnishing legal ground for an action.
Action in equity	Action in which person seeks equitable relief rather than damages.
Adamant	Firmly determined.
Adjudication	The legal process of resolving a dispute. The formal giving or pronouncing a judgment or decree in a court proceeding; also the judgment or decision given. It contemplates that the claims of all the parties thereto have been considered and set at rest.
Administrator	A person appointed by the court to administer the assets and liabilities of a decedent.

Administratrix	A woman appointed by the court to administer (i.e., manage or take charge of) the assets and liabilities of a decedent.
Admissible	Able to be admitted as evidence in a court of law.
Affiant	The person who makes and subscribes an affidavit.
Affidavit	A written or printed declaration or statement of facts, made voluntarily, and confirmed by the oath or affirmation of the party making it, taken before a person having authority to administer such oath or affirmation.
Affirm	To ratify, uphold, approve, make firm, confirm, establish, reassert. To assert as valid or confirmed.
Affront	To insult.
A fortiori	With stronger reason; much more.
Agree	To reach an agreement.
Agreement	Reaching a mutually acceptable compromise.
Aggrieved plaintiff	One whose legal right is invaded by an act complained of.
Allege	To state, recite, claim, assert, or charge.
All-nighter	All night study session, the night before an exam or paper is due.
Alter	To change, modify.
Alternative	Other possible solution.
Amend	To change for the better by removing defects or faults.
Amended complaint	A complaint which has been altered either by leave of court or within the statutory limitation.
Answer	The response of a defendant to the plaintiffs complaint, denying in part or in whole the allegations made by the plaintiff.
Appeal	To resort to a superior court to review the decision of an inferior court or administrative agency.
Appellant	The party who takes an appeal from one court or jurisdiction to another.
Appellee	The party in a cause against whom an appeal is taken; that is, the party who has an interest adverse to setting aside or reversing the judgment.
Applicability	How much something can be used or applied.

Approach	A way of doing something.
Arbitrator	A neutral person either chosen by the parties to a dispute or appointed by a court, to hear the parties claims and render a decision.
Argue	To give reasons for or against something; to debate.
Arguendo	In arguing; in the course of the argument. A statement or observation made by a judge or attorney as a matter of argument or hypothetical illustration.
Arrest	To deprive a person of his liberty by legal authority. Taking, under real or assumed authority, custody of another for the purpose of holding or detaining him to answer a criminal charge or civil demand.
Arrest warrant	A written order of the court which is made on behalf of the state, or United States, and is based upon a complaint issued pursuant to statute and/or court rule and which commands law enforcement officer to arrest a person and bring him before magistrate.
"As is" lease	A lease which contains no representations beyond those mentioned.
Assess	To determine the value of something.
Assume	To think.
Assumpsit	A promise or agreement by which one person assumes or undertakes to do some act or pay something to another.
Atmosphere	The mood or feeling.
Attitude	The way one feels or thinks about something.
Authority	The power to make a decision. Permission. Right to exercise powers; to implement and enforce laws; to exact obedience; to command. The right to command or to act; the right and power of public officers to require obedience to their orders lawfully issued in the scope of their official duty.
Aver	In a pleading, to declare or assert; to set out distinctly and formally; to allege.
Bailiff	A court officer or attendant who has charge of a court session in the matter of keeping order, custody of the jury, and custody of prisoners while in the court.
Balance of power	The power inherent in your position versus that in the position of the other side.

Bar (from recovery) To prevent; to defeat; to cut off.

Bargain A mutual undertaking, contract, or agreement. A contract or agreement between two parties, the one to sell or exchange goods or lands, and the other to buy or exchange them. An agreement to exchange a promise for a performance or to exchange performances.

Bargaining Negotiating with the purpose of coming to an agreement.

Bargaining power The power of one's position in the negotiation process.

Benefits Advantages.

Bind To obligate; to bring or place under definite duties or legal obligations. To affect one in a constraining or compulsory manner with a contract or judgment.

Bona fide In or with good faith; honestly, openly, and sincerely.

Bonding Doing any activity that links you more closely with a specific person or group of people.

Bottom line In this case, the furthest you are willing to go to reach an agreement.

Bound Denotes the condition of being constrained by judgment.

Breach The breaking or violating of a law, right, obligation, engagement, or duty, either by commission or omission.

Brushed aside To be ignored.

Burden of Proof The necessity or duty of affirmatively proving a fact or facts in dispute on an issue raised between the parties in a cause.

Burnt out Exhausted from overwork or stress.

Case at bar Case before the court.

Case law The aggregate of reported cases as forming a body of jurisprudence, or the law of a particular subject as evidenced or formed by the adjudged cases, in distinction to statutes and other sources of law.

Causal connection Proximate cause; that which, in a natural and continuous sequence, unbroken by any efficient intervening cause, produces injury, and without which the result would not have occurred.

Causation The act by which an effect is produced; an important doctrine in fields of negligence and criminal law.

Cause of action	The fact or facts which give a person a right to judicial redress or relief against another.
Caveat emptor	Let the buyer beware. This maxim summarizes the rule that a purchaser must examine, judge, and test for himself. This maxim is more applicable to judicial sales, auctions, and the like, than to sales of consumer goods where strict liability, warranty, and other consumer protection laws protect the consumer-buyer.
Charge	In a criminal case, the specific crime the defendant is accused of committing; accusation of a crime by a formal complaint, information or indictment.
Charge (the jury)	The final address by judge to jury before verdict, in which he sums up the case, and instructs jury as to the rules of law which apply to its various issues, and which they must observe.
Charlatan	One who pretends to more knowledge or skill than he possesses; a quack; a faker.
Cheesy	Used to describe something or someone as tacky or lacking in taste or style.
Civil action	Action brought to enforce, redress, or protect private rights.
Claim	A cause of action. Demand for money or property as of right.
Clueless	Having no idea what is going on; unaware.
Coerce	Compelled to compliance; constrained to obedience, or submission in a vigorous forcible manner.
Collective bargaining	The process where representatives from the union and management work out a contract specifying the conditions of employment.
Common law system	Law that develops and derives through judicial decisions, as distinguished from legislative enactments.
Compensate	To make equivalent return to, to recompense, or to pay.
Compensation	Payment to make good a loss.
Compensatory damages	Damages that will compensate the injured party for the injury sustained, and nothing more.
Complaint	The original or initial pleading by which an action is commenced under codes or Rules of Civil Procedure.

Compulsory nonsuit Name of a judgment given against the plaintiff when he is unable to prove a case, or when he refuses or neglects to proceed to trial and leaves the issue undetermined.

Consensus decision making Arriving at decisions through group discussion where the outcome is group agreement.

Concern Interest or worry.

Concession Compromise made by one side in order to reach an agreement; concessions from one side are expected to be matched by concessions from the other side.

Conclusions of law Findings of court as to law applicable on basis of facts found by jury.

Concur To agree with the result reached by another, but not necessarily with the reasoning or the logic used in reaching such a result.

Condition The term of a contract or the demand of the bargaining teams.

Condition precedent A condition which is to be performed before the agreement becomes effective, and which calls for the happening of some event or the performance of some act after the terms of the contract have been arrested on, before the contract shall be binding on the parties.

Confirm To make certain.

Confront To be faced with directly (this can be done in an aggressive manner).

Consider To examine; to inspect. To deliberate about and ponder over.

Constitution The organic and fundamental law of a nation or state establishing the character and conception of its government, laying the basic principles to which its internal life is to be conformed, organizing the government, and regulating, distributing, and limiting the functions of its different departments, and prescribing the extent and manner of the exercise of sovereign powers.

Constructive That which is established by the mind of the law in its act of construing facts, conduct, circumstances, or instruments. That which has not the character assigned to it in its own essential nature, but acquires such character in consequence of the way in which it is regarded by a rule or policy of law; hence, inferred, implied, or made out by legal interpretation.

Constructive eviction	Such arises when landlord, while not actually depriving tenant of possession, has done or suffered some act by which premises are rendered untenantable. Any disturbance of the tenant's possession by the landlord whereby the premises are rendered unfit or unsuitable for occupancy in whole or in substantial part for the purposes for which they were leased amounts to a constructive eviction, if the tenant so elects and surrenders his possession.
Contend	To assert; to maintain.
Contraband	In general, any property which is unlawful to produce or possess. Things and objects outlawed and subject to forfeiture and destruction upon seizure.
Contradictory	Something that goes against what you have previously said.
Conveyance	Generally, transfer of title to land from one person, or class of persons, to another by deed. Term may also include assignment, lease, mortgage or encumbrance of land.
Conviction	The result of a criminal trial which ends in a judgment or sentence that the accused is guilty as charged.
Convince/persuade	To make the other side agree that your point of view is correct.
Cool	Usually used to express approval of someone or something; something that is good, pleasing, interesting.
Counterclaim	A claim presented by a defendant in opposition to or deduction from the claim of the plaintiff.
Counterpart	Member of the opposing team.
Counterproposal	The other side's proposal in response to yours during negotiations.
Court of Common Pleas	Trial division of the Pennsylvania court system.
Covenant	An agreement, convention, or promise of two or more parties, by deed in writing, signed.
Cram	To study or review a subject in a hurried, intensive way, as in preparation for an exam.
Credibility	Worthiness of belief, that quality in a witness which renders his evidence worthy of belief.
Criminal division	Division of the court that deals specifically with those cases involving crimes against society.

Cross Examine	The examination of a witness upon a trial or hearing, or upon taking a deposition, by the party opposed to the one who produced him, upon his evidence given in chief, to test its truth, to further develop it, or for other purposes.
Custodial detention	Any act that indicates an intention to take a person into custody and subjects him to the actual control and will of the person making the arrest.
Custodial interrogation	Questioning initiated by law enforcement officers after a person has been taken into custody or otherwise deprived of his freedom of action in any significant way.
Custody	Actual imprisonment or physical detention or mere power, legal or physical, of imprisoning or of taking manual possession. Restraint of liberty.
Cutthroats	Students striving for good grades at any cost.
Damages	A pecuniary compensation or indemnity, which may be recovered in the courts by any person who has suffered loss, detriment, or injury, whether to his person, property, or rights, through the unlawful act or omission or negligence of another. A sum of money awarded to a person injured by the tort of another.
Deadlocked	When negotiations cannot proceed because both sides are unwilling to compromise.
Decedent	A deceased person.
Decedent's estate	Property, both real and personal, which person possesses at the time of his death, and title to it descends immediately to his heirs upon his death subject to the control of the probate court for the purposes of paying debts and claims and after distribution the estate ceases to exist.
Decide	To arrive at a determination. Includes the power and right to deliberate; to weigh the reasons for and against.
Decree	Judgment.
Deed	A conveyance of realty; a writing signed by grantor, whereby title to realty is transferred from one to another. A written instrument, signed, and delivered, by which one person conveys land, tenements, or hereditaments to another.
Defense	That which is offered and alleged by the party proceeded against in an action or suit, as a reason in law or fact why the plaintiff should not recover or establish what he

	seeks. That which is put forward to diminish plaintiff's cause of action or defeat recovery.
Deference	Giving way to others' views out of respect for their age and/or position.
Demand	To require/ask for something insistently.
Demands	Your opening position in a negotiation; what you want your counterpart to accept.
Demurrer	An allegation of a defendant, which, admitting the matters of fact alleged by complaint or bill to be true, shows that as they are therein set forth they are insufficient for the plaintiff to proceed upon or to oblige the defendant to answer.
Deny	To give a negative answer or reply to. To refuse to grant or accept.
Deter	To discourage or stop by fear. To stop or prevent from acting or proceeding by danger, difficulty, or other consideration which disheartens or countervails, the motive for the act.
Determine	To settle or decide by choice of alternatives or possibilities.
Directed verdict	In a case in which the party with the burden of proof has failed to present a prima facie case for jury consideration, the trial judge may order entry of a verdict without allowing the jury to consider it, because, as a matter of law, there can be only one such verdict.
Disconcerting	Upsetting.
Discretion	The exercise of judicial judgment, based on facts and guided by law, or the equitable decision of what is just and proper under the circumstances.
Dismiss	To send away; to discharge; to dispose of.
Dispute	To argue or to debate. To question the truth or validity of a claim.
Dissent	The term is most commonly used to denote the explicit disagreement of one or more judges of a court with the decision passed by the majority upon a case before them.
Distinguish	To point out an essential difference; to prove a case cited as applicable, inapplicable.

District magistrate	A public civil officer, possessing such power— legislative, executive, or judicial—as the government appointing him may ordain.
Diversionary	A tactical move to draw an opponent's attention away from a more important issue.
Document	To supply evidence.
Donee	The recipient of a gift.
Donor	The party conferring a power or gift.
Drawback	Disadvantage.
Duty	An element of negligence; an obligation, to which law will give recognition and effect, to comport to a particular standard of conduct toward another, and the duty is invariably the same, one must conform to legal standard of reasonable conduct in light of apparent risk.
Duty of care	The care demanded by the standard of reasonable conduct in like circumstances.
Elements	Material; substance; ingredient; factor. In the context of this case, it refers to the parts of negligence that must be proved by the prosecution to sustain a conviction.
Emotional distress	When connected with a physical injury, this term includes both the resultant mental sensation of pain and also the accompanying feelings of distress, fright, and anxiety. As an element of damages implies a relatively high degree of mental pain and distress; it is more than mere disappointment, anger, worry, resentment, or embarrassment, although it may include all of these, and it includes mental sensation of pain resulting from such painful emotions as grief, severe disappointment, indignation, wounded pride, shame, despair, and/or public humiliation.
En banc	Refers to a session where the entire membership of the court will participate in the decision rather than the regular quorum.
Equitable remedy	That kind of relief sought in a court with equity powers as, for example, in the case of one seeking an injunction or specific performance instead of money damages.
Err	To commit error: a mistaken judgment or incorrect belief as to the existence of effect of matters of fact, or a false or mistaken conception or application of the law. A mistake of law, or false or irregular application of it, such as

vitiates the proceedings and warrants the reversal of the judgment.

Error

A mistaken judgment or incorrect belief as to the existence or effect of matters of fact, or a false or mistaken conception or application of the law.

Error of law

An error of the court in applying the law to the case on trial, e.g., in ruling on the admission of evidence, or in charging the jury.

Escrow

A bank account generally held in the name of the depositor and an escrow agent which is returnable to depositor or paid to third person on the fulfillment of an escrow condition.

Estate

The total property of whatever kind that is owned by a decedent prior to the distribution of that property in accordance with the terms of a will, or, when there is no will by the laws of inheritance in the state of domicile of the decedent.

Etiquette

Rules of how to behave correctly.

Eventual

Something that may happen in the future.

Evidence

Any series of proof, or probative matter, legally presented at the trial of an issue, by the act of the parties and through the medium of witnesses, records, documents, exhibits, concrete objects, etc. for the purpose of inducing belief in the minds of the jury as to their contention.

Exclusionary rule

Commands that where evidence has been obtained in violation of the search and seizure protections guaranteed by the U.S. Constitution, the illegally obtained evidence cannot be used at the trial of the defendant. Held to be applicable to the States.

Executrix

A woman who has been appointed by will to execute such will or testament.

Expert testimony

Opinion evidence of some person who possesses a special skill or knowledge in some science, profession or business which is not common to the average man and which is possessed by the expert by reason of his special study or experience.

Exploit

To use for one's benefit or profit (this can be done at the expense of someone else).

Expose

To make known or reveal.

Factual findings	Determinations from the evidence of a case, either by court or an administrative agency, concerning facts averred by one party and denied by another.
Failure	Not doing something, not being successful.
Failure to state a claim	Failure of plaintiff to allege sufficient facts in the complaint to maintain an action.
Fair rental value	Present market value; such sum as the property will rent for to a lessee.
Felon	Person who commits or has committed a felony.
Fictitious injuries	Injuries that are feigned, imaginary, not real, false, not genuine, nonexistent.
File	To deposit in the custody or among the records of a court.
Final offer	Your last offer before breaking off negotiations.
Find	To discover; to determine; to locate; to ascertain and declare. To announce a conclusion upon a disputed fact or set of facts. To determine a controversy in favor of one of the parties.
Fish	In this case, trying to discover another person's goals or tactics by raising possibilities and watching their response.
Flexibility	The state of being flexible.
Flexible	Willing to negotiate, not rigid in your demands.
Follow	To conform to, comply with, or be fixed or determined by; to accept as authority.
Force	Power, violence, compulsion, or constraint exerted upon or against a person or thing.
Force majeure	A cause or event which neither party has control over such as natural disasters, strikes, or war.
Foreseeability	The ability to see or know in advance. The reasonable anticipation that harm or injury is a likely result from certain acts or omissions.
Foreseeable	An element of proximate cause that establishes by proof that actor, as person of ordinary intelligence and prudence, should reasonably have anticipated danger to others created by his negligent act.
Fourth Amendment	Constitutional law which guarantees people the right to be secure in their homes and property against

unreasonable searches and seizures and providing that no warrants shall issue except upon probable cause and then only as to specific places to be searched and persons and things to be seized.

Fraud	An intentional perversion of truth for the purpose of inducing another in reliance upon it to part with some valuable thing belonging to him or to surrender a legal right.
Fraudulent claims	Claims which are falsely made, or caused to be made, with the intent to deceive.
Fruit of the poisonous tree	Evidence which is spawned by or directly derived from an illegal search or illegal seizure or illegal interrogation. Such evidence is generally inadmissible against the defendant because of its original taint.
Fugitive	Used in criminal law with the implication of a flight, evasion or escape from arrest, prosecution or imprisonment.
Good chemistry	A good relation or feeling toward another person.
Good faith exception (to the Exclusionary rule)	Provides that evidence is not to be suppressed under such rule where that evidence was discovered by officers acting in good faith and in reasonable, though mistaken, belief that they were authorized to take those actions.
Governmental immunity	The federal, and derivatively, the state and local governments are free from liability for torts committed except in cases in which they have consented by statute to be sued.
Grant	To give or allow; to permit what is requested.
Grant certiorari	To affirmatively choose to hear a case from a lower court in order to inspect the proceedings and determine whether there have been any irregularities. Most commonly this is known as a discretionary action on the part of the Supreme Court of the United States.
Gravitate	To move toward or be attracted to something.
Guilty	Having committed a crime or other breach of conduct; justly charged with a crime.
Hang out	To relax (can be done alone or with other people).
Hardball, softball	Describes two approaches to negotiations; the first one suggests inflexibility, where you try to force the opposition to accept your conditions, while the latter suggests a more flexible approach, where you try to reach an acceptable compromise.

Have connections	To know people who can help you (business connections).
Heart Balm Act	Act that abolishes a right of action for alienation of affections, breach of promise to marry, and seduction of person over legal age of consent.
Hold	To adjudge or decide, spoken of a court, particularly to declare the conclusion of law reached by the court as to the legal effect of the facts disclosed.
Home court advantage	The advantage a team has in playing a game on their home court/field.
Impact	To influence/an influence.
Implicate	To show to have a connection with a crime, etc.
Implied warranty of habitability	Implied warranty of landlord that leased premises are properly maintained and are fit for habitation at time of letting and will remain so during time of tenancy.
Implied warranty of merchantability and fitness	A promise arising by operation of law, that something which is sold shall be merchantable and fit for the purpose for which the seller has reason to know that it is required.
Imprecise	Not clear.
Inadequate	Not sufficient.
Inconsistency	Ideas that do not follow logically.
Infer	To guess at or interpret.
Inference	A truth or proposition drawn from another which is supposed or admitted to be true. A process of reasoning by which a fact or proposition sought to be established is deduced as a logical consequence from other facts, or a state of facts, already proved or admitted.
Inflexibility	The state of being rigid.
Inflexible	Unwilling to compromise.
Informant	An undisclosed person who confidentially discloses material information of a law violation, thereby supplying a lead to officers for their investigation of a crime.
Initial	The first, the beginning.
Inquiry	Request for help or information.
Interrogation	Questioning.

Investigative stop/detention	Occurs when police stop and detain a person to investigate; such detention will rise to the level of an arrest unless the detention is for a relatively brief period and there are no coercive conditions present which constitute the functional equivalent of arrest.
Invitee	A person who enters another's land by invitation, express or implied.
Irreversible	Cannot be undone.
Judgment	The final decision of the court resolving the dispute and determining the rights and obligations of the parties.
Judgment as a matter of law (Rule 50)	Judgment where no reasonable jury could find for nonmoving party.
Judgment n.o.v.	A judgment entered by order of court for the plaintiff (or defendant) although there has been a verdict for the defendant (or plaintiff).
Jurisdiction	Defines the power of courts to inquire into facts, apply the law, make decisions, and declare judgment.
Jurisprudence	The philosophy of law, or the science which treats of the principles of positive law and legal relations.
Jury	A certain number of men and women selected according to law, and sworn to inquire of certain matters of fact, and declare the truth upon evidence to be laid before them.
Jury instructions	A direction given by the judge to the jury concerning the law of the case.
Justice of the peace	A judicial magistrate of inferior rank having (usually) jurisdiction limited to that prescribed by statute in civil matters and jurisdiction over minor criminal offenses, committing more serious crimes to higher courts.
Lame	Used to describe someone or something that is pathetic, ineffectual, weak, boring.
Landlord	The owner of an estate in land, or a rental property, who has leased it to another person, called the "tenant."
Lease	Any agreement which gives rise to relationship of landlord and tenant or lessor and lessee.
Leasehold	An estate in real property held by lessee/tenant under lease.
Leeway	A certain freedom before reaching limits or restriction.

Legislature	The department, assembly, or body of persons that makes statutory law for a state or nation.
Lessee	One who rents property from another. In the case of real estate, the lessee is also known as the tenant. He to whom a lease is made.
Leverage	Having an advantage due to power.
Liability	An obligation one is bound in law or justice to perform.
Liberty	Freedom from all restraints except such as are justly imposed by law.
Likelihood	The probability that something will happen.
Made a fool of myself	Usually used by a student to express that he embarrassed himself in responding to a professor's question.
Major	The main or most important.
Majority opinion	The opinion of an appellate court in which the majority of its members join.
Mandate	A command, order, or direction, written or oral, which court is authorized to give and person is bound to obey.
Material breach	Violation of contract which is substantially and significant and which usually excuses the aggrieved party from further performance under the contract and affords a right to sue for damages.
Material facts	Facts which are essential to the case and without which the case could not be supported. Facts which tend to establish any of the issues raised.
Matrimony	Marriage.
Mediation	A situation in which a neutral person (a mediator) works with labor and management to help them reach an agreement.
Mental suffering	When connected with a physical injury, this term includes both the resultant mental sensation of pain and also the accompanying feelings of distress, flight, and anxiety. As an element of damages implies a relatively high degree of mental pain and distress; it is more than mere disappointment, anger, worry, resentment, or embarrassment, although it may include all of these, and it includes mental sensation of pain resulting from such painful emotions as grief, severe disappointment, indignation, wounded pride, shame, despair, and/or public humiliation.

Mere encounters	Occurs where an officer approaches another person, but the person has no official obligation to stop or to respond to police questions or remarks; does not require reasonable suspicion or probable cause.
Merits	The substance, elements, or ground of a cause of action or defense.
Misrepresent facts	To present facts which are not correct.
Month-to-month lease	Tenancy where no lease is involved, rent being paid monthly. Statutes often require one month's notice to landlord of intent to terminate such tenancy.
Mortgage	An interest in land created by a written instrument providing security for the performance of a duty or the payment of a debt.
Motions	An application made to a court or judge for purpose of obtaining a rule or order directing some act to be done in favor of the applicant. Written or oral application to court for ruling or order, may be made before, during, or after trial.
Motion in limine	A pretrial motion requesting court to prohibit opposing counsel from referring to or offering evidence on matters so highly prejudicial to moving party that curative instructions cannot prevent predispositional effect on jury.
Motion to suppress evidence	To make an application to a court to eliminate from the trial of a criminal case evidence which has been secured illegally, generally in violation of the Fourth Amendment (search and seizure), the Fifth Amendment (privilege against self incrimination), or the Sixth Amendment (right to assistance of counsel, right of confrontation etc.), of U.S. Constitution.
Must	Important demand that you have to get if you are going to accept an agreement.
Musts	Important demands that you must get if you are going to accept an agreement.
Mutual	Something done or felt by each side toward the other.
Mutual gain	Where both sides profit.
Mutually beneficial	Good for both sides.
Name dropper	A person who seeks to impress others by frequently mentioning famous or important persons in a familiar way.

Natural and proximate consequences	Those consequences that a person by prudent human foresight can anticipate as likely to result from an act, because they happen so frequently from the commission of such an act that in the field of human experience they may be expected to happen again.
Negligence	The failure to use such care as a reasonably prudent and careful person would use under similar circumstances.
Negligent	Neglectful, careless, inattentive. Failing to do that which the reasonable man, guided by ordinary considerations which ordinarily regulate human affairs, would do.
Negotiations	The process of bargaining in an attempt to reach a mutually satisfying agreement/contract.
Nerd	A student who is constantly studying, who doesn't have a social life.
New Trial (Rule 59)	A request that the judge set aside the judgment or verdict and order a new trial on the basis that the trial was improper or unfair due to specified prejudicial errors that occurred, because of newly discovered evidence.
Nunc pro tunc	A phrase applied to acts allowed to be done after the time when they should be done, with a retroactive effect.
Oath	Any form of attestation by which a person signifies that he is bound in conscience to perform an act faithfully and truthfully.
Objection	Something which is presented in opposition, an adverse reason or argument. Used to call the court's attention to something improper.
Objective	Your goal; in this case what you hope to obtain.
Objective standard	Standard which does not consider the surrounding circumstances; standard applied consistently without looking into subjective considerations.
Obligation	That which a person is bound to do or forbear, any duty imposed by law, promise, contract, relations of society, courtesy, kindness, etc. That which constitutes a legal or moral duty and which renders a person liable to coercion and punishment for neglecting it.
Offer	A promise; a commitment to do or refrain from doing some specified thing in the future.
Opinion	The statement by a judge or court of the decision reached in regard to a cause tried or argued before them,

	expounding the law as applied to the case, and detailing the reasons upon which judgment is based.
Optimal	The best possible.
Option	Choice.
Oral argument	Statement before the court in support of, or in objection to, motion or other legal relief sought.
Order	Direction of a court or judge made or entered in writing, and not included in a judgment, which determines some point or directs commonly some step in the proceedings.
Outset	The beginning.
Outstanding (warrant)	Remaining undischarged; a warrant which has been issued but not yet executed upon its subject.
Overrule	To supersede; annul; reverse; make void. A judicial decision is said to be overruled when a later decision, rendered by the same court or by a superior court in the same system, expresses a judgment upon the same question of law directly opposite to that which was before given, thereby depriving the earlier opinion of all authority as precedent.
Pen register	A mechanical device that records the numbers dialed on a telephone by monitoring the electrical impulses caused when the dial on the telephone is released.
Perception	The way someone sees or regards something.
Persuasive authority	Source of law which need not be taken into account by a judge in deciding a case.
Physical force	Power, violence, compulsion, or constraint exerted upon or against a person or thing.
Plead	To make, deliver or file any pleading.
Pleadings	Formal allegations by the parties to a lawsuit of their respective claims and defenses, with the intended purpose being to provide notice of what is to be expected at trial.
Plurality opinion	Opinion of an appellate court in which more justices join than in any concurring opinion (though not a majority of the court). Distinguishable from a majority opinion in which a larger number of the justices on the panel join than not.
Pointless	There is no reason (in this case to continue negotiations).

Possession	Provides/involves right to exert control over specific land to exclusion of others.
Pray (for relief)	Demand for relief.
Precedent	An adjudged case or decision of a court, considered as furnishing example or authority for an identical or similar case afterwards arising or a similar question of law.
Preclude	To prohibit or prevent from doing something, e.g. injunction.
Preconceived	Determined in advance.
Predetermined	Determined in advance.
Prejudice	A forejudgment; bias; partiality; preconceived opinion.
Preliminary	Something in preparation to or coming before an event.
Preponderance of the evidence	Standard of proof in civil cases; evidence which is of greater weight or more convincing that the evidence which is offered in opposition to it.
Present	To show, to reveal.
Presuppose	To guess in advance.
Priority	How you rate something in terms of its importance (high priority, low priority).
Probable cause	Having more evidence for than against. A reasonable ground for belief in certain alleged facts. A set of probabilities grounded in the factual and practical considerations which govern the decisions of reasonable and prudent persons and is more than mere suspicion but less than the quantum of evidence required for conviction.
Procedural	That which prescribes method of enforcing rights or obtaining redress for their invasion.
Procedural Posture	The history of procedure of a given case.
Prolonged	Taking more time than expected.
Promise	A declaration which binds the person who makes it, either in honor, conscience, or law, to do or forbear a certain specific act, and which gives to the person to whom made a right to expect or claim the performance of some particular thing.
Proposal	What you offer as a basis for contract negotiations.

Proximate cause — That which in a natural and continuous sequence, unbroken by any efficient intervening cause, produces injury, and without which the result would not have occurred.

Public Policy — Community common sense and common conscience, extended and applied throughout the state to matters of public morals, health, safety, welfare, and the like.

Punctuality — Being on time.

Punitive damages — Damages based upon an entirely different public policy consideration—that of punishing the defendant or of setting an example for similar wrongdoers.

Pursuit — A chase (with the goal of apprehending or overtaking).

Push for — To urge someone to accept something strongly.

Rape — To have unlawful sexual intercourse with someone without his or her consent.

Reasonable Care — Such a degree of care, precaution, or diligence as may fairly and properly be expected or required, having regard to the nature of the action, or the subject-matter, and the circumstances surrounding the transaction.

Reasonable person — The standard to determine how someone (a reasonable person) should have acted in the same situation.

Reasonable suspicion — Justification for Fourth Amendment purposes in stopping defendant in public place. Quantum of knowledge sufficient to induce ordinarily prudent and cautious man under circumstances to believe criminal activity is at hand.

Reckless — Careless, heedless, inattentive; indifferent to consequences. According to circumstances it may mean desperately heedless, wanton or wilful, or it may mean only careless, inattentive, or negligent.

Record — A written account of some act, court proceeding, transaction, or instrument, drawn up, under authority of law, by a proper officer, and designed to remain as a memorial or permanent evidence of the matters to which it relates.

Recovery — The restoration or vindication of a right existing in a person, by the formal judgment or decree of a competent court, at his instance and suit, or the obtaining, by such judgment, of some right or property which has been taken or withheld from him.

Refute — To prove to be false or wrong, by argument or evidence.

Reject	To say no (to something).
Relinquish	To abandon, to give up, to surrender, to renounce something or right.
Rely	To look to for support or aid; depend.
Remand	The act of an appellate court when it sends a case back to the trial court and orders the trial court to conduct limited new hearings or an entirely new trial.
Remedy	To enforce a right or redress an injury.
Remitter	The procedural process by which an excessive verdict of a jury is reduced.
Rent	Consideration paid for use or occupation of property.
Rent Withholding Act	Allows rent to be withheld under certain circumstances and in compliance with certain provisions.
Res	Everything that may form an object of rights.
Respondent	In appellate practice, the party who contends against an appeal; the party against whom the appeal is taken, i.e. the appellee.
Responsible	Liable; legally accountable or answerable.
Restrain	To limit, confine, abridge, narrow down, restrict, obstruct, impede, hinder, stay, destroy. To prohibit from action, to put compulsion upon; to restrict; to hold or press back.
Restraint	Confinement, abridgement or limitation. Prohibition of action; holding or pressing back from action. Hindrance, confinement, or restriction of liberty.
Reverse	To overthrow, vacate, set aside, make void, annul, repeal, or revoke; as, to reverse a judgment, sentence or decree of a lower court by an appellate court.
Review	To re-examine judicially. A reconsideration; second view or examination; revision; consideration for purposes of correction. Used especially in the examination of a decision of a lower court by an appellate court.
Safeguard	A precaution, something that protects against loss or injury.
Scope of review	The extent to which a court may review a decision.
Search (4th Amendment)	Consists of looking for or seeking out that which is otherwise concealed from view.

Search incident to arrest	A police officer who has the right to arrest a person either with or without a warrant may search his person and the immediate area of the arrest for weapons.
Search warrant	An order in writing, issued by a justice or other magistrate, in the name of the state, directed to a sheriff, constable, or other officer, authorizing him to search for and seize any property that constitutes evidence of the commission of a crime.
Seizure	The taking of one physically or constructively into custody and detaining him, thus causing a deprivation of his freedom in a significant way, with real interruption of his liberty of movement. Such occurs not only when an officer arrests an individual, but whenever he restrains the individual's freedom to walk away.
Self-incrimination	Acts or declarations whether as testimony at trial or prior to trial by which one implicates himself or herself in a crime.
Set off	A counterclaim demand which defendant holds against plaintiff, arising out of a transaction extrinsic of plaintiffs cause of action.
Show of authority	Exhibition of a right and power to require obedience to one's orders.
Shy away	To avoid.
Sine qua non	That without which the thing cannot be.
Slacker	A student who is lazy, apathetic.
Slack off	To be lazy, idle, to neglect one's school work.
Snob	Someone who thinks he/she is better than everyone else.
Social Climber	A person who associates with socially prominent people in an attempt to gain higher social status.
Sound out	To ask questions to get an idea as to a person's feelings about a certain issue.
Specific performance	The remedy of requiring exact performance of a contract in the specific form in which it was made, or according to the precise terms agreed upon.
Stare decisis	To abide by, or adhere to, decided cases. Policy of courts to stand by precedent and not to disturb settled point. Doctrine that, when court has once laid down a principle of law as applicable to a certain state of facts, it will adhere to that principle, and apply it to all future cases,

	where facts are substantially the same; regardless of whether the parties and property are the same.
State of mind	A person's reasons and motives for acting as he did.
Statute of limitations	Statutes of the federal government and various states setting maximum time periods during which certain action can be brought or rights enforced.
Stop	To temporarily restrain a person's freedom to walk away. Permissible seizure within Fourth Amendment dimensions when such person is suspected of being involved in past, present or pending criminal activity.
Strategy	The plan you have for achieving your goals.
Stress	To emphasize.
Stress out	To worry, panic, fear. Feeling overwhelmed by school work, especially toward the end of the semester when reviewing for finals.
Strive	To attempt.
Submission	A yielding to authority, e.g. a citizen is bound to submit to the laws; a child to his parents.
Subsidiary	Under another's control.
Substantive	That part of law which creates, defines, and regulates rights and duties of parties.
Sufficient	Adequate, enough, as much as may be necessary.
Summary judgment	Procedural devise available for prompt and expeditious disposition of controversy without trial when there is no dispute as to either material fact or inferences to be drawn from undisputed facts, or if only question law is involved.
Superior Court	Appellate division of the Pennsylvania court system.
Suppress	To put a stop to a thing actually existing; to "suppress evidence" is to keep it from being used in a trial by showing that is was either gathered illegally or that it is irrelevant.
Suppression hearing	A pretrial proceeding in criminal cases in which a defendant seeks to prevent the introduction of evidence alleged to have been seized illegally. The ruling of the court then prevails at trial.
Suppression ruling	Ruling by a court that evidence sought to be admitted should be excluded because it was illegally acquired.

Supremacy Clause	The clause of Art. VI of the U.S. Constitution which declares that all laws made in pursuance of the Constitution and all treaties made under the authority of the United States shall be the "supreme law of the land" and shall enjoy legal superiority over any conflicting provision of a State constitution or law.
Survival action	Action for personal injuries which by statute survives death of injured person.
Sustain	To affirm, uphold or approve, as when an appellate court sustains the decision of a lower court.
Tenant	One who occupies another's land or premises in subordination to such other's title and with his assent, express or implied.
Terry **stop and frisk**	The situation where police officers who are suspicious of an individual run their hands lightly over the suspect's outer garments to determine if the person is carrying a concealed weapon. Reasonable suspicion which is sufficient for a stop and frisk is more than a mere hunch but less than probable cause.
Testify	To bear witness; to give evidence as a witness; to make a solemn declaration, under oath or affirmation, in a judicial inquiry, for the purpose of establishing or proving some fact.
Testimony	Evidence given by a competent witness under oath or affirmation.
Theft	The act of stealing; the taking of property without the owner's consent.
Tightrope act	A difficult balance.
Tort	A civil wrong.
Tortfeasor	A wrong-doer, an individual or business that commits or is guilty of a tort.
Totality of the circumstances	Test used to determine the constitutionality of various search and seizure procedures. This standard focuses on all the circumstances of a particular case, rather than any one factor.
Trading card/tradable	Demand that you are wiling to give up in trade for some of your other demands.
Trait	A distinguishing quality of personal character; characteristic.

Trespass	An unlawful interference with one's person, property, or rights.
Trier of fact	Term includes (a) the jury and (b) the court when the court is trying an issue of fact other than one relating to the admissibility of evidence.
Turn a blind eye	To pretend not to notice.
Ultimatum	A final proposal or terms whose rejection will result in the breaking off of negotiations.
Unanticipated	Unexpected.
Unbearable	Something you cannot stand.
Uniform Commercial Code	One of the Uniform Laws drafted by the National Conference of Commissioners on Uniform State Laws and the American Law Institute governing commercial transactions (including sales and leasing of goods, transfer of funds, commercial paper, bank deposits and collections, letters of credit, bulk transfers, warehouse receipts, bills of lading, investment securities, and secured transactions). The UCC has been adopted in whole or substantially by all states.
Unjust enrichment	General principle that one person should not be permitted unjustly to enrich himself at the expense of another, but should be required to make restitution of or for property or benefits received, retained or appropriated, where it is just and equitable that such restitution be made, and where such action involves no violation or frustration of law or opposition to public policy.
Unmeritorious claims	Claims which lack substance, elements, grounds for cause of action or defense.
Unyielding arbitration	A position of refusing to compromise. Parties unable to agree on a contract submit the final decision to a third party, an arbitrator.
Vacate	To annul; to set aside; to cancel or rescind. To render an act void.
Verdict	The formal decision or finding made by a jury, impaneled and sworn for the trial of a cause, and reported to the court, upon the matters or questions duly submitted to them upon the trial.
Vulnerable	Unprotected.
Warranty	A promise that a proposition of fact is true. An assurance by one party to agreement of existence of fact upon

which other party may rely. It is intended precisely to relieve promisee of any duty to ascertain facts for himself, and amounts to promise to indemnify promisee for any loss if the fact warranted proves untrue.

Wear someone out
To tire out, exhaust someone, to cause someone to become tired/exhausted.

What's up?
A greeting; hi, how are you?

Writ of attainder
At common law, the extinction of civil rights and capacities which took place whenever a person who had committed treason or felony received sentence of death for his crime.

Wrong
A violation of the legal rights of another, an invasion of right to the damage of the parties who suffer it, especially a tort.

Wrong-doer
One who commits an injury, a tort-feasor. One who invades a right to the damage of the party who suffers such invasion.

Wrongful death
Type of lawsuit brought on behalf of a deceased person's beneficiaries that alleges that death was attributable to the willful or negligent act of another.

Words from this glossary were taken from BLACK'S LAW DICTIONARY and MERRIAM WEBSTER'S COLLEGIATE DICTIONARY.

BLACK'S LAW DICTIONARY (6th ed. 1990).

MERRIAM WEBSTER'S COLLEGIATE DICTIONARY (10th ed. 1993).

APPENDIX B: PENNSYLVANIA AND U.S. CONSTITUTIONS

Constitution of the Commonwealth of Pennsylvania

PREAMBLE

WE, the people of the Commonwealth of Pennsylvania, grateful to Almighty God for the blessings of civil and religious liberty, and humbly invoking His guidance, do ordain and establish this Constitution.

ARTICLE I
DECLARATION OF RIGHTS

That the general, great and essential principles of liberty and free government may be recognized and unalterably established, WE DECLARE THAT—

§ 1. Inherent rights of mankind.

All men are born equally free and independent, and have certain inherent and indefeasible rights, among which are those of enjoying and defending life and liberty, of acquiring, possessing and protecting property and reputation, and of pursuing their own happiness.

§ 2. Political powers.

All power is inherent in the people, and all free governments are founded on their authority and instituted for their peace, safety and happiness. For the advancement of these ends they have at all times an inalienable and indefeasible right to alter, reform or abolish their government in such manner as they may think proper.

§ 3. Religious freedom.

All men have a natural and indefeasible right to worship Almighty God according to the dictates of their own consciences; no man can of right be compelled to attend, erect or support any place of worship, or to maintain any ministry against his consent; no human authority can, in any case whatever, control or interfere with the rights of conscience, and no preference shall ever be given by law to any religious establishments or modes of worship.

---

§ 4. Religion.

No person who acknowledges the being of a God and a future state of rewards and punishments shall, on account of his religious sentiments, be disqualified to hold any office or place of trust or profit under this Commonwealth.

§ 5. Elections.

Elections shall be free and equal; and no power, civil or military, shall at any time interfere to prevent the free exercise of the right of suffrage.

§ 6. Trial by jury.

Trial by jury shall be as heretofore, and the right thereof remain inviolate. The General Assembly may provide, however, by law, that a verdict may be rendered by not less than five-sixths of the jury in any civil case.

§ 7. Freedom of press and speech; libels.

The printing press shall be free to every person who may undertake to examine the proceedings of the Legislature or any branch of government, and no law shall ever by made to restrain the right thereof. The free communication of thoughts and opinions is one of the invaluable rights of man, and every citizen may freely speak, write and print on any subject, being responsible for the abuse of that liberty. No conviction shall be had in any prosecution for the publication of papers relating to the official conduct of officers or men in public capacity, or to any other matter proper for public investigation or information, where the fact that such publication was not maliciously or negligently made shall be established to the satisfaction of the jury; and in all indictments for libels the jury shall have the right to determine the law and the facts, under the direction of the court, as in other cases.

§ 8. Security from searches and seizures.

The people shall be secure in their persons, houses, papers and possessions from unreasonable searches and seizures, and no warrant to search any place or to seize any person or things shall issue without describing them as nearly as may be, nor without probable cause, supported by oath or affirmation subscribed by the affiant.

§ 9. Rights of accused in criminal prosecutions.

In all criminal prosecutions the accused hath a right to be heard by himself and his counsel, to demand the nature and cause of the accusation against him, to meet the witnesses face to face, to have compulsory process for obtaining witnesses in his favor, and, in prosecutions by indictment or information, a speedy public trial by an impartial jury of the vicinage; he cannot be compelled to give evidence against himself, nor can he be deprived of his life, liberty or property, unless by the judgment of his peers or the law of the land. The use of a suppressed voluntary admission or voluntary confession to impeach the credibility of a person may be permitted and shall not be construed as compelling a person to give evidence against himself.

§ 10. Initiation of criminal proceedings; twice in jeopardy; eminent domain.

Except as hereinafter provided no person shall, for any indictable offense, be proceeded against criminally by information, except in cases arising in the land or naval forces, or in the militia, when in actual service, in time of war or public danger, or by leave of the court for oppression or misdemeanor in office. Each of the several courts of common pleas may, with the approval of the Supreme Court, provide for the initiation of criminal proceedings therein by information filed in the manner provided by law. No person shall, for the same offense, be twice put in jeopardy of life or limb; nor shall private property be taken or applied to public use, without authority of law and without just compensation being first made or secured.

§ 11. Courts to be open; suits against the Commonwealth.

All courts shall be open; and every man for an injury done him in his lands, goods, person or reputation shall have remedy by due course of law, and right and justice administered without sale, denial or delay. Suits may be brought against the Commonwealth in such manner, in such courts and in such cases as the Legislature may by law direct.

§ 12. Power of suspending laws.

No power of suspending laws shall be exercised unless by the Legislature or by its authority.

§ 13. Bail, fines and punishments.

Excessive bail shall not be required, nor excessive fines imposed, nor cruel punishments inflicted.

§ 14. Prisoners to be bailable; habeas corpus.

All prisoners shall be bailable by sufficient sureties, unless for capital offenses when the proof is evident or presumption great; and the privilege of the writ of habeas corpus shall not be suspended, unless when in case of rebellion or invasion the public safety may require it.

§ 15. Special criminal tribunals.

No commission shall issue creating special temporary criminal tribunals to try particular individuals or particular classes of cases.

§ 16. Insolvent debtors.

The person of a debtor, where there is not strong presumption of fraud, shall not be continued in prison after delivering up his estate for the benefit of his creditors in such manner as shall be prescribed by law.

§ 17. Ex post facto laws; impairment of contracts.

No ex post facto law, nor any law impairing the obligation of contracts, or making irrevocable any grant of special privileges or immunities, shall be passed.

§ 18. Attainder.

No person shall be attainted of treason or felony by the Legislature.

§ 19. Attainder limited.

No attainder shall work corruption of blood, nor, except during the life of the offender, forfeiture of estate to the Commonwealth.

§ 20. Right of petition.

The citizens have a right in a peaceable manner to assemble together for their common good, and to apply to those invested with the powers of government for redress of grievances or other proper purposes, by petition, address or remonstrance.

§ 21. Right to bear arms.

The right of the citizens to bear arms in defense of themselves and the State shall not be questioned.

§ 22. Standing army; military subordinate to civil power.

No standing army shall, in time of peace, be kept up without the consent of the Legislature, and the military shall in all cases and at all times be in strict subordination to the civil power.

§ 23. Quartering of troops.

No soldier shall in time of peace be quartered in any house without the consent of the owner, nor in time of war but in a manner to be prescribed by law.

§ 24. Titles and offices.

The Legislature shall not grant any title of nobility or hereditary distinction, nor create any office the appointment to which shall be for a longer term than during good behavior.

§ 25. Reservation of powers in people.

To guard against the transgressions of the high powers which we have delegated, we declare that everything in this article is excepted out of the general powers of government and shall forever remain inviolate.

1967 Amendment. Joint Resolution No. 1 repealed former section 25 and renumbered section 26 to present section 25.

§ 26. No discrimination by Commonwealth and its political subdivisions.

Neither the Commonwealth nor any political subdivision thereof shall deny to any person the enjoyment of any civil right, nor discriminate against any person in the exercise of any civil right.

> **1967 Amendment.** Joint Resolution No. 1 added present section 26 and renumbered former section 26 to section 25.

§ 27. Natural resources and the public estate.

The people have a right to clean air, pure water, and to the preservation of the natural, scenic, historic and esthetic values of the environment. Pennsylvania's public natural resources are the common property of all the people, including generations yet to come. As trustee of these resources, the Commonwealth shall conserve and maintain them for the benefit of all the people.

> **1971 Amendment.** Joint Resolution No. 3 added section 27.

§ 28. Prohibition against denial or abridgment of equality of rights because of sex.

Equality of rights under the law shall not be denied or abridged in the Commonwealth of Pennsylvania because of the sex of the individual.

* * *

Constitution of the United States of America

WE THE PEOPLE of the United States, in Order to form a more perfect Union, establish Justice, insure domestic Tranquility, provide for the common defence, promote the general Welfare, and secure the Blessings of Liberty to ourselves and our Posterity, do ordain and establish this Constitution for the United States of America.

ARTICLE I.

SECTION 1. All legislative Powers herein granted shall be vested in a Congress of the United States, which shall consist of a Senate and House of Representatives.

SECTION 2. [1] The House of Representatives shall be composed of Members chosen every second Year by the People of the several States, and the Electors in each State shall have the Qualifications requisite for Electors of the most numerous Branch of the State Legislature.

[2] No Person shall be a Representative who shall not have attained to the Age of twenty five Years, and been seven Years a Citizen of the United States, and who shall not, when elected, be an Inhabitant of that State in which he shall be chosen.

[3] Representatives and direct Taxes shall be apportioned among the several States which may be included within this Union, according to their respective Numbers, which shall be determined by adding to the whole Number of free Persons, including those bound to Service for a Term of Years, and excluding Indians not taxed, three fifths of all other Persons. The actual Enumeration shall be made within three Years after the first Meeting of the Congress of the United States, and within every subsequent Term of ten Years, in such Manner as they shall by Law direct. The Number of Representatives shall not exceed one for every thirty Thousand, but each State shall have at Least one Representative; and until such enumeration shall be made, the State of New Hampshire shall be entitled to chuse three, Massachusetts eight, Rhode Island and Providence Plantations one, Connecticut five, New York six, New Jersey four, Pennsylvania eight, Delaware one, Maryland six, Virginia ten, North Carolina five, South Carolina five and Georgia three.

[4] When vacancies happen in the Representation from any State, the Executive Authority thereof shall issue Writs of Election to fill such Vacancies.

[5] The House of Representatives shall chuse their Speaker and other Officers; and shall have the sole Power of Impeachment.

SECTION 3. [1] The Senate of the United States shall be composed of two Senators from each State, chosen by the Legislature thereof, for six Years; and each Senator shall have one Vote.

[2] Immediately after they shall be assembled in Consequence of the first Election, they shall be divided as equally as may be into three Classes. The Seats of the

Senators of the first Class shall be vacated at the Expiration of the second Year, of the second Class at the Expiration of the fourth Year, and of the third Class at the Expiration of the sixth Year, so that one third may be chosen every second Year; and if Vacancies happen by Resignation, or otherwise, during the Recess of the Legislature of any State, the Executive thereof may make temporary Appointments until the next Meeting of the Legislature, which shall then fill such Vacancies.

[3] No person shall be a Senator who shall not have attained to the Age of thirty Years, and been nine Years a Citizen of the United States, and who shall not, when elected, be an Inhabitant of that State for which he shall be chosen.

[4] The Vice President of the United States shall be President of the Senate, but shall have no Vote, unless they be equally divided.

[5] The Senate shall chuse their other Officers, and also a President pro tempore, in the Absence of the Vice President, or when he shall exercise the Office of President of the United States.

[6] The Senate shall have the sole Power to try all Impeachments. When sitting for that Purpose, they shall be on Oath or Affirmation. When the President of the United States is tried, the Chief Justice shall preside: And no Person shall be convicted without the Concurrence of two thirds of the Members present.

[7] Judgment in Cases of Impeachment shall not extend further than to removal from Office, and disqualification to hold and enjoy any Office of honor, Trust or Profit under the United States: but the Party convicted shall nevertheless be liable and subject to Indictment, Trial, Judgment and Punishment, according to Law.

SECTION 4. [1] The Times, Places and Manner of holding Elections for Senators and Representatives, shall be prescribed in each State by the Legislature thereof; but the Congress may at any time by Law make or alter such Regulations, except as to the Place of Chusing Senators.

[2] The Congress shall assemble at least once in every Year, and such Meeting shall be on the first Monday in December, unless they shall by Law appoint a different Day.

SECTION 5. [1] Each House shall be the Judge of the Elections, Returns and Qualifications of its own Members, and a Majority of each shall constitute a Quorum to do Business; but a smaller Number may adjourn from day to day, and may be authorized to compel the Attendance of absent Members, in such Manner, and under such Penalties as each House may provide.

[2] Each House may determine the Rules of its Proceedings, punish its Members for disorderly Behavior, and, with the Concurrence of two-thirds, expel a Member.

3 Each House shall keep a Journal of its Proceedings, and from time to time publish the same, excepting such Parts as may in their Judgment require Secrecy; and the Yeas and Nays of the Members of either House on any question shall, at the Desire of one fifth of those Present, be entered on the Journal.

4 Neither House, during the Session of Congress, shall, without the Consent of the other, adjourn for more than three days, nor to any other Place than that in which the two Houses shall be sitting.

SECTION 6. 1 The Senators and Representatives shall receive a Compensation for their Services, to be ascertained by Law, and paid out of the Treasury of the United States. They shall in all Cases, except Treason, Felony and Breach of the Peace, be privileged from Arrest during their Attendance at the Session of their respective Houses, and in going to and returning from the same; and for any Speech or Debate in either House, they shall not be questioned in any other Place.

2 No Senator or Representative shall, during the Time for which he was elected, be appointed to any civil Office under the Authority of the United States, which shall have been created, or the Emoluments whereof shall have been encreased during such time; and no Person holding any Office under the United States, shall be a Member of either House during his Continuance in Office.

SECTION 7. 1 All Bills for raising Revenue shall originate in the House of Representatives; but the Senate may propose or concur with Amendments as on other Bills.

2 Every Bill which shall have passed the House of Representatives and the Senate, shall, before it become a Law, be presented to the President of the United States; If he approve he shall sign it, but if not he shall return it, with his Objections to that House in which it shall have originated, who shall enter the Objections at large on their Journal, and proceed to reconsider it. If after such Reconsideration two thirds of that House shall agree to pass the Bill, it shall be sent, together with the Objections, to the other House, by which it shall likewise be reconsidered, and if approved by two thirds of that House, it shall become a Law. But in all such Cases the Votes of both Houses shall be determined by yeas and Nays, and the Names of the Persons voting for and against the Bill shall be entered on the Journal of each House respectively. If any Bill shall not be returned by the President within ten Days (Sundays excepted) after it shall have been presented to him, the Same shall be a Law, in like Manner as if he had signed it, unless the Congress by their Adjournment prevent its Return, in which Case it shall not be a Law.

3 Every Order, Resolution, or Vote to which the Concurrence of the Senate and House of Representatives may be necessary (except on a question of Adjournment) shall be presented to the President of the United States; and before the Same shall take Effect, shall be approved by him, or being disapproved by him,

shall be repassed by two thirds of the Senate and House of Representatives, according to the Rules and Limitations prescribed in the Case of a Bill.

SECTION 8. [1] The Congress shall have Power To lay and collect Taxes, Duties, Imposts and Excises, to pay the Debts and provide for the common Defence and general Welfare of the United States; but all Duties, Imposts and Excises shall be uniform throughout the United States;

[2] To borrow money on the credit of the United States;

[3] To regulate Commerce with foreign Nations, and among the several States, and with the Indian Tribes;

[4] To establish an uniform Rule of Naturalization, and uniform Laws on the subject of Bankruptcies throughout the United States;

[5] To coin Money, regulate the Value thereof, and of foreign Coin, and fix the Standard of Weights and Measures;

[6] To provide for the Punishment of counterfeiting the Securities and current Coin of the United States;

[7] To establish Post Offices and post Roads;

[8] To promote the Progress of Science and useful Arts, by securing for limited Times to Authors and Inventors the exclusive Right to their respective Writings and Discoveries;

[9] To constitute Tribunals inferior to the supreme Court;

[10] To define and punish Piracies and Felonies committed on the high Seas, and Offenses against the Law of Nations;

[11] To declare War, grant Letters of Marque and Reprisal, and make Rules concerning Captures on Land and Water;

[12] To raise and support Armies, but no Appropriation of Money to that Use shall be for a longer Term than two Years;

[13] To provide and maintain a Navy;

[14] To make Rules for the Government and Regulation of the land and naval Forces;

[15] To provide for calling forth the Militia to execute the Laws of the Union, suppress Insurrections and repel Invasions;

[16] To provide for organizing, arming, and disciplining, the Militia, and for governing such Part of them as may be employed in the Service of the United States, reserving to the States respectively, the Appointment of the Officers, and the Authority of training the Militia according to the discipline prescribed by Congress;

[17] To exercise exclusive Legislation in all Cases whatsoever, over such District (not exceeding ten Miles square) as may, by Cession of particular States, and the

Acceptance of Congress, become the Seat of the Government of the United States, and to exercise like Authority over all Places purchased by the Consent of the Legislature of the State in which the Same shall be, for the Erection of Forts, Magazines, Arsenals, dock-Yards, and other needful Buildings;—And

[18] To make all Laws which shall be necessary and proper for carrying into Execution the foregoing Powers, and all other Powers vested by this Constitution in the Government of the United States, or in any Department or Officer thereof.

SECTION 9. [1] The Migration or Importation of such Persons as any of the States now existing shall think proper to admit, shall not be prohibited by the Congress prior to the Year one thousand eight hundred and eight, but a Tax or duty may be imposed on such Importation, not exceeding ten dollars for each Person.

[2] The Privilege of the Writ of Habeas Corpus shall not be suspended, unless when in Cases of Rebellion or Invasion the public Safety may require it.

[3] No Bill of Attainder or ex post facto Law shall be passed.

[4] No Capitation, or other direct, Tax shall be laid, unless in Proportion to the Census or Enumeration herein before directed to be taken.

[5] No Tax or Duty shall be laid on Articles exported from any State.

[6] No Preference shall be given by any Regulation of Commerce or Revenue to the Ports of one State over those of another: nor shall Vessels bound to, or from, one State, be obliged to enter, clear, or pay Duties in another.

[7] No Money shall be drawn from the Treasury, but in Consequence of Appropriations made by Law; and a regular Statement and Account of the Receipts and Expenditures of all public Money shall be published from time to time.

[8] No Title of Nobility shall be granted by the United States: And no Person holding any Office of Profit or Trust under them, shall, without the Consent of the Congress, accept of any present, Emolument, Office, or Title, of any kind whatever, from any King, Prince, or foreign State.

SECTION 10. [1] No State shall enter into any Treaty, Alliance, or Confederation; grant Letters of Marque and Reprisal; coin Money; emit Bills cf Credit; make any Thing but gold and silver Coin a Tender in Payment of Debts; pass any Bill of Attainder, ex post facto Law, or Law impairing the Obligation of Contracts, or grant any Title of Nobility.

[2] No State shall, without the Consent of the Congress, lay any Imposts or Duties on Imports or Exports, except what may be absolutely necessary for executing it's inspection Laws: and the net Produce of all Duties and Imposts, laid by any State on Imports or Exports, shall be for the Use of the Treasury of the United States; and all such Laws shall be subject to the Revision and Controul of the Congress.

[3] No State shall, without the Consent of Congress, lay any Duty of Tonnage, keep Troops, or Ships of War in time of Peace, enter into any Agreement or Compact with another State, or with a foreign Power, or engage in War, unless actually invaded, or in such imminent Danger as will not admit of delay.

ARTICLE II.

SECTION 1. [1] The executive Power shall be vested in a President of the United States of America. He shall hold his Office during the Term of four Years, and, together with the Vice President, chosen for the same Term, be elected, as follows:

[2] Each State shall appoint, in such Manner as the Legislature thereof may direct, a Number of Electors, equal to the whole Number of Senators and Representatives to which the State may be entitled in the Congress: but no Senator or Representative, or Person holding an Office of Trust or Profit under the United States, shall be appointed an Elector.

[3] The Electors shall meet in their respective States, and vote by Ballot for two Persons, of whom one at least shall not be an Inhabitant of the same State with themselves. And they shall make a List of all the Persons voted for, and of the Number of Votes for each; which List they shall sign and certify, and transmit sealed to the Seat of the Government of the United States, directed to the President of the Senate. The President of the Senate shall, in the Presence of the Senate and House of Representatives, open all the Certificates, and the Votes shall then be counted. The Person having the greatest Number of Votes shall be the President, if such Number be a Majority of the whole Number of Electors appointed; and if there be more than one who have such Majority, and have an equal Number of Votes, then the House of Representatives shall immediately chuse by Ballot one of them for President; and if no Person have a Majority, then from the five highest on the List the said House shall in like Manner chuse the President. But in chusing the President, the Votes shall be taken by States, the Representation from each State having one Vote; A quorum for this Purpose shall consist of a Member or Members from two thirds of the States, and a Majority of all the States shall be necessary to a Choice. In every Case, after the Choice of the President, the Person having the greatest Number of Votes of the Electors shall be the Vice President. But if there should remain two or more who have equal Votes, the Senate shall chuse from them by Ballot the Vice-President.

[4] The Congress may determine the Time of chusing the Electors, and the Day on which they shall give their Votes; which Day shall be the same throughout the United States.

[5] No Person except a natural born Citizen, or a Citizen of the United States, at the time of the Adoption of this Constitution, shall be eligible to the Office of President; neither shall any Person be eligible to that Office who shall not have

attained to the Age of thirty five Years, and been fourteen Years a Resident within the United States.

6 In Case of the Removal of the President from Office, or of his Death, Resignation, or Inability to discharge the Powers and Duties of the said Office, the Same shall devolve on the Vice President, and the Congress may by Law provide for the Case of Removal, Death, Resignation or Inability, both of the President and Vice President, declaring what Officer shall then act as President, and such Officer shall act accordingly, until the Disability be removed, or a President shall be elected.

7 The President shall, at stated Times, receive for his Services, a Compensation, which shall neither be encreased nor diminished during the Period for which he shall have been elected, and he shall not receive within that Period any other Emolument from the United States, or any of them.

8 Before he enter on the Execution of his Office, he shall take the following Oath or Affirmation:—"I do solemnly swear (or affirm) that I will faithfully execute the Office of President of the United States, and will to the best of my Ability, preserve, protect and defend the Constitution of the United States."

SECTION 2. 1 The President shall be Commander in Chief of the Army and Navy of the United States, and of the Militia of the several States, when called into the actual Service of the United States; he may require the Opinion, in writing, of the principal Officer in each of the executive Departments, upon any Subject relating to the Duties of their respective Offices, and he shall have Power to Grant Reprieves and Pardons for Offenses against the United States, except in Cases of Impeachment.

2 He shall have Power, by and with the Advice and Consent of the Senate, to make Treaties, provided two thirds of the Senators present concur; and he shall nominate, and by and with the Advice and Consent of the Senate, shall appoint Ambassadors, other public Ministers and Consuls, Judges of the supreme Court, and all other Officers of the United States, whose Appointments are not herein otherwise provided for, and which shall be established by Law: but the Congress may by Law vest the Appointment of such inferior Officers, as they think proper, in the President alone, in the Courts of Law, or in the Heads of Departments.

3 The President shall have Power to fill up all Vacancies that may happen during the Recess of the Senate, by granting Commissions which shall expire at the End of their next Session.

SECTION 3. He shall from time to time give to the Congress Information of the State of the Union, and recommend to their Consideration such Measures as he shall judge necessary and expedient; he may, on extraordinary Occasions, convene both Houses, or either of them, and in Case of Disagreement between them, with Respect to the Time of Adjournment, he may adjourn them to such Time as he shall think proper; he shall receive Ambassadors and other public Ministers;

he shall take Care that the Laws be faithfully executed, and shall Commission all the Officers of the United States.

SECTION. 4. The President, Vice President and all civil Officers of the United States, shall be removed from Office on Impeachment for, and Conviction of, Treason, Bribery, or other high Crimes and Misdemeanors.

ARTICLE III.

SECTION 1. The judicial Power of the United States, shall be vested in one su-preme Court, and in such inferior Courts as the Congress may from time to time ordain and establish. The Judges, both of the supreme and inferior Courts, shall hold their Offices during good Behaviour, and shall, at stated Times, receive for their Services, a Compensation, which shall not be diminished during their Con-tinuance in Office.

SECTION 2. [1] The judicial Power shall extend to all Cases, in Law and Equity, aris-ing under this Constitution, the Laws of the United States, and Treaties made, or which shall be made, under their Authority;—to all Cases affecting Ambassa-dors, other public Ministers and Consuls;—to all Cases of admiralty and mari-time Jurisdiction;—to Controversies to which the United States shall be a Party;—to Controversies between two or more States;—between a State and Cit-izens of another State;—between Citizens of different States;—between Citizens of the same State claiming Lands under Grants of different States, and between a State, or the Citizens thereof, and foreign States, Citizens or Subjects.

[2] In all Cases affecting Ambassadors, other public Ministers and Consuls, and those in which a State shall be Party, the supreme Court shall have original Juris-diction. In all the other Cases before mentioned, the supreme Court shall have ap-pellate Jurisdiction, both as to Law and Fact, with such Exceptions, and under such Regulations as the Congress shall make.

[3] Trial of all Crimes, except in Cases of Impeachment, shall be by Jury; and such Trial shall be held in the State where the said Crimes shall have been committed; but when not committed within any State, the Trial shall be at such Place or Places as the Congress may by Law have directed.

SECTION 3. [1] Treason against the United States, shall consist only in levying War against them, or in adhering to their Enemies, giving them Aid and Comfort. No Person shall be convicted of Treason unless on the Testimony of two Witnesses to the same overt Act, or on Confession in open Court.

[2] The Congress shall have power to declare the Punishment of Treason, but no Attainder of Treason shall work Corruption of Blood, or Forfeiture except during the Life of the Person attainted.

ARTICLE IV.

SECTION 1. Full Faith and Credit shall be given in each State to the public Acts, Records, and judicial Proceedings of every other State. And the Congress may by general Laws prescribe the Manner in which such Acts, Records and Proceedings shall be proved, and the Effect thereof.

SECTION 2. [1] The Citizens of each State shall be entitled to all Privileges and Immunities of Citizens in the several States.

[2] A Person charged in any State with Treason, Felony, or other Crime, who shall flee from Justice, and be found in another State, shall on Demand of the executive Authority of the State from which he fled, be delivered up, to be removed to the State having Jurisdiction of the Crime.

[3] No Person held to Service or Labour in one State, under the Laws thereof, escaping into another, shall, in Consequence of any Law or Regulation therein, be discharged from such Service or Labour, but shall be delivered up on Claim of the Party to whom such Service or Labour may be due.

SECTION 3. [1] New States may be admitted by the Congress into this Union; but no new States shall be formed or erected within the Jurisdiction of any other State; nor any State be formed by the Junction of two or more States, or Parts of States, without the Consent of the Legislatures of the States concerned as well as of the Congress.

[2] The Congress shall have Power to dispose of and make all needful Rules and Regulations respecting the Territory or other Property belonging to the United States; and nothing in this Constitution shall be so construed as to Prejudice any Claims of the United States, or of any particular State.

SECTION 4. The United States shall guarantee to every State in this Union a Republican Form of Government, and shall protect each of them against Invasion; and on Application of the Legislature, or of the Executive (when the Legislature cannot be convened) against domestic Violence.

ARTICLE V.

The Congress, whenever two thirds of both Houses shall deem it necessary, shall propose Amendments to this Constitution, or, on the Application of the Legislatures of two thirds of the several States, shall call a Convention for proposing Amendments, which, in either Case, shall be valid to all Intents and Purposes, as Part of this Constitution, when ratified by the Legislatures of three fourths of the several States, or by Conventions in three fourths thereof, as the one or the other Mode of Ratification may be proposed by the Congress; Provided that no Amendment which may be made prior to the Year One thousand eight hundred and eight shall in any Manner affect the first and fourth Clauses in the Ninth Section of the first Article; and that no State, without its Consent, shall be deprived of its equal Suffrage in the Senate.

ARTICLE VI.

[1] All Debts contracted and Engagements entered into, before the Adoption of this Constitution, shall be as valid against the United States under this Constitution, as under the Confederation.

[2] This Constitution, and the Laws of the United States which shall be made in Pursuance thereof; and all Treaties made, or which shall be made, under the Authority of the United States, shall be the supreme Law of the Land; and the Judges in every State shall be bound thereby, any Thing in the Constitution or Laws of any State to the Contrary notwithstanding.

[3] The Senators and Representatives before mentioned, and the Members of the several State Legislatures, and all executive and judicial Officers, both of the United States and of the several States, shall be bound by Oath or Affirmation, to support this Constitution; but no religious Test shall ever be required as a Qualification to any Office or public Trust under the United States.

ARTICLE VII.

The Ratification of the Conventions of nine States, shall be sufficient for the Establishment of this Constitution between the States so ratifying the Same.

DONE in Convention by the Unanimous Consent of the States present the Seventeenth Day of September in the Year of our Lord one thousand seven hundred and Eighty seven and of the Independence of the United States of America the Twelfth. In witness whereof We have hereunto subscribed our Names.

Amendments to the Constitution

First Amendment

Congress shall make no law respecting an establishment of religion, or prohibiting the free exercise thereof; or abridging the freedom of speech, or of the press; or the right of the people peaceably to assemble, and to petition the Government for a redress of grievances.

Second Amendment

A well regulated Militia, being necessary to the security of a free State, the right of the people to keep and bear Arms, shall not be infringed.

Third Amendment

No Soldier shall, in time of peace be quartered in any house, without the consent of the Owner, nor in time of war, but in a manner to be prescribed by law.

Fourth Amendment

The right of the people to be secure in their persons, houses, papers, and effects, against unreasonable searches and seizures, shall not be violated, and no

Warrants shall issue, but upon probable cause, supported by Oath or affirmation, and particularly describing the place to be searched, and the persons or things to be seized.

Fifth Amendment

No person shall be held to answer for a capital, or otherwise infamous crime, unless on a presentment or indictment of a Grand Jury, except in cases arising in the land or naval forces, or in the Militia, when in actual service in time of War or public danger; nor shall any person be subject for the same offence to be twice put in jeopardy of life or limb; nor shall be compelled in any criminal case to be a witness against himself, nor be deprived of life, liberty, or property, without due process of law; nor shall private property be taken for public use, without just compensation.

Sixth Amendment

In all criminal prosecutions, the accused shall enjoy the right to a speedy and public trial, by an impartial jury of the State and district wherein the crime shall have been committed, which district shall have been previously ascertained by law, and to be informed of the nature and cause of the accusation; to be confronted with the witnesses against him; to have compulsory process for obtaining witnesses in his favor, and to have the Assistance of Counsel for his defence.

Seventh Amendment

In Suits at common law, where the value in controversy shall exceed twenty dollars, the right of trial by jury shall be preserved, and no fact tried by a jury, shall be otherwise re-examined in any Court of the United States, than according to the rules of the common law.

Eighth Amendment

Excessive bail shall not be required, nor excessive fines imposed, nor cruel and unusual punishments inflicted.

Ninth Amendment

The enumeration in the Constitution, of certain rights, shall not be construed to deny or disparage others retained by the people.

Tenth Amendment

The powers not delegated to the United States by the Constitution, nor prohibited by it to the States, are reserved to the States respectively, or to the people.

Eleventh Amendment

The Judicial power of the United States shall not be construed to extend to any suit in law or equity, commenced or prosecuted against one of the United States by Citizens of another State, or by Citizens or Subjects of any Foreign State.

Twelfth Amendment

The Electors shall meet in their respective states, and vote by ballot for President and Vice-President, one of whom, at least, shall not be an inhabitant of the same state with themselves; they shall name in their ballots the person voted for as President, and in distinct ballots the person voted for as Vice-President, and they shall make distinct lists of all persons voted for as President, and of all persons voted for as Vice-President, and of the number of votes for each, which lists they shall sign and certify, and transmit sealed to the seat of the government of the United States, directed to the President of the Senate;—The President of the Senate shall, in the presence of the Senate and House of Representatives, open all the certificates and the votes shall then be counted;—The person having the greatest number of votes for President, shall be the President, if such number be a majority of the whole number of Electors appointed; and if no person have such majority, then from the persons having the highest numbers not exceeding three on the list of those voted for as President, the House of Representatives shall choose immediately, by ballot, the President. But in choosing the President, the votes shall be taken by states, the representation from each state having one vote; a quorum for this purpose shall consist of a member or members from two-thirds of the states, and a majority of all the states shall be necessary to a choice. And if the House of Representatives shall not choose a President whenever the right of choice shall devolve upon them, before the fourth day of March next following, then the Vice-President shall act as President, as in the case of the death or other constitutional disability of the President.—The person having the greatest number of votes as Vice-President, shall be the Vice-President, if such number be a majority of the whole number of Electors appointed, and if no person have a majority, then from the two highest numbers on the list, the Senate shall choose the Vice-President; a quorum for the purpose shall consist of two-thirds of the whole number of Senators, and a majority of the whole number shall be necessary to a choice. But no person constitutionally ineligible to the office of President shall be eligible to that of Vice-President of the United States.

Thirteenth Amendment

SECTION 1. Neither slavery nor involuntary servitude, except as a punishment for crime whereof the party shall have been duly convicted, shall exist within the United States, or any place subject to their jurisdiction.

SECTION 2. Congress shall have power to enforce this article by appropriate legislation.

Fourteenth Amendment

SECTION 1. All persons born or naturalized in the United States, and subject to the jurisdiction thereof, are citizens of the United States and of the State wherein they reside. No State shall make or enforce any law which shall abridge the privileges or immunities of citizens of the United States; nor shall any State deprive any person of life, liberty, or property, without due process of law; nor deny to any person within its jurisdiction the equal protection of the laws.

SECTION 2. Representatives shall be apportioned among the several States according to their respective numbers, counting the whole number of persons in each State, excluding Indians not taxed. But when the right to vote at any election for the choice of electors for President and Vice President of the United States, Representatives in Congress, the Executive and Judicial officers of a State, or the members of the Legislature thereof, is denied to any of the male inhabitants of such State, being twenty-one years of age, and citizens of the United States, or in any way abridged, except for participation in rebellion, or other crime, the basis of representation therein shall be reduced in the proportion which the number of such male citizens shall bear to the whole number of male citizens twenty-one years of age in such State.

SECTION 3. No person shall be a Senator or Representative in Congress, or elector of President and Vice President, or hold any office, civil or military, under the United States, or under any State, who, having previously taken an oath, as a member of Congress, or as an officer of the United States, or as a member of any State legislature, or as an executive or judicial officer of any State, to support the Constitution of the United States, shall have engaged in insurrection or rebellion against the same, or given aid or comfort to the enemies thereof. But Congress may by a vote of two-thirds of each House, remove such disability.

SECTION 4. The validity of the public debt of the United States, authorized by law, including debts incurred for payment of pensions and bounties for services in suppressing insurrection or rebellion, shall not be questioned. But neither the United States nor any State shall assume or pay any debt or obligation incurred in aid of insurrection or rebellion against the United States, or any claim for the loss or emancipation of any slave; but all such debts, obligations and claims shall be held illegal and void.

SECTION 5. The Congress shall have power to enforce, by appropriate legislation, the provisions of this article.

Fifteenth Amendment

SECTION 1. The right of citizens of the United States to vote shall not be denied or abridged by the United States or by any State on account of race, color, or previous condition of servitude.

SECTION 2. The Congress shall have power to enforce this article by appropriate legislation.

Sixteenth Amendment

The Congress shall have power to lay and collect taxes on incomes, from whatever source derived, without apportionment among the several States, and without regard to any census or enumeration.

Seventeenth Amendment

The Senate of the United States shall be composed of two Senators from each State, elected by the people thereof, for six years; and each Senator shall have one vote. The electors in each State shall have the qualifications requisite for electors of the most numerous branch of the State legislatures.

When vacancies happen in the representation of any State in the Senate, the executive authority of such State shall issue writs of election to fill such vacancies: *Provided*, That the legislature of any State may empower the executive thereof to make temporary appointments until the people fill the vacancies by election as the legislature may direct.

This amendment shall not be so construed as to affect the election or term of any Senator chosen before it becomes valid as part of the Constitution.

Eighteenth Amendment

SECTION 1. After one year from the ratification of this article the manufacture, sale, or transportation of intoxicating liquors within, the importation thereof into, or the exportation thereof from the United States and all territory subject to the jurisdiction thereof for beverage purposes is hereby prohibited.

SEC. 2. The Congress and the several States shall have concurrent power to enforce this article by appropriate legislation.

SEC. 3. This article shall be inoperative unless it shall have been ratified as an amendment to the Constitution by the legislatures of the several States, as provided in the Constitution, within seven years from the date of the submission hereof to the States by the Congress.

Nineteenth Amendment

The right of citizens of the United States to vote shall not be denied or abridged by the United States or by any State on account of sex.

Congress shall have power to enforce this article by appropriate legislation.

Twentieth Amendment

SECTION 1. The terms of the President and Vice President shall end at noon on the 20th day of January, and the terms of Senators and Representatives at noon on the 3d day of January, of the years in which such terms would have ended if this article had not been ratified; and the terms of their successors shall then begin.

SEC. 2. The Congress shall assemble at least once in every year, and such meeting shall begin at noon on the 3d day of January, unless they shall by law appoint a different day.

SEC. 3. If, at the time fixed for the beginning of the term of the President, the President elect shall have died, the Vice President elect shall become President. If a President shall not have been chosen before the time fixed for the beginning of his term, or if the President elect shall have failed to qualify, then the Vice President elect shall act as President until a President shall have qualified; and the Congress may by law provide for the case wherein neither a President elect nor a Vice President elect shall have qualified, declaring who shall then act as President, or the manner in which one who is to act shall be selected, and such person shall act accordingly until a President or Vice President shall have qualified.

SEC. 4. The Congress may by law provide for the case of the death of any of the persons from whom the House of Representatives may choose a President whenever the right of choice shall have devolved upon them, and for the case of the death of any of the persons from whom the Senate may choose a Vice President whenever the right of choice shall have devolved upon them.

SEC. 5. Sections 1 and 2 shall take effect on the 15th day of October following the ratification of this article.

SEC. 6. This article shall be inoperative unless it shall have been ratified as an amendment to the Constitution by the legislatures of three-fourths of the several States within seven years from the date of its submission.

Twenty-First Amendment

SECTION 1. The eighteenth article of amendment to the Constitution of the United States is hereby repealed.

SECTION 2. The transportation or importation into any State, Territory, or possession of the United States for delivery or use therein of intoxicating liquors, in violation of the laws thereof, is hereby prohibited.

SECTION 3. The article shall be inoperative unless it shall have been ratified as an amendment to the Constitution by conventions in the several States, as provided in the Constitution, within seven years from the date of the submission hereof to the States by the Congress.

Twenty-Second Amendment

SECTION 1. No person shall be elected to the office of the President more than twice, and no person who has held the office of President, or acted as President, for more than two years of a term to which some other person was elected President shall be elected to the office of the President more than once. But this Article shall not apply to any person holding the office of President when this Article was proposed by the Congress, and shall not prevent any person who may be holding the office of President, or acting as President, during the term within which this Article becomes operative from holding the office of President or acting as President during the remainder of such term.

SEC. 2. This article shall be inoperative unless it shall have been ratified as an amendment to the Constitution by the legislatures of three-fourths of the several

States within seven years from the date of its submission to the States by the Congress.

Twenty-Third Amendment

SECTION 1. The District constituting the seat of Government of the United States shall appoint in such manner as the Congress may direct:

A number of electors of President and Vice President equal to the whole number of Senators and Representatives in Congress to which the District would be entitled if it were a State, but in no event more than the least populous State; they shall be in addition to those appointed by the States, but they shall be considered, for the purposes of the election of President and Vice President, to be electors appointed by a State; and they shall meet in the District and perform such duties as provided by the twelfth article of amendment.

SEC. 2. The Congress shall have power to enforce this article by appropriate legislation.

Twenty-Fourth Amendment

SECTION 1. The right of citizens of the United States to vote in any primary or other election for President or Vice President, for electors for President or Vice President, or for Senator or Representative in Congress, shall not be denied or abridged by the United States or any State by reason of failure to pay any poll tax or other tax.

SEC. 2. The Congress shall have power to enforce this article by appropriate legislation.

Twenty-Fifth Amendment

SECTION 1. In case of the removal of the President from office or of his death or resignation, the Vice President shall become President.

SEC. 2. Whenever there is a vacancy in the office of the Vice President, the President shall nominate a Vice President who shall take office upon confirmation by a majority vote of both Houses of Congress.

SEC. 3. Whenever the President transmits to the President pro tempore of the Senate and the Speaker of the House of Representatives his written declaration that he is unable to discharge the powers and duties of his office, and until he transmits to them a written declaration to the contrary, such powers and duties shall be discharged by the Vice President as Acting President.

SEC. 4. Whenever the Vice President and a majority of either the principal officers of the executive departments or of such other body as Congress may by law provide, transmit to the President pro tempore of the Senate and the Speaker of the House of Representatives their written declaration that the President is unable to discharge the powers and duties of his office, the Vice President shall immediately assume the powers and duties of the office as Acting President.

Thereafter, when the President transmits to the President pro tempore of the Senate and the Speaker of the House of Representatives his written declaration that no inability exists, he shall resume the powers and duties of his office unless the Vice President and a majority of either the principal officers of the executive department or of such other body as Congress may by law provide, transmit within four days to the President pro tempore of the Senate and the Speaker of the House of Representatives their written declaration that the President is unable to discharge the powers and duties of his office. Thereupon Congress shall decide the issue, assembling within forty-eight hours for that purpose if not in session. If the Congress, within twenty-one days after receipt of the latter written declaration, or, if Congress is not in session, within twenty-one days after Congress is required to assemble, determines by two-thirds vote of both Houses that the President is unable to discharge the powers and duties of his office, the Vice President shall continue to discharge the same as Acting President; otherwise, the President shall resume the powers and duties of his office.

Twenty-Sixth Amendment

SECTION 1. The right of citizens of the United States, who are eighteen years of age or older, to vote shall not be denied or abridged by the United States or by any State on account of age.

SEC. 2. The Congress shall have power to enforce this article by appropriate legislation.

Twenty-Seventh Amendment

No law, varying the compensation for the services of the Senators and Representatives, shall take effect, until an election of Representatives shall have intervened.

APPENDIX C: SAMPLE BRIEF AND MEMORANDUM

Sample Brief

GRONER v. HEDRICK
Supreme Court of Pennsylvania
1961

PARTIES:

The appellant is Ms. Groner, the housekeeper. The appellees are Mr. and Mrs. Hedrick.

SUBSTANTIVE FACTS:

Ms. Groner went to work for the Hedrick family as a housekeeper and companion for Mrs. Hedrick's elderly mother. The Hedricks owned a Great Dane named "Sleepy" who was known to be an overly affectionate dog that often jumped up on people's shoulders. Ms. Groner was aware of the dog's temperament and had managed to keep him off her for the first four weeks of her employment. After four weeks of employment in the Hedrick household, the dog jumped up on Ms. Groner, the seventy-four year old, five feet two, 105 pound housekeeper, knocking her down and causing her to break her arm and her leg.

PROCEDURAL FACTS:

Ms. Groner sued the Hedrick family for injuries she sustained when knocked over by the dog. The jury in the Court of Common Pleas found for Mrs. Groner and awarded her damages. The judge, however, entered a judgment n.o.v. for the defendants stating that Ms. Groner had assumed the risk of injury from the dog. The housekeeper appealed.

LEGAL ISSUES:

1. Whether there is a legal difference between a vicious dog and an overly affectionate dog.

2. Whether the trial court erred when it entered a judgment n. o. v. stating that whether Ms. Groner had assumed the risk of injury from the dog was not a question for the jury.

HOLDINGS:

1. There is no legal difference between an overly affectionate dog and a vicious dog.

---

2. The entry of summary judgment was an error. It is for the jury to decide whether Ms. Groner assumed the risk of the dog because there are so many variables to consider. The Pennsylvania Supreme Court reversed the decision of the Court of Common Pleas.

RATIONALE:

1. Relying on *Owen v. Hampson*, the court held that it is immaterial whether an animal is vicious or overly friendly. Only the animal's ability to cause injury to persons or property is important to consider.

2. The court must draw all conclusions in favor of Ms. Goner, the petitioner, when reviewing a judgment n.o.v. Where the facts are disputed it is a question for the jury.

RULES:

1. A friendly dog can be equally dangerous as a vicious dog, and since it does not matter what the mood or mental state of the dog is at the time of injury, the difference is immaterial.

2. When facts are disputed and there are numerous variables to consider, it is for the jury to weigh the factors and make a determination. It is not for the judge to decide.

Memorandum

To: Professors Brostoff and Sinsheimer
From: Arthur Sandel
Date: November 1999
Re: Robert and Mrs. Hope; Negligence

QUESTIONS PRESENTED

I) Does Robert have a claim against a driver for negligence where Robert managed to jump away from his bicycle just before the driver crashed into it?

II) Can Mrs. Hope bring a negligence action against a driver for injuries caused by shock and fear for her son, where Mrs. Hope visually observed her son riding his bicycle outside their home, heard the accident while on her front porch, and arrived on the scene immediately thereafter to find her son lying on the street in front of driver's stopped automobile?

BRIEF ANSWER

I) Probably yes. Robert probably has a claim against the driver for negligence because Robert was in personal danger of physical impact given the direction of the driver's car in relation to him, and because he actually feared this danger of impact.

II) Probably no. Mrs. Hope probably cannot bring a negligence action against the driver since Mrs. Hope was on her front porch at the time of the incident, and thus probably was not in personal danger of physical impact with the driver's negligent force and therefore did not fear such physical impact.

FACTS

On the afternoon of June 13, 1997, Mrs. Hope was outside her suburban Pittsburgh home watching her ten-year-old son, Robert, riding his bicycle up and down their street. At approximately 3:00 p.m., Mrs. Hope walked over to her front porch to make a phone call on her cordless phone. While she was talking on the phone and looking at the ground, she heard the screeching of brakes and a crash. Immediately following this sensory perception, Mrs. Hope looked up and ran to see her son lying on the ground in front of a stopped automobile. The bicycle was crushed beneath the wheels of the auto. There were skid marks from the car's tires on the street.

Fearing the worst, Mrs. Hope fainted from the shock of seeing her son lying on the street. Mrs. Hope fell to the ground and struck her head on the concrete sidewalk. She suffered a severe concussion and head trauma that required treatment in the hospital for one week. Since having injured her head, Mrs. Hope has suffered from painful recurrent headaches.

Robert managed to jump away from his bike just before the car hit it. He suffered cuts and abrasions but was otherwise physically unharmed by the incident. However, since the incident, Robert has had nightmares and remains fearful of riding a bicycle.

DISCUSSION

I. Robert probably has a claim against the driver for negligence.

"[There is no] requirement of a physical impact as a precondition to recovery for damages proximately caused by the tort in only those cases . . . where the plaintiff was in personal danger of physical impact because of the direction of a negligent force against him and where plaintiff actually did fear the physical impact."

Niederman v. Brodsky, 261 A.2d 84, 90 (Pa. 1970).

In *Niederman*, the court found that an appellant's complaint alleged facts, which, if proven, would establish that "[a] negligent force was aimed at him and put him in personal danger of physical impact, and that he actually did fear the force. . . ." *Id.* at 90. This did away with the impact rule previously used in Pennsylvania. *See id.* at 85. The court credited its decision to high courts in neighboring states which had previously adopted the new rule. *See id.* (citing *Robb v. Pennsylvania RR. Co.*, 210 A.2d 709 (Del. 1965); *Falzone v. Busch*, 214 A.2d 12 (N.J. 1965); *Battalla v. New York*, 176 N.E.2d 729 (N.Y. 1961)).

Specifically, the complaint in *Niederman* alleged that appellee driver negligently struck down appellant's son, who at the time of this collision was standing next to appellant. *See id.* at 84. The *Niederman* court found that these alleged facts, if proven, would establish that appellee's car, a negligent force, cut a "destructive path" into appellant such that appellant was in personal danger and actually feared the force. *See id.* at 84-85. Since appellant's complaint satisfied the elements of the rule, the court afforded appellant a chance to recover for the physical and mental harm he sustained. *See id.* at 85.

A. Negligent Force

In order to prevail like the appellant in *Niederman*, Robert must allege facts which, if proven, will establish that the force in question was negligent. For the purposes of this memo, we assume that the car in this situation constituted a negligence force. Therefore the first element is met.

B. Aimed at the Plaintiff

Second, Robert must allege facts which, if proven, will establish that the negligent force in question was aimed at him, Robert's claim that he jumped away from his bicycle right before the driver struck and crushed his bicycle indicates that Robert will be able to satisfy the second element of the *Niederman* rule, Robert's account tends to show that before he jumped away from his bicycle, he was situated in the path of a negligent force.

The defense may claim that the force in question was not aimed specifically at Robert, since this would imply that the defendant had tried to hit Robert intentionally. Assuming arguendo that the defendant did not try to hit Robert intentionally, defense's argument still cannot overcome *Niederman*. In *Niederman*, the defendant hit a fire hydrant, a litter pole and basket, a newsstand, and Mr. Niederman's son before coming near Mr. Niederman. *See id.* at 84. Yet the court still saw fit to allow the case to go to trial, simultaneously establishing the rule. The only requirement is that the defendant's car cut a path toward the plaintiff, and that is what happened in Robert's situation.

C. Personal Danger of Physical Impact

Third, Robert must allege facts which, if proven, will establish that the negligent force put him in danger of physical impact. The fact that the car crushed the bicycle on which Robert was riding strongly suggests that Robert was in grave personal danger of physical impact. If Robert had not jumped from his bicycle prior to impact, there is a strong possibility that Robert's fate would closely resemble that of his bicycle.

The defense may claim that by leaping out of the way Robert took himself out of personal danger. However, the court set the standard that a plaintiff must show personal danger of an impact existed because of the direction of a negligent force. Therefore, according to the *Niederman* standard, it is enough that the car, moving in the trajectory it was, hit the bicycle. Whether Robert jumped out of the way is not relevant.

D. Fear of Physical Impact

Finally, Robert must allege facts which, if proven, will establish that he actually feared the physical impact. Robert's action of jumping off of his bicycle as the car approached him provides a strong inference that he actually feared the potential danger threatened by the car. Thus, Robert probably will be able to satisfy the last element of the Niederman rule, and accordingly be afforded a chance to recover for the physical and emotional injuries he has suffered.

The defense may claim that Robert did not jump out of the way because of fear. Jumping out of the way was an instinctual reaction. The fear only came after the accident. Furthermore, the fear that did finally manifest itself turned out to be of riding a bicycle, not of physical impact with the car. However, fear very often leads us to react instinctually to a situation where a rational reaction might injure us. Furthermore, Robert's fear of riding a bicycle is directly linked to having the bicycle upon which he was riding hit by a car. It can be inferred that Robert is apprehensive about riding the bicycle not because the bicycle itself will injure him, but because he feels a car might hit him while he is riding the bicycle.

II. Mrs. Hope probably does not have a claim against the driver for negligence.

A. Negligent Force

Again we assume the force in this issue was negligent in nature.

B. Aimed at the Plaintiff

It is improbable that a court would find that the force in question was aimed at Mrs. Hope. The direction of the car was not toward Mrs. Hope's porch on which she was standing at the time of the accident, because the accident occurred entirely on the street, and not the sidewalk or lawn. Furthermore, even if the car continued moving after the accident, it is unlikely that it would have reached Mrs. Hope's porch. Taking into account Mrs. Hope's distance from her son and her delayed awareness of the accident, a court probably will find that Mrs. Hope was physically removed from the path of danger threatened by driver's negligent force.

C. Personal Danger of Physical Impact

Under the *Niederman* rule, Mrs. Hope probably was not in personal danger of physical impact because the given facts lack evidence of a negligent force directed toward her. Unlike the appellant in *Niederman*, Mrs. Hope was not standing next to her son during the time the car approached, but instead was engaged in a phone conversation on her front porch. She became cognizant of danger in her surroundings only when she heard the screeching of brakes and a crash, and subsequently ran to see her son lying in front of a stopped automobile.

D. Fear of Physical Impact

In addition, Mrs. Hope probably will not be able to satisfy the final prong of the *Niederman* rule. Mrs. Hope's distance from her son and her delayed cognizance of the surrounding danger tend to support an inference that she did not actually fear impact. While Mrs. Hope might have felt fear, it was for her son's safety or her son being hit by the car. It was not fear over being herself hit by a car, which is the fear *Niederman* requires.

E. Good Faith Argument to Extend the Law

On the other hand, Mrs. Hope might be able to meet the recovery requirements set forth in *Niederman*. Mrs. Hope might be able to establish that she was in personal danger of physical impact because of the direction of a negligent force, if driver's car was traveling in the direction of Mrs. Hope's porch and if Mrs. Hope's porch is a close or reachable distance from the street. Also, Mrs. Hope's auditory perception of the screeching of brakes and a crash may be viewed by a court as sufficient for establishing that Mrs. Hope actually feared physical impact. Mrs. Hope's chance of successfully establishing this second element will be strongest if we can determine that driver's car was traveling toward Mrs. Hope's porch and her porch is close in distance to the street.

Although Mrs. Hope has a low chance of bringing a cause of action under the *Niederman* rule, she may be able to make a compelling argument for recovery given the rationale upon which the *Niederman* court relied in expanding the law of negligence beyond mere physical impact. According to the *Niederman* court, "the gravity of appellant's injury and the inherent humanitarianism of our judicial process and its responsiveness to the current needs of justice" represented the rationale controlling their decision. *Niederman*, 261 A.2d at 85. Specifically, this court found that a driver's conduct negligently created an unreasonable risk of causing bodily harm to an appellant present in the negligent driver's path of danger. *See id.* The *Niederman* court allowed appellant to seek recovery for substantial shock and fright and related physical injuries by reasoning that they were the proximate result of the threat of bodily harm created by the driver. *See id.*

Using *Niederman* as a guide, one may argue that the driver's conduct negligently created an unreasonable risk of causing emotional harm to Mrs. Hope, since the possibility that a close relative would contemporaneously witness or perceive negligent conduct was foreseeable. Arguably, Mrs. Hope contemporaneously perceived her son's ordeal. Mrs. Hope was supervising her son riding his bicycle at the time she heard the distinct sounds of a car crash, and immediately following this auditory perception, she recognized that her son was involved. Suffering from shock and fright, Mrs. Hope fainted from seeing her son lying on the street, and fell to the ground incurring severe head injuries. Like the appellant in *Niederman* was deemed to have apprehended a danger to himself, Mrs. Hope apprehended a danger to her son, and consequently suffered immediate and direct shock and fear. Thus, under the rationale relied on by the *Niederman* court in making its holding, Mrs. Hope may be given a chance to recover given the gravity of her injuries and the foreseeable circumstances in which they were incurred.

To see how the law has evolved since *Niederman*, please read the following case.

Janice A. NEFF, Individually and as Executrix of the Estate of William L. Neff, Appellant,
v.
William LASSO, Jr. and G. Thomas Pasquariello, T/A Pasquariello's Auto Shop Appellees.
Superior Court of Pennsylvania.
555 A.2d 1304 (Pa. Super. Ct. 1989)

[Some footnotes may have been omitted.]

KELLY, Judge:

The sole issue on appeal is whether a wife may recover against a tortfeasor for serious emotional distress caused by shock and fear for her husband who was fatally injured in an automobile accident, where the wife visually observed her husband's vehicle being followed by defendant's speeding vehicle, heard the impact between her husband's pickup and defendant's automobile and arrived on the scene immediately thereafter to find her husband lying unconscious. For the reasons which follow, we find that appellant has alleged sufficient facts to state a cause of action. Accordingly, we reverse the order of the trial court sustaining defendant's preliminary objections in the nature of a demurrer, reinstate appellant's cause of action, and remand for proceedings consistent with this opinion.

Appellant, Janice A. Neff, appeals from the order granting the preliminary objections in the nature of a demurrer made by appellees, William Lasso, Jr. and G. Thomas Pasquariello, t/a Pasquariello's Auto Shop, dismissing appellant's claim for negligent infliction of emotional distress.

I. STANDARD OF REVIEW

Our standard of review of an order granting preliminary objections in the nature of a demurrer was set forth in *Vattimo v. Lower Bucks Hosp., Inc.*, 502 Pa. 241, 465 A.2d 1231 (1983) as follows:

> All material facts set forth in the complaint as well as all inferences reasonably deducible therefrom are admitted as true [for the purpose of this review.] The question presented by the demurrer is whether, on the facts averred, the law says with certainty that no recovery is possible. Where a doubt exists as to whether a demurrer should be sustained, this doubt should be resolved in favor of overruling it.

465 A.2d at 1232-33 (citations omitted); *see also Mahoney v. Furches*, 503 Pa. 60, 66, 468 A.2d 458, 461-62 (1983). In reviewing the grant of a demurrer we are

not bound by the inferences drawn by the trial court nor are we bound by its conclusions of law. *See Drug House Inc. v. Keystone Bank*, 272 Pa. Super. 130, 132, 414 A.2d 704, 705 (1979). Moreover, the novelty of a claim or theory, alone, does not compel affirmance of a demurrer. *See Sinn v. Burd*, 486 Pa. 146, 150, 404 A.2d 672, 674 (1979); *Papieves v. Lawrence*, 437 Pa. 373, 376-77, 263 A.2d 118, 120 (1970); *Woodward v. Dietrich*, 378 Pa. Super. 111, 548 A.2d 301 (1988).

In light of our standard of review, the following is a summary of the relevant factual history of this case as stated in appellant's complaint. At approximately 3:55 p.m. on May 17, 1986, the decedent, William L. Neff, was driving his Chevrolet pickup truck on Allen Drive directly in front of his home. Appellee, William Lasso, Jr., traveling at an excessive rate of speed, followed decedent down Allen Drive. As decedent was attempting to make a left-hand turn into his driveway, appellee attempted to pass him on the left-hand side in a no passing zone. In doing so, appellee struck the rear left portion of decedent's pickup fatally injuring the decedent.

At the time of these events, appellant, Janice A. Neff, was standing in her home looking out her kitchen window. Appellant observed her husband arriving home and observed appellee following directly behind him at an excessive rate of speed. Appellant heard an impact between two vehicles. Appellant arrived at the accident scene immediately thereafter and found her husband lying unconscious on their front lawn. As a result, appellant suffered severe emotional distress.

Appellant, in her capacity as executrix of her husband's estate, filed a wrongful death and survival action. She also filed a separate claim on her own behalf for negligent infliction of emotional distress based upon the injuries she incurred as a result of appellee's negligence. Appellees, William Lasso and G. Thomas Pasquariello, filed preliminary objections in the nature of a demurrer in which they argued that appellant had failed to allege a cause of action for negligent infliction of emotional distress where she did not visually observe the accident. In her response, appellant asserted that seeing the impact was unnecessary and that she need only have had a contemporaneous sensory perception of the accident. The Honorable Richard D. Grifo concluded that "contemporaneous observance" of the accident as required by our Supreme Court's decision in *Sinn v. Burd, supra*, implied sight only and not hearing, and therefore he sustained the preliminary objections and dismissed Mrs. Neff's separate claim for negligent infliction of emotional distress. This timely appeal followed.

II. NEGLIGENT INFLICTION OF EMOTIONAL DISTRESS

Initially, we find it appropriate to briefly review the development of the cause of action for negligent infliction of emotional distress. In doing so, we will consider the development of the cause of action generally and then its development in Pennsylvania particularly.

A. EVOLUTION OF THE TORT OF NEGLIGENT INFLICTION OF EMOTIONAL DISTRESS: GENERALLY

Originally, courts allowed plaintiffs to maintain a cause of action for emotional distress only if certain limiting and qualifying factors were present. Early cases denied plaintiff's recovery unless the plaintiff had suffered a contemporaneous physical injury or impact accompanied by mental distress. A majority of courts gradually departed from the impact rule and adopted a rule allowing recovery for psychic injury where the plaintiff was in the physical zone of danger and was in fear for his own safety. This was known as the "zone of danger" rule. *See* W.P. Keeton, *Prosser & Keeton on Torts* (5th ed. 1984) at 363; Note, *The Next Best Thing to Being There?: Foreseeability of Media-Assisted Bystanders*, 17 S.W. U. L. Rev. 65 (1987); Bell, *The Bell Tolls: Toward Full Tort Recovery for Psychic Injury*, 36 U. Fla. L. R. 333 (1984); Note, *Administering the Tort of Negligent Infliction of Emotional Distress*, 4 Cardozo L. Rev. 487 (1983); Note, *Negligent Infliction of Emotional Distress: Keeping Dillon in Bounds*, 37 Wash. & Lee L. Rev. 1235 (1980); Comment, *Negligently Inflicted Mental Distress: The Case for an Independent Tort*, 59 Geo. L.J. 1237 (1971).

In 1968, the California Supreme Court rendered the landmark decision of *Dillon v. Legg*, 68 Cal. 2d 728, 69 Cal. Rptr. 72, 441 P.2d 912 (1968), which lowered the bystander barrier by permitting a mother, who was not within the zone of danger, to recover for psychic injury caused by witnessing her daughter's negligently caused death. The court adopted the position that liability for the negligent infliction of emotional distress would depend upon whether such injuries were foreseeable to the defendant at the time of the accident. The *Dillon* court set forth three factors—plaintiff's proximity to the decedent, the directness of her observance of the accident, and the closeness of her relationship to the accident victim—as guidelines for future courts to determine whether psychic injury was reasonably foreseeable. The California Supreme Court emphasized, however, that the reasonableness of imposing liability was ultimately a factual determination which is made on a case by case basis. 69 Cal. Rptr. at 80, 441 P.2d at 920. Thus, the factors were not to be applied formalistically to bar arguably valid claims. *See Ochoa v. Superior Court*, 39 Cal. 3d 159, 216 Cal. Rptr. 6611 703 P.2d 1 (1985). A majority of courts now recognize a cause of action based upon *Dillon's* three prong test, though some variety exists between courts recognizing the *Dillon* test with regard to the precise parameters of the cause of action. *See Witnessing Injury—Damages—Mental Anguish*, 5 A.L.R. 4th 833 (1981 & 1988 Supp.); *see also* Note, *The Next Best Thing to Being There? Foreseeability of Media-Assisted Bystanders, supra.*

B. EVOLUTION IN PENNSYLVANIA

In Pennsylvania, the tort of negligent infliction of emotional distress has followed a similar course of evolution. For decades, our Supreme Court uniformly applied the "impact rule," which barred recovery for fright, nervous shock or mental or emotional distress unless it was accompanied by a physical injury or impact upon the complaining party. *Kazatsky v. King David Memorial Park*, 515

Pa. 183, 191-92, 527 A.2d 988, 992 (1987) (collecting cases). However, in *Niederman v. Brodsky*, 436 Pa. 401, 261 A.2d 84 (1970), our Supreme Court abandoned the requirement of physical impact as a precondition to recovery where the plaintiff was in personal danger of physical impact from the negligent force and actually feared for his own safety.

Finally, in *Sinn v. Burd, supra,* our Supreme Court was presented with the question of whether to permit recovery for emotional distress by a plaintiff who, while outside the zone of danger, actually witnessed the accident causing serious injury to a close relative. In *Sinn*, the deceased child and her sister were standing by the family's mailbox located alongside the roadway. An automobile operated by the defendant struck the child and hurled her through the air, causing injuries which resulted in her death. The plaintiff-mother witnessed the accident from a position near the front door of her home. Our Supreme Court abandoned the zone of danger requirement, and permitted recovery for emotional distress by the plaintiff-mother who, while outside the zone of danger, actually witnessed the accident causing serious injury to her daughter.

In abandoning the "zone of danger" rule, the Court found that the *Niederman* test was unduly restrictive and prevented recovery in instances where there was no sound policy basis supporting such a result. The Court reasoned that the emotional impact upon a parent who witnesses the death of a child was "as great and as legitimate" as the apprehension of fear of impact under the zone of danger. 404 A.2d at 677. The Court explained:

> Applications of the zone of danger test to situations where the death or serious injury of a child is witnessed by a parent creates the very evil that the test was designed to eliminate, i.e., arbitrariness. It would bar recovery depending upon the position of the plaintiff at the time of the event, and ignores that the emotional impact was most probably influenced by the event witnessed—serious injury to or death of the child—rather than the plaintiff's awareness of personal exposure to danger.

404 A.2d at 678 (footnote omitted).

The Court adopted the *Dillon* parameters for determining whether the infliction of emotional distress was reasonably foreseeable. Thus, a cause of action for negligent infliction of emotional distress exists in Pennsylvania when the following criteria are met:

> (1) Whether plaintiff was located near the scene of the accident as contrasted with one who was a distance away from it;

> (2) Whether the shock resulted from a direct emotional impact upon plaintiff from the sensory and contemporaneous observance of the accident, as contrasted with learning of the accident from others after its occurrence;

> (3) Whether plaintiff and the victim were closely related as contrasted with an absence of any relationship or the presence of only a distant relationship.

Id. 404 A.2d at 685, *quoting Dillon v. Legg, supra,* 68 Cal. 2d at 740-41, 69 Cal. Rptr. at 80, 441 P.2d at 920. Applying the *Dillon* foreseeability requirements in *Sinn*, our Supreme Court found that the contemporaneous observance of the accident was the proximate cause of the plaintiff-mother's emotional injuries and therefore a cause of action should be recognized despite the fact that the plaintiff-mother was not within the zone of danger.

In the instant case, there is no question that appellant's pleading adequately satisfied requirements one and three. The question here is whether appellant has pled facts sufficient to meet the requirement that appellant's shock resulted from a "direct emotional impact from a sensory and contemporaneous observance of the accident." Specifically, we must determine whether visual awareness of the setting, simultaneous auditory perception of the impact, and immediate visual observation of the results of the impact seconds later is sufficient to constitute a "sensory and contemporaneous observance" within the meaning of those terms as used in *Sinn*.

III. SENSORY AND CONTEMPORANEOUS OBSERVANCE

Appellant argues that to require a visual observance of the moment of impact unrealistically elevates sight above the other senses and misperceives the distinction drawn in *Sinn* and its progeny. Appellant maintains that the cases which have considered the parameters of the "sensory and contemporaneous observation" requirement have not drawn the line between sight and hearing but have focused on whether the emotional blow was direct and immediate rather than distant and indirect. Thus, appellant asserts, for a cause of action to exist, the prospective plaintiff must be a percipient witness to the traumatic event.[1] For the reasons which follow, we agree.

A. PENNSYLVANIA SUPREME COURT DECISIONS

Following its decision in *Sinn*, our Supreme Court has been called upon three times to consider the parameters for pleading a cause of action for negligent infliction of emotional distress; specifically the contemporaneous observance requirement. *Brooks v. Decker*, 512 Pa. 365, 516 A.2d 1380 (1986); *Mazzagatti v. Everingham*, 512 Pa. 266, 516 A.2d 672 (1986); and *Yandrich v. Radic*, 495 Pa. 243, 433 A.2d 459 (1981). In each case, the Court concluded that the plaintiff had failed to allege that his shock resulted from a "sensory and contemporaneous observance" of the accident.

In *Yandrich*, the Court denied recovery to a plaintiff-father who did not witness the accident and who did not arrive at the accident scene until after his son had been taken to the hospital. The father's emotional injuries resulted from seeing his son at the hospital and remaining there with him until he died five days later.

---

1   Percipient is defined as: "capable of or characterized by perception." Perception is defined as: "1. obs: consciousness; 2. a: a result of perceiving: OBSERVATION; b: a mental image: CONCEPT: 3. a: awareness of the elements of environment through physical sensation <color>; b: physical sensation interpreted in the light of experience; 4. a: a quick, acute, and intuitive cognition: APPRECIATION: b: a capacity of comprehension." *Webster's Ninth New Collegiate Dictionary* (1986) at 872.

Our Supreme Court sustained the grant of demurrer in an Opinion in Support of Affirmance. The Court held that the father's pleadings had not satisfied the *Sinn* criteria and, therefore, his emotional distress was not foreseeable as a matter of law. 433 A.2d at 461 (Wilkinson, J.). In a separate Opinion in Support of Affirmance, Justice Nix (now Chief Justice), in addressing the question of whether the policies underlying its decision in *Sinn* would support the extension of liability when the plaintiff had been notified of the accident, gave the following explanation for the denial of recovery:

> Where a parent or close blood relative actually witnesses a traumatic serious injury to a loved one, we expressed in *Sinn* that the emotional impact reverberating from that event was at least as potent as that which flowed from the personal exposure to danger under the zone of danger theory articulated in *Niederman*.

> In *Sinn* we also recognized the traditional view that solatiurn was not compensable. In *Sinn* we noted that damages were not to be awarded to allay the grief resulting from the loss, but rather to compensate for the shock of actually witnessing the event.

433 A.2d at 462-63 (Nix, J.) (footnote omitted). Recovery was denied because the plaintiff had been informed of the event by a third person and thus had not suffered an emotional injury resulting from a direct and contemporaneous sensory experience of the event itself.

In *Mazzagatti*, the Court considered whether a cause of action exists where a close relative does not observe the accident itself, but instead arrives at the scene of the accident and observes the victim a few minutes afterwards. The Court declined to extend liability reasoning that any other interpretation of the *Sinn* foreseeability test would ignore several basic principles of tort liability. "These principles, which require that the defendant's breach of a duty of care proximately cause the plaintiff's injury, have established the jurisprudential concept that at some point along the causal chain, the passage of time and the span of distance mandate the cut-off point for liability." 516 A.2d at 676. (Citations omitted).

The Court in *Mazzagatti* determined that the critical element for establishing such liability was the contemporaneous observance of the injury to the close relative. Our Supreme Court explained that:

> We believe that where the close relative is not present at the scene of the accident, but instead learns of the accident from a third party, the close relative's *prior knowledge of the injury to the victim serves as a buffer against the full impact of observing the accident scene. By contrast, the relative who contemporaneously observes the tortious conduct has no time span in which to brace his or her emotional system.* The negligent tortfeasor inflicts upon this bystander a injury separate and apart from the injury to the victim. *See Sinn v. Burd, supra,* 486 Pa. at 158-62, 404 A.2d at 678-80 . . . Where, as here, the plaintiff has no contemporaneous sensory perception of the injury, the emotional distress results more from the particular emotional makeup of the plaintiff rather than from the nature of defendant's actions.

516 A.2d at 679. (Emphasis added). Based upon the above reasoning, the Court in *Mazzagatti* held that a plaintiff who does not experience a contemporaneous

observance of the injury to a close relative does not state a cause of action for the negligent infliction of emotional distress under the parameters enunciated in *Sinn v. Burd, supra.*

Similarly, in *Brooks v. Decker, supra,* our Supreme Court denied recovery to a plaintiff-father who did not witness the accident. In *Brooks*, as the plaintiff drove towards his home an ambulance passed him and turned onto his street. The ambulance stopped shortly thereafter where a crowd of people had gathered. Plaintiff, who followed the ambulance, noticed a bicycle that belonged to his son on the ground. As plaintiff exited his vehicle to investigate, he discovered his son had been the victim of an automobile accident. Relying upon its reasoning in *Mazzagatti*, our Supreme Court held in *Brooks* that a father who alleged that he sustained an actual injury upon seeing the broken body of his son who had been struck by an automobile while riding a bicycle, but who failed to allege that he witnessed the accident or his son's injuries, failed to state a cause of action for negligent infliction of emotional distress. 516 A.2d at 1383.

A comparison of the facts alleged in the instant case with the facts as alleged in *Sinn, Yandrich, Mazzagatti,* and *Brooks,* discloses that we are dealing with a case that falls between the facts in *Sinn,* which involved the actual visual observance of the moment of impact and those in *Yandrich, Mazzagatti,* and *Brooks,* which involved no comtemporaneous observance of the impact, visual or otherwise. Although appellant did not visually witness the impact, she experienced a contemporaneous sensory awareness of the accident and its personal import based upon her visual and aural observations before, during, and after the moment of impact. Thus, we must determine whether our Supreme Court in abandoning the "zone of danger" rule intended to limit relief for negligent infliction of emotional distress to those plaintiffs who visually witnessed the impact.

Our reading of *Sinn, Yandrich, Mazzagatti,* and *Brooks* leads us to conclude that our Supreme Court, in considering the parameters of the "sensory and contemporaneous observance" requirement, focused upon whether the emotional shock was immediate and direct rather than distant and indirect, and not upon the sense employed in perceiving the accident. We concede however, these decisions are inconclusive for purposes of deciding the narrow question before us. Consequently, we look to persuasive authority of non-binding precedent from this and other jurisdictions to determine whether actual *visual* observance ought to be deemed necessary to satisfy the "sensory and contemporaneous observance" requirement.

B. PENNSYLVANIA PERSUASIVE AUTHORITY

Our research discloses no Pennsylvania appellate court cases addressing the narrow question of whether visual perception of the impact is necessary to satisfy the *Sinn* requirement that the "shock resulted from a direct emotional impact upon plaintiff from the sensory and contemporaneous observance of the accident." Our research has, however, disclosed two Pennsylvania trial court decisions which allowed the plaintiffs to recover for emotional injury where the plaintiffs *heard* the impact and immediately thereafter *visually* observed the injured relative. *Kratzer v. Unger*, 17 Pa. D & C 3d 771 (1981); *Anfuso v. Smith*, 15 Pa. D & C 3d 389 (1980).

In *Kratzer*, the plaintiff-foster mother heard a loud thump and turned to see that her foster son had been struck by the defendant's automobile and was lying unconscious in the road. Relying on *Sinn*, the defendant argued that the plaintiff had failed to state a cause of action where the perception of the accident's happening was auditory rather than visual. The trial court disagreed and found that a cause of action for negligent infliction of emotional distress existed. The trial court reasoned that:

> Clearly our Supreme Court focused upon the first-hand observation by plaintiff of her son's fatal accident in *Sinn v. Burd.* However, *we cannot believe that the court intended thereby to limit recovery to those situations where the shocking event might manifest itself through the eyesight of the witness, to the exclusion of other types of sensory observation.* The important element is the immediate and direct awareness of what has occurred, and the appellate court's concern was to limit recovery to persons 'on the scene' when such a tragedy happens, as opposed to those who might learn of it from someone else who had been present. There is no rational reason to believe that what an eyewitness sees will be any more or less shocking than what an 'earwitness' hears.

17 Pa. D & C 3d at 773. (Emphasis added).

In *Anfuso*, the plaintiff-mother observed her daughter shortly before the child was struck by an automobile, heard the impact, and witnessed the accident scene immediately thereafter. The trial court rejected the contention that visual perception of the impact was the only sensory observance sufficient to give rise to a cause of action and concluded that the facts as pleaded established that the plaintiff-mother was a "participient witness" to the impact. Finding no basis in logic or fairness for rejecting the claim, the trial court concluded that the "sensory and contemporaneous observance" requirement was satisfied by the pleading that the plaintiff-mother saw her child immediately prior to impact, heard the squeal of tires and the impact with the child, and witnessed the accident scene immediately afterwards.

In addition to the above trial court decisions, we note that the District Court for the Eastern District of Pennsylvania addressed this precise question in *Bliss v. Allentown Public Library*, 497 F. Supp. 487 (E.D. Pa. 1980). Applying its construction of Pennsylvania's law, the Eastern District Court held that a complaint alleging that the mother heard a metal sculpture fall upon her child and turned to see her child lying on the floor with a statute positioned across the child's arm stated a cause of action for negligent infliction of emotional harm, even though the mother was not looking at the child at the exact moment of impact. The court reasoned that to deny the mother's claim because of the position of her eyes at the split second that the accident occurred would ignore the reality that the entire incident produced the emotional injury for which she sought redress. The court concluded that requiring a direct visual perception would defeat the policy underlying *Sinn*. The court held that the mother had identified herself sufficiently as a "percipient witness" to state a cause of action for negligent infliction of emotional harm. 497 F. Supp. at 489.

C. OTHER JURISDICTIONS

This particular question has also been addressed by the appellate courts of California, Florida, New Hampshire and Texas. *Krouse v. Graham*, 19 Cal. 3d 59, 137 Cal. Rptr. 863, 562 P.2d 1022 (1977); *Champion v. Gray*, 478 So. 2d 17 (Fla. 1985); *Corso v. Merrill*, 119 N.H. 647, 406 A.2d 300 (1979); *Bedgood v. Madalin*, 589 S.W.2d 797 (Tex. Civ. App. 1979). A review of these cases reveals that the requirement of actual observance of the event has been construed since *Dillon* to include *sensory perception* of the accident generally and not strict *visual* observance of the event. *Versland v. Caron Transport*, 206 Mont. 313, 317, 671 P.2d 583, 586 (1983). *See also Prosser & Keeton*, at 366 n.74 (1984 & 1988 Supp.).

In *Krouse v. Graham, supra*, the plaintiff was seated in the driver's seat of a parked car. His wife was removing groceries from the back seat when the defendant driver smashed into the car, killing plaintiff's wife. In response to plaintiffs claim for emotional injury under *Dillon*, the court specifically held that direct impact from a sensory and contemporaneous observance did not require visual perception of the impact causing the injury. 137 Cal. Rptr. at 872, 562 P.2d at 1031. The court concluded that the plaintiff must have perceived that his wife was struck because "he knew her position an instant before the impact, observed the defendant's vehicle approach . . . and realized that defendant's car must have struck her." 137 Cal. Rptr. at 872, 562 P.2d at 1031. Thus, he was deemed a percipient witness and recovery for negligent infliction of emotional distress was granted. *Compare Parsons v. Superior Court*, 81 Cal. App. 3d 506, 146 Cal. Rptr. 495 (1978) (recovery denied because plaintiff neither "saw, heard, or otherwise sensorily perceived the injury-producing event").

In *Champion v. Gray, supra*, the Florida Supreme Court adopted the *Dillon* foreseeability requirements and allowed the mother to recover after she heard the accident, came immediately to the accident scene, and, upon seeing the body of her daughter who had been hit by a drunk driver, suffered such severe emotional distress and shock that she collapsed and died. In reaching its conclusion, the court reasoned that the price of death or significant discernible physical injury, when caused by psychological trauma resulting from negligent injury imposed upon a close family member within the *sensory perception of the physically injured person*, is too great a harm to require direct physical contact before a cause of action exists. The injury is foreseeable where the physically injured party is directly involved in this event which caused the original injury. Therefore, if the plaintiff "sees it, hears it, or arrives upon the scene while the injured party is still there, the person is likely involved." 478

So. 2d at 20. We note that the last contingency is concededly beyond the scope of recovery which our Supreme Court is willing to recognize.

In *Corso v. Merrill, supra*, the New Hampshire Supreme Court adopted the *Dillon* foreseeability requirements and allowed the plaintiff-mother to recover after she heard a thud, looked outside and saw her daughter lying in the street. The court stated that in order to prove the injury was foreseeable the emotional injury must be directly attributable to the emotional impact of the plaintiff's *observations or contemporaneous sensory perception of the accident and immediate viewing of the accident*. 406 A.2d at 306. (Emphasis added). To ensure against unreasonable and unlimited liability the New Hampshire Supreme Court indicated that they would require a relatively close connection in both time and geography between the negligent act and the resulting injury. The court reasoned that, such requirements were consistent with general principles of liability based upon reasonable foreseeability. The court concluded that Mrs. Corso's auditory perceptions from inside the house followed by her immediate observance of the accident scene met the test of reasonable foreseeability and stated a cause of action for negligent infliction of emotional distress. *Accord Oberreuter v. Orion Industries, Inc.*, 342 N.W.2d 492 (Iowa 1984) (recovery for negligent infliction of emotional distress is intended to compensate the plaintiff for emotional trauma caused by plaintiffs "visceral participation" in the event).

In *Bedgood v. Madalin, supra*, a cause of action for negligent infliction of emotional distress was held to exist where the father who was located 100 feet from the place where his eleven year old son was struck by an automobile, heard the impact, heard a loud scream by his son, reached the scene within less than one minute after impact, and found the boy apparently unconscious and bleeding profusely from a torn artery. The court concluded that the circumstances were sufficient to permit a finding that tortfeasors could have reasonably foreseen that their negligence would cause mental anguish. *Cf. Landreth v. Reed*, 570 S.W.2d 486 (Tex. Civ. App. 1978) (allowing minor plaintiff to recover for injuries sustained by her as a result of shock and trauma in witnessing efforts to revive her infant sister after she was removed from a swimming pool was appropriate where plaintiff was located near the scene of the accident, the shock resulted from a direct emotional impact on plaintiff from a contemporaneous perception of the accident).

Finally, it appears that English courts also recognize a cause of action for negligent infliction of emotional distress where there's an immediate sensory observance without actual visual observance of the impact. For example, in *Hambrook v. Stokes Brothers, Ltd.*, 41 The Times L.R. 125, 1 K.B. 141 (1925), a mother was allowed to recover for emotional injuries she sustained not by reason of what she saw or what she was told by any bystander but on the assumption that the shock was caused by her own sight of the lorry, running uncontrolled down the hill, and knowing her children were in the lorry's path. Hale, *The Lot of Negligent Frightener*, 22 B.U.L. L. Rev. 508, 512 (1942).

Our analysis of the foregoing persuasive authorities convinces us that the "sensory and contemporaneous observance" requirement should not be limited to visual observance. Well reasoned opinions in this and other jurisdictions persuade us that the logical and practical focus of the second prong of the *Dillon* test should be whether the observance was direct and immediate as opposed to indirect and removed and not upon the particular sensory vehicle which gave rise to the awareness of the event and its personal import. It is the immediate sensory awareness and not the source (*i.e.* visual, tactile, aural, gustatory or olfactory), of the awareness which must control.

IV. APPLICATION

With these principles in mind, we now consider the question of whether appellant's "shock resulted from a direct emotional impact upon her from a sensory and contemporaneous observance of the accident," keeping in mind that our focus is on the degree of appellant's awareness of the negligent act rather than the source of her awareness. A review of the record discloses that appellant has pled that she was standing in her kitchen looking out towards the street. She observed her husband's pickup traveling down the street followed by Mr. Lasso, who was operating his automobile at an excessive rate of speed. Although she no longer could see the two vehicles, appellant heard a collision and immediately realized her husband's pickup was involved in the collision. She arrived on the scene immediately thereafter to find her husband lying unconscious on their front lawn. As a result, she suffered a severe and emotional shock for which she now seeks recovery. We find that appellant has pled sufficient facts to state a claim that she was a percipient witness and her injuries were foreseeable under the circumstances.

It may be true that unlike visual observance, aural awareness may rarely, standing alone, give rise to a sufficient awareness of the nature and import of the event to cause severe emotional injury. However, aural perception (hearing the impact) when considered together with prior and subsequent visual observance (seeing Mr. Lasso's car speeding behind her husband's pickup and seeing her husband lying unconscious immediately after the impact), may produce a full, direct, and immediate awareness of the nature and import of the negligent conduct which may foreseeably result in emotional injury, and which is not buffered by the intervention of a third party or the effects of the removal of the awareness temporally or geographically from the impact and its consequences. To deny appellant's claim solely because she did not see the precise moment of the impact would ignore the plain reality that the *entire incident* produced the emotional injury for which the plaintiff seeks redress, and would be contrary to the very policy and purpose of the Court in *Sinn* when it abandoned the "zone of danger" rule, *i.e.* eliminating arbitrariness. Therefore, we conclude that "sensory and contemporaneous observance" is not limited to visual sensory perception but properly includes an aural sensory awareness as well. Succinctly, it is not the source of the awareness, rather, it is the degree of the awareness arising from all of the individual's senses and memory which must be determinative of whether the plaintiffs emotional shock resulted from a "sensory and contemporaneous observance" of the accident.

CONCLUSION

Having found that appellee has alleged a claim for negligent infliction of emotional distress, we reverse the order of the trial court, reinstate appellant's claim and remand for trial. Jurisdiction relinquished.

APPENDIX E

**AURELIA DAVIS, as next friend of LaSHONDA D.,
PETITIONER,**

v.

MONROE COUNTY BOARD OF EDUCATION et al.
United States Supreme Court
526 U.S. 629 (1999)

[Some footnotes may have been omitted.]

JUSTICE O'CONNOR delivered the opinion of the Court.

Petitioner brought suit against the Monroe County Board of Education and other defendants, alleging that her fifth-grade daughter had been the victim of sexual harassment by another student in her class. Among petitioner's claims was a claim for monetary and injunctive relief under Title IX of the Education Amendments of 1972 (Title IX), 86 Stat. 373, as amended, 20 U.S.C. § 1681 et seq. The District Court dismissed petitioner's Title IX claim on the ground that "student-on-student," or peer, harassment provides no ground for a private cause of action under the statute. The Court of Appeals for the Eleventh Circuit, sitting en banc, affirmed. We consider here whether a private damages action may lie against the school board in cases of student-on-student harassment. We conclude that it may, but only where the funding recipient acts with deliberate indifference to known acts of harassment in its programs or activities. Moreover, we conclude that such an action will lie only for harassment that is so severe, pervasive, and objectively offensive that it effectively bars the victim's access to an educational opportunity or benefit.

I

Petitioner's Title IX claim was dismissed under Federal Rule of Civil Procedure 12(b)(6) for failure to state a claim upon which relief could be granted. Accordingly, in reviewing the legal sufficiency of petitioner's cause of action, "we must assume the truth of the material facts as alleged in the complaint." *Summit Health, Ltd. v. Pinhas*, 500 U.S. 322, 325 (1991).

A

Petitioner's minor daughter, LaShonda, was allegedly the victim of a prolonged pattern of sexual harassment by one of her fifth-grade classmates at Hubbard Elementary School, a public school in Monroe County, Georgia. According to petitioner's complaint, the harassment began in December 1992, when the classmate, G. F., attempted to touch LaShonda's breasts and genital area and made vulgar statements such as "'I want to get in bed with you'" and "'I want to feel your boobs.'" Complaint ¶ 7. Similar conduct allegedly occurred on or about January 4 and January 20, 1993. *Ibid.* LaShonda reported each of these incidents to her mother and to her classroom teacher, Diane Fort. *Ibid.* Petitioner, in turn, also contacted Fort, who allegedly assured petitioner that the school principal, Bill Querry, had been informed of the incidents. *Ibid.* Petitioner contends that, notwithstanding these reports, no disciplinary action was taken against G. F. *Id.* ¶ 16.

G. F.'s conduct allegedly continued for many months. In early February, G. F. purportedly placed a door stop in his pants and proceeded to act in a sexually suggestive manner toward LaShonda during physical education class. *Id.* ¶ 8. LaShonda reported G. F.'s behavior to her physical education teacher, Whit Maples. *Ibid.* Approximately one week later, G. F. again allegedly engaged in harassing behavior, this time while under the supervision of another classroom teacher, Joyce Pippin. *Id.* ¶ 9. Again, LaShonda allegedly reported the incident to the teacher, and again petitioner contacted the teacher to follow up. *Ibid.*

Petitioner alleges that G. F. once more directed sexually harassing conduct toward LaShonda in physical education class in early March, and that LaShonda reported the incident to both Maples and Pippen. *Id.* ¶ 10. In mid-April 1993, G. F. allegedly rubbed his body against LaShonda in the school hallway in what LaShonda considered a sexually suggestive manner, and LaShonda again reported the matter to Fort. *Id.* ¶ 11.

The string of incidents finally ended in mid-May, when G. F. was charged with, and pleaded guilty to, sexual battery for his misconduct. *Id.* ¶ 14. The complaint alleges that LaShonda had suffered during the months of harassment, however; specifically, her previously high grades allegedly dropped as she became unable to concentrate on her studies, *id.* ¶ 15, and, in April 1993, her father discovered that she had written a suicide note, *ibid.* The complaint further alleges that, at one point, LaShonda told petitioner that she "'didn't know how much longer she could keep [G. F.] off her.'" *Id.* ¶ 12.

Nor was LaShonda G. F.'s only victim; it is alleged that other girls in the class fell prey to G. F.'s conduct. *Id.* ¶ 16. At one point, in fact, a group composed of LaShonda and other female students tried to speak with Principal Querry about G. F.'s behavior. *Id.* ¶ 10. According to the complaint, however, a teacher denied the students' request with the statement, "'If [Querry] wants you, he'll' call you.'" *Ibid.*

Petitioner alleges that no disciplinary action was taken in response to G. F.'s behavior toward LaShonda. *Id.* ¶ 16. In addition to her conversations with Fort and Pippen, petitioner alleges that she spoke with Principal Querry in mid-May 1993. When petitioner inquired as to what action the school intended to take against G. F., Querry simply stated, "'I guess I'll have to threaten him a little bit harder.'" *Id.* ¶ 12. Yet, petitioner alleges, at no point during the many months of his reported misconduct was G. F. disciplined for harassment. *Id.* ¶ 16. Indeed, Querry allegedly asked petitioner why LaShonda "'was the only one complaining.'" *Id.* ¶ 12.

Nor, according to the complaint, was any effort made to separate G. F. and LaShonda. *Id.* ¶ 16. On the contrary, notwithstanding LaShonda's frequent complaints, only after more than three months of reported harassment was she even permitted to change her classroom seat so that she was no longer seated next to G. F. *Id.* ¶ 13. Moreover, petitioner alleges that, at the time of the events in question, the Monroe County Board of Education (Board) had not instructed its personnel on how to respond to peer sexual harassment and had not established a policy on the issue. *Id.* ¶ 17.

B

On May 4, 1994, petitioner filed suit in the United States District Court for the Middle District of Georgia against the Board, Charles Dumas, the school district's superintendent, and Principal Querry. The complaint alleged that the Board is a recipient of federal funding for purposes of Title IX, that "[t]he persistent sexual advances and harassment by the student G. F. upon [LaShonda] interfered with her ability to attend school and perform her studies and activities," and that "[t]he deliberate indifference by Defendants to the unwelcome sexual advances of a student upon LaShonda created an intimidating, hostile, offensive and abus[ive] school environment in violation of Title IX." *Id.* ¶¶ 27, 28. The complaint sought compensatory and punitive damages, attorney's fees, and injunctive relief. *Id.* ¶ 32.

The defendants (all respondents here) moved to dismiss petitioner's complaint under Federal Rule of Civil Procedure 12(b)(6) for failure to state a claim upon which relief could be granted, and the District Court granted respondents' motion. See 862 F. Supp. 363, 368 (M.D. Ga. 1994). With regard to petitioner's claims under Title IX, the court dismissed the claims against individual defendants on the ground that only federally funded educational institutions are subject to liability in private causes of action under Title IX. *Id.* at 367. As for the Board, the court concluded that Title IX provided no basis for liability absent an allegation "that the Board or an employee of the Board had any role in the harassment." *Ibid.*

Petitioner appealed the District Court's decision dismissing her Title IX claim against the Board, and a panel of the Court of Appeals for the Eleventh Circuit reversed. 74 F.3d 1186, 1195 (1996). Borrowing from Title VII law, a majority of the panel determined that student-on-student harassment stated a cause of action against the Board under Title IX: "[W]e conclude that as Title VII encompasses a claim for damages due to a sexually hostile working environment created by co-workers and tolerated by the employer, Title IX encompasses a claim for damages due to a sexually hostile educational environment created by a fellow student or students when the supervising authorities knowingly fail to act to eliminate the harassment." *Id.* at 1193. The Eleventh Circuit panel recognized that petitioner sought to state a claim based on school "officials' failure to take action to stop the offensive acts of those over whom the officials exercised control," *ibid.*, and the court concluded that petitioner had alleged facts sufficient to support a claim for hostile environment sexual harassment on this theory, *id.* at 1195.

The Eleventh Circuit granted the Board's motion for rehearing en banc, 91 F.3d 1418 (1996), and affirmed the District Court's decision to dismiss petitioner's Title IX claim against the Board, 120 F.3d 1390 (1998). The en banc court relied, primarily, on the theory that Title IX was passed pursuant to Congress' legislative authority under the Constitution's Spending Clause, U.S. Const., Art 1, § 8, cl. 1, and that the statute therefore must provide potential recipients of federal education funding with "unambiguous notice of the conditions they are assuming when they accept" it. 120 F.3d at 1399. Title IX, the court reasoned, provides recipients with notice that they must stop their employees from engaging in discriminatory conduct, but the statute fails to provide a recipient with sufficient notice of a duty to prevent student-on-student harassment. *Id.* at 1401.

Writing in dissent, four judges urged that the statute, by declining to identify the perpetrator of discrimination, encompasses misconduct by third parties: "The identity of the perpetrator is simply irrelevant under the language" of the statute. *Id.* at 1412 (Barkett, J., dissenting). The plain language, the dissenters reasoned, also provides recipients with sufficient notice that a failure to respond to student-on-student harassment could trigger liability for the district. *Id.* at 1414.

We granted certiorari, 524 U.S. ___ (1998), in order to resolve a conflict in the Circuits over whether, and under what circumstances, a recipient of federal educational funds can be liable in a private damages action arising from student-on-student sexual harassment, compare 120 F.3d 1390 (CA11 1998) (case below), and *Rowinsky v. Bryan Independent School Dist.*, 80 F.3d 1006, 1008 (CA5) (holding that private damages action for student-on-student harassment is available under Title IX only where funding recipient responds to these claims differently based on gender of victim), *cert. denied*, 519 U.S. 861 (1996), with *Doe v. University of Illinois*, 138 F.3d 653, 668 (CA7 1998) (upholding private damages action under Title IX for funding recipient's inadequate response to known student-on-student harassment), *cert. pending*, No. 98-126, *Brzonkala v. Virginia Polytechnic Institute and State University*, 132 F.3d 949, 960-961 (CA4 1997) (same), vacated and District Court decision affirmed en banc, 169 F.3d 820 (CA4 1999) (not addressing merits of Title IX hostile environment sexual harassment claim and directing District Court to hold this claim in abeyance pending this Court's decision in the instant case), and *Oona, R. S. v. McCaffrey*, 143 F.3d 473, 478 (CA9 1998) (rejecting qualified immunity claim and concluding that Title IX duty to respond to student-on-student harassment was clearly established by 1992-1993), *cert. pending*, No. 98-101. We now reverse.

II

Title IX provides, with certain exceptions not at issue here, that

> "[n]o person in the United States shall, on the basis of sex, be excluded from participation in, be denied the benefits of, or be subjected to discrimination under any education program or activity receiving Federal financial assistance." 20 U.S.C. § 1681(a).

Congress authorized an administrative enforcement scheme for Title IX. Federal departments or agencies with the authority to provide financial assistance are entrusted to promulgate rules, regulations, and orders to enforce the objectives of § 1681, see § 1682, and these departments or agencies may rely on "any . . . means authorized by law," including the termination of funding, *ibid.*, to give effect to the statute's restrictions.

There is no dispute here that the Board is a recipient of federal education funding for Title IX purposes. 74 F.3d at 1189. Nor do respondents support an argument that student-on-student harassment cannot rise to the level of "discrimination" for purposes of Title IX. Rather, at issue here is the question whether a recipient of federal education funding may be liable for damages under Title IX under any circumstances for discrimination in the form of student-on-student sexual harassment.

A

Petitioner urges that Title IX's plain language compels the conclusion that the statute is intended to bar recipients of federal funding from permitting this form of discrimination in their programs or activities. She emphasizes that the statute prohibits a student from being "subjected to discrimination under any education program or activity receiving Federal financial assistance." 20 U.S.C. § 1681 (emphasis supplied). It is Title IX's "unmistakable focus on the benefited class," *Cannon v. University of Chicago*, 441 U.S. 677, 691 (1979), rather than the perpetrator, that, in petitioner's view, compels the conclusion that the statute works to protect students from the discriminatory misconduct of their peers.

Here, however, we are asked to do more than define the scope of the behavior that Title IX proscribes. We must determine whether a district's failure to respond to student-on-student harassment in its schools can support a private suit for money damages. See *Gebser v. Lago Vista Independent School Dist.*, 524 U.S. 274, 283 (1998) ("In this case, . . . petitioners seek not just to establish a Title IX violation but to recover damages . . ."). This Court has indeed recognized an implied private right of action under Title IX, see *Cannon v. University of Chicago, supra*, and we have held that money damages are available in such suits, *Franklin v. Gwinnett County Public Schools*, 503 U.S. 60 (1992). Because we have repeatedly treated Title IX as legislation enacted pursuant to Congress' authority under the Spending Clause, however, *see, e.g., Gebser v. Lago Vista Independent School Dist., supra*, at 287 (Title IX); *Franklin v. Gwinnett County Public Schools, supra*, at 74-75, and n.8 (Title IX); *see also Guardians Assn. v. Civil Serv. Comm'n of New York City*, 463 U.S. 582, 598-599 (1983) (opinion of

White, J.) (Title VI), private damages actions are available only where recipients of federal funding had adequate notice that they could be liable for the conduct at issue. When Congress acts pursuant to its spending power, it generates legislation "much in the nature of a contract: in return for federal funds, the States agree to comply with federally imposed conditions." *Pennhurst State School and Hospital v. Halderman*, 451 U.S. 1, 17 (1981). In interpreting language in spending legislation, we thus "insis[t] that Congress speak with a clear voice," recognizing that "[t]here can, of course, be no knowing acceptance [of the terms of the putative contract] if a State is unaware of the conditions [imposed by the legislation] or is unable to ascertain what is expected of it." *Ibid.*; *see also id.* at 24-25.

Invoking *Pennhurst*, respondents urge that Title IX provides no notice that recipients of federal educational funds could be liable in damages for harm arising from student-on-student harassment. Respondents contend, specifically, that the statute only proscribes misconduct by grant recipients, not third parties. Respondents argue, moreover, that it would be contrary to the very purpose of Spending Clause legislation to impose liability on a funding recipient for the misconduct of third parties, over whom recipients exercise little control. *See also Rowinsky v. Bryan Independent School Dist.*, 80 F.3d at 1013.

We agree with respondents that a recipient of federal funds may be liable in damages under Title IX only for its own misconduct. The recipient itself must "exclud[e] [persons] from participation in, . . . den[y] [persons] the benefits of, or . . . subjec[t] [persons] to discrimination under" its "program[s] or activit[ies]" in order to be liable under Title IX. The Government's enforcement power may only be exercised against the funding recipient, see § 1682, and we have not extended damages liability under Title IX to parties outside the scope of this power. See *National Collegiate Athletic Assn. v. Smith*, 525 U.S. 459, ___ n.5 (1999) (slip op., at 7 n.5) (rejecting suggestion "that the private right of action available under . . . § 1681(a) is potentially broader than the Government's enforcement authority"); *cf. Gebser v. Lago Vista Independent School Dist.*, *supra*, at 289 ("It would be unsound, we think, for a statute's express system of enforcement to require notice to the recipient and an opportunity to come into voluntary compliance while a judicially implied system of enforcement permits substantial liability without regard to the recipient's knowledge or its corrective actions upon receiving notice").

We disagree with respondents' assertion, however, that petitioner seeks to hold the Board liable for G. F.'s actions instead of its own. Here, petitioner attempts to hold the Board liable for its own decision to remain idle in the face of known student-on-student harassment in its schools. In *Gebser*, we concluded that a recipient of federal education funds may be liable in damages under Title IX where it is deliberately indifferent to known acts of sexual harassment by a teacher. In that case, a teacher had entered into a sexual relationship with an eighth grade student, and the student sought damages under Title IX for the teacher's misconduct. We recognized that the scope of liability in private damages actions under

Title IX is circumscribed by *Pennhurst's* requirement that funding recipients have notice of their potential liability. 524 U.S. at 287-288. Invoking *Pennhurst*, *Guardians Assn.*, and *Franklin*, in *Gebser* we once again required "that 'the receiving entity of federal funds [have] notice that it will be liable for a monetary award'" before subjecting it to damages liability. *Id.* at 287 (quoting *Franklin v. Gwinnett County Public Schools*, 503 U.S. at 74). We also recognized, however, that this limitation on private damages actions is not a bar to liability where a funding recipient intentionally violates the statute. *Id.* at 74-75; *see also Guardians Assn. v. Civil Serv. Comm'n of New York City, supra*, at 597-598 (opinion of White, J.) (same with respect to Title VI). In particular, we concluded that *Pennhurst* does not bar a private damages action under Title IX where the funding recipient engages in intentional conduct that violates the clear terms of the statute.

Accordingly, we rejected the use of agency principles to impute liability to the district for the misconduct of its teachers. 524 U.S. at 283. Likewise, we declined the invitation to impose liability under what amounted to a negligence standard—holding the district liable for its failure to react to teacher-student harassment of which it knew or should have known. *Ibid.* Rather, we concluded that the district could be liable for damages only where the district itself intentionally acted in clear violation of Title IX by remaining deliberately indifferent to acts of teacher-student harassment of which it had actual knowledge. *Id.* at 290. Contrary to the dissent's suggestion, the misconduct of the teacher in *Gebser* was not "treated as the grant recipient's actions." Post, at 8. Liability arose, rather, from "an official decision by the recipient not to remedy the violation." *Gebser v. Lago Vista Independent School Dist., supra*, at 290. By employing the "deliberate indifference" theory already used to establish municipal liability under Rev. Stat. § 1979, 42 U.S.C. § 1983, see *Gebser v. Lago Vista Independent School Dist., supra*, at 290-291 (citing *Board of Comm'rs of Bryan Cty. v. Brown*, 520 U.S. 397 (1997), and *City of Canton v. Harris*, 489 U.S. 378 (1989)), we concluded in *Gebser* that recipients could be liable in damages only where their own deliberate indifference effectively "cause[d]" the discrimination, 524 U.S. at 291; *see also Canton v. Harris, supra*, at 385 (recognizing that a municipality will be liable under § 1983 only if "the municipality itself causes the constitutional violation at issue" (emphasis in original)). The high standard imposed in *Gebser* sought to eliminate any "risk that the recipient would be liable in damages not for its own official decision but instead for its employees' independent actions." 524 U.S. at 290-291.

Gebser thus established that a recipient intentionally violates Title IX, and is subject to a private damages action, where the recipient is deliberately indifferent to known acts of teacher-student discrimination. Indeed, whether viewed as "discrimination" or "subject[ing]" students to discrimination, Title IX "[u]nquestionably . . . placed on [the Board] the duty not" to permit teacher-student harassment in its schools, *Franklin v. Gwinnett County Public*

Schools, supra, at 75, and recipients violate Title IX's plain terms when they remain deliberately indifferent to this form of misconduct.

We consider here whether the misconduct identified in *Gebser*—deliberate indifference to known acts of harassment—amounts to an intentional violation of Title IX, capable of supporting a private damages action, when the harasser is a student rather than a teacher. We conclude that, in certain limited circumstances, it does. As an initial matter, in *Gebser* we expressly rejected the use of agency principles in the Title IX context, noting the textual differences between Title IX and Title VII. 524 U.S. at 283; *cf. Faragher v. City of Boca Raton,* 524 U.S. 775, 791-792 (1998) (invoking agency principles on ground that definition of "employer" in Title VII includes agents of employer); *Meritor Savings Bank, FSB v. Vinson,* 477 U.S. 57, 72 (1986) (same). Additionally, the regulatory scheme surrounding Title IX has long provided funding recipients with notice that they may be liable for their failure to respond to the discriminatory acts of certain non-agents. The Department of Education requires recipients to monitor third parties for discrimination in specified circumstances and to refrain from particular forms of interaction with outside entities that are known to discriminate. *See, e.g.,* 34 C.F.R. §§ 106.31(b)(6), 106.31(d), 106.37(a)(2), 106.38(a), 106.51(a)(3) (1998).

The common law, too, has put schools on notice that they may be held responsible under state law for their failure to protect students from the tortious acts of third parties. See Restatement (Second) of Torts § 320, and Comment a (1965). In fact, state courts routinely uphold claims alleging that schools have been negligent in failing to protect their students from the torts of their peers. *See, e.g., Rupp v. Bryant,* 417 So. 2d 658, 666-667 (Fla. 1982); *Brahatcek v. Millard School Dist.,* 202 Neb. 86, 99-100, 273 N.W.2d 680, 688 (1979); *McLeod v. Grant County School Dist. No. 128,* 42 Wash. 2d 316, 320, 255 P.2d 360, 362-363 (1953).

This is not to say that the identity of the harasser is irrelevant. On the contrary, both the "deliberate indifference" standard and the language of Title IX narrowly circumscribe the set of parties whose known acts of sexual harassment can trigger some duty to respond on the part of funding recipients. Deliberate indifference makes sense as a theory of direct liability under Title IX only where the funding recipient has some control over the alleged harassment. A recipient cannot be directly liable for its indifference where it lacks the authority to take remedial action.

The language of Title IX itself—particularly when viewed in conjunction with the requirement that the recipient have notice of Title IX's prohibitions to be liable for damages—also cabins the range of misconduct that the statute proscribes. The statute's plain language confines the scope of prohibited conduct based on the recipient's degree of control over the harasser and the environment in which the harassment occurs. If a funding recipient does not engage in harassment directly, it may not be liable for damages unless its deliberate indifference "subject[s]" its students to harassment. That is, the deliberate indifference must, at a minimum, "cause [students] to undergo" harassment or "make them liable or vulnerable" to it. *Random House Dictionary of the English Language* 1415 (1966) (defining "subject" as "to cause to undergo the action of something specified; expose" or "to make liable or vulnerable; lay open; expose"); *Webster's Third New International Dictionary of the English Language* 2275 (1961) (defining "subject" as "to cause to undergo or submit to: make submit to a particular action or effect: EXPOSE"). Moreover, because the harassment must occur "under" "the operations of" a funding recipient, see 20 U.S.C. § 1681(a); § 1687 (defining "program or activity"), the harassment must take place in a context subject to the school district's control, *Webster's Third New International Dictionary of the English Language, supra,* at 2487 (defining "under" as "in or into a condition of subjection, regulation, or subordination"; "subject to the guidance and instruction of"); *Random House Dictionary of the English Language, supra,* at 1543 (defining "under" as "subject to the authority, direction, or supervision of").

These factors combine to limit a recipient's damages liability to circumstances wherein the recipient exercises substantial control over both the harasser and the context in which the known harassment occurs. Only then can the recipient be said to "expose" its students to harassment or "cause" them to undergo it "under" the recipient's programs. We agree with the dissent that these conditions are satisfied most easily and most obviously when the offender is an agent of the recipient. Post, at 8. We rejected the use of agency analysis in *Gebser,* however, and we disagree that the term "under" somehow imports an agency requirement into Title IX. See *ibid.* As noted above, the theory in *Gebser* was that the recipient was directly liable for its deliberate indifference to discrimination. See *supra,* at 11. Liability in that case did not arise because the "teacher's actions [were] treated" as those of the funding recipient, post, at 8; the district was directly liable for its own failure to act. The terms "subjec[t]" and "under" impose limits, but nothing about these terms requires the use of agency principles.

Where, as here, the misconduct occurs during school hours and on school grounds—the bulk of G. F.'s misconduct, in fact, took place in the classroom—the misconduct is taking place "under" an "operation" of the funding recipient. See *Doe v. University of Illinois,* 138 F.3d at 661 (finding liability where school fails to respond properly to "student-on-student sexual harassment that takes place while the students are involved in school activities or otherwise under the supervision of school employees"). In these circumstances, the recipient retains substantial control over the context in which the harassment occurs. More importantly, however, in this setting the Board exercises significant control over the harasser. We have observed, for example, "that the nature of [the State's] power [over public schoolchildren] is custodial and tutelary, permitting a degree of supervision and control that could not be exercised over free adults." *Vernonia School Dist. 47J v. Acton,* 515 U.S. 646, 655 (1995). On more than one occasion, this Court has recognized the importance of school officials' "comprehensive authority . . ., consistent with fundamental constitutional safeguards, to prescribe and control conduct in the schools." *Tinker v. Des Moines Independent Community School Dist.*, 393 U.S. 503, 507 (1969); *see also New Jersey v. T. L. O.*, 469 U.S. 325, 342 n.9 (1985) ("The maintenance of discipline in the schools requires not only that students be restrained from assaulting one another, abusing drugs and alcohol, and committing other crimes, but also that students conform themselves to the standards of conduct prescribed by school authorities"); 74 F.3d at 1193 ("The ability to control and influence behavior exists to an even greater extent in the classroom than in the workplace . . ."). The common law, too, recognizes the school's disciplinary authority. See Restatement (Second) of Torts § 152 (1965). We thus conclude that recipients of federal funding may be liable for "subject[ing]" their students to discrimination where the recipient is deliberately indifferent to known acts of student-on-student sexual harassment and the harasser is under the school's disciplinary authority.

At the time of the events in question here, in fact, school attorneys and administrators were being told that student-on-student harassment could trigger liability under Title IX. In March 1993, even as the events alleged in petitioner's complaint were unfolding, the National School Boards Association issued a publication, for use by "school attorneys and administrators in understanding the law regarding sexual harassment of employees and students," which observed that districts could be liable under Title IX for their failure to respond to student-on-student harassment. See National School Boards Association Council of School Attorneys, Sexual Harassment in the Schools: Preventing and Defending Against Claims v, 45 (rev. ed.). Drawing on Equal Employment Opportunity Commission guidelines interpreting Title VII, the publication informed districts that, "if [a] school district has constructive notice of severe and repeated acts of sexual harassment by fellow students, that may form the basis of a [T]itle IX claim." *Id.* at 45. The publication even correctly anticipated a form of *Gebser's* actual notice requirement: "It is unlikely that courts will hold a school district liable for sexual harassment by students against students in the absence of actual knowledge or notice to district employees." Sexual Harassment in the Schools, *supra*, at 45. Although we do not rely on this publication as an "indicium of congressional notice," see post, at 19, we do find support for our reading of Title IX in the fact that school attorneys have rendered an analogous interpretation.

Likewise, although they were promulgated too late to contribute to the Board's notice of proscribed misconduct, the Department of Education's Office for Civil Rights (OCR) has recently adopted policy guidelines providing that student-on-student harassment falls within the scope of Title IX's proscriptions. See Department of Education, Office of Civil Rights, Sexual Harassment Guidance: Harassment of Students by School Employees, Other Students, or Third Parties, 62 Fed. Reg. 12034, 12039-12040 (1997) (OCR Title IX Guidelines); *see also* Department of Education, Racial Incidents and Harassment Against Students at Educational Institutions, 59 Fed. Reg. 11448, 11449 (1994).

We stress that our conclusion here—that recipients may be liable for their deliberate indifference to known acts of peer sexual harassment—does not mean that recipients can avoid liability only by purging their schools of actionable peer harassment or that administrators must engage in particular disciplinary action. We thus disagree with respondents' contention that, if Title IX provides a cause of action for student-on-student harassment, "nothing short of expulsion of every student accused of misconduct involving sexual overtones would protect school systems from liability or damages." See Brief for Respondents 16; *see also* 120 F.3d at 1402 (Tjoflat, J.) ("[A] school must immediately suspend or expel a student accused of sexual harassment"). Likewise, the dissent erroneously imagines that victims of peer harassment now have a Title IX right to make particular remedial demands. See post, at 34 (contemplating that victim could demand new desk assignment). In fact, as we have previously noted, courts should refrain from second guessing the disciplinary decisions made by school administrators. *New Jersey v. T. L. O., supra,* at 342-343 n.9.

School administrators will continue to enjoy the flexibility they require so long as funding recipients are deemed "deliberately indifferent" to acts of student-on-student harassment only where the recipient's response to the harassment or lack thereof is clearly unreasonable in light of the known circumstances. The dissent consistently mischaracterizes this standard to require funding recipients to "remedy" peer harassment, post at 5, 10, 16, 30, and to "ensur[e] that . . . students conform their conduct to" certain rules, post at 13. Title IX imposes no such requirements. On the contrary, the recipient must merely respond to known peer harassment in a manner that is not clearly unreasonable. This is not a mere "reasonableness" standard, as the dissent assumes. See post, at 26. In an appropriate case, there is no reason why courts, on a motion to dismiss, for summary judgment, or for a directed verdict, could not identify a response as not "clearly unreasonable" as a matter of law.

Like the dissent, see post, at 11-15, we acknowledge that school administrators shoulder substantial burdens as a result of legal constraints on their disciplinary authority. To the extent that these restrictions arise from federal statutes, Congress can review these burdens with attention to the difficult position in which such legislation may place our Nation's schools. We believe, however, that the standard set out here is sufficiently flexible to account both for the level of disciplinary authority available to the school and for the potential liability arising from certain forms of disciplinary action. A university might not, for example, be expected to exercise the same degree of control over its students that a grade school would enjoy, see post, at 14, and it would be entirely reasonable for a school to refrain from a form of disciplinary action that would expose it to constitutional or statutory claims.

While it remains to be seen whether petitioner can show that the Board's response to reports of G. F.'s misconduct was clearly unreasonable in light of the known circumstances, petitioner may be able to show that the Board "subject

[ed]" LaShonda to discrimination by failing to respond in any way over a period of five months to complaints of G. F.'s in-school misconduct from LaShonda and other female students.

B

The requirement that recipients receive adequate notice of Title IX's proscriptions also bears on the proper definition of "discrimination" in the context of a private damages action. We have elsewhere concluded that sexual harassment is a form of discrimination for Title IX purposes and that Title IX proscribes harassment with sufficient clarity to satisfy *Pennhurst*'s notice requirement and serve as a basis for a damages action. See *Gebser v. Lago Vista Independent School Dist.*, 524 U.S. at 281; *Franklin v. Gwinnett County Public Schools, supra*, at 74-75. Having previously determined that "sexual harassment" is "discrimination" in the school context under Title IX, we are constrained to conclude that student-on-student sexual harassment, if sufficiently severe, can likewise rise to the level of discrimination actionable under the statute. See *Bennett v. Kentucky Dept. of Ed.*, 470 U.S. 656, 665-666 (1985) (rejecting claim of insufficient notice under *Pennhurst* where statute made clear that there were some conditions placed on receipt of federal funds, and noting that Congress need not "specifically identif[y] and proscrib[e]" each condition in the legislation). The statute's other prohibitions, moreover, help give content to the term "discrimination" in this context. Students are not only protected from discrimination, but also specifically shielded from being "excluded from participation in" or "denied the benefits of" any "education program or activity receiving Federal financial assistance." § 1681(a). The statute makes clear that, whatever else it prohibits, students must not be denied access to educational benefits and opportunities on the basis of gender. We thus conclude that funding recipients are properly held liable in damages only where they are deliberately indifferent to sexual harassment, of which they have actual knowledge, that is so severe, pervasive, and objectively offensive that it can be said to deprive the victims of access to the educational opportunities or benefits provided by the school.

The most obvious example of student-on-student sexual harassment capable of triggering a damages claim would thus involve the overt, physical deprivation of access to school resources. Consider, for example, a case in which male students physically threaten their female peers every day, successfully preventing the female students from using a particular school resource—an athletic field or a computer lab, for instance. District administrators are well aware of the daily ritual, yet they deliberately ignore requests for aid from the female students wishing to use the resource. The district's knowing refusal to take any action in response to such behavior would fly in the face of Title IX's core principles, and such deliberate indifference may appropriately be subject to claims for monetary damages. It is not necessary, however, to show physical exclusion to demonstrate that students have been deprived by the actions of another student or students of an educational opportunity on the basis of sex. Rather, a plaintiff must establish sexual harassment of students that is so severe, pervasive, and objectively offensive, and that so undermines and detracts from the victims' educational experience, that the victim-students are effectively denied equal access to an institution's resources and opportunities. *Cf. Meritor Savings Bank, FSB v. Vinson*, 477 U.S. at 67.

Whether gender-oriented conduct rises to the level of actionable "harassment" thus "depends on a constellation of surrounding circumstances, expectations, and relationships," *Oncale v. Sundowner Offshore Services, Inc.*, 523 U.S. 75, 82 (1998), including, but not limited to, the ages of the harasser and the victim and the number of individuals involved, see OCR Title IX Guidelines 12041-12042. Courts, moreover, must bear in mind that schools are unlike the adult workplace and that children may regularly interact in a manner that would be unacceptable among adults. *See, e.g.,* Brief for National School Boards Association et al. as Amici Curiae 11 (describing "dizzying array of immature . . . behaviors by students"). Indeed, at least early on, students are still learning how to interact appropriately with their peers. It is thus understandable that, in the school setting, students often engage in insults, banter, teasing, shoving, pushing, and gender-specific conduct that is upsetting to the students subjected to it. Damages are not available for simple acts of teasing and name-calling among school children, however, even where these comments target differences in gender. Rather, in the context of student-on-student harassment, damages are available only where the behavior is so severe, pervasive, and objectively offensive that it denies its victims the equal access to education that Title IX is designed to protect.

The dissent fails to appreciate these very real limitations on a funding recipient's liability under Title IX. It is not enough to show, as the dissent would read this opinion to provide, that a student has been "teased," post, at 25, or "called . . . offensive names," post, at 27-28. Comparisons to an "overweight child who skips gym class because the other children tease her about her size," the student "who refuses to wear glasses to avoid the taunts of 'four-eyes,'" and "the child who refuses to go to school because the school bully calls him a 'scardy-cat' at recess," post, at 25, are inapposite and misleading. Nor do we contemplate, much less hold, that a mere "decline in grades is enough to survive" a motion to dismiss. *Ibid.* The drop-off in LaShonda's grades provides necessary evidence of a potential link between her education and G. F.'s misconduct, but petitioner's ability to state a cognizable claim here depends equally on the alleged persistence and severity of G. F.'s actions, not to mention the Board's alleged knowledge and deliberate indifference. We trust that the dissent's characterization of our opinion will not mislead courts to impose more sweeping liability than we read Title IX to require.

Moreover, the provision that the discrimination occur "under any education program or activity" suggests that the behavior be serious enough to have the systemic effect of denying the victim equal access to an educational program or activity. Although, in theory, a single instance of sufficiently severe one-on-one peer harassment could be said to have such an effect, we think it unlikely that Congress would have thought such behavior sufficient to rise to this level in light of the inevitability of student misconduct and the amount of litigation that would be invited by entertaining claims of official indifference to a single instance of one-on-one peer harassment. By limiting private damages actions to cases having a systemic effect on educational programs or activities, we reconcile the general principle that Title IX prohibits official indifference to known peer sexual harassment with the practical realities of responding to student behavior, realities that Congress could not have meant to be ignored. Even the dissent suggests that Title IX liability may arise when a funding recipient remains indifferent to severe, gender-based mistreatment played out on a "widespread level" among students. Post, at 31.

The fact that it was a teacher who engaged in harassment in *Franklin* and *Gebser* is relevant. The relationship between the harasser and the victim necessarily affects the extent to which the misconduct can be said to breach Title IX's guarantee of equal access to educational benefits and to have a systemic effect on a program or activity. Peer harassment, in particular, is less likely to satisfy these requirements than is teacher-student harassment.

C

Applying this standard to the facts at issue here, we conclude that the Eleventh Circuit erred in dismissing petitioner's complaint. Petitioner alleges that her daughter was the victim of repeated acts of sexual harassment by G. F. over a 5-month period, and there are allegations in support of the conclusion that G. F.'s misconduct was severe, pervasive, and objectively offensive. The harassment was not only verbal; it included numerous acts of objectively offensive touching, and, indeed, G. F. ultimately pleaded guilty to criminal sexual misconduct. Moreover, the complaint alleges that there were multiple victims who were sufficiently disturbed by G. F.'s misconduct to seek an audience with the school principal. Further, petitioner contends that the harassment had a concrete, negative effect on her daughter's ability to receive an education. The complaint also suggests that petitioner may be able to show both actual knowledge and deliberate indifference on the part of the Board, which made no effort whatsoever either to investigate or to put an end to the harassment.

On this complaint, we cannot say "beyond doubt that [petitioner] can prove no set of facts in support of [her] claim which would entitle [her] to relief." *Conley v. Gibson*, 355 U.S. 41, 45-46 (1957). *See also Scheuer v. Rhodes*, 416 U.S. 232, 236 (1974) ("The issue is not whether a plaintiff will ultimately prevail but whether the claimant is entitled to offer evidence to support the claims"). Accordingly, the judgment of the United States Court of Appeals for the Eleventh Circuit is reversed, and the case is remanded for further proceedings consistent with this opinion.

It is so ordered.

JUSTICE KENNEDY, with whom THE CHIEF JUSTICE, JUSTICE SCALIA, and JUSTICE THOMAS join, dissenting.

The Court has held that Congress' power "'to authorize expenditure of public moneys for public purposes is not limited by the direct grants of legislative power found in the Constitution.'" *South Dakota v. Dole*, 483 U.S. 203, 207 (1987) (quoting *United States v. Butler*, 297 U.S. 1, 66 (1936)). As a consequence, Congress can use its Spending Clause power to pursue objectives outside of "Article I's 'enumerated legislative fields'" by attaching conditions to the grant of federal funds. 483 U.S. at 207. So understood, the Spending Clause power, if wielded without concern for the federal balance, has the potential to obliterate distinctions between national and local spheres of interest and power by permitting the federal government to set policy in the most sensitive areas of traditional state concern, areas which otherwise would lie outside its reach.

A vital safeguard for the federal balance is the requirement that, when Congress imposes a condition on the States' receipt of federal funds, it "must do so unambiguously." *Pennhurst State School and Hospital v. Halderman*, 451 U.S. 1, 17 (1981). As the majority acknowledges, "legislation enacted . . . pursuant to the spending power is much in the nature of a contract," and the legitimacy of Congress' exercise of its power to condition funding on state compliance with congressional conditions "rests on whether the State voluntarily and knowingly accepts the terms of the 'contract.'" *Ibid.*; see ante, at 9. "'There can, of course, be no knowing acceptance [of the terms of the putative contract] if a State is unaware of the conditions [imposed by the legislation] or is unable to ascertain what is expected of it.'" *Ibid.* (quoting *Pennhurst*, 451 U.S. at 17).

Our insistence that "Congress speak with a clear voice" to "enable the States to exercise their choice knowingly, cognizant of the consequences of their participation," *Pennhurst, supra* at 17, is not based upon some abstract notion of contractual fairness. Rather, it is a concrete safeguard in the federal system. Only if States receive clear notice of the conditions attached to federal funds can they guard against excessive federal intrusion into state affairs and be vigilant in policing the boundaries of federal power. *Cf.* Dole, *supra* at 217 (O'CONNOR, J., dissenting) ("If the spending power is to be limited only by Congress' notion of the general welfare, the reality, given the vast financial resources of the Federal Government, is that the Spending Clause gives 'power to the Congress to tear down the barriers, to invade the states' jurisdiction, and to become a parliament of the whole people, subject to no restrictions save such as are self-imposed'" (quoting Butler, *supra*, at 78)). While the majority purports to give effect to these principles, it eviscerates the clear-notice safeguard of our Spending Clause jurisprudence.

Title IX provides:

> "No person in the United States shall, on the basis of sex be [1] excluded from participation in, [2] be denied the benefits of, or [3] be subjected to discrimination

under any education program or activity receiving Federal financial assistance." 20 U.S.C. § 1681(a).

To read the provision in full is to understand what is most striking about its application in this case: Title IX does not by its terms create any private cause of action whatsoever, much less define the circumstances in which money damages are available. The only private cause of action under Title IX is judicially implied. See *Cannon v. University of Chicago*, 441 U.S. 677 (1979).

The Court has encountered great difficulty in establishing standards for deciding when to imply a private cause of action under a federal statute which is silent on the subject. We try to conform the judicial judgment to the bounds of likely congressional purpose but, as we observed in *Gebser v. Lago Vista Independent School District*, 524 U.S. 274 (1998), defining the scope of the private cause of action in general, and the damages remedy in particular, "inherently entails a degree of speculation, since it addresses an issue on which Congress has not specifically spoken." *Id.* at 284.

When the statute at issue is a Spending Clause statute, this element of speculation is particularly troubling because it is in significant tension with the requirement that Spending Clause legislation give States clear notice of the consequences of their acceptance of federal funds. Without doubt, the scope of potential damages liability is one of the most significant factors a school would consider in deciding whether to receive federal funds. Accordingly, the Court must not imply a private cause of action for damages unless it can demonstrate that the congressional purpose to create the implied cause of action is so manifest that the State, when accepting federal funds, had clear notice of the terms and conditions of its monetary liability.

Today the Court fails to heed, or even to acknowledge, these limitations on its authority. The remedial scheme the majority creates today is neither sensible nor faithful to Spending Clause principles. In order to make its case for school liability for peer sexual harassment, the majority must establish that Congress gave grant recipients clear and unambiguous notice that they would be liable in money damages for failure to remedy discriminatory acts of their students. The majority must also demonstrate that the statute gives schools clear notice that one child's harassment of another constitutes "discrimination" on the basis of sex within the meaning of Title IX, and that—as applied to individual cases—the standard for liability will enable the grant recipient to distinguish inappropriate childish behavior from actionable gender discrimination. The majority does not carry these burdens.

Instead, the majority finds statutory clarity where there is none and discovers indicia of congressional notice to the States in the most unusual of places. It treats the issue as one of routine statutory construction alone, and it errs even in this regard. In the end, the majority not only imposes on States liability that was unexpected and unknown, but the contours of which are, as yet, unknowable. The majority's opinion purports to be narrow, but the limiting principles it proposes are illusory. The fence the Court has built is made of little sticks, and it cannot contain the avalanche of liability now set in motion. The potential costs to our schools of today's decision are difficult to estimate, but they are so great that it is most unlikely Congress intended to inflict them.

The only certainty flowing from the majority's decision is that scarce resources will be diverted from educating our children and that many school districts, desperate to avoid Title IX peer harassment suits, will adopt whatever federal code of student conduct and discipline the Department of Education sees fit to impose upon them. The Nation's schoolchildren will learn their first lessons about federalism in classrooms where the federal government is the ever-present regulator. The federal government will have insinuated itself not only into one of the most traditional areas of state concern but also into one of the most sensitive areas of human affairs. This federal control of the discipline of our Nation's schoolchildren is contrary to our traditions and inconsistent with the sensible administration of our schools. Because Title IX did not give States unambiguous notice that accepting federal funds meant ceding to the federal government power over the day-to-day disciplinary decisions of schools, I dissent.

I

I turn to the first difficulty with the majority's decision. Schools cannot be held liable for peer sexual harassment because Title IX does not give them clear and unambiguous notice that they are liable in damages for failure to remedy discrimination by their students. As the majority acknowledges, Title IX prohibits only misconduct by grant recipients, not misconduct by third parties. Ante, at 9. ("The recipient itself must 'exclud[e] [persons] from participation in, . . . den[y] [persons] the benefits of, or . . . subjec[t] [persons] to discrimination under' its 'program[s] or activit[ies]' in order to be liable under Title IX"). The majority argues, nevertheless, that a school "subjects" its students to discrimination when it knows of peer harassment and fails to respond appropriately.

The mere word "subjected" cannot bear the weight of the majority's argument. As we recognized in *Gebser*, the primary purpose of Title IX is "to prevent recipients of federal financial assistance from using the funds in a discriminatory manner." *Gebser*, 524 U.S. at 292. We stressed in *Gebser* that Title IX prevents discrimination by the grant recipient, whether through the acts of its principals or the acts of its agents. See *id.* at 286 (explaining that Title IX and Title VI "operate in the same manner, conditioning an offer of federal funding on a promise by the recipient not to discriminate, in what amounts essentially to a contract between the Government and the recipient of funds"). "[W]hereas Title VII aims centrally to compensate victims of discrimination, Title IX focuses more on 'protecting' individuals from discriminatory practices carried out by recipients of federal funds." *Id.* at 287. The majority does not even attempt to argue that the school's failure to respond to discriminatory acts by students is discrimination by the school itself.

A

In any event, a plaintiff cannot establish a Title IX violation merely by showing that she has been "subjected to discrimination." Rather, a violation of Title IX occurs only if she is "subjected to discrimination under any education program or activity," 20 U.S.C. § 1681(a), where "program or activity" is defined as "all of the operations of" a grant recipient, § 1687.

Under the most natural reading of this provision, discrimination violates Title IX only if it is authorized by, or in accordance with, the actions, activities, or policies of the grant recipient. See *Webster's Third New International Dictionary* 2487 (1981) (defining "under" as "required by: in accordance with: bound by"); *American Heritage Dictionary of the English Language* 1395 (1981) (defining "under" as "[w]ith the authorization of; attested by; by virtue of"); *Random House Dictionary of the English Language* 2059 (2d ed.1987) (defining "under" as "authorized, warranted, or attested by" or "in accordance with"); *see also* 43 *Words and Phrases* 149-152 (1969) (citing cases defining "under" as, *inter alia*, "'in accordance with' and 'in conformity with'"; "indicating subjection, guidance or control, and meaning 'by authority of'"; "'by,' 'by reason of,' or 'by means of'"; and "'by virtue of,' which is defined . . . as meaning 'by or through the authority of'"). This reading reflects the common legal usage of the term "under" to mean pursuant to, in accordance with, or as authorized or provided by. *See, e.g., Gregory v. Ashcroft*, 501 U.S. 452, 469 (1991) ("Because Congress nowhere stated its intent to impose mandatory obligations on the States under its § 5 powers, we concluded that Congress did not do so."); ante, at 1, ("Among petitioner's claims was a claim for monetary and injunctive relief under Title IX . . .").

It is not enough, then, that the alleged discrimination occur in a "context subject to the school district's control." Ante, at 14. The discrimination must actually be "controlled by"—that is, be authorized by, pursuant to, or in accordance with, school policy or actions. Compare ante, at 14 (defining "under" as "in or into a condition of subjection, regulation, or subordination") (emphasis added) with *ibid.* (defining "under" as "subject to the guidance and instruction of") (emphasis added).

This reading is also consistent with the fact that the discrimination must be "under" the "operations" of the grant recipient. The term "operations" connotes active and affirmative participation by the grant recipient, not merely inaction or failure to respond. See *Black's Law Dictionary* 1092 (6th ed. 1990) (defining "operation," as an "[e]xertion of power; the process of operating or mode of action; an effect brought about in accordance with a definite plan; action; activity").

Teacher sexual harassment of students is "under" the school's program or activity in certain circumstances, but student harassment is not. Our decision in *Gebser* recognizes that a grant recipient acts through its agents and thus, under certain limited circumstances, even tortious acts by teachers may be attributable to the school. We noted in *Gebser* that, in contrast to Title VII, which defines "employer" to include "any agent"—Title IX "contains no comparable reference to an educational institution's 'agents,' and so does not expressly call for application of agency principles." *Gebser, supra*, at 283. As a result, we declined to incorporate principles of agency liability, such as a strict application of vicarious liability, that would conflict with the Spending Clause's notice requirement and Title IX's express administrative enforcement scheme.

Contrary to the majority's assertion, ante, at 12, however, we did not abandon agency principles altogether. Rather, we sought in *Gebser* to identify those employee actions which could fairly be attributed to the grant recipient by superimposing additional Spending Clause notice requirements on traditional agency principles. *Gebser*, 524 U.S. at 288 ("Title IX contains important clues that Congress did not intend to allow recovery in damages where liability rests solely on principles of vicarious liability or constructive notice"). We concluded that, because of the Spending Clause overlay, a teacher's discrimination is attributable to the school only when the school has actual notice of that harassment and is "deliberately indifferent." The agency relation between the school and the teacher is thus a necessary, but not sufficient, condition of school liability. Where the heightened requirements for attribution are met, the teacher's actions are treated as the grant recipient's actions. In those circumstances, then, the teacher sexual harassment is "under" the operations of the school.

I am aware of no basis in law or fact, however, for attributing the acts of a student to a school and, indeed, the majority does not argue that the school acts through its students. See ante, at 10 ("We disagree with respondents' assertion . . . that petitioner seeks to hold the Board liable for G. F.'s actions instead of its own. Here, petitioner attempts to hold the Board liable for its own decision to remain idle in the face of known student-on-student harassment in its schools"). Discrimination by one student against another therefore cannot be "under" the school's program or activity as required by Title IX. The majority's imposition of liability for peer sexual harassment thus conflicts with the most natural interpretation of Title IX's "under a program or activity" limitation on school liability. At the very least, my reading undermines the majority's implicit claim that Title IX imposes an unambiguous duty on schools to remedy peer sexual harassment.

B
1

Quite aside from its disregard for the "under the program" limitation of Title IX, the majority's reading is flawed in other respects. The majority contends that a school's deliberate indifference to known student harassment "subjects" students to harassment—that is, "cause[s] [students] to undergo" harassment. Ante, at 13. The majority recognizes, however, that there must be some limitation on the third-party conduct that the school can fairly be said to cause. In search of a principle, the majority asserts, without much elaboration, that one causes discrimination when one has some "degree of control" over the discrimination and fails to remedy it. Ante, at 13.

To state the majority's test is to understand that it is little more than an exercise in arbitrary line-drawing. The majority does not explain how we are to determine what degree of control is sufficient—or, more to the point, how the States were on clear notice that the Court would draw the line to encompass students.

Agency principles usually mark the outer limits of an entity's liability for the actions of an individual over whom it exercises some control. *Cf. Faragher v. Boca Raton*, 524 U.S. 775 (1998) (applying agency principles to delimit Title VII employer liability); *Burlington Industries, Inc. v. Ellerth*, (1998) (same). The Court, for example, has not recognized liability for the actions of nonagents under Title VII, which contains an express private right of action and is not Spending Clause legislation. The majority nonetheless rejects out-of-hand an agency limitation on Title IX liability based on its cramped reading of *Gebser*. As noted above, the *Gebser* Court rejected the wholesale importation of federal common-law agency principles into Title IX to expand liability beyond that which the statute clearly prohibited; it did not, as the majority would have it, reject the proposition that school liability is limited by agency principles. Indeed, to suppose that Congress would have rejected well-established principles of agency law in favor of the majority's vague control principle turns *Gebser* on its head. *Gebser* contemplated that Title IX liability would be less expansive than Title VII liability, not more so. See *Gebser, supra*, at 286-287.

One would think that the majority would at least limit its control principle by reference to the long-established practice of the Department of Education (DOE). For the first 25 years after the passage of Title IX—until 1997—the DOE's regulations drew the liability line, at its most expansive, to encompass only those to whom the school delegated its official functions. See 34 C.F.R. § 106.51(a)(3) (1998) ("A [grant] recipient shall not enter into any contractual or other relationship which directly or indirectly has the effect of subjecting employees or students to discrimination prohibited by this subpart, including relationships with employment and referral agencies, with labor unions, and with organizations providing or administering fringe benefits to employees of the recipient"). It is perhaps reasonable to suppose that grant recipients were on notice that they could not hire third parties to do for them what they could not do themselves. For example, it might be reasonable to find that a school was on notice that it could not circumvent Title IX's core prohibitions by, for example, delegating its admissions decisions to an outside screening committee it knew would discriminate on the basis of gender.

Given the state of gender discrimination law at the time Title IX was passed, however, there is no basis to think that Congress contemplated liability for a school's failure to remedy discriminatory acts by students or that the States would believe the statute imposed on them a clear obligation to do so. When Title IX was enacted in 1972, the concept of "sexual harassment" as gender discrimination had not been recognized or considered by the courts. *See generally* C. MacKinnon, *Sexual Harassment of Working Women: A Case of Sex Discrimination* 59-72 (1979). The types of discrimination that were recognized—discriminatory admissions standards, denial of access to programs or resources, hiring, etc.—could not be engaged in by students. *See, e.g.*, 20 U.S.C. § 1681(a)(2) (referencing application of Title IX prohibitions to school admissions).

2

The majority nonetheless appears to see no need to justify drawing the "enough control" line to encompass students. In truth, however, a school's control over its students is much more complicated and limited than the majority acknowledges. A public school does not control its students in the way it controls its teachers or those with whom it contracts. Most public schools do not screen or select students, and their power to discipline students is far from unfettered.

Public schools are generally obligated by law to educate all students who live within defined geographic boundaries. Indeed, the Constitution of almost every State in the country guarantees the State's students a free primary and secondary public education. *See, e.g.*, Cal. Const., Art. IX, § 5; Colo. Const., Art IX, § 2; Ga. Const., Art VIII, § 1, ¶ 1; Ind. Const., Art. VIII, § 1; Md. Const., Art. VIII, § 1; Mo. Const., Art. IX, § 1(a); Neb. Const., Art. VII, § 1; N.J. Const., Art. VIII, § 4 ¶ 1; N.M. Const., Art. XII, § 1; N.Y. Const., Art. XI, § 1; N.D. Const., Art. VIII, §§ 1 and 2; Okla. Const., Art. XIII, § 1; S.C. Const., Art. XI, § 3; Tex. Const., Art VII, § 1; Va. Const., Art. VIII, § 1; Wash. Const., Art. IX, §§ 1 and 2; Wyo. Const., Art. VII, §§ 1 and 9. In at least some States, moreover, there is a continuing duty on schools to educate even students who are suspended or expelled. *See, e.g., Phillip Leon M. v. Board of Education*, 199 W. Va. 400, 484 S.E.2d 909 (1996) (holding that the education clause of the West Virginia Constitution confers on students a fundamental right to an education and requires that a county school board provide alternative educational programs, such as an alternative school, to students who are expelled or suspended for an extended period for bringing guns to school). Schools that remove a harasser from the classroom and then attempt to fulfill their continuing-education obligation by placing the harasser in any kind of group setting, rather than by hiring expensive tutors for each student, will find themselves at continuing risk of Title IX suits brought by the other students in the alternative education program.

In addition, federal law imposes constraints on school disciplinary actions. This Court has held, for example, that due process requires "[a]t the very minimum," that a student facing suspension "be given some kind of notice and afforded some kind of hearing." *Goss v. Lopez*, 419 U.S. 565, 579 (1975) (emphasis added).

The Individuals with Disabilities Education Act (IDEA), 20 U.S.C. 1400 et seq. (1994 ed., Supp. III), moreover, places strict limits on the ability of schools to take disciplinary actions against students with behavior disorder disabilities, even if the disability was not diagnosed prior to the incident triggering discipline. *See, e.g.*, § 1415(f)(1) (parents entitled to hearing when school proposes to change disabled student's educational placement); § 1415(k)(1)(A) (school authorities can only "order a change in the placement of a child with a disability . . . to an appropriate interim alternative educational setting, another setting, or suspension" for up to "10 school days" unless student's offense involved a weapon or illegal drugs); § 1415(k)(8) ("[A] child who has not been determined to be eligible for special education . . . and who has engaged in behavior that violated any [school rule], may assert any of the protections" of the subchapter if the school "had knowledge . . . that the child was a child with a disability before the behavior that precipitated the disciplinary action occurred"); § 1415(k)(8)(B)(ii) (school "deemed to have knowledge that a child is a child with a disability if . . . the behavior or performance of the child demonstrates the need for such [special education and related] services"). "Disability," as defined in the Act, includes "serious emotional disturbance," § 1401(3)(A)(i), which the DOE, in turn, has defined as a "condition exhibiting . . . over a long period of time and to a marked degree that adversely affects a child's educational performance" an "inability to build or maintain satisfactory interpersonal relationships with peers and teachers" or "[i]nappropriate types of behavior or feelings under normal circumstances." 34 C.F.R. § 300.7(b)(9) (1998). If, as the majority would have us believe, the behavior that constitutes actionable peer sexual harassment so deviates from the normal teasing and jostling of adolescence that it puts schools on clear notice of potential liability, then a student who engages in such harassment may have at least a colorable claim of severe emotional disturbance within the meaning of IDEA. When imposing disciplinary sanction on a student harasser who might assert a colorable IDEA claim, the school must navigate a complex web of statutory provisions and DOE regulations that significantly limit its discretion.

The practical obstacles schools encounter in ensuring that thousands of immature students conform their conduct to acceptable norms may be even more significant than the legal obstacles. School districts cannot exercise the same measure of control over thousands of students that they do over a few hundred adult employees. The limited resources of our schools must be conserved for basic educational services. Some schools lack the resources even to deal with serious problems of violence and are already overwhelmed with disciplinary problems of all kinds.

Perhaps even more startling than its broad assumptions about school control over primary and secondary school students is the majority's failure to grapple in any meaningful way with the distinction between elementary and secondary schools, on the one hand, and universities on the other. The majority bolsters its argument that schools can control their students' actions by quoting our decision in *Vernonia School Dist. 47J v. Acton*, 515 U.S. 646, 655 (1995), for the proposition that "'the nature of [the State's] power [over public school children] is custodial and tutelary, permitting a degree of supervision and control that could not be exercised over free adults.'" Ante, at 15. Yet the majority's holding would appear to apply with equal force to universities, which do not exercise custodial and tutelary power over their adult students.

A university's power to discipline its students for speech that may constitute sexual harassment is also circumscribed by the First Amendment. A number of federal courts have already confronted difficult problems raised by university speech codes designed to deal with peer sexual and racial harassment. *See, e.g.,* *Dambrot v. Central Michigan University*, 55 F.3d 1177 (CA6 1995) (striking down university discriminatory harassment policy because it was overbroad, vague, and not a valid prohibition on fighting words); *UWM Post, Inc. v. Board of Regents of University of Wisconsin System*, 774 F. Supp. 1163 (E.D. Wis. 1991) (striking down university speech code that prohibited, *inter alia*, "'discriminatory comments'" directed at an individual that "'intentionally . . . demean'" the "'sex . . . of the individual'" and "'[c]reate an intimidating, hostile or demeaning environment for education, university related work, or other university-authorized activity'"); *Doe v. University of Michigan*, 721 F. Supp. 852 (E.D. Mich. 1989) (similar); *IOTA XI Chapter of Sigma Chi Fraternity v. George Mason University*, 993 F.2d 386 (CA4 1993) (overturning on First Amendment grounds university's sanctions on a fraternity for conducting an "ugly woman contest" with "racist and sexist" overtones).

The difficulties associated with speech codes simply underscore the limited nature of a university's control over student behavior that may be viewed as sexual harassment. Despite the fact that the majority relies on the assumption that schools exercise a great deal of control over their students to justify creating the private cause of action in the first instance, it does not recognize the obvious limits on a university's ability to control its students as a reason to doubt the propriety of a private cause of action for peer harassment. It simply uses them as a factor in determining whether the university's response was reasonable. See ante, at 18.

3

The majority's presentation of its control test illustrates its own discomfort with the rule it has devised. Rather than beginning with the language of Title IX itself, the majority begins with our decision in *Gebser* and appears to discover there a sweeping legal duty—divorced from agency principles—for schools to remedy third-party discrimination against students. The majority then finds that the DOE's Title IX regulations and state common law gave States the requisite notice that they would be liable in damages for failure to fulfill this duty. Only then does the majority turn to the language of Title IX itself—not, it appears, to find a duty or clear notice to the States, for that the majority assumes has already been established, but rather to suggest a limit on the breathtaking scope of the liability the majority thinks is so clear under the statute. See ante, at 14 ("These factors [('subjects' and 'under')] combine to limit a recipient's damages liability to circumstances wherein the recipient exercises substantial control over both the harasser and the context in which the known harassment occurs").

Our decision in *Gebser* did not, of course, recognize some ill-defined, free-standing legal duty on schools to remedy discrimination by third parties. In particular, *Gebser* gave schools no notice whatsoever that they might be liable on the majority's novel theory that a school "subjects" a student to third-party discrimination if it exercises some measure of control over the third party. We quoted the "subjected to discrimination" language only once in *Gebser*, when we quoted the text of Title IX in full, and we did not use the word "control." Instead, we affirmed that Title IX prohibits discrimination by the grant recipient. See *Gebser*, 524 U.S. at 286; *id.* at 291-292; *supra*, at 5.

Neither the DOE's Title IX regulations nor state tort law, moreover, could or did provide States the notice required by our Spending Clause principles. The majority contends that the DOE's Title IX regulations have "long provided funding recipients with notice that they may be liable for their failure to respond to the discriminatory acts of certain non-agents." Ante, at 12. Even assuming that DOE regulations could give schools the requisite notice, they did not do so. Not one of the regulations the majority cites suggests that schools may be held liable in money damages for failure to respond to third-party discrimination.

In addition, as discussed above, the DOE regulations provide no support for the proposition that schools were on notice that students were among those "non-agents" whose actions the schools were bound to remedy. Most of the regulations cited by the majority merely forbid grant recipients to give affirmative aid to third parties who discriminate. See 34 C.F.R. § 106.31(b)(6) (1998) (A grant "recipient shall not, on the basis of sex," "[a]id or perpetuate discrimination against any person by providing significant assistance to any agency, organization, or person which discriminates on the basis of sex in providing any aid, benefit or service to students or employees"); *see also* § 106.37(a)(2) (A grant recipient shall not "[t]hrough solicitation, listing, approval, provision of facilities or other services, assist any foundation, trust, agency, organization, or person which provides assistance to any of such recipient's students in a manner which discriminates on the basis of sex"); § 106.38(a) (A grant recipient "which assists any agency, organization or person in making employment available to any of its students . . . [s]hall assure itself that such employment is made available without discrimination on the basis of sex [and] [s]hall not render such services to any agency, organization, or person which discriminates on the basis of sex in its employment practices"). The others forbid grant recipients to delegate the provision of student (or employee) benefits and services to third parties who engage in gender discrimination in administering what is, in effect, the school's program. See § 106.51(a)(3) ("A [grant] recipient shall not enter into any contractual or other relationship which directly or indirectly has the effect of subjecting employees or students to discrimination prohibited by this subpart, including relationships with employment and referral agencies, with labor unions, and with organizations providing or administering fringe benefits to employees of the recipient"); *see also* § 106.31(d) (A grant recipient "which requires participation by any applicant, student, or employee in any education program or activity not operated wholly by such recipient, or which facilitates, permits, or considers such participation as part of or equivalent to an education program or activity operated by such recipient, including participation in educational consortia and cooperative employment and student-teaching assignments" must take steps to assure itself that the education program or activity is not discriminating on the basis of gender and "shall not facilitate, require, permit, or consider such participation" if the program is discriminating). None of the regulations suggests a generalized duty to remedy discrimination by third parties over whom the school may arguably exercise some control.

Requiring a school to take affirmative steps to remedy harassment by its students imposes a much heavier burden on schools than prohibiting affirmative aid or effective delegation of school functions to an entity that discriminates. Notice of these latter responsibilities, then, can hardly be said to encompass clear notice of the former. In addition, each of the DOE regulations is predicated on a grant recipient's choice to give affirmative aid to, or to enter into voluntary association with, a discriminating entity. The recipient, moreover, as the regulations envision, is free to terminate that aid or association (or could have so provided through contract). The relationships regulated by the DOE are thus quite different from school-student relationships. The differences confirm that the regulations did not provide adequate notice of a duty to remedy student discrimination.

The majority also concludes that state tort law provided States the requisite notice. It is a non sequitur to suppose, however, that a State knows it is liable under a federal statute simply because the underlying conduct might form the basis for a state tort action. In any event, it is far from clear that Georgia law gave the Monroe County Board of Education notice that it would be liable even under state law for failure to respond reasonably to known student harassment. *See, e.g., Holbrook v. Executive Conference Center, Inc.*, 219 Ga. App. 104, 106, 464 S.E.2d 398, 401 (1996) (holding that school districts are entitled to sovereign immunity for claims based on their supervision of students unless the school displayed "wilfulness, malice, or corruption").

The majority's final observation about notice confirms just how far it has strayed from the basic Spending Clause principle that Congress must, through the clear terms of the statute, give States notice as to what the statute requires. The majority contends that schools were on notice because they "were being told" by a 1993 National School Boards Association publication that peer sexual harassment might trigger Title IX liability. Ante, at 16. By treating a publication designed to help school lawyers prevent and guard against school liability as a reliable indicium of congressional notice, the majority has transformed a litigation manual—which, like all such manuals, errs on the side of caution in describing potential liability—into a self-fulfilling prophecy. It seems schools cannot even discuss potential liabilities amongst themselves without somehow stipulating that Congress had some specified intent.

II

Our decision in *Gebser* makes clear that the Spending Clause clear-notice rule requires both that the recipients be on general notice of the kind of conduct the statute prohibits, and—at least when money damages are sought—that they be on notice that illegal conduct is occurring in a given situation. *See, e.g., Gebser*, 524 U.S. at 287-288 (rejecting vicarious liability because it would hold schools liable even when they did not know that prohibited discrimination was occurring).

Title IX, however, gives schools neither notice that the conduct the majority labels peer "sexual harassment" is gender discrimination within the meaning of the Act nor any guidance in distinguishing in individual cases between actionable discrimination and the immature behavior of children and adolescents. The majority thus imposes on schools potentially crushing financial liability for student conduct that is not prohibited in clear terms by Title IX and that cannot, even after today's opinion, be identified by either schools or courts with any precision.

The law recognizes that children—particularly young children—are not fully accountable for their actions because they lack the capacity to exercise mature judgment. *See, e.g.,* 1 E. Farnsworth, *Farnsworth on Contracts* § 4.4 (2d ed. 1998) (discussing minor's ability to disaffirm a contract into which he has entered). It should surprise no one, then, that the schools that are the primary locus of most children's social development are rife with inappropriate behavior by children who are just learning to interact with their peers. The amici on the front lines of our schools describe the situation best:

> "Unlike adults in the workplace, juveniles have limited life experiences or familial influences upon which to establish an understanding of appropriate behavior. The real world of school discipline is a rough-and-tumble place where students practice newly learned vulgarities, erupt with anger, tease and embarrass each other, share offensive notes, flirt, push and shove in the halls, grab and offend." Brief for National School Boards Association et al. as Amici Curiae 10-11 (hereinafter school amici).

No one contests that much of this "dizzying array of immature or uncontrollable behaviors by students," *ibid.*, is inappropriate, even "objectively offensive" at times, ante at 19, and that parents and schools have a moral and ethical responsibility to help students learn to interact with their peers in an appropriate manner. It is doubtless the case, moreover, that much of this inappropriate behavior is directed toward members of the opposite sex, as children in the throes of adolescence struggle to express their emerging sexual identities.

It is a far different question, however, whether it is either proper or useful to label this immature, childish behavior gender discrimination. Nothing in Title IX suggests that Congress even contemplated this question, much less answered it in the affirmative in unambiguous terms.

The majority, nevertheless, has no problem labeling the conduct of fifth graders "sexual harassment" and "gender discrimination." Indeed, the majority sidesteps the difficult issue entirely, first by asserting without analysis that respondents do not "support an argument that student-on-student harassment cannot rise to the level of discrimination' for purposes of Title IX," ante, at 7, and then by citing *Gebser* and *Franklin v. Gwinnett County Public Schools*, 503 U.S. 60 (1992), for the proposition that "[w]e have elsewhere concluded that sexual harassment is a form of discrimination for Title IX purposes and that Title IX proscribes harassment with sufficient clarity to satisfy *Pennhurst*'s notice requirement and serve as a basis for a damages action," ante, at 19.

Contrary to the majority's assertion, however, respondents have made a cogent and persuasive argument that the type of student conduct alleged by petitioner should not be considered "sexual harassment," much less gender discrimination actionable under Title IX:

> "[A]t the time Petitioner filed her complaint, no court, including this Court had recognized the concept of sexual harassment in any context other than the employment context. Nor had any Court extended the concept of sexual harassment to the misconduct of emotionally and socially immature children. The type of conduct alleged by Petitioner in her complaint is not new. However, in past years it was properly identified as misconduct which was addressed within the context of student discipline. The Petitioner now asks this Court to create out of whole cloth a cause of action by labeling childish misconduct as 'sexual harassment,' to stigmatize children as sexual harassers, and have the federal court system take on the additional burden of second guessing the disciplinary actions taken by school administrators in addressing misconduct, something this Court has consistently refused to do." Brief for Respondents 12-13 (citation omitted).

See also Brief for Independent Women's Forum as Amicus Curiae 19 (questioning whether "at the primary and secondary school level" it is proper to label "sexual misconduct by students" as "sexual harassment" because there is no power relationship between the harasser and the victim).

Likewise, the majority's assertion that *Gebser* and *Franklin* settled the question is little more than ipse dixit. *Gebser* and *Franklin* themselves did nothing more than cite *Meritor Savings Bank, FSB v. Vinson*, 477 U.S. 57, 64 (1986), a Title VII case, for the proposition that "when a supervisor sexually harasses a subordinate because of the subordinate's sex, that supervisor 'discriminate[s]' on the basis of sex." See *Franklin, supra*, at 74; *Gebser*, 524 U.S. at 282-283. To treat that proposition as establishing that the student conduct at issue here is gender discrimination is to erase, in one stroke, all differences between children and adults, peers and teachers, schools and workplaces.

In reality, there is no established body of federal or state law on which courts may draw in defining the student conduct that qualifies as Title IX gender discrimination. Analogies to Title VII hostile environment harassment are inapposite, because schools are not workplaces and children are not adults. The norms of the adult workplace that have defined hostile environment sexual harassment, *see, e.g., Oncale v. Sundowner Offshore Services, Inc.*, 523 U.S. 75 (1998), are not easily translated to peer relationships in schools, where teenage romantic relationships and dating are a part of everyday life. Analogies to Title IX teacher sexual harassment of students are similarly flawed. A teacher's sexual overtures toward a student are always inappropriate; a teenager's romantic overtures to a classmate (even when persistent and unwelcome) are an inescapable part of adolescence.

The majority admits that, under its approach, "[w]hether gender-oriented conduct rises to the level of actionable 'harassment' . . . 'depends on a constellation of surrounding circumstances, expectations, and relationships, including, but not limited to, the ages of the harasser and the victim and the number of individuals involved.'" Ante, at 20 (citations omitted). The majority does not explain how a school is supposed to discern from this mishmash of factors what is actionable discrimination. Its multifactored balancing test is a far cry from the clarity we demand of Spending Clause legislation.

The difficulties schools will encounter in identifying peer sexual harassment are already evident in teachers' manuals designed to give guidance on the subject. For example, one teachers' manual on peer sexual harassment suggests that sexual harassment in kindergarten through third grade includes a boy being "put down" on the playground "because he wants to play house with the girls" or a girl being "put down because she shoots baskets better than the boys." *Minnesota Dept. of Education, Girls and Boys Getting Along: Teaching Sexual Harassment Prevention in the Elementary Classroom* 65 (1993). Yet another manual suggests that one student saying to another, "You look nice" could be sexual harassment, depending on the "tone of voice," how the student looks at the other, and "who else is around." N. Stein & L. Sjostrom, *Flirting or Hurting? A Teacher's Guide on Student-to-Student Sexual Harassment in Schools (Grades 6 through 12)* 14 (1994). Blowing a kiss is also suspect. *Ibid.* This confusion will likely be compounded once the sexual-harassment label is invested with the force of federal law, backed up by private damages suits.

The only guidance the majority gives schools in distinguishing between the "simple acts of teasing and name-calling among school children," said not to be a basis for suit even when they "target differences in gender," ante at 21, and actionable peer sexual harassment is, in reality, no guidance at all. The majority proclaims that "in the context of student-on-student harassment, damages are available only in the situation where the behavior is so serious, pervasive, and objectively offensive that it denies its victims the equal access to education that Title IX is designed to protect." Ante, at 21. The majority does not even purport to explain, however, what constitutes an actionable denial of "equal access to education." Is equal access denied when a girl who tires of being chased by the boys at recess refuses to go outside? When she cannot concentrate during class because she is worried about the recess activities? When she pretends to be sick one day so she can stay home from school? It appears the majority is content to let juries decide.

The majority's reference to a "systemic effect," ante at 22, does nothing to clarify the content of its standard. The majority appears to intend that requirement to do no more than exclude the possibility that a single act of harassment perpetrated by one student on one other student can form the basis for an actionable claim. That is a small concession indeed.

The only real clue the majority gives schools about the dividing line between actionable harassment that denies a victim equal access to education and mere inappropriate teasing is a profoundly unsettling one: On the facts of this case, petitioner has stated a claim because she alleged, in the majority's words, "that the harassment had a concrete, negative effect on her daughter's ability to receive an education." Ante, at 23. In petitioner's words, the effects that might have been visible to the school were that her daughter's grades "dropped" and her "ability to concentrate on her school work [was] affected." App. to Pet. for Cert. 97a. Almost all adolescents experience these problems at one time or another as they mature.

III

The majority's inability to provide any workable definition of actionable peer harassment simply underscores the myriad ways in which an opinion that purports to be narrow is, in fact, so broad that it will support untold numbers of lawyers who will prove adept at presenting cases that will withstand the defendant school districts' pretrial motions. Each of the barriers to run- away litigation the majority offers us crumbles under the weight of even casual scrutiny.

For example, the majority establishes what sounds like a relatively high threshold for liability—"denial of equal access" to education—and, almost in the same breath, makes clear that alleging a decline in grades is enough to survive 12(b)(6) and, it follows, to state a winning claim. The majority seems oblivious to the fact that almost every child, at some point, has trouble in school because he or she is being teased by his or her peers. The girl who wants to skip recess because she is teased by the boys is no different from the overweight child who skips gym class because the other children tease her about her size in the locker room; or the child who risks flunking out because he refuses to wear glasses to avoid the taunts of "four- eyes"; or the child who refuses to go to school because the school bully calls him a "scaredy-cat" at recess. Most children respond to teasing in ways that detract from their ability to learn. The majority's test for actionable harassment will, as a result, sweep in almost all of the more innocuous conduct it acknowledges as a ubiquitous part of school life.

The string of adjectives the majority attaches to the word "harassment"—"severe, pervasive, and objectively offensive"—likewise fails to narrow the class of conduct that can trigger liability, since the touchstone for determining whether there is Title IX liability is the effect on the child's ability to get an education. Ante at 20. Indeed, the Court's reliance on the impact on the child's educational experience suggests that the "objective offensiveness" of a comment is to be judged by reference to a reasonable child at whom the comments were aimed. Not only is that standard likely to be quite expansive, it also gives schools—and juries—little guidance, requiring them to attempt to gauge the sensitivities of, for instance, the average seven year old.

The majority assures us that its decision will not interfere with school discipline and instructs that, "as we have previously noted, courts should refrain from second guessing the disciplinary decisions made by school administrators." Ante, at 17. The obvious reason for the majority's expressed reluctance to allow courts and litigants to second-guess school disciplinary decisions is that school officials are usually in the best position to judge the seriousness of alleged harassment and to devise an appropriate response. The problem is that the majority's test, in fact, invites courts and juries to second-guess school administrators in every case, to judge in each instance whether the school's response was "clearly unreasonable." A reasonableness standard, regardless of the modifier, transforms every disciplinary decision into a jury question. *Cf. Doe v. University of Illinois*, 138 F.3d 653, 655 (CA7 1998) (holding that college student had stated a Title IX claim for peer sexual harassment even though school officials had suspended two male students for 10 days and transferred another out of her biology class).

Another professed limitation the majority relies upon is that the recipient will be liable only where the acts of student harassment are "known." *See, e.g.*, ante, at 13; *id.* at 16. The majority's enunciation of the standard begs the obvious question: known to whom? Yet the majority says not one word about the type of school employee who must know about the harassment before it is actionable.

The majority's silence is telling. The deliberate indifference liability we recognized in *Gebser* was predicated on notice to "an official of the recipient entity with authority to take corrective action to end the discrimination." *Gebser, supra*, at 290. The majority gives no indication that it believes the standard to be any different in this context and—given its extensive reliance on the *Gebser* standard throughout the opinion—appears to adopt the *Gebser* notice standard by implication. At least the courts adjudicating Title IX peer harassment claims are likely to so conclude.

By choosing not to adopt the standard in explicit terms, the majority avoids having to confront the bizarre implications of its decision. In the context of teacher harassment, the *Gebser* notice standard imposes some limit on school liability. Where peer harassment is the discrimination, however, it imposes no limitation at all. In most cases of student misbehavior, it is the teacher has authority, at least in the first instance, to punish the student and take other measures to remedy the harassment. The anomalous result will be that, while a school district cannot be held liable for a teacher's sexual harassment of a student without notice to the school board (or at least to the principal), the district can be held liable for a teacher's failure to remedy peer harassment. The threshold for school liability, then, appears to be lower when the harasser is a student than when the harasser is a teacher who is an agent of the school. The absurdity of this result confirms that it was neither contemplated by Congress nor anticipated by the States.

The majority's limitations on peer sexual harassment suits cannot hope to contain the flood of liability the Court today begins. The elements of the Title IX claim created by the majority will be easy not only to allege but also to prove. A female plaintiff who pleads only that a boy called her offensive names, that she told a teacher, that the teacher's response was unreasonable, and that her school performance suffered as a result, appears to state a successful claim.

There will be no shortage of plaintiffs to bring such complaints. Our schools are charged each day with educating millions of children. Of those millions of students, a large percentage will, at some point during their school careers, experience something they consider sexual harassment. A 1993 Study by the American Association of University Women Educational Foundation, for instance, found that "fully 4 out of 5 students (81%) report that they have been the target of some form of sexual harassment during their school lives." *Hostile Hallways: The AAUW Survey on Sexual Harassment in America's Schools* 7 (1993). The number of potential lawsuits against our schools is staggering.

The cost of defending against peer sexual harassment suits alone could overwhelm many school districts, particularly since the majority's liability standards will allow almost any plaintiff to get to summary judgment, if not to a jury. In addition, there are no damages caps on the judicially implied private cause of action under Title IX. As a result, school liability in one peer sexual harassment suit could approach, or even exceed, the total federal funding of many school districts. Petitioner, for example, seeks damages of $500,000 in this case. App. to Pet. for Cert. 101a. Respondent school district received approximately $679,000 in federal aid in 1992-1993. Brief for the School Amici 25 n.20. The school district sued in *Gebser* received only $120,000 in federal funds a year. 524 U.S. at 289-290. Indeed, the entire 1992-1993 budget of that district was only $1.6 million. See Tr. of Oral Arg. in No. 96-1866, p. 34.

The limitless liability confronting our schools under the implied Title IX cause of action puts schools in a far worse position than businesses; when Congress established the express cause of action for money damages under Title VII, it prescribed damage caps. See *Gebser, supra*, at 286 ("It was not until 1991 that Congress made damages available under Title VII, and even then, Congress carefully limited the amount recoverable in any individual case, calibrating the maximum recovery to the size of the employer. See 42 U.S.C. § 1981a(b)(3). Adopting petitioners' position would amount, then, to allowing unlimited recovery of damages under Title IX where Congress has not spoken on the subject of either the right or the remedy, and in the face of evidence that when Congress expressly considered both in Title VII it restricted the amount of damages available"). In addition, in contrast to Title VII, Title IX makes no provision for agency investigation and conciliation of complaints (prior to the filing of a case in federal court) that could weed out frivolous suits or settle meritorious ones at minimal cost.

The prospect of unlimited Title IX liability will, in all likelihood, breed a climate of fear that encourages school administrators to label even the most innocuous of childish conduct sexual harassment. It would appear to be no coincidence that, not long after the DOE issued its proposed policy guidance warning that schools could be liable for peer sexual harassment in the fall of 1996, see 61 Fed. Reg. 42728, a North Carolina school suspended a 6-year-old boy who kissed a female classmate on the cheek for sexual harassment, on the theory that "[u]nwelcome is unwelcome at any age." Los Angeles Times, Sept. 25, 1996, p. A11. A week later, a New York school suspended a second-grader who kissed a classmate and ripped a button off her skirt. Buffalo News, Oct. 2, 1996, p. A16. The second grader said that he got the idea from his favorite book "Corduroy," about a bear with a missing button. *Ibid.* School administrators said only, "We were given guidelines as to why we suspend children. We follow the guidelines." *Ibid.*

At the college level, the majority's holding is sure to add fuel to the debate over campus speech codes that, in the name of preventing a hostile educational environment, may infringe students' First Amendment rights. See *supra*, at 14. Indeed, under the majority's control principle, schools presumably will be responsible for remedying conduct that occurs even in student dormitory rooms. As a result, schools may well be forced to apply workplace norms in the most private of domains.

Even schools that resist overzealous enforcement may find that the most careful and reasoned response to a sexual harassment complaint nonetheless provokes litigation. Speaking with the voice of experience, the school amici remind us, "[h]istory shows that, no matter what a school official chooses to do, someone will be unhappy. Student offenders almost always view their punishment as too strict, and student complainants almost always view an offender's punishment as too lax." Brief for the School Amici 12.

A school faced with a peer sexual harassment complaint in the wake of the majority's decision may well be beset with litigation from every side. One student's demand for a quick response to her harassment complaint will conflict with the alleged harasser's demand for due process. Another student's demand for a harassment-free classroom will conflict with the alleged harasser's claim to a mainstream placement under the Individuals with Disabilities Education Act or with his state constitutional right to a continuing, free public education. On college campuses, and even in secondary schools, a student's claim that the school should remedy a sexually hostile environment will conflict with the alleged harasser's claim that his speech, even if offensive, is protected by the First Amendment. In each of these situations, the school faces the risk of suit, and maybe even multiple suits, regardless of its response. See *Doe v. University of Illinois*, 138 F.3d, at 679 (Posner, C.J., dissenting from denial of rehearing en banc) ("Liability for failing to prevent or rectify sexual harassment of one student by another places a school on a razor's edge, since the remedial measures that it takes against the alleged harasser are as likely to expose the school to a suit by him as a failure to take those measures would be to expose the school to a suit by the victim of the alleged harassment").

The majority's holding in this case appears to be driven by the image of the school administration sitting idle every day while male students commandeer a school's athletic field or computer lab and prevent female students from using it through physical threats. See ante, at 20. Title IX might provide a remedy in such a situation, however, without resort to the majority's unprecedented theory of school liability for student harassment. If the school usually disciplines students for threatening each other and prevents them from blocking others' access to school facilities, then the school's failure to enforce its rules when the boys target the girls on a widespread level, day after day, may support an inference that the school's decision not to respond is itself based on gender. That pattern of discriminatory response could form the basis of a Title IX action.

(Contrary to the majority's assertion, see ante at 22, we do not suggest that mere indifference to gender-based mistreatment—even if widespread—is enough to trigger Title IX liability. We suggest only that a clear pattern of discriminatory enforcement of school rules could raise an inference that the school itself is discriminating. Recognizing that the school itself might discriminate based on gender in the enforcement of its rules is a far cry from recognizing Title IX liability based on the majority's expansive theory that a school "subjects" its students to third-party discrimination when it has some control over the harasser and fails to take corrective action.)

Even more important, in most egregious cases the student will have state-law remedies available to her. The student will often have recourse against the offending student (or his parents) under state tort law. In some cases, like this one, the perpetrator may also be subject to criminal sanctions. And, as the majority notes, the student may, in some circumstances, have recourse against the school under state law. Ante, at 13.

Disregarding these state-law remedies for student misbehavior and the incentives that our schools already have to provide the best possible education to all of their students, the majority seeks, in effect, to put an end to student misbehavior by transforming Title IX into a Federal Student Civility Code. See Brief for Independent Women's Forum as Amicus Curiae 2 (urging the Court to avoid that result). I fail to see how federal courts will administer school discipline better than the principals and teachers to whom the public has entrusted that task or how the majority's holding will help the vast majority of students, whose educational opportunities will be diminished by the diversion of school funds to litigation. The private cause of action the Court creates will justify a corps of federal administrators in writing regulations on student harassment. It will also embroil schools and courts in endless litigation over what qualifies as peer sexual harassment and what constitutes a reasonable response.

In the final analysis, this case is about federalism. Yet the majority's decision today says not one word about the federal balance. Preserving our federal system is a legitimate end in itself. It is, too, the means to other ends. It ensures that essential choices can be made by a government more proximate to the people than the vast apparatus of federal power. Defining the appropriate role of schools in teaching and supervising children who are beginning to explore their own sexuality and learning how to express it to others is one of the most complex and sensitive issues our schools face. Such decisions are best made by parents and by the teachers and school administrators who can counsel with them. The delicacy and immense significance of teaching children about sexuality should cause the Court to act with great restraint before it displaces state and local governments.

Heedless of these considerations, the Court rushes onward, finding that the cause of action it creates is necessary to effect the congressional design. It is not. Nothing in Title IX suggests that Congress intended or contemplated the result the Court reaches today, much less dictated it in unambiguous terms. Today's decision cannot be laid at the feet of Congress; it is the responsibility of the Court.

The Court must always use great care when it shapes private causes of action without clear guidance from Congress, but never more so than when the federal balance is at stake. As we recognized in *Gebser*, the definition of an implied cause of action inevitably implicates some measure of discretion in the Court to shape a sensible remedial scheme. *Gebser*, 524 U.S. at 284. Whether the Court ever should have embarked on this endeavor under a Spending Clause statute is open to question. What should be clear beyond any doubt, however, is that the Court is duty-bound to exercise that discretion with due regard for federalism and the unique role of the States in our system. The Court today disregards that obligation. I can conceive of few interventions more intrusive upon the delicate and vital relations between teacher and student, between student and student, and between the State and its citizens than the one the Court creates today by its own hand. Trusted principles of federalism are superseded by a more contemporary imperative.

Perhaps the most grave, and surely the most lasting, disservice of today's decision is that it ensures the Court's own disregard for the federal balance soon will be imparted to our youngest citizens. The Court clears the way for the federal government to claim center stage in America's classrooms. Today's decision mandates to teachers instructing and supervising their students the dubious assistance of federal court plaintiffs and their lawyers and makes the federal courts the final arbiters of school policy and of almost every disagreement between students. Enforcement of the federal right recognized by the majority means that federal influence will permeate everything from curriculum decisions to day-to-day classroom logistics and interactions. After today, Johnny will find that the routine problems of adolescence are to be resolved by invoking a federal right to demand assignment to a desk two rows away.

As its holding makes painfully clear, the majority's watered-down version of the Spending Clause clear-statement rule is no substitute for the real protections of state and local autonomy that our constitutional system requires. If there be any doubt of the futility of the Court's attempt to hedge its holding about with words of limitation for future cases, the result in this case provides the answer. The complaint of this fifth grader survives and the school will be compelled to answer in federal court. We can be assured that like suits will follow—suits, which in cost and number, will impose serious financial burdens on local school districts, the taxpayers who support them, and the children they serve. Federalism and our struggling school systems deserve better from this Court. I dissent.

APPENDIX F: ANSWER KEY

Matching Exercise (page 11)

A.	14		L.	4
B.	8		M.	9
C.	7		N.	12
D.	21		O.	17
E.	19		P.	10
F.	11		Q.	6
G.	2		R.	15
H.	3		S.	18
I.	5		T.	20
J.	1		U.	16
K.	13			

Article Exercise (page 26)

"George Pavlicic is not asking for ___ damages because of a broken heart or a mortified spirit. He is asking for the return of things he bestowed with an attached condition precedent, a condition which was never met. In demanding the return of his gifts, George cannot be charged with ___ Indian giving. Although he has reached the Indian summer of his life and now at ___ 80 years of age might, in the usual course of human affairs, be regarded as beyond the marrying age, everyone has the unalienable right under his own constitution as well as that of the United States to marry when he pleases, if and when he finds the woman who will marry him. George Pavlicic believed that he found that woman in Sara Jane. He testified that he asked her at least 30 times if she would marry him and on each occasion she answered in the affirmative. There is nothing in the law which required him to ask ___ 31 times. But even so, he probably would have continued asking her had she not taken his last $5,000 and decamped to another city. Moreover he has to accept ___ 30 offers of marriage as the limit she now had married someone else. Of course, mere multiplicity of ___ proposals does not make for ___ certainty of acceptance. The testimony, however, is to the effect that on the occasion of each proposal by George, Sara Jane accepted—not only accepted not only the proposal but the gift which invariably accompanied it.

The Act of 1935 in no way alters or modifies the law on ___ ante-nuptial conditional gifts as expounded in ___ 28 C.J. 651, and quoted by us with approval in the case *Stranger v. Epler*, 382 Pa. 411, 415, 115 A.2d 197, 199, namely:

> "A gift to a person to whom the donor is engaged to be married, made in ___ contemplation of ___ marriage, although absolute in ___ form, is conditional; and upon breach of the marriage engagement by the donee the property may be recovered by the donor."

Law School Vocabulary (page 42)

A.	17		L.	6
B.	3		M.	8
C.	7		N.	15
D.	4		O.	9
E.	19		P.	18
F.	10		Q.	13
G.	11		R.	14
H.	1		S.	2
I.	5		T.	20
J.	21		U.	16
K.	12			

The Corpus Juris Game Answers (p. 50)

	Executive Branch	Judicial Branch	Legislative Branch	Court System I	Court System II	Verbs
100 points	Attorney General	Jurisdiction	Congress	Appellate process	Precedent	To bind
200 points	To enforce	Case law	House of Represen-tatives	Trial court	Mandatory/ binding authority	To nominate
300 points	Agency	Dual Court System	Statue	Issues of law	Acquittal	To veto
400 points	Power of appointment	Jury	Senate	Stare decis	Secondary sources of law	To amend
500 points	Advice and consent of Senate	To overturn; to invalidate; to void; to strike down	To override	Petition for Certiorari	Error of law	To act contrary

Matching Exercise (page 51)

A.	5		I.	16
B.	9		J.	3
C.	12		K.	6
D.	7		L.	10
E.	1		M.	13
F.	15		N.	8
G.	2		O.	11
H.	4		P.	14

Matching Exercise (page 123)

A.	2		J.	3
B.	5		K.	9
C.	8		L.	14
D.	15		M.	7
E.	4		N.	16
F.	11		O.	10
G.	13		P.	12
H.	1		Q.	18
I.	6		R.	17

Article Exercise (page 145)

"Dennis has only pled that the police responded to a call for assistance. A mere response to a call for assistance or aid does not create a special relationship between the police and the person in need of ___ aid. . . . In *Yates,* the Yates family call the police to break up a gang fight behind their home. The police arrived but instead of stopping the fight, they remained in their car. After the car departed, a shot was fired at the rear of the Yates' house which struck and killed their daughter. This court refused to find a special relationship where the police 'did not assure the Yates family that they would protect them from the dangers caused by a gang fight. The focus of *Melendez* is on the individual and any danger unique to the individual from which the police specifically promise protection.' . . .

In *Rankin,* the plaintiff was stabbed on a local Philadelphia train. The plaintiff alleged that a police officer witnessed the stabbing and failed to prevent it. He further alleged that the officer escorted him from the train, told him to sit down on a bench, and told him he would be 'alright.' The plaintiff subsequently passed out and was left on the bench without___ medical attention for some four hours. . . . This court concluded that a special relationship existed because the three elements of the *Thomas* test were met. We inferred that the third element was met by the allegation that the police escorted the plaintiff from the train, seated him, and reassured him. In the case now before us, there are simply no facts led from which we can make such an inference. Without the third element of a voluntary assumption by the officer in this case to protect the decedent, there can be no special relationship, no duty, and hence no liability."

Matching Exercise (page 146)

A.	7	K.	15
B.	18	L.	8
C.	10	M.	13
D.	3	N.	9
E.	17	O.	19
F.	1	P.	16
G.	14	Q.	2
H.	4	R.	5
I.	6	S.	12
J.	11		

Matching Exercise (page 225)

A.	7	K.	17
B.	16	L.	6
C.	4	M.	8
D.	1	N.	3
E.	14	O.	19
F.	5	P.	13
G.	11	Q.	18
H.	2	R.	9
I.	10	S.	12
J.	15		

Negotiation Terms Exercise (page 279)

1. must have
2. compromise
3. mutually beneficial
4. impasse
5. objectives
6. hard strategy
7. bargaining power
8. disclosure

Negotiation Terms Matching Exercise (page 280)

1.	H		11.	N
2.	P		12.	C
3.	R		13.	O
4.	S		14.	T
5.	J		15.	B
6.	E		16.	G
7.	M		17.	D
8.	A		18.	F
9.	Q		19.	K
10.	L		20.	I

Answers to Internet Scavenger Hunt (page 289)

1) Describe the functions of the National Aeronautics and Space Administration.

NASA is authorized to conduct research for the solution of problems of flight within and outside the Earth's atmosphere; to develop, construct, test, and operate aeronautical space vehicles for research purposes; to operate a space transportation system including the space shuttle, upper stages, space program, space station, and related equipment; and to perform such other activities as may be required for the exploration of space.

Which federal regulation gives you the answer? **14 C.F.R. § 1201.102 (1999)**

- Start at Barco Law Library Home Page
- Click **Executive Branch**
- Click **Code of Federal Regulations**
- Click **Title 14—Aeronautics and Space—Jan. 1, 1999**
- Search with the phrase **National Aeronautics and Space Administration**
- Click **Part 1201—Statement of Organization and General Information** (TEXT)

2) Using JURIST, find the title of an article dealing with the Second Amendment of the U.S. Constitution. Include the author's name and the name of the scholarly journal in which the article was published.

***The Commonplace Second Amendment*, Professor Eugene Volokh, New York University Law Review**

- Start at Barco Law Library Home Page
- Click **General Legal Research Sources**
- Click **JURIST**
- Click **Online Artists**
- Click **Constitutional Law**
- Click **"The Commonplace Second Amendment"**

3) What are the act and bill numbers of a recent 1998 Pennsylvania statute amending the Judicial Code to allow arraignments by audio-video communication?

Act 67; Senate Bill 770

- Start at Barco Law Library Home Page
- Click **Pennsylvania Law**
- Click **Recent PA Legislation**
- Click **General Legislation 1998**
- Scroll down to **Act 67 (SB 770)** and click

When was the bill signed by the Pennsylvania Senate? **June 2, 1998**

When was it signed by the Pennsylvania House of Representatives? **June 3, 1998**

When did the Governor receive the bill for approval? **June 3, 1998**

When did he approve the bill? **June 11, 1998**

- Start at Barco Law Library Home Page
- Click **PA Electronic Bill Room**
- Type **sb770 for 1997-1998 Session**
- Click **Bill History**
- Scroll to bottom of history for answers

4) What is the street address of the U.S. Court of International Trade?

One Federal Plaza, New York, NY 10278-0001

How many judges sit on the court? **Nine**

- Start at Barco Law Library Home Page
- Click **General Legal Research Sources**
- Click **US Government**
- Click **Judicial**
- Click **Other Courts**
- Click **US Court of International Trade**
- Click **About the Court**

5) Go to the home page of the American Bar Association (http://www.abanet.org).

Who would you contact for a lawyer referral in Pittsburgh?

Allegheny County Bar Association Lawyer Referral Service (LRS).

What is the phone number you would call? **(412) 261-5555**

- Start at ABA Home Page
- Click **Public Information**
- Click **Lawyer Referral**
- Click **Pennsylvania**
- Scroll down to answers under **Allegheny County**

6) What is the total cost of obtaining a marriage license in Allegheny County?

$40.00

- Start at Barco Law Library Home Page
- Click **Allegheny County & Pittsburgh**
- Click **Register of Wills**

- Click **Planning to Marry?**
- Scroll down to answer.

7) What is the name of the 1999 Cornell Law School International Law Journal Symposium?

The International Criminal Court: Consensus and Debate on the International Adjudication of Genocide, Crimes Against Humanity, War Crimes, and Aggression.

- Start at Barco Law Library Home Page
- Click **General Legal Research Sources**
- Click **Cornell Legal Informational Institute**
- Click **Cornell Law School**
- Click **International Law Journal**
- Click **Globe Icon**
- Click **Symposium**

What will be the volume and number of the corresponding symposium issue of the Cornell International Law Journal?   **Volume 32, Number 3**

- All of the above, and then click **Symposium Issue**

8) What are the functions of the United States Office of the Solicitor General?

Supervise and conduct government litigation in the United States Supreme Court; review all cases decided adversely to the government in the lower courts to determine whether they should be appealed and, if so, what position should be taken; determine whether the government will participate as an amicus curiae, or intervene, in cases in any appellate court.

- Start at Barco Law Library Home Page
- Click **Executive Branch**
- Click **President, Vice-President, Cabinet**
- Click **Department of Justice**
- Click **Organizations & Information**
- Click **Alphabetical List**
- Click **Office of the Solicitor General**
- Click **About the OSG**
- Click **Functions of the Office**

Within the Justice Department, which positions are above the Solicitor General?

Attorney General; Deputy Attorney General

- Start at Barco Law Library Home Page
- Click **Executive Branch**
- Click **President, Vice-President, Cabinet**
- Click **Department of Justice**
- Click **Organizations & Information**
- Click **Organization Chart**

9) How much time does the U.S. Supreme Court allow each side to present oral arguments? **Half hour**

Which Supreme Court rule tells you this? **Rule 28.3**

- Start at Barco Law Library Home Page
- Click **Courts and Cases**
- Click **U.S. Supreme Court**
- Click **Supreme Court Resources**
- Click **Supreme Court Rules 10/95**
- Click **Rule 28. Oral Argument**

10) Using LEXIS or Westlaw, find a case where the facts include the United States arresting and prosecuting the skin of an afghan urial (a type of sheep).

United States v. One Afghan Urial Ovis Orientalis Blanfordi Fully Mounted Sheep, **964 F.2d 474 (5th Cir. 1992).**

- Start at either **LEXIS or Westlaw**
- The easiest way to find the case is to search the term "afghan urial." There is only one case where the afghan urial is a named party.

Where does this case constitute binding precedent?

All federal courts in the Fifth Circuit (Louisiana, Mississippi, and Texas).

- Start at Barco Law Library Home Page
- Click **Courts and Cases**
- Click **Federal Judiciary**
- Click **About U.S. Courts**
- Click **Understanding the Federal Courts**
- Click **Directory of the U.S. Court of Appeals**